In War's Wake

War has diverse and seemingly contradictory effects on liberal democratic institutions and processes. It has led democracies to abandon their principles, expanding executive authority and restricting civil liberties, but it has also prompted the development of representative parliamentary institutions. War has undercut socioeconomic reform, but it has also laid the basis for the modern welfare state. This landmark volume brings together distinguished political scientists, historians, and sociologists to explore the impact of war on liberal democracy – a subject far less studied than the causes of war but hardly less important. Three questions drive the analysis: How does war shape the transition to and durability of democracy? How does war influence democratic contestation? How does war transform democratic participation? Employing a wide range of methods, this volume assesses what follows in the wake of war. It is an urgent question for scholars, and even more for citizens, especially in our anxious post–9/11 age.

Elizabeth Kier is associate professor of political science at the University of Washington. She won the Edgar S. Furniss Book Award for *Imagining War: French and British Military Doctrine between the Wars*. She has been a visiting scholar at the Danish Institute for International Studies, the Belfer Center for Science and International Affairs at Harvard University, the Center for International Security and Cooperation at Stanford University, and the John M. Olin Institute for Strategic Studies at Harvard University. Her research has also been supported by the Social Science Research Council–MacArthur Fellowship in Peace and International Security. She is an associate editor of *Security Studies* and is on the editorial board of *International Security*.

Ronald R. Krebs is associate professor of political science at the University of Minnesota. His most recent book is *Fighting for Rights: Military Service and the Politics of Citizenship*. A former McKnight Land-Grant Professor at the University of Minnesota, his research has been supported by the United States Institute of Peace, a Donald D. Harrington Faculty Fellowship at the University of Texas at Austin, the John M. Olin Institute for Strategic Studies at Harvard University, the Belfer Center for Science and International Affairs at Harvard University, and the Miller Center of Public Affairs at the University of Virginia.

In War's Wake

International Conflict and the Fate of Liberal Democracy

Edited by

ELIZABETH KIER
University of Washington

RONALD R. KREBS
University of Minnesota

CAMBRIDGE
UNIVERSITY PRESS

CAMBRIDGE UNIVERSITY PRESS
Cambridge, New York, Melbourne, Madrid, Cape Town, Singapore,
São Paulo, Delhi, Dubai, Tokyo, Mexico City

Cambridge University Press
32 Avenue of the Americas, New York, NY 10013-2473, USA

www.cambridge.org
Information on this title: www.cambridge.org/9780521157704

First published 2010

Printed in the United States of America

A catalog record for this publication is available from the British Library.

Library of Congress Cataloging in Publication data
In war's wake : international conflict and the fate of liberal
democracy / [edited by] Elizabeth Kier, Ronald R. Krebs.
    p. cm.
Includes bibliographical references and index.
ISBN 978-0-521-19481-5 – ISBN 978-0-521-15770-4 (pbk.)
 1. Politics and war. 2. Democracy. I. Kier, Elizabeth, 1958–
II. Krebs, Ronald R., 1974– III. Title.
JZ6385.I59   2010
321.8–dc22   2010012379

ISBN 978-0-521-19481-5 Hardback
ISBN 978-0-521-15770-4 Paperback

To the memory of Charles Tilly –
Whose passionate scholarship inspires us still

Contents

PART III. WAR AND DEMOCRATIC STATES:
GOVERNMENT BY THE PEOPLE OR OVER THE PEOPLE?

Contributors

Deborah Avant
Professor of Political Science and Director of International Studies,
University of California, Irvine

Nancy Bermeo
Nuffield Professor of Comparative Politics, Oxford University

Miguel Angel Centeno
Professor of Sociology and International Affairs, Princeton University

Rieko Kage
Associate Professor of Political Science, University of Tokyo

Elizabeth Kier
Associate Professor of Political Science, University of Washington

Ronald R. Krebs
Associate Professor of Political Science, University of Minnesota

Daniel Kryder
Associate Professor of Politics and Director of the Gordon Center for
American Public Policy, Brandeis University

Edward D. Mansfield
Hum Rosen Professor of Political Science and Director of the Christopher
H. Browne Center for International Politics, University of Pennsylvania

Jack Snyder
Robert and Renée Belfer Professor of International Relations in the
Department of Political Science and the Saltzman Institute of War
and Peace Studies, Columbia University

Paul Starr
Professor of Sociology and Public Affairs and Stuart Professor of
  Communications and Public Affairs, Princeton University

Mark R. Wilson
Associate Professor of History, University of North Carolina, Charlotte

Jay Winter
Charles J. Stille Professor of History, Yale University

Acknowledgments

It was over coffee in Harvard Square nearly ten years ago that we first recognized our common interest in war and democracy. But those first glimmers of recognition of common interests did not yield anything like a common project until a few years ago. Those initial conversations led to two productive workshops, one hosted at the University of Texas at Austin (where Krebs was a visiting faculty Fellow) in May 2007 and the other at the University of Washington (where Kier sits on the faculty) in March 2008. The result is this interdisciplinary volume grappling with the consequences of international conflict for democracy.

We are, first and foremost, grateful to our collaborators in this intellectual journey – the contributors to the volume, whose insights have enriched us intellectually and whose good humor and responsiveness have made putting this project together a pleasure. We are also thankful for the substantial contribution of the many scholars who participated in the two workshops by writing papers and serving as discussants: Zoltan Barany, Gad Barzilai, Bill Brands, Jim Burk, Jim Caporaso, Dan Chirot, Dana Cloud, Christopher Dandeker, Willie Forbath, Jamie Galbraith, Oren Gross, Steve Hanson, Peter Katzenstein, Sandy Levinson, Gary Marx, Joel Migdal, Brian Rathbun, Gretchen Ritter, Hugh Rockoff, Bat Sparrow, Peter Trubowitz, Jeff Tulis, and Michael Young. We would like to single out Sid Tarrow for his unstinting enthusiasm for this project, as well as his excellent guidance. The anonymous reviewers for Cambridge University Press also deserve our thanks: Their careful reading of the volume markedly improved it.

Our debts are also institutional. At the University of Texas at Austin, financial support came from the Donald D. Harrington Fellows Program, under whose auspices Krebs was a visitor in the Department of Government in 2006–2007; the College of Communication; the College of Liberal Arts; the Department of Government; the Law School; and the LBJ Library and Museum. The LBJ Library and Museum also graciously hosted the workshop, "The Politics of Peace and the Consequences of War," and expertly guided our event-planning and publicity. Thanks also to Aaron Herold for his fine work as the rapporteur. At the University of Washington, our workshop, "War and Democracy: The Domestic Political Consequences of International Conflict," received primary funding from the Institute for National Security Education and Research as well as substantial support from the Center for West European Studies; the Marc Lindenburg Center for Humanitarian Action, International Development and Global Citizenship; and the Department of Political Science. As always, Ann Buscherfeld and Phil Shekleton at the University of Washington made administrative tasks easy and workshop planning a pleasure.

Lew Bateman of Cambridge University Press has been supportive of this project from the start and has been a thoughtful and patient guide as it has progressed. We are grateful to the entire staff of Cambridge University Press, especially Emily Spangler and Anne Lovering Rounds who shepherded this manuscript to production. Finally, we thank Kristan Seibel for creating the index.

An edited volume is a leap of faith – on the part of the editors, the contributors, the press, and the many institutions that financially support the project. We hope this volume justifies that collective leap. The experience of co-editing a volume can lead the editors to leap at each other's throats. Or so we've been told, since, fortunately, that did not happen to us. Although we did sometimes argue (in which case the other was almost always wrong!), more often we agreed, and always we enjoyed the give and take through the long yet delightful process.

I

Introduction

War and Democracy in Comparative Perspective

Elizabeth Kier and Ronald R. Krebs

Democracies often compromise their principles during crises: executive authority grows, rights of due process are set aside, and free expression suffers. But war's effects on liberal-democratic institutions and processes are diverse, often contradictory, and not always negative. Fear of the Soviet Union helped create the U.S. national security state, but the demands of war mobilization contributed to the advance of parliamentary institutions in nineteenth-century Europe. The Vietnam War promoted political alienation, but the vast social networks forged by America's earlier large-scale wars built a vigorous civil society. War can undermine progressive reform, or so Lyndon Johnson believed as he refrained from mobilizing the public to wage war in Vietnam, hoping thereby to save the Great Society. But European preparations for the total wars of the twentieth century laid the basis for the modern welfare state. Big wars may have big effects, but limited wars can also have substantial and pro-democratic consequences, as the Argentine junta discovered when its defeat in the Falklands delegitimized its rule and facilitated the transition to democracy. Victory, too, can usher in more open and democratic politics, as Israel learned after the Yom Kippur War.

Few questions are as important as war's effects on democracy – and few questions are as neglected. Scholars routinely allude to war's transformative power, but studies of war's effects on democratic institutions and politics are rare. Stein and Russett's call, nearly three decades ago, for research on the domestic political consequences of international conflict has, by and large, gone unanswered.[1] Consumed with avoiding the destruction of the world wars and the potential devastation of a nuclear war, political scientists have focused on the *causes* of war, not its consequences. Sociologists have explored how war

---

[1] Stein and Russett 1980. Other reviews include Kasza 1996; Mayhew 2005; Thompson 1993. An important recent exception is Davenport 2007. Fine studies, however, have been conducted on veterans' capacity and will for political action and on war and social memory. Productive research programs also exist on war and state-building, spawned by the seminal work of Charles Tilly, and on war and leadership tenure.

and military service affect individuals, but have been skeptical that international conflict has enduring consequences for society and politics.[2] Historians have traced the legacies of particular wars for particular regimes, but have not generally searched for patterns across cases. Although scholars have produced a substantial literature on how democracies fight wars and on their immediate domestic political consequences, there have been few systematic studies of democratic politics in war's wake.

Basic theoretical and normative questions remain unanswered. What are the consequences of international conflict for liberal democracy? Do liberal-democratic polities emerge from war unscathed, at least in the long run, or do increases in executive authority endure? Do wars stifle political participation and breed reactionary politics, or does mass mobilization foster new forms of civic engagement and facilitate postwar reform? Do wars bolster authoritarian rule, or can international conflict weaken antidemocratic forces? In short, are we correct to fear for the fate of liberal democracies at war, or can international conflict also advance democratization and deepen democracy?

Questions about the consequences of international conflict for democratic institutions and practices are as compelling as ever. Although the United States has been enmeshed in two wars since 2003, neither the nation's political leaders nor the scholarly community have addressed the possible long-term ramifications of war for American democracy. This problem is not just an American one. Many other countries also reconsidered the "balance" between liberty and security after 2001: glorification of terrorism is now a crime in Britain, and antiterrorism laws threaten to suppress political opposition in the Philippines. These choices remind us that it makes a great difference to the lives of citizens and to the quality of governance not just whether polities are democratic, but where they lie within the spectrum of liberal democracy.

This volume explores the effects of international conflict over the last two centuries on both democratizing countries and consolidated liberal democracies. Such conflicts include total wars, in which the boundaries between home-front and battlefront and between state and society have eroded, as well as limited conflicts, in which those boundaries remain more stable. They include conventional wars fought between the uniformed militaries of sovereign states, as well as counterinsurgencies waged against irregulars. The states studied in depth in this volume are generally located in the industrialized world, where the bulk of interstate conflict has historically taken place and where most democracies reside. But the developing world also looms large, especially in those chapters examining the effects of wars on democratization. Although the volume privileges no methodology, nearly all the authors develop historically contingent generalizations. The chapters focus on conflict's long-term effects, which are the most difficult to conceptualize and the least studied.

---

[2] MacLean and Elder Jr. 2007; Modell and Haggerty 1991. But see also Kestnbaum 2009. A notable exception is the "bellicist" literature on state-building, associated especially with the political/historical sociologist Charles Tilly.

They also share a comparative (cross-national) perspective. Most importantly, war's consequences belong to no single discipline. This volume engages with the findings and claims of historians, sociologists, political scientists, and lawyers to begin to unravel war's consequences for democracy.

This introduction has three sections. First, we clarify what we mean by war and democracy and identify how individual chapters speak to each. The volume's organizing structure emerges from this disentangling of its central concepts. Second, we explore how two central features of international conflict – scale and outcome – have been thought to shape democratic institutions and practices, and we highlight how this volume's chapters develop and sometimes challenge these conventional wisdoms. Third, we reflect on the relationship between war and democracy in contemporary world politics. Recent changes in both war and democracy may limit how lessons from the past apply to the future. Nevertheless, we contend that those interested in the future should study the past, as this volume does. If decisions about war and peace are to be made wisely, only through examination of the past can policymakers and citizens alike grasp what is at stake at home as well as abroad.

CENTRAL CONCEPTS

Two concepts – war and democracy – structure this volume. Understanding their relationship to each other depends on first understanding each alone.[3]

Unpacking Democracy

In his classic work on democratic theory, Robert Dahl suggested that regimes can be situated along two continuums. The first is *contestation*, or the extent to which political opposition is sanctioned and protected among those permitted to participate in governance. The second is *participation*, or the proportion of the population that can and does meaningfully engage in contestation, whatever its extent.[4] Liberal democracies rank high on both dimensions; illiberal democracies allow superficial participation but restrict the scope of the population's political involvement; liberal autocracies permit substantial contestation but define the political community narrowly; and despotic regimes rank low across the board.

These two categories are often conceived narrowly, as encompassing only formal democratic procedures and political rights.[5] In contrast, we understand

---

[3] This discussion draws and expands upon Krebs 2009.

[4] Dahl 1971.

[5] Dahl himself argues that high participation and high contestation produce only "polyarchal" democracy, which he associates with several fundamental political institutions, among them elected government officials; free, fair, and frequent elections; inclusive suffrage; freedom of expression; freedom of the press; and freedom of association. Dahl, however, sees these formal rights, structures, and procedures as necessary but not sufficient features of the ideal liberal democracy, which he maintains no actual regime has achieved (though polyarchies have come

these concepts to include not only formal rights and procedures, but also the substantive policies, social and economic structures, and informal practices that democratic theorists have identified as crucial to the health and operation of liberal democracy – that is, that render contestation and participation more or less "effective."[6] Participation suffers if ethnicity or religion structures the rights and obligations of citizenship or if deep and abiding economic inequality plagues society. Contestation suffers if the wealthy control the political agenda, if authorities can arbitrarily silence citizens, and if citizens are ill-informed or lack equal access to the polls or the basic privacy requisite to define and pursue their interests. Simply put, the greater the degree of (effective) contestation and the broader and deeper (effective) participation, the more closely a regime approaches the liberal-democratic ideal. Only regimes with high levels of effective participation and contestation are likely to be democratic in the sense of being "responsive" to their citizens – that is, likely to translate popular will into public policy.[7]

This distinction between participation and contestation, broadly conceived, structures much of this volume. Democratic regimes allow for broad and equal participation in politics (or positive freedom, "freedom to"), without limitations imposed on the basis of ascriptive categories (e.g., ethnicity, race, religion, gender, sexual orientation) or the origins of citizenship (naturalized vs. native-born). The right to vote is a minimum criterion for democracy, but it is a thin form of participation: Those regimes that Nancy Bermeo identifies as "electoral democracies" in her chapter might rank high on participation if narrowly defined, as would those that Fareed Zakaria calls "illiberal democracies."[8] Participation also includes various forms of more costly political activities, from writing legislators and contributing money and time to political campaigns to organizing social movements and marching in protests. The political mobilization of populations marks the advance of participation, while public apathy signals its decline. Even democracies with universal suffrage vary in the depth and breadth of participation. Moreover, participation hinges on socioeconomic security, education, and equality: Wealthier and

closest). For Dahl's evolving views of polyarchy's defining institutions, see Dahl 1971, 3; Dahl 1997, 94–95; Dahl 1998, 83–99. On polyarchy versus ideal liberal democracy, see Dahl 1971, 8; Dahl 1998, 37–40. See also Bailey and Braybrooke 2003, 107–109.

[6] Dahl (1997, 95) similarly argues that polyarchic institutions "guarantee a very broad set of rights that are necessary to each of the institutions; to this extent, then, polyarchy is also a form of substantive democracy."

[7] Our expansive understanding of participation and contestation has much in common with Charles Tilly's view of democracy as defined by "broad, equal, protected, and mutually binding consultation." Participation parallels breadth (what portion of the population enjoys rights) and equality (regarding access to rights and subjection to obligations). Contestation rests on liberal protections from arbitrary state action and the rule of law, which overlap with Tilly's categories of protection and mutually binding consultation. We further agree with Tilly that regimes are democratic to "the extent [that] … the state behaves in conformity to the expressed demands of its citizens." See Tilly 2007, 13–15.

[8] Zakaria 2003.

better educated citizens are more likely to participate in politics than poorer and less educated citizens.[9] To inquire into the effects of war on participation is not only to ask whether and when war leads to the expansion (or contraction) of the franchise. It is also, as in the chapters in Part II, to inquire into war's impact on associational life (Kage), on the mobilization of societal actors (Kier, Wilson), and on how those actors imagine politics and their interests (Kier, Winter).

Liberal regimes value and safeguard contestation. In principle, these regimes protect individual liberties (or negative freedoms, "freedom from"), specifically those that nurture the formation and expression of political opposition. These regimes also limit the scope of unchecked executive authority, which defines the boundaries of effective opposition. Finally, such regimes enshrine the rule of law, which guarantees that the outcomes of political contest will be honored. Evaluating a polity's level of contestation requires going beyond formal constitutional guarantees. One must also examine the processes that shape the political agenda and determine the breadth of political debate, whether civil liberties are protected in practice, and whether informal means of social control are circumscribed. The chapters in Part III focus on the effects of international conflict on various dimensions of contestation – on the constraints on executive authority (Krebs), on the will and capacity of democratic publics and their representatives to monitor and control foreign affairs (Avant), and on states' surveillance and policing capacity (Kryder).

Charles Tilly, the distinguished political sociologist with whom many of this volume's chapters engage, made famous the insight that war mobilization was a central driver of European state-building: "war made the state, and the state made war."[10] Some commentators view increases in state strength as inimical to liberal democracy, and for good reason: Strong states often can, if they so desire, eviscerate formal constitutional guarantees. But there is no necessary contradiction between state power and democratic governance.[11] First, the essence of the liberal state lies in the rule of law and the essence of the democratic state in accountability to the general public. As long as authorities remain bound to the rule of law, answerable to public, and compelled to justify publicly their policy stances, even a capacitous state may remain constitutional.[12] In fact, state power, liberal commitments, and democratic institutions grew together over the twentieth century. Second, domestic legitimacy is an important but oft-ignored component of state strength. Various regime types historically have enjoyed legitimacy, but liberal democracies have, since the French Revolution, had a legitimacy advantage. Autocratic

---

[9] Schlozman et al. 2005.

[10] Tilly 1975, 42.

[11] As Tilly argued in Tilly 2004, 36; Tilly 2006, 23–24; Tilly 2007, 15–22.

[12] Finn 1991. However, if state strength is understood to include "autonomy" from societal pressures, as in Theda Skocpol's now-classic formulation, then a stronger state will necessarily be a less democratic and liberal one.

regimes may be relatively autonomous from society, but they are weak over the long run. Paul Starr suggests, in his chapter in this volume and elsewhere, that this autocratic weakness is among the reasons for modern liberal polities' resilience and their surprisingly strong performance in war.[13] Third, effective states are necessary for democratic governance. As Tilly has pointed out, weak states cannot protect citizens from harassment by the state's own agents because they cannot follow through on promises of meaningful contestation. Others have similarly argued that poor, corrupt, and dysfunctional states provide a weak foundation for democratic polities.[14]

Rather than explore the effects of international conflict on institutions, actors, interests, and political dynamics within existing democratic regimes (as in Parts II and III), the chapters in Part I examine the effects of war on democratic transition and consolidation. The earliest social-scientific analysis of democratization focused on various structural conditions, but this scholarship could not explain how these same structures had previously coexisted with stable autocracy or how countries moved from one stable regime to another. Subsequent analysis thus highlighted the role of elite pacts and civil-military bargaining, as well as domestic and transnational nonstate actors, in encouraging, and even driving, autocratic leaders to relinquish their hold on power. In these accounts, war, and especially defeat, is often an important piece of the democratization puzzle.[15] The chapters in Part I debate this relationship between war and democratic transition (Mansfield and Snyder, Starr) and explore how war-induced transitions shape the durability of new democracies (Bermeo).

Unpacking War

Scholars commonly speak of "war" as a causal force, but it is more useful to disaggregate this phenomenon into threat, mobilization, and warfare. Intensifying security threats need not yield corresponding increases in authorities' extraction of societal resources, and preparations for war need not culminate in warfare. These distinct processes can have distinct effects on participation and contestation. As the United States was demobilizing its military and scaling back the government's role in the economy after World War II, Americans discovered that emerging threats could also prompt measures striking at individual freedoms, even without large-scale mobilization or war. Similarly, few countries have mobilized extensive national resources after September 11, 2001, and the struggle against terrorism has entailed, at most, limited warfare, but many polities have rethought societal standards regarding expression, detention, and surveillance.

---

[13] Starr 2007.
[14] Rose and Shin 2001; Tilly 2007, 15–16.
[15] Acemoglu and Robinson 2006, 31–32, 65–68; Bermeo 2007.

States' hunger for war-making resources – mobilization – may alone, in times of both peace and war, affect the quality of existing democracies and the potential for new ones. Mobilization may lead to greater political representation (increased participation) or lead states to reduce the scope of legitimate politics (decreased contestation).[16] Although Europe was at peace after 1870, preparations for war – taxation, military conscription – intensified, with ramifications for democratic politics. Interstate military competition led leaders to extend the sphere of state intervention and thereby transformed the state into a target of popular claims-making.[17] The expansion of participation coincided with the rise of nationalism, which the state promoted partly to serve its military ends and partly in a futile effort to preserve the political status quo by controlling mass politics.[18] Increased participation and decreased contestation preceded, and were independent of, the outbreak of war in 1914.

Warfare, or organized armed conflict between groups, may accelerate these processes and activate new ones. Wartime mobilization of societal resources – people, money, and materials – can intensify bargaining between state and societal actors. Battlefield valor has provided populations seeking first-class citizenship with a powerful argument to use against recalcitrant authorities.[19] Combat experience may also encourage political engagement.[20] Warfare may even boost participation in states that are not combatants: World War I caused European demand for raw materials to plummet, shook the dominance of South American elites who controlled the export industries, mobilized the working class, and catalyzed mass politics in these narrow democracies.[21]

Separating these three processes is necessary: It is important for both theory and policy to understand what is causing what. This volume focuses on mobilization and warfare, devoting less attention to threat alone. The authors examine the effects of industrial and military mobilization on the broadening of citizenship (Starr); postwar associational life (Kage); the power, ends, and strategy of labor (Kier); postwar debate over the state's role in the economy (Wilson); and democratic control over foreign policy (Avant). For others, war itself is central to the analysis – as a potential cause of democratization (Mansfield and Snyder), as a selection mechanism (Starr), as the crucible in which postwar institutions are forged (Bermeo), as the inspiration for political commitments and mobilization (Winter), as the test of institutional mettle (Krebs), as an opportunity to expand claimed executive authority, specifically with regard to federal policing (Kryder), and as the driver of institutional emulation (Avant).

---

[16] For an early effort to focus on the consequences of mobilization, separate of warfare, see Barnett 1992.

[17] Tilly 1992, chap. 4.

[18] Posen 1993.

[19] Krebs 2006.

[20] Leal 1999.

[21] Albert 1988, chap. 6.

HOW WAR MATTERS

Two important dimensions of conflict figure centrally in the existing literature on the consequences of war: scale and outcome. Any examination of how international conflict drives democratization or shapes democratic participation and contestation must begin with these features of conflict. Many chapters in this volume, however, question whether these dimensions produce the effects that the conventional wisdom supposes or whether they are sufficient to explain outcomes of interest.

Reconsidering Scale

International conflict varies in its intensity, duration, and cost. Bellicist historical sociologists, notably Tilly, as well as students of American political development, normally presume that only large-scale wars produce substantial and lasting state-building.[22] This claim was central to Arthur Marwick's research program on total war and social change, and legal scholars have assumed that the more intense the threat, the greater and perhaps more enduring are the resulting restrictions on civil liberties and expansion of executive authority.[23] The bellicist tradition is right to underline the potential importance of conflict's scale, but its effects on democracy vary. Large-scale war is neither necessary nor sufficient to produce large-scale and lasting effects on democratic polities.

Scholars have long noted that large-scale warfare expands participation. The demands of mass mobilization leave state officials little choice: Desperate for money and men, they often feel compelled to grant concessions –such as representative government, the franchise, and social welfare provisions – so that they may retain the cooperation and loyalty of subordinate classes.[24] Although this practice of state bargaining with societal actors during wartime is longstanding, unusual levels of mobilization marked the first half of the twentieth century, and thus these cases – the focus of the chapters in Part II – are "easy" for the conventional wisdom. In other words, if conventional accounts of large-scale war hold, we should observe war's effects most readily in these cases. Michael Mann's pithy take on this payback logic – "the people sacrificed but not for nothing"[25] – captures an essential truth: The enormous sacrifices that modern warfare demands of populations spurred both the expectations, and the reality, of new rights in Europe. But that story is both more complex and uncertain than the usual accounts imply.

[22] Andreski 1954; Lustick 1997; Porter 1994; Tilly 1992. On American political development, see Mayhew 2005.

[23] Marwick 1974. From the large legal literature, see, among many others, Cole 2005 [2003]; Gross and Ní Aoláin 2006. See also Gibler and Hutchinson 2007.

[24] Andreski 1954; Tilly 1992, 83, 99–103; Tilly 2004, 214–216, 237. For an unusually sensitive reading of Tilly's corpus from this angle, see Tarrow 2009.

[25] Mann 1992, 159.

These bargaining or payback arguments justly highlight the importance of a conflict's scale. However, just as the effect of war on state-building varies, separate of scale, according to the *type* of war – whether it is global or not and whether it is internal or external[26] – the *type* of mobilization is critical, as Martin Shaw has noted.[27] In his work on war mobilization and state-building, Michael Barnett similarly distinguishes among international, accommodational, and restructural modes, arguing that only the last influences state-society relations.[28] But scholars have not jumped through the window Barnett opened: His insight only *began* to consider the different strategies states use to mobilize societal resources, and he did not theorize how the type of mobilization shaped democratic institutions.

Several chapters in this volume take up this challenge. Focusing on military recruitment – that is, the mobilization of human resources for soldiering – Deborah Avant distinguishes between mass-conscript citizen armies and voluntary professional forces, arguing that the former encourage contestation, specifically democratic oversight of foreign policy, and that the latter undermine it. Focusing on the mobilization of industrial labor, Elizabeth Kier distinguishes among normative, remunerative, and coercive strategies, arguing that these strategies shape the labor movement's wartime and postwar power and preferences, and thus the prospect for reform. Finally, focusing on wartime industrial mobilization, Mark Wilson distinguishes between procurement efforts run by civilians and those headed by military officers, arguing that during World War II, British civilian control promoted state intervention in the economy and opened the path to a strong welfare state, thus enhancing participation. In contrast, militarized procurement in the United States facilitated a relatively laissez-faire approach to the postwar economy and foreclosed the adoption of expansive social rights. These chapters introduce new ways of thinking about war mobilization and suggest new directions for theorizing about mobilization's effects on participation and contestation.

Payback arguments imply that wartime concessions are retained and that the state's wartime promises to citizens are routinely fulfilled. Yet states often fail to uphold their end of the bargain. During World War I, W.E.B. Dubois urged African Americans temporarily to put aside their grievances: "First Your Country, Then Your Rights." Afterward, a disillusioned Dubois bitterly observed that he "did not realize the full horror of war and its wide impotence as a method of social reform."[29] As Kier relates, British and Italian workers made important gains during and immediately after World War I, but with only a few years of peace, these achievements largely vanished, especially in Italy: Once the threat had passed and the economy had demobilized, the state

[26] Rasler and Thompson 1985; Thies 2006.
[27] Shaw 1987, 148.
[28] Barnett 1992.
[29] Quoted in Wynn 1977, 49.

revoked many of its concessions. The scale of conflict cannot explain when states honor their wartime commitments to citizens.

In at least two ways, however, the type of war mobilization may affect whether wartime gains become permanent and whether wartime leverage translates into peacetime reform. First, mobilization may shape the power and preferences of societal actors. When mobilization spurs them to work within the system, rather than rendering them quiescent or radicalizing them, wartime reform is more lasting. As Kier shows, Britain's reliance on normative appeals during World War I encouraged labor's reformist goals, thereby strengthening labor's position and laying the groundwork for the postwar expansion of citizenship rights; Italy's coercive mobilization radicalized its labor movement, polarized its politics, and ultimately undermined Italian liberalism.

Second, mobilization may structure postwar debate in ways that can advantage particular policy stances and actors to the benefit or detriment of democracy. In this regard, Wilson emphasizes the impact of how mobilization is organized: The heavily militarized U.S. approach allowed the business community and Republicans to portray World War II as a victory for free enterprise and thereby made state intervention a hard sell. The rhetoric of mobilization may also generate postwar expectations and provide groups with political weapons. The inclusive American mobilization rhetoric of World War II, reinforced by the rhetoric of the Cold War, sparked an enduring liberal turn in American citizenship discourse.[30] This in turn propelled a steady expansion in participation as marginalized groups, notably African Americans, seized on this liberal rhetoric to insist that they be granted full rights and privileges.[31] The rhetoric of mobilization can also, however, work to exclude groups from the political process and inhibit contestation. The total wars of the twentieth century required women's inclusion in the workforce, but gendered mobilization rhetoric ensured their swift return to hearth and home once peace came.[32] In Israel, republican discourse, in which rights follow from the fulfillment of duties, has historically blocked Arab citizens' claims to full rights.[33]

Although experts disagree on whether international conflict shapes democratization[34] – a division reflected in the chapters by Starr and by Edward Mansfield and Jack Snyder in Part I – it seems likely that the process of mobilization affects whether democracy emerges. In Africa, the lessons taught in wars of liberation and the capacities those wars bequeathed helped insulate new regimes from praetorian rule: Those African states most likely to avoid military rule were also those that had fought their way to independence.[35] In this volume, Bermeo shows that war-induced transitions to democracy yield

[30] Primus 1999.
[31] Klinkner and Smith 2000.
[32] Higgonet et al. 1987.
[33] Krebs 2006.
[34] For representative pieces on both sides of the debate, see Rasler and Thompson 2004; Reiter 2001.
[35] Frazer 1994.

durable regimes compared to democracies born in peace, and she attributes this longevity in part to how the combatants were organized. Short-lived rebel armies fed by lootable commodities are unlikely to build the political institutions necessary for democracy, whereas belligerent forces with effective organization and broad support are more likely to generate viable political parties led by popular leaders. Yet, such "conflict democracies" are also thin, for those same factors that render these democracies durable – organizationally strong liberation parties and popular "big man" executives – may also ensure that participation remains shallow and contestation narrow. What appears to exert the greatest effect is not the scale of war, civil or international, but how forces are mobilized and organized to prosecute those conflicts.

Several chapters in this volume follow the conventional view that the scale of war is crucial (note, especially, Starr and Kage), and the underlying presumption that large events produce large effects is intuitive and common. But it is wrong to assume that is always the case. Research on complexity and path dependence warns against an exclusive focus on large-scale mobilizations and intense and long wars.[36] Small events can have large effects, and large events can have small effects. System-altering wars often have been limited in their intensity and duration, and large-scale wars have sometimes had limited international consequences.[37] The same can be true of their domestic impact: Even small-scale conflicts may have enduring consequences for democratic practice.[38] Limited wars can enhance participation in ways that bargaining accounts do not anticipate: In the United States, the Vietnam War led to the extension of the franchise to eighteen-year-olds, who were "old enough to carry a gun, but not to vote." Yet limited wars may also erode confidence in government and promote political alienation.[39]

By emphasizing the importance of limited mobilizations and small and medium-sized wars, several chapters in this volume add an important corrective to prior scholarship that tends to focus only on large-scale conflicts. Daniel Kryder sees threats (great and small) and mobilizations (limited and large-scale) as influencing the development of policing and surveillance institutions in the United States. But Kryder insists that while America's large-scale wars have prompted grand federal claims of intrusive policing authority, actual growth in corresponding federal institutional capacity has been more closely tied to threats to the domestic order, which differ in both scale and type from the total wars that have been at the heart of studies of state-building. Ronald Krebs explores how limited wars have varying effects on contestation, depending on how they are framed: What Krebs calls "transformative" limited wars ultimately curb executive authority, while those limited wars legitimated in "restorative" terms serve to normalize extensive wartime

[36] Jervis 1997; Pierson 2004.
[37] Levy 1990.
[38] Centeno 2002, 25.
[39] Sparrow 2002.

executive power. Krebs argues that the "restorative" French withdrawal from Algeria entrenched the expansive authority granted the presidency under the constitution of the Fifth Republic, which was designed to cope with the rigors of war, while the "transformative" U.S. campaign in Vietnam sparked a backlash against the "imperial presidency." Avant finds that even minor military campaigns can have enduring effects: She maintains that the proliferation of unpopular peacekeeping missions led U.S. decision-makers to rely on private security contractors and that, as a result, legislative oversight of U.S. military operations eroded and democratic contestation suffered. In keeping with recent elaborations of historical institutionalism, Avant, Krebs, and Kryder all imply that relatively small-scale events can produce relatively large and long-term consequences. Students of the effects of war and democracy must be attentive to more limited conflicts and mobilizations, as well as the large-scale wars to which they have traditionally devoted their scholarly energies.

Reconsidering Outcome

Wars can end in stalemate, victory, or defeat, with varying effects on the prospects for and the quality of democracy. It makes a difference to postwar politics if the military is crowned in glory or shrouded in disgrace and if the existing regime is seen as prudent and opportunistic or vainglorious and reckless. Military defeat can undermine the power of traditional ruling elites and spark popular mobilization and revolution.[40] Leaders defeated in war often lose power and sometimes their lives.[41] Failure in war can also lead to political learning and less tumultuous policy changes.[42] Yet not all scholars agree that defeat drives democracy. Skocpol and her collaborators posit a link between the vibrancy of civil society and the health of democracy, and argue that associational life flowers among victorious populations and withers among the defeated.[43] Nor is there a consensus that the outcome of war structures postwar democracy. In fact, those in this volume who focus on mobilization (Kage, Kier, Wilson) discount the importance of a war's outcome. Nevertheless, this volume reveals that the outcome of war has important effects on the participants' domestic politics and institutions, that neither victory nor defeat can lay exclusive claim to the mantle of democracy, and that the existing literature has only scratched the surface of how the ending of war alters the course of democracy. This volume offers a more nuanced portrait of how war outcomes can influence democratization as well as participation and contestation in existing democracies.

[40] Skocpol 1979; Tilly 1993.
[41] From the burgeoning literature on war and "leadership tenure," see Bueno de Mesquita and Siverson 1995; Chiozza and Goemans 2004.
[42] Hall 1993; Legro 2005.
[43] Skocpol, Ganz, and Munson 2000; Skocpol et al. 2002.

A war's outcome – whether victory or defeat – can drive the transition to and deepening of democracy. While quantitative studies duel over the effects of war on democratization – and Mansfield and Snyder come down firmly in the camp opposed to any causal relationship – many students of comparative politics closer to the ground assert that war outcomes, and specifically stalemate and defeat, can bolster democratic forces. Scholars have generally left this relationship undertheorized,[44] but there are notable exceptions: Building on Tilly, Leonard Wantchekon argues that warring factions facing prolonged stalemates in civil wars are likely to choose democracy, and Jack Goldstone maintains that military debacles and foreign occupation – more than state crises and revolutions – are crucial catalysts of liberal-democracy.[45] Bermeo's contribution to this volume deepens our understanding of the relationship between war and democratization by specifying several mechanisms that link military outcomes with the construction of "conflict democracies." Decisive defeat in interstate war, she notes, can open the door to foreign powers with democratizing agendas, and battlefield stalemate in civil war can nurture accords that constrain "spoilers." Military defeat can also prompt demoralized militaries to exit the political arena and to rethink their support for authoritarian rule. Military failure can reinvigorate established democracies as well by helping to roll back wartime measures limiting contestation. In a related vein, Krebs illustrates how the U.S. failure in Vietnam led to the subsequent backlash against the Cold War national-security state.

Defeat and stalemate can promote democracy, but so can victory. Scholars have found that democracies tend to win their wars, partly because they can mobilize greater resources, but perhaps more importantly because they choose their wars wisely and fight effectively.[46] Building on this finding, Starr argues that international conflict is a powerful selection mechanism that operates in favor of democracies and helps account for the global democratic trend. Wars eliminate authoritarian regimes from the international system, and democratic victories in harsh battlefield tests enhance the worldwide appeal of their ideals and institutions. Napoleon's relentless march across Europe, Avant similarly argues, contributed to the widespread adoption of the citizen army and thus promoted an institution that sustained democratic control. However, because military victory helps wartime institutional innovations endure and become the "new normal," it can as easily work to reduce contestation as to promote it. The French public's readiness to credit the Fifth Republic with extricating France from Algeria, Krebs maintains, helped consolidate the new constitution's expansive conception of executive authority.

Whether military missions end in victory or defeat often has important, if indeterminate, effects on postwar politics, but these are not natural

---

[44] Bermeo 2003b.
[45] Goldstone 1991; Wantchekon 2004.
[46] Lake 1992; Reiter and Stam 2002. But see Desch 2008; Downes 2009.

categories: The attribution of success or failure is a social construction. Many scholars of international relations implicitly resist this notion even though few would deny that whether a candidate for office wins a debate has less to do with his performance than with how he has managed the audience's expectations.[47] There are limits: Leaders who surrender unconditionally are hard-pressed to deny that the outcome was anything but a devastating defeat. But wars often conclude without a clear outcome. Israel beat back Arab armies in 1973, but the victory was bitter for the Israeli public, which hailed its commanders' tactical brilliance but generally remembered the war as the *mehdal*, the blunder. Krebs and Avant in particular are sensitive to how framing and "myth-making" shape public assessments of both the conflict and the domestic institutions justified in its name.

Some conflict-related processes, notably mobilization, may have effects independent of the war's outcome. Britain and the United States were among the victors of World War II, yet they emerged with very different relationships to the welfare state, Wilson argues, thanks to how they managed war production. Britain and Italy were both on the winning side in World War I, and thus that war's outcome cannot explain the great variation in the preferences of labor and the fate of socioeconomic reform in the two countries; Kier thus turns to the mode of mobilization. Challenging Skocpol's U.S.-centered account, Rieko Kage examines cross-national evidence from World War II and argues that large-scale mobilization nurtures civic engagement among the defeated and the victorious alike and, to a lesser extent, among noncombatants as well. Future research might consider how the scope and organization of mobilization interact with the outcome of war.

What War Does[48]

What is the causal status of war vis-à-vis democracy? First, war may be an interruption. It may disrupt or even temporarily suspend the state's democratic development or encourage a pro-democratic detour, but "interruption" accounts assume that the state ultimately returns to its "normal" – that is, prewar – course. This view is reflected in Mansfield and Snyder's argument that war-related processes sometimes jump-start democratization, but that regimes inevitably slide back into authoritarianism if the underlying conditions favorable to democracy are absent. In their view, war neither inhibits nor encourages democratization, regardless of its scale, type, or outcome. The other authors in the volume acknowledge that many wartime innovations are short-lived, but they find that international conflict has enduring and significant effects on democratic institutions and practices.

---

[47] For an important exception in the international relations literature, see Johnson and Tierney 2006.
[48] With apologies to Miguel Centeno, the language of whose chapter title we have shamelessly appropriated.

Second, war may be a catalyst – an event or process that accelerates the *pace* of change, but does not alter the ultimate outcome. World War I advanced the franchise in Britain, but all adult men and women would have eventually been granted the right to vote. Mansfield and Snyder adopt this view as well. They acknowledge that Portugal's defeat in Angola spurred the transition to democracy, but they see Portugal's democratization as inevitable. Other authors agree that international conflict may influence only the timing of events, but they disagree about what this implies about war's significance. Starr explicitly argues that timing may not be everything, but it can be crucial: Particular outcomes may be due to a combination of causes brought together only in the crucible of war. And even if the eventual outcome is the same from a macrosocietal perspective, the ramifications for individuals could be great.

Third, wars may be transformative, radically altering the trajectory of politics. Wars can create opportunities for action that were previously either unfeasible or unimaginable. In accounts of institutional, ideational, and policy change, war often plays this role, serving as a "critical juncture," an exogenous shock that unhinges previously settled arrangements and that brings new institutions, ideas, or policies into view.[49] This is where conflict's contribution to postwar politics is most marked. Krebs shows how the Algerian War allowed de Gaulle to create the strong presidential regime that he had envisioned since World War II but had been unable to attain. Winter documents how the brutality of World War I altered many veterans' visions of the good society, led some to challenge traditional notions of *raison d'état*, and gave rise to a commitment to human rights whose time might never have come if not for the world wars. By "making war on war," these veterans transformed and strengthened European democracy.

Many war-induced effects on participation and contestation are not the product of intentional design, yet that does not make them any less powerful. In Avant's retelling, for instance, Revolutionary France turned to the *levée en masse* primarily for military reasons, but broad recruitment nevertheless facilitated democratic control. Rebel groups create strong military organizations to fight effectively, not to foster democracy, but Bermeo finds that the strong parties that often result are important building blocks for durable democracies. War's impact on democracy may be powerful, but it is also normally contingent: Its effects are possible, not necessary. It is no accident that nearly every chapter studies "war with adjectives"[50] – distinguishing the effects of total versus limited wars, restorative versus transformative wars, civil wars versus interstate wars – and that intervening variables figure centrally. Mobilization for war or the experience of war are not always the most important factors driving the transition to or the deepening of democracy; various long-term processes and large-scale social structures may matter more. Indeed, Kryder's account of war's impact on federal surveillance

[49] Capoccia and Kelemen 2007; Pierson 2004.
[50] Collier and Levitsky 1997.

and policing institutions in the United States suggests that domestic politics sometimes has the greatest influence. Yet if war shapes state-building, as Tilly persuasively argued and as most scholars now accept, it is not surprising to find that international conflict can also leave a lasting imprint on democratic institutions and practices.

Academic lawyers are also actively debating the long-run impact of international conflict. One view, whose most forceful proponents emerge out of the law-and-economics research program, parallels this "interruption" account: In their view, wartime measures restricting individual liberties and expanding executive authority generally do not survive demobilization, and the few that are retained are presumptively rational adjustments to postwar circumstances.[51] Two alternative accounts maintain that war's causal impact is more profound: They argue that international conflict can "transform" democratic contestation, but they disagree on the direction of the claimed transformation. Some observe a "statist," or perhaps more accurately an "authoritarian," ratchet in which these legal and institutional changes often do become permanent for reasons less rational than psychological, political, and bureaucratic.[52] In contrast, other legal scholars, while also skeptical of these measures' necessity, are more hopeful: They observe a "libertarian" ratchet, in which illiberal conflict measures provoke a political backlash against state power that, over the long-term, deepens democratic institutions and practices.[53]

Krebs argues that all three positions have failed to specify the conditions under which their favored causal mechanism operates, and he suggests that how war is framed helps explain when each account holds. While the other chapters do not explicitly engage the legal scholarship, their conclusions, with the exception of Mansfield and Snyder, echo a "transformative" account in either of its variants. However, nearly all the contributors see the effects of conflict on political institutions as more contingent, with other factors – from scale to political rhetoric to the type of mobilization – intervening. The interdisciplinary group assembled for this volume generally agrees that international conflict does not unvaryingly prompt either a race to the authoritarian bottom or steady progress toward liberal nirvana.

The legal literature also highlights an important limitation of this volume: This volume's chapters tend to focus on *interstate* conflict, not civil wars or internal threats. They do not systematically address the possibility and reality of "permanent emergency" that has shaped political and legal orders around the globe.[54] This important topic is worthy of sustained theoretical and empirical examination.

[51] For the most tightly argued statement, see Posner and Vermeule 2007.
[52] For the best work in this vein, see Cole 2005 [2003]; Donohue 2008; Gross and Ní Aoláin 2006.
[53] For the most nuanced account in the context of free speech in the United States, see Stone 2004.
[54] On the impact of never-ending crises, see especially Gross and Ní Aoláin 2006.

THE FUTURE OF WAR AND DEMOCRACY

The use of military force makes for good television, but its ubiquity in the media belies the reality: War is becoming passé. Interstate war, suppressed by the superpower nuclear rivalry, did not return with the end of the Cold War. Intrastate wars reached their apogee in 1992 and have fallen by three-quarters since. Even conflicts to which governments are not a party are declining. The number of fatalities in interstate and intrastate wars has fallen steeply since the late 1960s.[55] These trends might suggest that this volume's chapters, which focus largely on the interstate wars of the first half of the twentieth century, are of historical interest alone. But that conclusion does not follow. Even if current trends are irreversible – and we are skeptical that international politics has any permanent trajectory – armed conflict and military organizations may still influence democratic institutions and processes, though not for the good. As Starr and Miguel Centeno both argue, the end of the mass army (at least in the industrialized world) has foreclosed an important path to expanded participation and perhaps contestation. But insecurity and limited wars are still with us, with democratic contestation at home ranking among their likely victims.

From the latter half of the nineteenth through the late twentieth centuries, industrialized societies paid a heavy price for security, mobilizing vast societal resources for the production of war materiel and supporting mass armies through universal conscription. Whether these efforts enhanced security is debatable, but they did inadvertently broaden democracy. State-society bargaining helped drive the episodic and often unwilling expansion of participation. Other mechanisms – from socialization to the deployment of military sacrifice – also hinged on the mass mobilization that only large-scale war, or its prospect, can entail. And these effects sometimes extended to contestation. The mass army may have underpinned democratic control over foreign policy, and the state's hunger for resources may have led to the reluctant acceptance of checks on executive authority and protections for individual liberties.[56]

Today, the forces for peace in the industrialized world are numerous: the destructiveness of conventional and nuclear warfare, the depth of globalization, the density of international institutions and law, and the deepening popular commitments to norms controlling the use of force. The era of the mass army is also over: Its strategic rationale is less compelling, and citizens in industrialized states are unwilling to support obligatory military service.

Centeno reminds us not to extrapolate too readily from the experiences of the industrialized world. Perhaps developing nations have learned the horrible lessons of the world wars, and perhaps the spread of democracy will facilitate that learning process.[57] It is also possible that their state institutions

[55] Human Security Report Project, http://www.hsrgroup.org/.
[56] Holmes 2003.
[57] Cederman 2001.

and economies are too weak to support large-scale mobilization and warfare. Developing nations have often decoupled military mobilization from societal extraction, thanks to mercenaries, financing from abroad, or the armed forces' control of vast economic enterprises. States have, therefore, been able to mount military campaigns without making concessions to mass publics, foreclosing one war-induced route to democratization. But the decline of mass armies and large-scale warfare in the industrialized world need not portend their obsolescence elsewhere. As developing nations industrialize and as their state institutions strengthen, mobilization and warfare that had been beyond their capabilities may become conceivable. Contrary to Starr's implication, the conjuncture between war and equality may have disappeared only in the so-called West.

The decline of large-scale warfare in the industrialized world does not mean that democratic theorists and policymakers can safely avoid thinking about the implications of international conflict for politics at home. How industrialized states cope with smaller-scale threats and how they design their armed forces may be particularly worrisome for democratic contestation. We cannot easily imagine that moderate levels of conflict would prompt contractions in participation, but we can envision how more limited conflicts might reduce contestation.

First, insecurity alone (even in the absence of mobilization or substantial warfare) can render increased executive authority attractive and can prompt reductions in individual freedoms, especially those of minorities. Sustained by fear of "the next attack" after 9/11, Americans and their representatives in Congress acceded to measures concentrating power in the executive branch and permitting the abrogation of various rights with only minimal congressional or judicial oversight. It has been the fear of terrorism, not war in Iraq or Afghanistan, that has driven the perceived need to limit contestation. Moreover, many nations whose military forces are not engaged abroad have been similarly rethinking the "balance" between security and liberty and between executive dispatch and legislative deliberation. Even if the "War on Terror" recedes from popular consciousness, its revival in the future remains possible.

Second, *how* states raise military forces and prosecute (even limited) missions may be as important for contestation as the extent of mobilization. The increasing reliance on volunteers and private military contractors may, as Avant suggests, limit the capacity of democratic publics to contest state action and may promote norms that devalue public engagement. This may be even more likely and consequential through a process Avant does not explore. Even if national economies are not mobilized to wage war, foreign policy must still be legitimated before democratic audiences. The result, in Michael Mann's memorable phrase, is "spectator sport militarism": the mobilization of societal sentiment, including warrior worship and the fetishization of military technology. When forces are raised through voluntary means, soldiers are particularly valorized and alternative voices are silenced.[58] When such militarism is coupled with missions that appear never-ending – think the "long war" – contestation especially suffers. Moreover, the increased reliance on professional forces around the globe may also weaken civilian control of the military. Volunteers often identify and are identified as "citizen-soldiers" in Western democracies, but the long-serving professionals that inhabit today's militaries are, compared to the citizen-soldiers who served in the mass armies of the nineteenth and twentieth centuries, increasingly distant from the societies they are charged with protecting. Some fear that this gap has led to the creation of a distinct military caste and has eroded civilian authority at the highest levels of foreign and defense policy-making.[59]

This volume's historical concerns have contemporary significance. Its authors place their bets on the past as the only guide to an unknown future. Yet our knowledge of the past effects of international conflict on democratic institutions and processes remains unsure. We suggest four paths for future research.

First, *cross-national comparison.* Democratic polities' choices after 9/11 sparked an explosion of research, but the literature has generally been too focused on the American experience. More comparative historical studies are needed across the range of questions identified.

Second, *conceptual and data development.* The databases commonly used in the literature on democracy (Polity, Freedom House) are not sufficiently fine-grained to capture many important but subtle changes, including those in Europe and North America, since 2001. The development of more refined measures of participation and contestation, and the collection of historical data based upon them, would facilitate statistical testing of these chapters' hypotheses as well as others.

Third, *theoretical extension.* This volume's chapters help advance scholars' understanding of the factors, beyond scale and outcome, that may affect war's consequences for democracy. But theoretical development remains rudimentary. More analysis is needed, especially on the domestic context in which war's effects play out. For instance, how do civil law and common law regimes differ in their response to the pressures of international conflict? Or presidential versus semipresidential versus parliamentary regimes? How does the nature of civil society shape civic organizations' responses to war, and how do variations in economic structures and principles influence the type of mobilization and its effect on participation and contestation?

Fourth, *beyond the industrialized world and beyond interstate war.* This volume's chapters generally focus on old, rich democracies and on major-power interstate wars in the first half of the twentieth century. Because this volume is an initial foray into less-charted terrain, and because a narrower empirical scope helps preserve the project's coherence, that choice made sense. But it

---

[58] Bacevich 2007; Mann 1992, 183–187.
[59] Cohen 2000; Kohn 2002.

is crucial that research be conducted on less developed democracies entering the international system in subsequent decades. Do the processes uncovered in these chapters yield insight into states differently situated – economically, politically, and temporally? What purchase do these processes have in cases of ethnic and civil wars? Have the internationalization of war and the proliferation of peacekeepers and nongovernmental actors altered the dynamics between war and democratization?

We know that war is destructive, but the ancient Greek philosopher Heraclitus reminds us that war is also generative: "War is the father of all things." Whether its role is as uniform and universal as Heraclitus suggests is debatable. But at various moments and for various reasons, the modern social sciences have neglected, or rather occluded, war, impeding this debate. This volume brings war back into the story of democracy and aims to spark such debate once more.

PART I

WAR AND DEMOCRATIC TRANSITIONS

New and Durable Democracies?

2

Does War Influence Democratization?

Edward D. Mansfield and Jack Snyder

Contrarians have been fascinated by the idea that war can lead to progress.[1] In particular, there is a long tradition of viewing war as a midwife of democracy. For Americans raised on the history of the U.S. Revolutionary War, the idea of fighting for freedom seems intuitively plausible. More scholarly analyses note that prosecuting a war requires governments to raise armies and revenue, which places substantial demands on society. In exchange for meeting these demands, citizens in nondemocratic countries have sometimes pressed for an expansion of the franchise, stimulating democratic reforms.

An opposing school of thought, however, notes that in order to wage war countries often militarize society, centralize power, and restrict civil liberties, thereby promoting the rise of authoritarianism and the establishment of garrison states. Although scholars have advanced these competing claims for well over half a century, they have not been thoroughly or conclusively tested.[2] The purpose of our chapter is to help fill this important gap in the literature.

We begin by conducting a statistical analysis of the influence of war on democratization spanning the nineteenth and twentieth centuries. We examine the effects of both interstate and other external wars on subsequent democratic transition, using four different measures of democratization. Our results provide no support for the view that war inhibits democratization; instead, they furnish some scattered support for the view that war promotes democratization. However, further historical analysis of the cases drawn from the statistical analysis casts doubt on the claim that war has any strong, systematic impact on regime change. In a number of cases – including Britain and Germany after World War I; Portugal after its colonial wars in Angola,

For helpful comments and suggestions, we are grateful to Nancy Bermeo, James Caporaso, Page Fortna, Stacie Goddard, Beth Kier, Ron Krebs, two anonymous reviewers, and the other participants at a conference held at the University of Washington. For research assistance, we are grateful to Rumi Morishima.

[1] Nef 1963.
[2] Krebs 2009.

Mozambique, and Guinea Bissau from 1961 to 1975; and Argentina after the Falklands War – war did stimulate democratization. But in many other cases comprising our sample, the association between war and regime change was more coincidental than causal. Taken together, the quantitative and narrative case evidence in this chapter provides little indication that war either stimulates or inhibits democratization. Our results suggest that the most powerful causes of democratization are not war but rather economic development, the character of the international neighborhood around the transitional state, and the legacy of the state's prior political institutions.

THE LINKS BETWEEN WAR AND DEMOCRATIZATION

Some scholars have argued that war undermines democracy by creating a garrison state, providing an excuse for the curtailment of liberties, and offering opportunities to revile the domestic opposition as traitors.[3] Others have argued the opposite. War, they claim, fosters democratization by breaking the power of elites, mobilizing the masses, and creating incentives for the state to bargain with the people it needs to contribute to the war effort.[4]

It may be that both positions are correct, but under different circumstances. War might undermine democratic liberties by reinforcing conformity in the short run but promote democracy in the long run by making elites more dependent on the support of energized mass groups. War might strengthen the absolutist state in continental powers that commandeer men and materiel for war through coercion, whereas it might strengthen democratic institutions in states that finance war through market loans secured by strict legal guarantees.[5] Short wars might bolster dictators seeking prestige through military victories, whereas long, costly wars or extended military rivalries that require the mobilization of vast military resources might stimulate democracy by creating a need for nationalism and popular government.[6] Victories might help incumbent elites, whereas defeats may sweep them from power and lay the foundation for democrats to obtain office.[7] International wars may rally the masses around the ruling elites, whereas civil wars may topple them.[8]

But these claims cannot be evaluated simply by logical arguments and apt illustrations. A case could easily be made for the opposite of any of the propositions that we just laid out. Systematic tests supplemented by the tracing of specific causal mechanisms are needed to sort out these claims and counterclaims.

In this chapter, we focus on the general argument that war increases the likelihood of democratization by enhancing popular groups' freedom to

[3] See Hintze 1975; Dolman 2004.
[4] See Andreski 1954; Tilly 1992.
[5] See Downing 1992; Tilly 1992.
[6] Posen 1993.
[7] Goemans 2000.
[8] Stein 1976.

contend for political power, by expanding the scope of political participation, and by strengthening the institutions that make democracy work.[9] Specifically, we will look for the following proposed mechanisms, which have been highlighted in previous research:

(1) War breaks the power of antidemocratic elites – sweeping them from power, sapping their resources, or discrediting them – and opens the door for more democratic forces.[10]

(2) War leads to the mobilization of mass groups that had previously played little role in politics or had been weakly organized, increasing their capacity for collective action, developing civil society networks, heightening their political consciousness, placing arms or economic resources in their hands, or expanding their repertoires of political action in ways that forge tools for successful democratization.[11]

(3) War induces antidemocratic elites to bargain with mass groups in order to gain their cooperation with the war effort, resulting in broader political inclusion and greater political power for pro-democracy mass groups.[12]

(4) War strengthens institutions and ideologies that facilitate democratic rule, including state administrative capacity, rule of law, economic capacity, national consolidation, and patriotism.[13]

MEASURING DEMOCRATIZATION

To test the effects of war on democratization, we need to develop a measure of regime change. Consistent with much existing research, we use the Polity IV data as well as indices developed by Ted Robert Gurr and his colleagues for this purpose.[14] This data set includes yearly information on a variety of domestic institutions for a very broad cross-section of countries from 1800 to 2004. The Polity data have been widely used in studies of international relations and comparative politics, and they cover a wider array of countries and a longer time period than any alternative compilation.[15] Gurr, Keith Jaggers, and Will Moore combine annual measures of the competitiveness of the process through which a country's chief executive is selected, the openness of this process, the extent to which institutional constraints exist on a chief executive's decision-making authority, the competitiveness of political participation

[9] Krebs 2009. To make this point, Krebs draws on Dahl 1971.
[10] Tilly 2003.
[11] Feldman 1966.
[12] Tilly 1992, chap. 4.
[13] Ibid., chap. 3.
[14] See Gurr, Jaggers, and Moore 1989; Jaggers and Gurr 1995; Marshall and Jaggers 2005.
[15] For some alternative data on regime type and regime change, see Bollen 1980; Gastil 1980 and 1990; Gasiorowski 1996; Przeworski et al. 2000. For an analysis of these compilations and the Polity data, see Munck and Verkuilen 2002.

within a country, and the degree to which binding rules govern political participation to create 11-point indices of each state's democratic (*Democracy*) and autocratic (*Autocracy*) characteristics.[16] The difference between these indices (*Regime = Democracy – Autocracy*) provides a summary measure of regime type that ranges from –10 to 10. Jaggers and Gurr define democracies as states where *Regime* > 6 and autocracies as states where *Regime* < –6.[17] The remaining states (i.e., those where –7 < *Regime* < 7) are coded as mixed, or anocracies.

The relatively few statistical studies of the effects of political-military conflict on democratization have measured regime change using some variant of Jaggers and Gurr's summary index.[18] However, in addition to this index, which we refer to as the composite index, there is reason to analyze democratization along some of the specific institutional dimensions that make it up. Particularly important are the competitiveness of political participation, the openness of executive recruitment, and the extent of the constraints placed on the chief executive. We emphasize these factors and analyze them separately because each has been featured in the theoretical literature on war and democratization. Furthermore, these factors are not closely related. On average, the correlation between any given pair of measures of democratization is quite modest, indicating that they are not tapping the same institutional characteristics.[19] Finally, unlike these factors, the remaining variables that make up *Regime* are coded in a way that makes distinguishing between democracies and autocracies quite difficult. For each of these three institutional factors, a state's regime type is assessed using the following coding rules.

The competitiveness of political participation is measured using a 5-point scale. We code as autocratic those states characterized by what Gurr, Jaggers, and Moore refer to as "suppressed competition," a category that includes totalitarian dictatorships, despotic monarchies, and military dictatorships in which no significant political activity is allowed outside of the ruling regime.[20] We code states characterized by "competitive competition" as democratic. In such states, competitive political groupings (usually political parties) are stable and enduring, and their competition rarely leads to violence or widespread disruption. We code as anocratic states falling into any of Gurr, Jaggers, and Moore's three intermediate categories of the competitiveness of political participation (restricted/transitional, factional, and transitional competition).[21] Gurr, Jaggers, and Moore claim that "transitions to Competitive [i.e., full democracy] are not complete until a national election is held on a fully

---

[16] See Gurr, Jaggers, and Moore 1989, 36–39; Jaggers and Gurr 1995.
[17] Jaggers and Gurr 1995.
[18] See Mousseau and Shi 1999; James, Solberg, and Wolfson 1999; Oneal and Russett 2000; Reiter 2001; Gleditsch 2002; Reuveny and Li 2003; Rasler and Thompson 2004; Pevehouse 2005.
[19] Mansfield and Snyder 2005.
[20] Gurr, Jaggers, and Moore 1989, 18.
[21] Ibid., 19.

competitive basis."[22] Based on this variable, distinguishing among autocracies, anocracies, and democracies is fairly straightforward.

The openness of executive recruitment is measured using a 4-point scale. We code as autocratic those regimes with hereditary absolute rulers or with rulers who seized power by force. We code as anocratic those regimes with dual executives, in which a hereditary ruler shares authority with an appointed or elected governing minister. We code as democratic those regimes that Gurr, Jaggers, and Moore classify as having an open system of executive recruitment, regardless of whether the executive is popularly elected or selected through some other regularized process. We rely on the case studies conducted later in this chapter to identify any nondemocratic "false positives" that might result from the use of this measure.

Institutional constraints on the chief executive are measured using a 7-point scale. We classify regimes as autocratic if the chief executive has unlimited authority or if the executive's authority falls in an intermediate category whereby the institutional constraints faced by this individual are less than "slight to moderate."[23] We classify regimes as democratic if "accountability groups [such as legislatures] have effective authority equal to or greater than the executive in most areas of activity," or if the constraints on the executive are more than "substantial" based on the Polity scale.[24] Substantial constraints exist when the executive has more effective authority than the legislature, but the legislature can block appointments, funds, or bills proposed by the executive. Regimes in which executive constraints lie in the range between "slight" and "substantial" are classified as anocratic.

The sample analyzed in this chapter includes all states coded as members of the interstate system by the Correlates of War (COW) Project during the nineteenth and twentieth centuries.[25] For each measure of regime type (the composite index and the three component indices), we measure democratization over five-year intervals. We analyze regime change over five years because, in various cases, the data needed to code a state's regime type are missing for years immediately surrounding the change. As such, certain instances of democratization are omitted from the sample when very short intervals are analyzed, a problem that is ameliorated by considering the effects of transitions occurring over five-year periods. To measure democratization, we code each state, i, as democratic, autocratic, or anocratic in every year, t. We then measure i's regime type in year t-5. *Democratization* is a variable that equals 1 if state i changes from either an autocracy or an anocracy in year t-5 to a democracy in year t. It equals 0 otherwise.[26]

[22] Ibid., 19.
[23] Ibid., 14–16.
[24] Ibid., 16.
[25] COW Project 2005.
[26] As we explain below, war is measured in year t-6. Consequently, states that are not members of the international system in year t-6 are excluded from our sample. Note that the COW Project and the Polity Project usually agree on when states are formed and when they dissolve.

In the following analysis, we code *Democratization* in two somewhat different ways to make sure that our results do not depend on which coding procedure is used. Over a given ten-year period from t-9 to t, for example, during which a state was nondemocratic until year t-5 and then democratic from year t-4 onward, we would observe five instances in which *Democratization* equals 1: from t-9 to t-4, from t-8 to t-3, from t-7 to t-2, from t-6 to t-1, and from t-5 to t. One might consider only the initial instance to be a case of democratization since the regime change occurs in year t-4, or one might consider all five instances to be cases of democratization. Since we see no conceptual basis for choosing between these two procedures, we use both. We conduct one set of tests where only the first episode is considered a case of democratization (in this example, from t-9 to t-4). The following four cases are coded as missing. We also conduct a second set of tests after coding all five cases as instances of democratization. It is important to recognize that no democratizing country is omitted altogether, regardless of which procedure is used. The only difference based on these procedures is whether, for a given country, democratization is coded as a single event in the data set or an event occurring over a longer period. Estimating our statistical models using both coding procedures will help to assess the robustness of the following results.

It is also important to note that the Polity data include various yearly observations in which a country is coded as –66, –77, or –88 because its institutions are in flux, are difficult to code, or are controlled by a foreign power. We follow the Polity Project in transforming these "standardized authority codes" into values of *Regime* and each of the three component indices, thereby reducing the number of missing observations in our sample.[27] We refer to this as the Adjusted Polity procedure.[28] However, we also include a set of results in which the values –66, –77, and –88 are treated as missing to ensure that transforming these values in the way that the Polity Project suggests does not unduly influence our findings. We refer to this as the Polity procedure.

MEASURING WAR

Most studies of conflict's effect on democratization have focused on the influence of militarized interstate disputes (MIDs).[29] MIDs are a broad class of conflicts ranging in intensity from wars to disputes involving threats to use

---

However, the Polity Project considers the following pairs of states to be separate countries: (1) Sardinia and Italy, (2) Prussia and Germany, (3) the Ottoman Empire and Turkey, (4) Serbia and Yugoslavia, and (5) Russia and the Soviet Union. The COW Project considers each of these pairs to be a single country. Like previous studies, we follow the Polity Project on this issue.

[27] Marshall and Jaggers 2005.

[28] The Polity Project refers to this transformed Polity variable as "Polity2."

[29] See Mousseau and Shi 1999; James, Solberg, and Wolfson 1999; Oneal and Russett 2000; Reiter 2001; Gleditsch 2002; Reuveny and Li 2003; Rasler and Thompson 2004; Pevehouse 2005.

force but no actual fatalities.[30] Disputes that do not escalate to war constitute the vast majority of MIDs. However, the main causal mechanisms through which war is alleged to cause democratization (such as breaking the grip of authoritarian elites and mobilizing masses) seem more relevant to war than to lower-intensity disputes. Consequently, we analyze wars rather than MIDs in the following empirical analysis.

Like most quantitative studies of war, we rely on the COW Project's definition of and data on war.[31] These data cover the period from 1816 to 1997. The COW Project defines two types of external wars, which are conflicts in which a state (or group of states) actively fights a foreign enemy. Interstate wars are hostilities between members of the interstate system that generate at least 1,000 battle fatalities. To be considered a participant, a state must have suffered at least 100 fatalities or have sent at least 1,000 troops into combat. Extrasystemic wars are imperial or colonial actions in which a nation-state engages in military conflict against a nonstate actor, leading to at least 1,000 battle deaths. States are considered participants in such wars if they sustained – in combination with any allies – at least 1,000 deaths in battle during each year of the conflict. Since existing arguments suggest that any type of external war might promote democratization, we analyze both interstate and extrasystemic wars.

Initially, we analyze interstate and extrasystemic wars together. To this end, we create a variable, *All War*, that equals 1 if state i is involved in either type of external war in year t-6, 0 otherwise. However, we also examine these types of wars separately to determine if their effects on democratization differ. To this end, we define two variables. *Interstate War* equals 1 if state i is embroiled in a war with another nation-state in year t-6, 0 otherwise. *Extrasystemic War* equals 1 if state i is involved in a foreign war against a nonstate actor in year t-6. Recall that *Democratization* is measured from year t-5 to year t. Measuring war in year t-6 reduces the possibility that our results will be undermined by any simultaneity bias that might exist if a state's regime type in t-5 influences whether it is enmeshed in a war. Nonetheless, we will analyze the impact of war when it is measured in year t-5 in a set of additional tests described later.

THE CONTROL VARIABLES

In addition to external war, it is important to account for various factors that previous studies have linked to democratization. Due to our interest in tracking the effects of war on democratization over the last two centuries and across as many countries as possible, accumulating data on some of these factors is quite difficult. Nonetheless, we include a series of control

---

[30] See Gochman and Maoz 1984; Jones, Bremer, and Singer 1996.
[31] See Small and Singer 1982; Sarkees 2000.

variables in the following analyses, all of which are measured in year t-5 unless otherwise noted.

First, we include the natural logarithm of (1) each state's per capita energy consumption (*Development*), (2) each state's national population (*Population*), and (3) the ratio of each state's total military personnel in year t-6 to its total military personnel in year t-11 (*Military Personnel*). Further, we include the percentage of its population located in urban centers (*Urban Population*) and the length of time it has been a sovereign entity (*Years Sovereign*). Data on these variables are taken from the COW Project's National Material Capabilities version 3.02 and State System Membership List version 2004.1.[32] Many studies have concluded that heightened economic development promotes democratization, and per capita energy consumption is a widely used measure of development. In addition, various studies have argued that smaller countries may be better able to create and maintain democratic forms of government.[33] The log of the ratio of military personnel in year t-6 to t-11 is included to test the argument that as the government draws a larger portion of society into the military, citizens will demand a more democratic polity.[34] We analyze the percentage of the population living in urban centers because it is commonly held that urbanization contributes to democratization.[35] The length of time that a state has been sovereign is included because it has been argued that states are more likely to democratize as they age.[36]

Second, various recent studies have concluded that democratization is characterized by geographical diffusion.[37] More specifically, these studies have found that the probability of a state experiencing a democratic transition increases as the number of established democracies neighboring it rises. To analyze this claim, we measure the number of each state's democratic neighbors (*Democratic Neighbors*) using data drawn from Polity IV and from the COW project's Direct Contiguity Data version 3.1. We consider countries to be neighbors if they were separated by a land or river border or by 400 miles of water or less.

Third, we follow some recent research on democratization in including a dummy variable indicating whether state i is a major power (*Major Power*) based on the COW Project's definition of such powers.[38] We also control for this state's regime score (*Regime Score*) in year t-5 based on which of the four measures (the composite index or the three component indices) is being used to measure democratization. It may be, for example, that anocratic states are more likely to democratize than their autocratic counterparts. If so, the

[32] See Singer 1987; COW Project 2005.
[33] See Dahl and Tufte 1973; Kurzman and Leahey 2004.
[34] Andreski 1954.
[35] See Huntington 1991, 39; Wejnert 2005.
[36] Pevehouse 2005.
[37] See Gleditsch 2002; Rasler and Thompson 2004; Pevehouse 2005; Gleditsch and Ward 2006.
[38] See Mousseau, Hegre, and Oneal 2003; COW Project 2005.

coefficient of this variable would be positive. Finally, to account for any temporal dependence in the data, we include a spline function with three knots representing the length of time, as of t-5, since state i last experienced a democratic transition.[39]

RESULTS

Our analysis spans the period from 1827 to 1997, since these are the years for which we are able to obtain data for all of the variables included in our model. The sample of cases that we analyze includes all nondemocratic states in year t-5, based on the composite index, the openness of executive recruitment, the competitiveness of political participation, and the constraints on the chief executive, respectively. Democracies are removed from the sample because they cannot democratize and, therefore, are out of the "risk set." Since, in all cases, the observed value of our dependent variable is dichotomous, we estimate our models using logistic regression. To account for the grouped nature of the data by country, the standard error for each estimated coefficient is clustered by country. The results for the composite index are shown in Table 2.1. In Table 2.2, we present the estimated effects of war involvement on democratization for each component variable. The estimated coefficients of the control variables are omitted to conserve space.

These results provide only scattered support for the view that war promotes democratization. The general pattern of results does not differ markedly between international and extrasystemic wars, although the results are marginally stronger based on extrasystemic wars. Nor does this pattern vary much depending on whether we code only the first episode of democratization for a given country (t-9 to t-4 in our earlier example) and consider the remaining cases to be missing or whether we consider all cases in which the observed value of *Democratization* equals 1. Finally, the overall pattern of results is much the same, regardless of whether we measure regime type using the Polity or the Adjusted Polity coding procedure. There is, however, some variation in the strength of war's effect depending on which measure of regime type is analyzed: The results are strongest based on the openness of executive recruitment and weakest based on the competitiveness of political participation.

Initially, we consider the impact of war on democratization when the composite index is used to measure regime type. As shown in Table 2.1, eleven of the twelve estimated coefficients associated with war are positive, indicating that war increases the odds of democratization. These results, however, are relatively weak: Merely three of the estimated coefficients are statistically significant. Only when we focus on Extrasystemic War and code just the first

---

[39] Beck, Katz, and Tucker 1998.

TABLE 2.1. *Effects of War on Democratization, Based on the Composite Index, 1827–1997*

	All War				Interstate War				Extrasystemic War			
	Adj. Polity		Polity		Adj. Polity		Polity		Adj. Polity		Polity	
Variables	Model 1	Model 2	Model 3	Model 4	Model 5	Model 6	Model 7	Model 8	Model 9	Model 10	Model 11	Model 12
	1st episode	All incidence	1st episode	All incidence	1st episode	All incidence	1st episode	All incidence	1st episode	All incidence	1st episode	All incidence
Population	-0.005	0.006	-0.009	0.004	0.008	0.007	0.008	0.004	0.004	0.014	-0.003	0.008
	(0.126)	(0.108)	(0.134)	(0.104)	(0.131)	(0.108)	(0.136)	(0.105)	(0.122)	(0.106)	(0.130)	(0.104)
Development	0.148*	0.063	0.116+	0.032	0.149*	0.066	0.114+	0.032	0.135+	0.053	0.106+	0.025
	(0.072)	(0.079)	(0.063)	(0.078)	(0.071)	(0.079)	(0.060)	(0.077)	(0.070)	(0.078)	(0.061)	(0.079)
Urban Population	0.003	0.011	0.005	0.015	0.003	0.010	0.004	0.015	0.005	0.012	0.006	0.016
	(0.009)	(0.012)	(0.009)	(0.011)	(0.009)	(0.012)	(0.009)	(0.011)	(0.009)	(0.012)	(0.010)	(0.012)
Military Personnel	-0.161	-0.194+	-0.158	-0.231+	-0.136	-0.177	-0.121	-0.212+	-0.147	-0.163	-0.148	-0.213+
	(0.138)	(0.117)	(0.136)	(0.122)	(0.122)	(0.109)	(0.127)	(0.115)	(0.148)	(0.111)	(0.141)	(0.121)
Years Sovereign	0.016***	0.018***	0.016***	0.018***	0.015***	0.019***	0.016***	0.019***	0.015***	0.018***	0.015***	0.018***
	(0.003)	(0.004)	(0.003)	(0.004)	(0.003)	(0.004)	(0.004)	(0.004)	(0.003)	(0.004)	(0.003)	(0.004)
Major Power	-1.379	-0.960+	-1.761*	-1.182+	-1.331	-0.734	-1.807+	-1.039	-1.688+	-1.115	-2.061*	-1.312
	(0.879)	(0.559)	(0.846)	(0.676)	(1.084)	(0.572)	(1.036)	(0.731)	(0.921)	(0.717)	(0.871)	(0.832)
All War	0.513	0.602+	0.490	0.534								
	(0.361)	(0.337)	(0.410)	(0.441)								
Interstate War					0.153	0.449	-0.177	0.329				
					(0.836)	(0.425)	(0.847)	(0.548)				

	(1)	(2)	(3)	(4)	(5)	(6)	(7)	(8)	(9)	(10)	(11)	(12)
Extrasystemic War									1.157**	0.961	1.121*	0.794
									(0.402)	(0.658)	(0.551)	(1.185)
Adj. Polity Level	0.028	0.009			0.030	0.012			0.026	0.008		
	(0.026)	(0.023)			(0.026)	(0.023)			(0.026)	(0.022)		
Polity Level			0.024	0.008			0.026	0.011			0.022	0.009
			(0.028)	(0.028)			(0.028)	(0.029)			(0.028)	(0.027)
Dem. Neighbors	0.256**	0.192**	0.287**	0.232**	0.261**	0.186*	0.302***	0.232**	0.279**	0.212**	0.307***	0.244**
	(0.088)	(0.075)	(0.094)	(0.082)	(0.092)	(0.077)	(0.092)	(0.082)	(0.086)	(0.079)	(0.088)	(0.079)
Duration	-0.166**	-0.593***	-0.173**	-0.572***	-0.167**	-0.593***	-0.172**	-0.571***	-0.168**	-0.598***	-0.176**	-0.574***
	(0.058)	(0.047)	(0.058)	(0.047)	(0.058)	(0.047)	(0.058)	(0.048)	(0.058)	(0.048)	(0.059)	(0.049)
Spline 1	-0.000+	-0.001***	-0.000+	-0.001***	-0.000+	-0.001***	-0.000+	-0.001***	-0.000+	-0.001***	-0.000+	-0.001***
	(0.000)	(0.000)	(0.000)	(0.000)	(0.000)	(0.000)	(0.000)	(0.000)	(0.000)	(0.000)	(0.000)	(0.000)
Spline 2	0.000	0.000***	0.000	0.000***	0.000	0.000***	0.000	0.000***	0.000	0.000***	0.000	0.000***
	(0.000)	(0.000)	(0.000)	(0.000)	(0.000)	(0.000)	(0.000)	(0.000)	(0.000)	(0.000)	(0.000)	(0.000)
Spline 3	-0.000	-0.000***	-0.000	-0.000***	-0.000	-0.000***	-0.000	-0.000***	-0.000	-0.000***	-0.000	-0.000***
	(0.000)	(0.000)	(0.000)	(0.000)	(0.000)	(0.000)	(0.000)	(0.000)	(0.000)	(0.000)	(0.000)	(0.000)
Constant	-3.607+	-0.609	-3.592	-0.984	-3.791+	-0.625	-3.867+	-0.986	-3.764*	-0.728	-3.717+	-1.057
	(1.950)	(1.878)	(2.185)	(1.858)	(2.047)	(1.876)	(2.252)	(1.865)	(1.901)	(1.854)	(2.139)	(1.854)
Log likelihood	-300.308	-417.668	-281.495	-384.033	-300.939	-418.655	-281.993	-384.753	-299.026	-417.571	-280.505	-384.142
N	6207	6408	5766	5920	6207	6408	5766	5920	6207	6408	5766	5920

Note: Entries are logistic regression coefficient estimates with robust standard errors in parentheses. First episode indicates that only the first episode of democratization is coded as valid; all incidence indicates that all cases of democratization are analyzed. The Polity2 data fill in observations that are coded as -66, -77, or -88 by the Polity Project. The Polity data code these observations as missing. Statistical significance is indicated as follows: +$p < 0.10$, *$p < 0.05$, **$p < 0.01$, ***$p < 0.001$.

TABLE 2.2. *Effects of War on Democratization, Based on the Three Component Indices, 1827–1997*

	Competitiveness of Participation				Openness of Executive Recruitment				Executive Constraints			
	Coeff.	S.E.	Log likelihood	N	Coeff.	S.E.	Log likelihood	N	Coeff.	S.E.	Log likelihood	N
All war												
Adj. Polity, first episode	0.316	(0.643)	−193.646	6539	1.184**	(0.372)	−334.712	2652	0.782+	(0.416)	−324.217	5772
Adj. Polity, all incidence	0.105	(0.512)	−298.323	6662	1.314**	(0.401)	−497.399	2899	0.610+	(0.340)	−469.343	5982
Polity, first episode	0.440	(0.597)	−180.490	6079	1.536***	(0.371)	−273.818	2428	0.563	(0.512)	−308.243	5363
Polity, all incidence	0.174	(0.566)	−272.217	6182	1.730***	(0.487)	−401.863	2600	0.298	(0.432)	−427.750	5522
Interstate war												
Adj. Polity, first episode	0.385	(0.568)	−193.622	6539	1.209**	(0.410)	−335.599	2652	0.442	(0.693)	−325.576	5772
Adj. Polity, all incidence	0.075	(0.435)	−266.992	6662	0.785	(0.478)	−471.955	2899	0.872*	(0.409)	−468.398	5982
Polity, first episode	0.490	(0.520)	−180.487	6079	1.354**	(0.459)	−276.752	2428	0.210	(0.689)	−308.904	5363
Polity, all incidence	0.092	(0.497)	−239.708	6182	1.177*	(0.498)	−340.658	2600	0.537	(0.577)	−427.387	5522
Extrasystemic war												
Adj. Polity, first episode	−0.166	(1.437)	−193.766	6539	0.807	(0.568)	−338.836	2652	1.314+	(0.793)	−324.007	5772
Adj. Polity, all incidence	0.368	(0.855)	−266.865	6662	1.267*	(0.495)	−471.102	2899	−0.002	(0.917)	−471.056	5982
Polity, first episode	−0.067	(1.458)	−180.741	6079	1.515*	(0.619)	−277.833	2428	1.591*	(0.707)	−306.376	5363
Polity, all incidence	0.453	(0.887)	−239.544	6182	1.235*	(0.594)	−341.680	2600	0.222	(1.150)	−427.968	5522

Note: Entries are logistic regression coefficient estimates with robust standard errors in parentheses. Control variables are included when generating each of these coefficient estimates, but are not presented to conserve space. First episode indicates that only the first episode of democratization is coded as valid; all incidence indicates that all cases of democratization are analyzed. The Adjusted Polity data fill in observations that are coded as -66, -77, or -88 by the Polity Project. The Polity data code these observations as missing. Statistical significance is indicated as follows: $+p < 0.10$, $*p < 0.05$, $**p < 0.01$, $***p < 0.001$.

episode of democratization (models 9 and 11 in Table 2.1) does war have a strong impact on democratic transitions.

Taken as a whole, the results in Table 2.2 continue to provide only scattered evidence that war promotes democratization. First, there is no evidence of this sort when democratization is measured using the competitiveness of political participation. The estimated coefficients of *All War* and *Interstate War* are positive in each case, and the estimated coefficient of *Extrasystemic War* is positive in two out of four cases. None of these coefficients, however, is statistically significant. Second, there is some evidence that war stimulates democratization when constraints on the chief executive are used to measure regime change. The estimated coefficients of *All War* and *Interstate War* are positive in each case. However, only two of the former coefficients and one of the latter coefficients are statistically significant (at the 0.10 level). The estimated coefficient of *Extrasystemic War* is positive in three instances, and it is significant (at the 0.10 level) in two of them. Finally, there is considerable evidence that war fosters democratization based on the openness of executive recruitment. Each estimated coefficient associated with war is positive, and these estimates are statistically significant in ten out of twelve cases. Thus, the extent to which war stimulates democratic transitions seems to depend on the variable used to measure regime type and regime change.

Turning to the control variables, there is strong evidence that the number of years a state has been sovereign and the extent to which a state has democratic neighbors are directly related to democratization. In each case shown in Table 2.1 and in most cases when the component indices are used to measure democratization, the coefficient estimates of *Years Sovereign* and *Democratic Neighbors* are positive and statistically significant. There is also some indication that heightened economic development spurs democratization. In Table 2.1, each estimated coefficient of *Development* is positive. This coefficient is statistically significant when we consider only the initial episode of democratization, but not when we analyze all such episodes. There continues to be scattered evidence that development prompts transitions to democracy when we focus on the competitiveness of political participation and the constraints on the chief executive, but not when we address the openness of executive recruitment. Further, we find limited evidence that major powers are less likely to democratize than other states. The coefficient estimate of *Major Power* is always negative; however, it is only significant in six instances based on the composite index, and it is rarely significant based on any other measure of democratization.

The remaining control variables do not have any clear influence on the likelihood of a democratic transition. Each estimated coefficient of *Military Personnel* in Table 2.1 is negative, and four of them are marginally significant, but both the sign and the significance of these coefficients vary across the three component indices. Finally, we find little evidence that a state's regime score in year *t*-5, the percentage of its population located in urban centers, and its population size are associated with democratization.

Some Additional Statistical Tests

We conducted a set of additional tests to ensure that our results are not overly sensitive to coding decisions and the estimation procedures used to generate our initial results. First, we code war in year t-5 – the beginning of each five-year interval (t-5 to t) used to measure democratization – instead of year t-6.[40] Second, we analyze whether war affects any regime change, regardless of whether it is in a democratic or an autocratic direction and regardless of the magnitude of this change. To this end, we analyze the effects of war (as well as the control variables and country-specific fixed effects) on the change in *Regime* from year t-5 to t. We then do likewise for the change in each of the three component indices. Third, democratization is a rare event. To ensure that this rarity is not biasing our results, we re-estimate our earlier models using a rare events logit specification.[41] In each of these analyses, we continue to find that the overall pattern of results mirrors the findings in Tables 2.1 and 2.2. The regression coefficients of war are usually positive, but they are statistically significant in only about one-third of these cases.

Next, we address whether civil war influences democratization. Although our focus has been on the impact of external wars, it is possible that civil war might also influence regime change. To examine this issue, we started by estimating the models presented in Tables 2.1 and 2.2 after replacing interstate war and extrasystemic war with a variable that equals 1 if state i is experiencing a civil war in year t-6, 0 otherwise. Then we estimate the same models, but measure civil war in year t-5 rather than t-6. While the estimated coefficients of civil war tend to be positive, there is not a single instance in which it is statistically significant. Consequently, our results provide no indication that civil violence affects democratization.

Finally, we analyze whether the effects of external war on democratization are contingent on the length of the war or whether states won or lost the conflict. We also analyze whether the effects of war depend on the extent of a state's military buildup prior to hostilities (as measured by *Military Personnel*). Our tests, however, yield no systematic evidence that war's influence on democratization is contingent on any of these factors.

CASES AND CAUSAL MECHANISMS

To understand better the causal mechanisms behind our statistical results, we examined over forty cases drawn from the data set used in the preceding statistical analysis in which international or extrasystemic (mainly colonial) wars preceded democratization. These cases, which are listed in the Appendix,

---

[40] In our original analysis, *Military Personnel* was defined as the ratio of each state's total military personnel in year t-6 to its total military personnel in year t-11. In this analysis, military personnel is measured in years t-5 and t-10.

[41] King and Zeng 2001.

were generated using the composite index and the three component indices of regime change. In addition, they include the set of cases in which war was measured in year t-6 (the results in Tables 2.1 and 2.2) as well as those cases in which war was measured in year t-5. Broadly speaking, we were looking for evidence of any of the four mechanisms summarized at the outset of this paper that have been emphasized in studies arguing that war is an important cause of democracy. A case offers stronger support for any of these mechanisms to the extent that war directly triggers them and the postwar democratic advance is fairly large and long-lasting, reaching a high level of democracy noticeably above levels previously achieved in the country.

In fact, we find relatively few cases in which these causal mechanisms are unambiguously at work. Much more often, we see a spurious or a weak relationship between war and democratization. For example, there are various cases where (1) a democratic country becomes autocratic during war and then returns to its prewar democratic state once hostilities end; (2) the war is causally unrelated to the democratization; (3) democratization causes the war more than the war causes democratization; (4) any democratization caused by war is minimal or short-lived; or (5) the causal mechanism is highly idiosyncratic – that is, one not envisioned by existing theories.

In contrast, several of the factors captured by our control variables are causally important in affecting the level of postwar democracy: the country's level of economic development, whether the country had democratic neighbors, and whether the country benefited from a legacy of previous democratic institutions. If war is a cause of democratization, it is a weak, sporadic cause compared to the usual suspects.

Valid Cases

Among the instances of democratization preceded by war identified in our statistical findings, we find five cases in which war seems to lead directly to significant democratization through the mechanisms identified by the theories. Even here, however, we have reservations about claiming that the causal mechanisms of the theories are the main causes of the democratization.

One textbook case of war expanding democracy, discussed at length in Elizabeth Kier's chapter (Chapter 7), is the United Kingdom after World War I. According to Polity, Britain's score for the competitiveness of participation goes from its historic norm of 3 up to 5 in 1922. Kier's story about wartime bargaining to include labor seems plausible as an account of this development. Of course, background socioeconomic factors and a long-term trajectory of democratic institution-building underpinned Britain's rise to complete democracy. Any positive effect of the war in culminating this process depended on these underlying factors.

Another valid supporting case from our statistical results is Germany's democratization after World War I. Gerald Feldman's *Army, Industry, and Labor in Germany, 1914–1918*, is the *locus classicus* for the argument that wartime economic mobilization can induce illiberal elites to bargain with labor, producing political inclusion.[42] It is hard to imagine the emergence of a Weimar-style democracy, with the Social Democratic Party in its ruling coalition, without Imperial Germany's military defeat by the Entente. True, this is an example of war breaking the power of an illiberal elite, which is also one of our valid mechanisms. However, to the extent that it was American doughboys more than German workers that set the stage for the Weimar Republic, the story is theoretically less interesting.

Another valid case is Italy after World War II, where Allied occupation made the country permanently more democratic than it had ever been before. Existing research reveals that military intervention and occupation by a democracy rarely produce successful democratization, and then only in countries that enjoy facilitating conditions – for example, those with highly developed economies, a favorable neighborhood, or a recent history of democracy.[43] Two additional cases of this type, West Germany and Japan after World War II, do not appear as war-caused democratizations in our results – West Germany because we code it as a new state and Japan because the democratization occurred after our five-year time horizon. The U.S. military intervention unseating Manuel Noriega as dictator of Panama similarly installed a democratic successor regime, but this falls below the level of casualties needed to qualify as a war.

A fourth valid case is Portugal, which democratized in 1976 after the old autocratic regime was discredited by its defeat in a colonial war in Angola. Still, an undeniable factor was Europe's highly democratic neighborhood and the democratic transition the previous year in Greece. Shortly afterwards, Spain democratized when its dictator died, without any push from war. Undeniably, the Angolan war had a causal impact on Portugal's regime change, but it seems unlikely that the war was the only streetcar that could have taken Portugal to democracy.

A fifth, and quite interesting, case is Finland's democratization in 1944 after its peace treaty with the Soviet Union, when it leaped from its long-standing score of 4 on the composite index to a maximally democratic score of 10. During the interwar period, conservative and monarchist parties had been reluctant to include the large socialist parties in governing coalitions. Gradually, centrist parties grew stronger, and in 1937, democratic socialists were included in the government. Powerful conservatives, however, remained wary and the democratic opening remained incomplete before the war.[44] Finland's war of national survival against the Soviet Union strengthened bonds of patriotism that mitigated the divisive factors of class and political ideology. In 1944, the largest socialist parties moved toward the center and insisted on a liberal-democratic platform that would shore up their nation's independence in the face of Soviet influence. Meanwhile, the defeat of Nazi Germany,

[42] Feldman 1966.
[43] See Peceny 1999; Edelstein 2004.
[44] Kirby 1979, 95–96.

Finland's ally in the war against the Soviet Union, made an extreme antidemo-cratic stance less feasible for conservatives.[45] War reshaped Finland's domestic political landscape in a way that made full democratization feasible.

Are there other valid cases of war leading to democracy that our statistical procedure failed to identify? One classic from the historical literature is Great Britain during the Crimean War. Olive Anderson chronicles how the middle class supported Lord Palmerston's rhetorically liberal policy of imperialism and then elbowed its way into governmental administrative positions to replace the incompetent aristocrats who were making a hash of the war effort.[46] This recon-ciliation of middle and upper classes around a more efficient imperial policy may have helped set the stage for the Second Reform Bill of 1867. It does not appear in our results as a case of war leading to democracy. We do, however, record a case of further British democratization: Gladstone's Third Reform Bill of 1884, which expanded the franchise to include poorer laborers shortly after a series of minor colonial wars under Disraeli's Conservative government. Liberal opposi-tion to colonial wars figured prominently in Gladstone's famous 1880 electoral campaign in Midlothian and thus helped to usher in the franchise reform.[47]

Overall, the Victorian era offers ambiguous support for the theory. Wars and political reforms were frequent during this period, so it would be hard for them to be totally disconnected in time, if not in causality. Plausible causal connections seem indiscriminately diverse, including everything and its oppo-site. At one juncture, foreign war cements a class alignment in favor of limited democratization; at the next, it serves as a rallying point for expanded suf-frage. Above all, obvious background causes of British democratization – the Industrial Revolution, the growth of the middle and working classes, the con-vergence of elite and mass economic interests, the institutional legacy of Whig liberalism – seem more directly related to democratization than does war.

Our coding rules may have led us to miss instances of international war leading to democratization, but, after cross-checking against Nancy Bermeo's list (Chapter 4), we do not believe that we have missed obviously valid ones. Many of Bermeo's cases involve civil wars that precede democratization, such as occurred in El Salvador and Guatemala.[48] Since the hypothesis that civil war leads to democratization failed our statistical tests, we do not review civil war cases here.

Spurious Cases

We find about twenty cases in our statistical results for which any causal claim that war led to democracy would be spurious. In three cases, the state's

[45] See Puntila 1975, chaps. 6–9; Kirby 1979, 158–169.
[46] Anderson 1967.
[47] Vincent 1966, 124, 162, 247.
[48] Another difference stems from our different treatment of new states. We code several of Bermeo's cases as democracies from the inception of the state (e.g., Cyprus and India). We

postwar regime score was higher than its wartime score but no higher (or not appreciably higher) than its prewar score. In two cases (France in 1946 and Belgium in 1920), this was because a democracy was conquered by an authoritarian regime but then liberated by a coalition of democracies. In the third case, democracy in Greece was disrupted by factional divisions over war policy in World War I and the subsequent war with Turkey, but then returned to exactly the same level under the same political leader, Eleftherios Venizelos, in 1926.[49]

In five cases, the state's armed participation in an international or extra-systemic war was irrelevant to the later democratization: Colombia's democratization in 1957 following its token participation in the Korean War; Brazil's democratization in 1949 following its token participation in World War II; South Africa's democratization following its military intervention in Namibia; and France's minor "democratization" in 1930 and Spain's major democratization in 1931, several years after both fought against the Rif rebels in Morocco. France and Spain won the war, and it was not a contentious factor leading to their later domestic reforms. Although General Franco's Moroccan-based forces later squelched Spain's democracy in the civil war, the Spanish military neither supported nor opposed democratization in 1931.[50]

In a couple of cases, war was a side effect of authoritarian breakdown, not a cause of subsequent democratization. For example, the unraveling of the Ching Dynasty created an opening for the Sino-Tibetan War of 1912, and the dynasty's final collapse led later to a weak constitutional regime in China in 1917. Likewise, Turkey experienced a series of wars – the Balkan Wars of 1912–1913, World War I, and the subsequent war against Greece – in the aftermath of the collapse of the Ottoman Empire and the Young Turk Revolution. Eventually, Ataturk succeeded in forging a single-party-dominated, modernizing, constitutional nation-state, which our results show as leading to a partial postwar democratization in 1927, based on the "openness of executive recruitment." In these cases, regime collapse led both to war and eventually to limited democratization, but it would be a spurious inference to say that war caused the democratization.

In several cases, our tests identified wars leading to highly ephemeral or illusory democratic transitions, typically involving increases in the openness of executive recruitment: Communist regimes in Hungary, Romania, Bulgaria, and Yugoslavia immediately after World War II; South Vietnam shortly before

---

code Russia as a new state after the Soviet collapse and thus not democratized by the Soviet war in Afghanistan, which would be in any case a debatable causal inference. We likewise missed the democratization of Bangladesh by the 1971 Indo-Pakistani War, because it was a new state created by the war. It might be argued that this was a false negative due to our coding rule. However, handling a few new states differently would not have appreciably changed our overall results, given the large number of false positives that we identify in other categories.

[49] Mansfield and Snyder 2005, 154.
[50] Payne 1987, 31.

the helicopters lifted off from the embassy roof; Egypt after the war with Israel, when King Farouk gave way to Gamal Abdel Nasser; Uganda in 1979 when President Milton Obote stole an election after he was installed by foreign military intervention; Iran's biased electoral regime after Saddam Hussein's Iraq attacked. In short, bending over backward to look for democratizations spurred by war, we checked a number of regime-type variables, including the marginally relevant openness of executive recruitment, which led to numerous false positives in this part of our statistical analysis.

Ambiguous and Dubious Cases

We identified twelve ambiguous cases where war preceded an improvement in the country's democracy score, but where the causal mechanism or the validity of the democracy measure is debatable.

1. *Cases in which Democratization Caused the War*

In four cases, democratization was underway before the war and contributed in a significant way to causing it. There may also have been some reciprocal causation of the war on later democratization, but the fact that democratization was already underway suggests that underlying causal factors were more basic than the happenstance of war.

One such case is the First Schleswig-Holstein War, which is significant because of its seminal role in the broader politics of liberalism and nationalism of mid-nineteenth-century Europe. In the period leading up to the revolutionary year of 1848, nationalist liberals became increasingly assertive in Prussia, Denmark, and the German-populated Danish provinces of Schleswig and Holstein. German nationalists in Schleswig-Holstein, encouraged by the rising power of national liberals in neighboring Prussia as a result of new constitutional reforms, declared themselves independent of Danish authority. Danish liberal nationalists, who gained control of Denmark's cabinet in the course of the revolutionary events of 1848, opposed the secession of Schleswig, which had a Danish majority. To appease the nationalists, the Danish king invaded Schleswig-Holstein, and Prussia invaded to back the German nationalists.[51] Thus, democratization occurred first and caused the war. Later, when the Danish king died, Denmark undertook an even more far-reaching reform, which Polity codes as a democratic transition in 1853 and which our statistical procedure identifies as an instance of postwar democratization. It is probably true that the mobilization of nationalist sentiment as a result of the war helped the liberal cause in 1853, but this was a second-order effect of the earlier democratization process.

A similar problem of causal inference occurs when our model identifies a substantial movement toward democracy in Pakistan under Zulfikar Ali Bhutto following the 1971 war with India that broke apart Pakistan and

---

[51] See Carr 1963; Mansfield and Snyder 2005, 196–197.

Bangladesh. In fact, this gets causality backwards: The victory of the East Pakistan-based Awami League in free elections in 1971 led to a crackdown there by the Pakistani military, refugee flows into India, and an Indian invasion to establish Bangladesh. Thus, botched democratization caused the war, and both Pakistan and Bangladesh became more democratic (at least for a time) after their bloody divorce.[52]

Argentina democratized dramatically in 1983 after its military junta's defeat in the Falklands War. However, the causal story is complicated by the fact that political liberalization preceded the war and helped to trigger it in ways that were not foreseen by the junta. Unpopular because of economic mismanagement, the junta allowed significant increases in press freedom and the organization of multiple political parties in 1981. The newly organizing mass forces included nationalists who competed for attention by clamoring for Britain to hand over the Malvinas (Falkland) Islands to Argentine sovereignty. The junta, in an effort to avoid the increasing inevitability of elections or to position itself to win them, gambled for political resurrection by invading the islands. Military failure completed the discrediting of the military regime and cleared the way for a liberal-democratic electoral victory. This is a case both of democratization causing war and of war causing democratization.[53]

In another case of reciprocal causality, the defeat of Napoleon III in the Franco-Prussian War led to the postwar democratization of France by breaking what was left of the power of the "empire" and by creating an opportunity for popular forces to mobilize against the Prussian invaders and against the French elite. However, this story is complicated by two considerations. Liberal democracy was brought not so much by mass mobilization for guerrilla war and the Paris Commune as by the repression of armed mass action and the assertion of power by bourgeois elites. In fact, the rise to power of these bourgeois liberals was already well underway in the final years of Napoleon III's rule. Constraints on the executive jumped from 3 to 5 in 1869, a partial but noteworthy democratization even before the war began. To contain this liberalization, Napoleon's foreign minister, the Duke of Gramont, schemed to provoke a war with Prussia as a way of rallying French liberal nationalist opinion to the empire. In this way, he boasted, "I will be the French Bismarck." The liberal opposition, led by Adolphe Thiers, ruefully agreed that either a French or a Prussian victory in such a war would "take our liberty away."[54] After the war, Thiers was among the elites who worked to establish a liberal regime amid the ashes of the military defeat and the Commune.

2. The Mechanisms Present in Embryo
In a few nineteenth-century Latin American cases, the mechanisms envisioned in theories of war as a cause of democratization were present in an embryonic

---

[52] Mansfield and Snyder 2005, 244–246.
[53] Ibid., 219–221.
[54] Ibid., 190–193.

state. War temporarily broke down forces of authoritarian control, created opportunities for mass forces to mobilize, and induced elites to bargain with masses. However, the insufficient development of the basic facilitating conditions of democracy – economic development, literacy, an urban middle class – left liberalism stillborn. Democracy gave way to patronage politics. Economic elites regrouped around authoritarians. Without well-laid tracks, war is a streetcar to nowhere.

For example, Peru's score on the openness of executive recruitment moved from its historic norm of 0 to a new equilibrium of 4 in 1886 following Chilean military occupation as a result of Peru's defeat in the War of the Pacific over nitrate deposits. The war broke the political and economic power of a corrupt, pseudoconstitutional elite that had pocketed the proceeds of the country's guano deposits. Chile, a semidemocratic constitutional regime, installed a weak, pseudodemocratic ruler in Lima. Chile's occupation was effectively resisted by an indigenous peasant insurgency led by a white military officer, Andrés Cáceres. The remnants of Peru's elite at first collaborated with the occupiers, fearing Cáceres more than the Chileans, but later co-opted Cáceres and established an oligarchical, authoritarian, but ostensibly constitutional regime. This case offers caricatures of three of our targeted causal mechanisms: war breaking the power of authoritarian elites, war mobilizing mass groups into politics, and bargaining between old elites and mass groups. However, Peru lacked any facilitators of meaningful democratic consolidation: neither economic development, nor mass literacy, nor a middle class, nor a legacy of useable institutions, nor popular national patriotism. As a result, says Carlos Forment, "this enclave of Jacobin democracy ... did not transform political life in any lasting way."[55] Bolivia's democratization after the War of the Pacific follows much the same pattern.

In a similar case, Mexico's score based on the openness of executive recruitment jumped from 0 to 4 in 1867 following the military defeat and execution of the French-installed Emperor Maximilian. Before the French intervention, the liberal head of state, Benito Juárez, was stymied by conservatives, clericals, and local authorities in his attempts to carry out a program of reform. The resulting civil war and anarchy led to international intervention by European creditors and tempted Napoleon III to use Mexico as a test case for his pet theories of liberal imperialism. The popular war of resistance against French occupation and their puppet Maximilian created an opportunity to develop capacities for mass democratic collective action. "In rebel-held enclaves, local militias promoted democratic habits at a time when the rest of political society was militarized and authoritarian groups controlled the central state," observes Forment.[56] "Public-spirited citizens who had been active in civic groups and economic networks before the war played a prominent role in organizing and leading militia units." "Militiamen also undermined the public authority of

[55] Forment 2003, 383. See also Klarén 2000, chaps. 6–8.
[56] Forment 2003, 334.

the Church in rebel-held areas, although it was local residents who determined how and to what extent this would be done."[57] After defeating the French, the rebels purged the bureaucracy of collaborators, slashed the army budget, and attempted to discredit authoritarianism as antinational. Juárez was elected to the presidency but failed to win a majority for a more centralizing constitution. Localism and patronage politics reasserted themselves, though in not quite so hierarchical a form as before. Eventually, authoritarianism returned, and Mexican society once again turned to armed rebellion to overthrow it.[58]

This case manifests several of the expected mechanisms linking war and democratization: the mobilization of mass groups, the breaking of the power of elites, and even some bargaining between elites and masses. However, lacking a favorable setting in which to institutionalize these gains, the polity slipped back into illiberal patterns. The causal mechanisms triggered by war led in this environment only to successful rebellion and stillborn liberalization.

Our statistical results also identify a case of democratization in Colombia in 1867, following Ecuador's unsuccessful military intervention in New Granada (Colombia) in 1863, but any direct connection between the war and the later political changes is doubtful.[59]

3. Oscillations

In a few cases, we observe oscillations between incomplete democratization and autocratization during or following wars. For example, during the Spanish-Cuban War of 1868–1878, and shortly after the inconclusive Spanish-Chilean War over nitrate-rich islands, Spain's regime score, based on the constraints on the chief executive, spikes from 1 in 1867 to 7 in 1871. In 1873, the score dips to 1, then it rises to 7 in 1876, where it remains (unaffected by the much more consequential Spanish-American War of 1898) until 1923, when it drops to 1 with the dictatorship of Primo de Rivera. These wars may occasionally have had a temporary influence on factional politics, but they failed to produce a sustained effect on mass politics in the way that theories of war as a cause of democratization would predict. Since these colonial "conflicts were basically between Spaniards, they failed even to produce a sense of national unity, much less Spanish nationalism," says Stanley Payne.[60] Similar oscillations between dictatorial and electoral regimes marked Thailand's politics in the years after the Vietnam War. We also identified cases of French oscillations between autocracy and democracy following episodes of minor colonial warfare in Algeria in the mid-nineteenth century. Theories of war as a cause of democratization have little if anything to contribute to understanding these dynamics.

[57] Ibid., 337.
[58] Ibid., 338–341, 359.
[59] Bushnell 1993, chap. 5.
[60] Payne 1987, 7.

CONCLUSION

In a few prominent instances, war has provided an impetus to democratization for the reasons that are outlined in logically plausible theories. However, our statistical tests fail to reveal any strong, systematic pattern in which war causes democratization. Moreover, an overview of the cases that underpin our statistical findings suggests that there are many false positives in which international or colonial war precedes some kind of democratization but does not cause democracy in any meaningful way. Background factors like economic development, the character of the neighborhood, and the legacy of prior political institutions are, in almost all cases, far more important to democratization than any processes triggered by war. Indeed, the efficacy of wartime mechanisms in producing meaningful democratization is determined almost entirely by those contextual factors. The breaking of elite power, the mobilization of mass networks of collective action, elite-mass bargaining, and efforts to create democratic institutions lead to true democratization only where conditions are ripe. Elsewhere they lead, at most, to short-lived rebellions and superficial constitutionalism that relapses into corruption and authoritarianism.

APPENDIX
STATES THAT FOUGHT WARS PRIOR TO DEMOCRATIZATION

Interstate war and composite index

Country	Year (t)	War experienced
Argentina	1987*	Falklands (1982)
Colombia	1868*, 1869**	Ecuadorian-Columbian (1863)
Colombia	1957, 1958, 1959**	Korean (1950–1953)
Finland	1944*, 1945, 1946, 1947, 1948	Russo-Finnish (1939–1940), World War II (1939–1945)
France	1877#**	Franco-Prussian (1870–1871)
France	1946, 1947**, 1949#*, 1950#	World War II (1939–1945)
Greece	1926, 1927#, 1928#**	Greco-Turkish (1919–1922)
Greece	1945*, 1946#, 1947#**	World War II (1939–1945)
Italy	1947#, 1948#, 1949#, 1950#, 1951#**	World War II (1939–1945)
Pakistan	1976#*	Bangladesh (1971)
Syria	1954**	Palestine (1948–1949)

Interstate war and competitiveness of participation

Country	Year (t)	War experienced
Belgium	1920, 1921, 1922, 1923	World War I (1914–1918)
Denmark	1853*	First Schleswig-Holstein (1848)
Finland	1944*, 1945, 1946, 1947, 1948	Russo-Finnish (1939–1940), World War II (1939–1945)
France	1946, 1947**, 1949#*, 1950#	World War II (1939–1945)
Greece	1926, 1927#, 1928#**	Greco-Turkish (1919–1922)
Italy	1947#, 1948#, 1949#, 1950#, 1951#**	World War II (1939–1945)
United Kingdom	1922, 1923, 1924**	World War I (1914–1918)

Interstate war and openness of executive recruitment

Country	Year (t)	War experienced
Belgium	1920, 1921, 1922, 1923	World War I (1914–1918)
Bolivia	1884*	Pacific (1879–1883)
Brazil	1949*, 1950#	World War II (1939–1945)
Bulgaria	1919**, 1920*, 1921, 1922	World War I (1914–1918)
Bulgaria	1946*, 1947, 1948#, 1949#	World War II (1939–1945)
Egypt	1953*, 1954, 1955**	Palestine (1948–1949)
Ethiopia	1947**	World War II (1939–1945)
Germany	1919*, 1920, 1921, 1922, 1923#	World War I (1914–1918)
Greece	1926, 1927#, 1928#**	Greco-Turkish (1919–1922)
Greece	1946#, 1947#**	World War II (1939–1945)
Hungary	1948, 1950#, 1951#**	World War II (1939–1945)
Iran	1985#*, 1986#	Iran-Iraq (1980–1988)
Iraq	1979**	Yom Kippur (1973)
Italy	1948#, 1949#, 1950#, 1951#**	World War II (1939–1945)

Country	Year (*t*)	War experienced
Mexico	1867*, 1869, 1870, 1871	Franco-Mexican (1862–1867)
Pakistan	1976#*	Bangladesh (1971)
Paraguay	1941**	Chaco (1932–1935)
Peru	1888, 1889**	Pacific (1879–1883)
Romania	1948, 1949#, 1950#, 1951#**	World War II (1939–1945)
South Vietnam	1970*, 1971	Vietnamese (1965–1975)
Syria	1954**	Palestine (1948–1949)
Thailand	1978#	Vietnamese (1965–1975)
Turkey	1927#	Greco-Turkish (1919–1922)
Uganda	1983*	Ugandan-Tanzanian (1978–1979)
Yugoslavia	1946#*, 1947#**	World War II (1939–1945)

Interstate war and executive constraints

Country	Year (*t*)	War experienced
Argentina	1987*	Falklands (1982)
Colombia	1868*, 1869**	Ecuadorian-Columbian (1863)
Colombia	1957, 1958, 1959**	Korean (1950–1953)
France	1871#, 1872#, 1873#**	Franco-Mexican (1862–1867)
France	1875#*	Franco-Prussian (1870–1871)
France	1946, 1947**, 1949#*, 1950#	World War II (1939–1945)
Greece	1926, 1927#, 1928#**	Greco-Turkish (1919–1922)
Greece	1945*, 1946#, 1947#**	World War II (1939–1945)
Italy	1946#, 1947#, 1948#, 1949#, 1950#	World War II (1939–1945)
Pakistan	1976#*	Bangladesh (1971)
Spain	1870#*, 1871, 1872**	Spanish-Chilean (1865–1866)
Syria	1954**	Palestine (1948–1949)

Extrasystemic war and composite index

Country	Year (*t*)	War experienced
France	1877#, 1878#, 1879#, 1880#, 1881#	Franco-Algerian of 1871 (1871–1872), Franco-Tonkin (1873–1885)
France	1950#*	Franco-Indochinese of 1945 (1945–1954)
Portugal	1976, 1977, 1978, 1979#, 1980#	Angolan-Portuguese (1961–1975)
South Africa	1993#, 1994**	Namibian (1975–1988)
Spain	1931, 1932**	Riff Rebellion (1921–1926)
United Kingdom	1880**	British-Ashanti of 1873 (1873–1874)
United Kingdom	1882*, 1883, 1884	British-Kaffir of 1877 (1877–1878), British-Afghan of 1878 (1878–1879), British-Zulu of 1879 (1879)

Extrasystemic war and competitiveness of participation

Country	Year (*t*)	War experienced
France	1930*, 1931, 1932, 1933**	Riff Rebellion (1921–1926), Franco-Druze (1925–1927)
France	1950#*	Franco-Indochinese of 1945 (1945–1954)
Portugal	1976, 1977, 1978, 1979#, 1980#	Angolan-Portuguese (1961–1975)
United Kingdom	1924*, 1925, 1926	British-Afghan of 1919 (1919), British-Afghan of 1919 (1919), Iraqi-British (1920, 1921), Moplah Rebellion (1921–1922)

Extrasystemic war and openness of executive recruitment

Country	Year (*t*)	War experienced
China	1917*, 1918#	Sino-Tibetan of 1912 (1912–1913)
France	1848, 1849, 1850, 1851#, 1852	Franco-Algerian of 1839 (1839–1847), Franco-Moroccan (1844), Uruguayan Dispute (1845–1852)

Country	Year (*t*)	War experienced
Italy	1927#, 1928#, 1929#, 1930#, 1931#	Italo-Libyan (1920–1932)
Spain	1873#*, 1874#, 1875#, 1876, 1877	Spanish-Cuban of 1868 (1868–1878)
Spain	1931, 1932**	Riff Rebellion (1921–1926)

Extrasystemic war and executive constraints

Country	Year (*t*)	War experienced
France	1950#*	Franco-Indochinese of 1945 (1945–1954)
Portugal	1976, 1977, 1978, 1979#, 1980#	Angolan-Portuguese (1961–1975)
Spain	1870#, 1871**	Spanish-Santo Dominican (1863–1865)
Spain	1878, 1879#, 1880#	Spanish-Cuban of 1868 (1868–1878)
Spain	1931, 1932**	Riff Rebellion (1921–1926)

Note: Years listed are *t*, where democratization is measured from year *t*-5 to year *t*. Polity procedure and measurement is indicated as follows: # cases from Adjusted Polity variable only, * war at *t*-5 only, ** war at *t*-6 only.

3

Dodging a Bullet

Democracy's Gains in Modern War

Paul Starr

That war drives state-building is virtually a truism of historical sociology, summed up in the late Charles Tilly's well-known aphorism that states make war, and war makes states.[1] But if war and state-building merely reinforce each other, why have liberal democracies flourished and proliferated during the past two centuries when war reached unprecedented dimensions? Why not militaristic autocracies? What role, if any, has war played in the formation and spread of liberal-democratic regimes?

To raise these questions is not to suggest that war is one of democracy's primary causes, but rather to ask how democracy and, more particularly, liberal democracy dodged a bullet – a bullet that, according to many ancient and plausible theories, might well have been fatal. The belief that democracy is a liability in war has been a staple of political thought, beginning with Thucydides. If liberalism and democracy had been sources of severe military disadvantage during the past two centuries, liberal-democratic regimes should have perished in wars as they were conquered and eliminated by other states, or when their own populations rose up to overthrow them in the wake of defeat, or because they were forced to abandon their institutions in order to survive. That this was not their fate suggests a range of possibilities. At a minimum, their institutions have not been a disabling handicap in war, and no consistent relationship may exist between war and democracy. Alternatively, war may have contributed to the spread of democratic regimes if democracy itself or features correlated with democracy have increased the chances of a regime's survival in war, or if war has promoted changes favorable to democratic institutions.

As these reflections suggest, war may affect the population of liberal democracies in two ways. War can act as a selection mechanism insofar as it results

This chapter builds on arguments scattered through my book *Freedom's Power* (New York: Basic Books, 2007), and incorporates material from "War and Liberalism," *The New Republic*, March 5 and 12, 2007.

[1] Tilly 1992.

in the elimination or establishment of different types of regimes, and it can affect regimes from within by acting as a catalyst in bringing about changes that advance or damage one or another aspect of liberalism and democracy.

War as a selection mechanism raises a Darwinian problem. Through much of history, wars have often functioned as "elimination contests," to use Norbert Elias's term, with its wry overtones of a tournament.[2] Tilly argues that war was central to the winnowing process that took Europe from about 500 "more or less independent political units" at the beginning of the sixteenth century to only 25 by the beginning of the twentieth.[3] Moreover, according to Tilly, this process led to the emergence of the national state as the virtually exclusive state form and consigned to history's graveyard two other types that he categorizes as "tribute-taking empires" and "fragmented systems of sovereignty," such as federations of city-states.[4] To be sure, history has been no neat linear progression, and wars have also worked in the opposite way. Redrawn maps at the end of wars have added new states, imperial wars have turned nations into empires, and civil wars have fragmented power and sovereignty. But the net effect of war in modern Europe, as Tilly presents it, was to winnow down states and state types roughly in line with their military capacity. In his work on state formation, Tilly makes no suggestion that liberalism or democracy advanced as a result of this winnowing-out process, though elsewhere he identifies conquest as one of several developments that under certain conditions fostered democratization.[5]

Besides eliminating or creating democratic regimes, war may also have a catalytic effect in bringing about institutional change within a regime that already has some elements of constitutionalism or democracy. Catalysts, of course, are never sufficient causes of their own, and some may object that they only affect the timing of events, as if time were homogenous. But historical developments are unlikely to play out exactly the same way at different times; the specific sequence and context are often critical.[6] Like such shocks as natural disasters and economic crises, wars may bring to the surface suppressed problems in a society, release pent-up demands for change, and concentrate at a particular moment what would otherwise be slow-moving developments. Every society has stalled tendencies and blocked initiatives. Wars may open up a path for realizing some of those latent possibilities by bringing into alignment an array of forces that would otherwise be unsynchronized and less consequential. Wars seem more likely to have those kinds of catalytic effects

---

[2] Elias 1993.

[3] Tilly 1975, 15.

[4] Tilly 1992.

[5] In his books on democracy and democratization, Tilly hardly mentions war, and he is not a proponent of the hypothesis that war generally leads to democratization. "[T]he social world's order," Tilly (2003, 9) writes, "does not reside in general laws, repeated large-scale sequences, or regular relationships among variables. We should not search for a single set of circumstances or a repeated series of events that everywhere produces democracy."

[6] Pierson 2004.

on a given country the higher the level of mobilization, the longer the duration of the fighting, the greater the casualties and the costs (possibly including the costs of defeat), the more global the conflict, and thereby the greater the potential effect of the outcome on the postwar structure of international politics. High-impact catalytic wars may have many of these characteristics, sometimes with radical repercussions. "All great convulsions in the history of the world, and more particularly in modern Europe, have been at the same time wars and revolutions," Elie Halévy writes.[7] Tilly makes a related point: "All of Europe's great revolutions, and many of its lesser ones, began with the strains imposed by war."[8]

But why might the effects of these convulsions in the past two centuries have favored liberal democracy? Much may depend on preexisting institutions that affect *how* a country mobilizes and fights. Here it also makes sense to break down the compound concept of liberal democracy because the effects on constitutionalism and the protection of individual liberties may differ from the effects on such aspects of democracy as the breadth of citizenship. The idea that constitutional government and liberalism are unsuited to the rigors of war has a long genealogy, and for a time the historical evidence was at least ambiguous. When classical liberalism had its heyday in the mid-1800s, the conditions of world politics were relatively benign. As the twentieth century began, it seemed reasonable to suppose that, like a plant that grows only in bright sunshine, liberalism flourishes only in peace. And while liberal governments have since performed effectively in war, wartime has continued to furnish examples of the curtailment of constitutional liberties. Yet many of the landmark expansions of the franchise in both Europe and the United States also occurred in close conjunction with major wars. Insofar as these two cross-cutting developments occur together, they form a pattern that might be called the *skew of war* – that is, a tendency to move societies in both an illiberal and a democratic direction.

The puzzle of war's impact on regimes, therefore, resolves into two questions that correspond to war's Darwinian and catalytic potentials: First, why didn't war winnow out liberal democracies? And second, why weren't liberal democracies transformed from within into the "garrison states" that many in the mid-twentieth century feared they would become?

The answers, this chapter claims, hinge on historically contingent relationships. Through most of human history, war did not create any tendency toward democracy; if we had data on all wars in all societies throughout history, anyone looking for a causal relationship between war and democracy would almost certainly come up with nothing. The connection, such as there is, has depended on a peculiar and likely temporary conjuncture. The advent of "the nation in arms" in the late eighteenth century and the later rise of total war created an isomorphic fit between mass democracy and the demands of

[7] Halévy 1966, 212.
[8] Tilly 1992, 186.

war-making in the modern world. While democracy spread for many reasons unrelated to war, warfare contributed to that process because of both selection effects (war killed off more authoritarian regimes because of liberal democracies' military success during the past two centuries) and catalytic effects (the role of war in promoting the extension of the franchise and mobilizing civic engagement). These relationships would not have existed, however, if war had not earlier had a formative, toughening influence on constitutional liberalism, enabling liberal states subsequently to meet the challenges of war and to withstand its pressures. History offers no guarantee that these relationships will continue, and there is some reason to suspect that they are coming to an end. If there is no longer a fit between democracy and the exigencies of war-making – if war now skews regimes in an illiberal direction without any compensating democratic tendencies – the future of the liberal democracies may depend more than ever on the capacity to create collective international means to protect liberty as well as security.

WAR AS A SELECTION MECHANISM:
THE DARWINIAN PROBLEM

It is a striking pattern: More than half of the seventy-three democracies established after 1945 and still in existence in 2003 emerged in the immediate aftermath of war or as part of a peace settlement – a pattern traceable in part, Nancy Bermeo (Chapter 4) finds, to the greater durability of postconflict democracies compared to democracies established in peacetime.[9] In contrast, many authoritarian governments collapsed (and did not reestablish themselves) after wars, particularly after failing militarily. But is this a mere coincidence – perhaps only a reflection of the Allied victory in 1945 and the subsequent hegemony of the United States – or is it part of a longer-run pattern? Edward D. Mansfield and Jack Snyder (Chapter 2) find only scattered evidence of a positive relationship between war and democracy over the period from 1816 to 1997. But, among several problems in their approach, they consider only states that exist continuously before and after wars, excluding states that wars eliminate.

A regime can die as a result of war in three ways: by being defeated and wiped off the map, by being defeated and having a new regime imposed upon it, or – whether or not defeated – by being overthrown from within during the conflict or immediately in its wake. Failure in war has often been a prelude to revolution, and nothing has had more dire consequences for a regime than starting a war and losing it. From 1818 to 1975, according to Bueno de Mesquita et al., defeated regimes were more often overthrown from within than were victors, and the probability of collapse was greatest for regimes that lost wars they had initiated. The vast majority of these overturned regimes were authoritarian.[10]

---

[9] See also Bermeo 2003b.
[10] See Bueno de Mesquita et al. 1992, Appendix.

Autocracies were more likely to suffer this fate not only because changes of leadership in a democracy do not necessarily require the regime's over-throw, but also because authoritarian regimes have lost wars more often than democracies. According to Lake, of the 26 wars that pitted autocratic against democratic states between 1816 and 1965, democracies won 21 (81 percent); of the 121 individual countries that participated in those 26 wars, the win-ners had a mean score of 5.60 and the losers a mean of 2.55 on an 11-point democracy index.[11] A more extensive analysis by Reiter and Stam finds that between 1816 and 1990 democracies won more than three-fourths of the wars in which they were involved.[12] Although the cause of democratic regimes' winning record is disputed, even the skeptics acknowledge that democracy has been correlated with military victory during the past two centuries.[13] Democracies have also been far less likely to initiate wars that they end up losing. According to Reiter and Stam, when democracies have attacked first, they have won 93 percent of the wars, whereas dictatorships that have struck first have lost four out of ten times. When attacked, democracies have also been more successful, prevailing in 63 percent of the cases, compared with just 34 percent for dictatorships.[14] "Given democracies' greater propensity to win wars and greater propensity to emerge from defeat with the *regime* intact, war should lead to greater democratization," McLaughlin et al. hypothesize, and their data on levels of warfare and democratization in the international system from 1816 to 1992 are consistent with that hypothesis.[15] Taken together, these findings suggest that democracy has spread partly by process of elimination, precipitated in some cases by authoritarian governments' self-inflicted injuries when they gambled on war and lost.

War may function as a selection mechanism for democracy, regardless of whether democracy itself has been a cause of military victory or has merely been correlated with factors such as wealth that are causally effective. Either way, war has favored the survival of democratic over authoritarian regimes, though the question of causation is crucial in explaining democratic military success and the growing prevalence of democratic regimes.

While providing relevant evidence on the relationship of war and regime type, the quantitative studies of Lake, Reiter and Stam, Desch, and Mansfield and Snyder (the last in Chapter 2) have three limitations from the standpoint of understanding the historical impact of war on the population of regimes. First, they count all wars equally, but not all wars matter equally for sur-vival. The conflict between Honduras and El Salvador in the Football War of 1969 weighs as much in their results as the conflict between Germany and the United States during World War II. Yet the statistical relationships would be less impressive if World War II was among the one-fourth of wars lost by

[11] Lake 1992.
[12] Reiter and Stam 2002.
[13] See Desch 2002, 2008.
[14] Reiter and Stam 2002.
[15] McLaughlin et al. 1999.

democracies. From the standpoint of the Darwinian problem of the life and death of regimes, the Football War was irrelevant, whereas World War II was a war of elimination, and it was the Nazi regime that was eliminated.

Second, the studies typically conceptualize the effects of war as involving only the participating states, even though global wars involving great powers have far-ranging repercussions, even for nonbelligerents. World War I, according to Tilly, brought not only "significant shifts with respect to breadth [of citizenship], equality, consultation, and protection" among all fifteen European countries involved in the war. Thanks to the war, "the Austro-Hungarian, Ottoman, and Russian empires collapsed. Germany, Hungary, Ireland, and Russia all broke into revolution and/or civil war. Elsewhere, widespread demands for democratization arose. ... [E]very country [of a list of eighteen major European states] that had not done so earlier installed manhood suffrage, and a majority enacted female suffrage as well."[16] The outcome of World War II led to decolonization in Africa and Asia, and influenced the kind of regimes that were established there. A method that looks only at the belligerents misses these effects.

A related point has to do with the meaning attached to wars and their long-term impact on political understanding. The great revolutionary and world wars have been understood as tests of ideas, sometimes democratic ideas. If the Axis had prevailed in World War II, it would have confirmed the ancient belief in the weakness and incompetence of democracies and would likely have had wide and lasting ramifications for regime formation as well as political ideology.

These types of effects of war help to explain why some wars have triggered waves of democratization. In European history, of the four major clustered transitions to democracy – the 1840s, World War I, World War II, and the collapse of the Soviet bloc in 1989 – two have been directly related to war, and the fourth was arguably related. The Soviet war in Afghanistan contributed to the exhaustion of the Soviet military in the years leading up to Gorbachev's announcement that he would not use force to defend Soviet-bloc governments in Eastern Europe. Those regimes fell soon afterward.

As Mansfield and Snyder have ably demonstrated, it is possible to construct a study of war's influence on democracy that excludes these larger effects and, therefore, supports the misleading conclusion that democracy is largely unrelated to war; amazingly, their study does not register an effect of World War II on Germany and Japan. The two cases, they explain, "do not appear as war-caused democratization in our results – West Germany because we code it as a new state [they do not count new states] and Japan because the democratization occurred after than our five-year time horizon."

Nonetheless, the fact remains that the defeat of Nazi Germany and fascist Japan removed two of the major sources of antidemocratic military power in the world. Earlier in American history, the Union's defeat of the

---

[16] Tilly 2003, 216.

Confederacy eliminated what might have become another major illiberal military power. War also contributed to the collapse of France's Second Empire,[17] Wilhelmine Germany, the Austro-Hungarian Empire, the Russian Empire, the Ottoman Empire, fascist Italy, and the Soviet Union, as well as various authoritarian governments in the Third World. Even though not all of these were replaced by democracies, the destruction of these regimes led to the predominance of liberal democracies among the great powers and the establishment of a hegemonic model of constitutional government emulated by other states.

How best to account for democratic military success and the gains achieved by democracy through war during the past two centuries? According to one view, democracy itself has nothing to do with the military victory of democratic regimes. Desch argues that "the association between democracy and victory appears to be spurious: [F]actors such as wealth and power that makes states more likely to win their wars also make it more likely that they will be democratic."[18] In Desch's view, most of the wars included in the analyses of Lake and Reiter and Stam are not "fair tests" of the hypothesis that democracy itself is the cause of victory, chiefly because of "gross mismatches" (the democracies were so much stronger that the outcome was a foregone conclusion) or "asymmetrical interests" (the democracies had more at stake and, therefore, fought harder). For example, Desch disqualifies the war in the Pacific in World War II as a fair test because Japan was grossly mismatched against the United States and its allies. After deleting all such cases, he is left with just eight wars that meet his restricted criteria, and though democracies won five of those, the data no longer provide any basis for confident generalization.[19] As an alternative, Desch offers the "theory that power is the best explanation of victory in war," a proposition that few would dispute, particularly if power is defined in classic Weberian terms as the capacity to overcome resistance. The relevant question, however, is whether liberalism and democracy are advantages, liabilities, or of no consequence in the creation and mobilization of the kind of power that decides wars.

Realists and materialists would generally agree with Desch's view that "regime type hardly matters" in producing the power that decides wars.

---

[17] Neither the collapse of Napoleon III's regime after the Franco-Prussian War nor the collapse of the Argentine junta after the Falklands War makes it on to Mansfield and Snyder's list of legitimate examples of war-caused democratization. They argue that these are cases of "reciprocal causality" because there were democratic tendencies before the wars and the regimes tried to use war to strengthen their position. But the regimes' desperation does not prove that democratization *caused* these wars, and we cannot run history over again to see whether they would have democratized in the absence of war. In both cases, what we know is this: The regimes gambled on war, lost, and were replaced by democracies. Both instances surely qualify as legitimate cases.

[18] Desch 2008.

[19] Desch 2008, 31–35.

Similarly, Tilly's work on war and state formation, which has been aptly characterized as a form of "political materialism,"[20] treats constitutionalism and law as irrelevant fictions. In an influential essay building on the work of Lane, Tilly argues that the state is best conceptualized as a "protection racket" whose basic functions (war-making, state-making, protection, and extraction) come down to "eliminating or neutralizing enemies" and acquiring the means to do so.[21] And in respect to the latter, he focuses wholly on the state's capacity to extract wealth and labor through such mechanisms as taxation and conscription, ignoring the effect of different regimes on economic growth. Whether a regime is constitutional or democratic plays no part in Tilly's analysis of state power.

An alternative perspective emphasizes the positive contribution of constitutional liberalism and democracy to state capacity and performance, including performance in war. The basic counterintuitive proposition of the liberal theory of power is that constitutionally limited power, as Holmes suggests, can be "more powerful than unlimited power."[22] Or to put the point another way, how fast a vehicle can run depends not only on the engine but also on the brakes. Constitutional constraints, besides protecting citizens from tyranny, protect the state itself by inhibiting capricious or overreaching decisions by political leaders, such as ill-considered decisions to go to war. By binding those in power, making their behavior more predictable and reliable, and thereby increasing the trust and the confidence of citizens, creditors, and investors, constitutionalism amplifies the long-term wealth and power of a state (including its capacity to wage war). Credible commitments to property rights are only one aspect of this pattern.[23] Other aspects of constitutional liberalism, such as the separation of powers and requirements of transparency in government, limit the ability of officials to pursue their own private interests and to hide incompetence and corruption. Public discussion is a vital error-correction mechanism.

Modern democratic liberalism extends the same logic, both constraining and enlarging the state's power. To make the government accountable to the entire public is a way not just of limiting the power of officials but also of strengthening public responsibility and patriotism. Rights to education and other requirements for human development and security aim to advance equal opportunity and personal dignity, and to promote a more creative and productive society (with indirect, though sometimes conscious and deliberate, effects on the human and technological capabilities for war). Liberalism has thereby served as a method not only to protect rights from power, but also to create power to achieve rights – and to project both soft and hard power internationally.

[20] Collins 1999.
[21] Lane 1979; Tilly 1985.
[22] Holmes 1991, 1995.
[23] North 1990.

These various aspects of constitutional liberalism and democracy, so obviously relevant to war-related capacities, seem to have become increasingly important in the eighteenth and nineteenth centuries as the financial and human resources required for military superiority increased. This is where the structure of regimes intersects with the history of warfare. Something changed in the modern world that led war to begin tilting the population of regimes toward democracy. Perhaps the growing wealth of democracies began to give them an edge in war. And perhaps the rise of large-scale warfare with mass armies also conveyed an advantage to regimes that were best positioned to generate and mobilize wealth and popular support.

The mechanisms associated with constitutional liberalism and democracy may have even improved state performance of the extractive tasks that Tilly specifically emphasizes – finance and conscription. The differences in fiscal effort and tax resistance in Britain and France in the eighteenth century when they were repeatedly at war with each other illustrate how constitutional liberalism affected compliance with fiscal demands. According to Brewer, even though they were far more heavily taxed per capita than the French, the British accepted the taxation imposed upon them as legitimate because both taxes and spending were subject to parliamentary approval and investigation, whereas France clothed its finances in secrecy, lacked the mechanisms for obtaining the consent of the propertied classes, and thereby brought upon itself the fiscal crisis that preceded the Revolution. Precisely because it was suspicious of malfeasance, Brewer argues, Parliament enlarged the power of the British state: "Public scrutiny reduced peculation, parliamentary consent lent greater legitimacy to government action."[24] In a related vein, Levi argues that citizens have been more likely to comply with conscription the more democratic a regime and the more universalistic its rules.[25] And because the soldiers in a democratic army, as George Washington learned, could not "be drove" but had to be led, democracy may have promoted qualities of leadership that improved military performance.[26]

Reiter and Stam's analysis of the military success of democracies is consistent with some of these arguments. They maintain that democracies tend to win wars for two sets of reasons – self-selection[27] (i.e., democracies initiate wars only when the odds are overwhelmingly in their favor) and military effectiveness. The former arises out of democracy's role in both constraining and informing decisions. Drawing on historical cases as well as quantitative analysis, they argue that whereas democratic leaders usually refuse to launch a war unless they are virtually certain of victory, authoritarian regimes are far

[24] Brewer 1989.
[25] Levi 1997.
[26] For an example, see Fischer 2004, quote at 6, but, more generally, see all.
[27] Reiter and Stam use the term "selection effects." But because I here use "selection" in its Darwinian sense, I have substituted "self-selection" to characterize Reiter and Stam's argument about different regimes' initiation of wars.

more prone either to miscalculate the odds of victory or to gamble on war even when they recognize the risks. Dictators are prone to miscalculate because they have poor information and wax overconfident as a result of making decisions in secret, suppressing political opposition, and refusing to tolerate public criticism. And they may be willing to gamble on a high-risk attack because, though they may get overthrown if they lose, they do not have to face the voters at an election and are, therefore, more likely than democratic leaders to be able to ride out a defeat. In response to Desch's argument that many wars are not "fair tests" because of gross mismatches, Reiter and Stam insist that gross mismatches are precisely what one should expect to find because democracies initiate wars only when they are virtually certain of winning.[28]

The second set of factors has to do with how well states fight once wars have begun. Here Reiter and Stam look at the outcomes of individual battles during the past two centuries, using a database originally created by military historians for other purposes. The key factors in democracies' war-fighting advantage, according to Reiter and Stam, are greater initiative among the soldiers of democratic armies than among soldiers of autocratic regimes (which they attribute to differences in political culture) and better military leadership (which they attribute in part to the greater ability of democracies to make merit rather than political loyalty the basis of military promotion). Unlike Lake, Reiter and Stam find that neither overall wealth nor military support from other countries explains why democracies are more likely than dictatorships to win wars that their adversaries have initiated.[29] But even if that is a valid generalization when counting all wars the same, the contrary cases of the two world wars – where the outcomes clearly did turn on both wealth and coalitions – simply matter more to the fate of regimes and the course of world politics.

Total war could have given totalitarianism an edge. Lacking accountability to voters, internal checks and balances, a free press, and independent power

---

[28] Reiter and Stam (2003). Lake (2003) makes a similar rebuttal to Desch, arguing that his theory also predicts gross mismatches because authoritarian regimes' unconstrained rent-seeking saps their wealth, while their imperialist bias generates overwhelming countercoalitions. For further evidence on democracies' selecting conflicts that they can win, see Gelpi and Greisdorf (2001). Desch tendentiously refers to all those who hold that democracy is causally related to winning wars as "triumphalists" and argues that this error contributed to the hubris of the Bush administration in going to war in Iraq. But if the self-selection argument is right, the edge that democracies have historically enjoyed comes in large part from being more cautious and hesitant about initiating war than authoritarian regimes have been. The Bush administration overrode those cautionary objections and limits on executive power. Desch is so anxious to make a political point that he misses the opportunity to read Reiter and Stam's evidence as bolstering the case for constitutional constraints on the executive that he wants to make.

[29] Another analysis of the same data on battle outcomes also finds that democracy is associated with military effectiveness, but that the relationship depends entirely on democracies' advantages in human capital and stable civil-military relations, as well as Western culture (Biddle and Long 2004).

centers in civil society, the fascist and Communist regimes had a relatively free hand in conscripting, taxing, and otherwise extracting resources from their societies. If that were the sole determinant of state capacity and military performance, they should have prevailed. But by virtue of their political structure, the totalitarian states also suppressed initiative, lagged in critical technological innovations, and lacked means of self-correction. These deficiencies had fateful consequences for the creation of wealth and power. As it turned out, the modern forms of despotism were not a winning national strategy in the twentieth century. As before, governments with constitutionally limited powers proved to be more powerful than governments with unlimited powers. Moreover, by the end of World War II, the liberal democracies had learned that it was imperative for them to build international alliances and institutions to have any chance of stopping aggressive wars and maintaining peace and security. Whether or not the "democratic peace" is a generalizable pattern, the recent pattern of cooperation among the liberal democracies has enabled them to maintain their regimes and conserve their power.

With the ascendancy of the United States, a variety of secondary forces have come into play that make it difficult to distinguish any general relationship of war and democracy in the past two centuries from the singular effect of American hegemony. Of course, if war had served as a selection mechanism to kill off liberal democracies earlier, the world would never have reached this point. It is only because democracies repeatedly avoided elimination through war that the second set of effects came into play – war as a catalyst in the extension of democracy.

WAR AS CATALYST

No one doubts that wars have large short-run effects; the harder question is whether those effects last or get washed out by later developments. For example, for the period 1950 to 1990, Przeworski et al. find that in the short term, wars cut economic growth in half and authoritarian regimes suffered more damage than democracies did, but over the long term, even the dictatorships' economic growth was little affected.[30] Some evidence seems to bear out the intuition that the greater the scale, duration, costs, and global reach of war, the more likely it will leave a lasting effect on state capacities. In Latin America, according to Centeno, a history of limited wars of limited duration has failed to have the state-building effects that Tilly attributes to war-making in Europe.[31] Conversely, Rasler and Thompson provide evidence that global wars have had precisely those effects on their participants. But this contrast underlines that the context of war, not just its dimensions, may be what matters.[32] In certain circumstances, limited wars do have large effects, as in the

[30] Przeworski et al. 2000.
[31] Centeno 2002.
[32] Rasler and Thompson 1985, 1989.

case of the Falklands War, which brought about the collapse of the Argentine junta that started it.

Our concern here, however, is not with state-building in general or regime change (the subject of the previous section), but with the catalytic effects of war within liberal and democratic regimes. In liberal democracies today, war raises anxieties about the suspension or compromise of constitutional liberties, but it would be a mistake to see war only as a source of deviation from constitutional traditions. Taking Britain and the United States as paradigmatic cases, the modern liberal state has had three principal moments in the development of rights: the inception of constitutional government, the extension of democratic citizenship to groups previously excluded from the political community, and the establishment of social rights. And war has played a role in each phase.

In both England and the United States, war had a formative influence in the shaping of constitutional government. In seventeenth- and eighteenth-century England, the need to raise armies and obtain new revenue led the monarchy to concede authority to Parliament, which under the pressure of war authorized taxes and debt but introduced new methods of oversight, control, and accountability to curb corruption and waste, and thereby made the state even stronger. The suspicion of centralized power was even more acute among the American revolutionaries, whose original national charter, the Articles of Confederation, established a government without fiscal powers or an executive. It is sometimes said that the United States owes its distinctive political development to the security afforded by the protection of the Atlantic Ocean, but this is to forget the country's beginnings, when its trade was shut out of European ports as well as the Mississippi, and the republic might well have collapsed and been dismembered by foreign powers. War was the formative experience for the federalists who wrote the Constitution; they had come of age during the Revolution, and many believed that the weakness of the Confederation, particularly its dependence on the states for revenue, had caused them needless privation as soldiers, prolonged the fighting, and nearly cost them victory. Of the fifty-five delegates who attended the Constitutional Convention, twenty-six had served in the war, eighteen of them as officers.[33] Nearly half the delegates in Philadelphia, in other words, were veterans, presided over by their former commanding general. Their bitter memories of an impotent Confederation may help explain why the Constitution they wrote so radically extended the federal government's fiscal and war powers. War, in other words, may have been the source of a healthy constitutional realism and an endowment of powers that, although not fully exploited in the early republic, proved sufficient for the national government to overcome secession and later enabled it to meet other challenges.

---

[33] McGuire 2003, 53.

War has also had a connection with the second phase of democratic development – the extension of the franchise. In the United States, constitutional amendments have been rare events, but wars have helped to overcome the obstacles. The expansion of voting rights to African Americans after the Civil War in the Fifteenth Amendment, to women after World War I in the Nineteenth Amendment, and to eighteen-year-olds during the Vietnam War in the Twenty-Sixth Amendment were all cases of war-related democratization. In Europe, the end of both world wars saw not just the replacement of authoritarian regimes, but also further extensions of the franchise in democratic countries, as well as expansions of social rights – the third phase in the formation of modern liberal democracy. Relatively few wars have been of sufficient magnitude to catalyze democratization or occurred at a moment when such effects were possible.[34] Nonetheless, in the states that have served as models of constitutionalism and democracy, war served in precisely that role as a catalyst.

These moves toward broader citizenship in the nineteenth and twentieth centuries admit both functional and class interpretations. Large-scale war, especially total war, made it imperative for states to generate popular loyalty; concessions of wider political and social rights served, in effect, as a way of buying that commitment or rewarding it after the fact. War also created tighter labor markets and strengthened the ability of groups previously denied their full rights to make claims on the state. Both lines of interpretation are consistent with Andreski's proposition that the higher the military participation ratio (the proportion of the population under arms), the more likely war will have a socially leveling impact.[35] Here again is an isomorphic fit between total war and mass democracy. It is scarcely surprising that total wars requiring mass conscription and popular participation would break down social hierarchies.

War may also have long-term consequences for democracy because of the impact of wartime mobilization on the organization of civil society. Here the effects of war may depend not on war itself, but on how it is fought. In the United States, Skocpol finds, the most fertile periods for launching large civic organizations – specifically, cross-class, chapter-based national federations that went on to enroll at least 1 percent of the population – were the periods during and immediately after the Civil War, World War I, and World War II. War, she writes, can be deleterious to civic life, "especially when authoritarian bureaucrats take over all aspects of economic and social life and suppress voluntary efforts. But this was not the way big wars were fought in the United States."[36] From the nineteenth to the mid-twentieth century, elites found that to mobilize successfully for war, as for elections and other purposes, they needed to create representative, membership organizations that reached from the national down

[34] Barbalet 1988.
[35] Andreski 1954.
[36] Skocpol 2003, 60.

to the state and local levels. The federal constitutional structure created incentives to organize on that basis, but that structure enjoyed such prestige that many groups organized themselves into national federations even when they were not pursuing political influence. In wartime, the national government drew on these federations for such purposes as recruiting soldiers, providing social support to the troops, and selling war bonds. Wars thereby drew not only soldiers but also civilians into public commitments and enabled them to gain organizational skills that some of them put to use in building new associations afterward. In short, given deeply entrenched models of association, war ratcheted up the level of civic engagement.

The expansion of social rights may also be related to the historical ratchet effect of war on state capacity – that is, the tendency for taxes and spending not to shrink back fully to prewar levels after expanding sharply during war.[37] The evidence on the "displacement hypothesis" is contradictory; it is certainly not a law of public finance. Yet, taking into account the scope of government intervention as well as the level of spending, there is evidence of a ratchet-like pattern for the largest global wars.[38] The twentieth-century democratic state, particularly its fiscal and bureaucratic apparatus, was the quintessential legacy of catalytic war.

But by virtue of the same mechanism, why didn't war ratchet up the suppression of civil liberties? Infringements of free speech, attacks on dissenters and suspect minorities, governmental suspensions of habeas corpus – these have been the historical companions of war. But in the established democracies, once wars have ended, their illiberal effects have typically been reversed, while the democratizing and state-building effects have remained.

The skew of war has been temporary in the United States, Britain, and other major liberal democracies for several reasons. First, infringements of civil liberties and human rights have generated protest and opposition, albeit often after the fact, from both organized forces in civil society and the courts, and these groups and institutions have been able to reassert themselves when the sense of crisis has passed. The long-run danger of infringements during wartime – of emergency laws and states of exception – is that they become normalized and integrated into official doctrine. This was Justice Jackson's fear when he dissented from the Supreme Court's decision in *Korematsu* (1944) approving Japanese internment and argued that the Court should never have taken up the case in the midst of war; the majority opinion, he warned, would lie about "like a loaded gun," ready to be used by some future administration oblivious to liberty. But while Jackson's worry has often been cited approvingly, *Korematsu* itself has never been cited as a valid precedent, and the decision is long discredited. It ought to be some comfort that that particular loaded gun has never gone off. The same year as *Korematsu*, one legal commentator, Wiley Rutledge, wrote, "War is a contradiction of all that

---

[37] Peacock and Wiseman 1961.
[38] Rasler and Thompson 1985.

democracy implies."[39] If that had literally been true, the United States would have suspended its national election in 1944, yet the nation voted, despite the shadow of war, as it had eighty years earlier in the midst of the Civil War. War has injured and imperiled liberty, but the surviving, healthy core institutions of democracy have been able to repair the injuries.

What is especially surprising is that, on the whole, despite bouts of collective anxiety and repression, the liberal democracies also grew more liberal as well as more democratic over the course of the twentieth century. Instead of collapsing in the face of war, the institutions and ideas of constitutional liberalism shaped and limited policies to meet the challenge. And when they mattered most, in the world wars and Cold War, those choices proved successful.

The explanation for this deepening of liberalism also lies in the particular adversaries that the liberal states faced in the twentieth century. Fascism and Communism posed threats to liberal democracy that were simultaneously ideological and strategic. In opposing and fighting totalitarian regimes, the democracies appealed for international as well as domestic support on the basis of ideals of freedom and equality, and in the process were forced to confront such contradictions as racial injustice at home and their own role as colonial powers. Those facing repression, including political dissenters, could appeal to the banner of liberty that the democracies held up as the very heart of their own cause.

Finally, the effects of the world wars, like other wars, have depended on the meaning that societies have attached to their collective experience. A war seared into collective memory as a horror will likely influence political choices differently from a war celebrated as a triumph. Consider two contrasting interpretations of Europe's turn away from war-making in the second half of the twentieth century. In *Coercion, Capital, and European States*, Tilly's main thrust is to explain the triumph of the national state over other political forms; he views the recent decline in the military's share of government budgets as the result of the expansion of other state functions, as if military spending were merely being crowded out.[40] But this is to underestimate the significance of the change in political culture and institutions since 1945. In *Where Have All the Soldiers Gone?*, Sheehan argues that Europeans drew lessons from the horrors of the world wars, and their revulsion was itself an important source of change, including the movement toward a new transnational form of political organization, which has supported guarantees of what have become European, not merely national, standards of human rights and social protection.[41] If we are to understand why liberty has survived war in the democracies, this, too, must be part of the story.

[39] Quoted in Brandon 2003.
[40] Tilly 1992.
[41] Sheehan 2008.

THE END OF THE CONJUNCTURE?

There is an implicit assumption in much work on democratization that when states become democracies, especially rich democracies, they remain democracies. In fact, that has been the recent pattern. Since 1950, according to Przeworski et al., no democracy that has reached a high level of economic development (per capita income of $6,000 or more) has turned authoritarian.[42] But this durability has been due to an unmentioned factor. Democracies have been winning the modern wars of elimination, and in certain contexts, albeit far from universally, wars have had a catalytic effect in extending democracy. This surprising bias of war has been enough to change the course of world politics. War is not democracy's primary cause, but the military success of democracies has been an essential and necessary condition for their predominance among the great powers, and that predominance has set in motion secondary effects favorable to constitutionalism and democracy elsewhere in the world.

Humanity has thereby avoided the fate that so many feared. The danger of states making war and war-making states is a spiral of force, ending in a thoroughly militarized world. But because liberal democracy and liberal internationalism proved an effective strategy for creating power and prevailing in conflict, a different self-reinforcing cycle set in, at least for a time. Liberal democracies fought and won wars, which led to further democratization, which helped to protect individual liberties once the war emergencies ended.

Unfortunately, there is nothing inevitable about this cycle. If the positive effects of war on political and social equality depend on a high military participation ratio, the connection may have disappeared. More broadly, Crenson and Ginsberg argue that Western governments have "found ways of raising armies, collecting taxes, and administering programs that do not require much involvement on the part of ordinary citizens."[43] The active commitment of citizens may not be as irrelevant to political outcomes and governmental performance as Crenson and Ginsberge suggest, but war is a clear case in their favor. The kind of technological war now waged by the advanced societies no longer requires mass enlistment or popular mobilization, and consequently seems to generate no pressure to expand rights or benefits. Indeed, if the recent experience of the United States is any indication, the ability to wage war without conscription and with so little call for personal sacrifice from the public may reduce the high threshold for starting wars that has been partly responsible for democracies' military success. And if reversing the illiberal effects of war depends on bringing war to a close, what of a global "war on terror," which it will be impossible ever to say has come to an end? The threat of terrorism puts at perpetual risk the equilibrium on which

---

[42] Przeworski et al. 2000.
[43] Crenson and Ginsberg 2002, x.

liberty rests. In a world where one country's political instabilities, economic miscalculations, and failures in public health so easily propagate to the rest of the world, the need is evident for international arrangements to protect security. But if war no longer works to the advantage of liberal democracy, there will also be greater need than ever for an alert global civil society as well as international institutions to protect rights and liberties. They may have to be the catalysts now.

4

Armed Conflict and the Durability of Electoral Democracy

Nancy Bermeo

How do the legacies of armed conflict affect new democracies? This chapter focuses on a small part of this larger question. It examines an intriguing puzzle that emerges from the statistical analysis of the entire set of new electoral democracies emerging between 1946 and 2001. Briefly put, the puzzle is this: Democracies that emerge during or after armed conflict tend to last longer than democracies that emerge in peacetime.

Why would democracies emerging during or after conflict enjoy this advantage? There are good reasons to expect the opposite outcome – that is, that *conflict democracies*, as I call them, would be less likely to endure. Careful scholars have shown us that war and violence often undercut the sense of trust that workable democracy requires.[1] Yet, the durability advantage withstands statistical controls for level of development, past democratic experience, regional effects, and other variables we normally associate with democratic longevity. In fact, the probability of a democracy enduring or failing is affected more by this historical variable than by most others.[2]

To argue that conflict democracies have a durability advantage is not to argue that war, or armed conflict more generally, leads to democracy. Quite the contrary, in keeping with the argument made by Edward D. Mansfield and Jack Snyder (Chapter 2), the research that exposes the durability puzzle concludes that there is no clear association between armed conflict and the emergence of democracy. Raymond Hicks and I find that the chances of armed conflict being followed by a democratic regime change are slim indeed: worse

The author thanks David Art, Tom Carothers, Consuelo Cruz, Raymond Hicks, Gergo Hudecz, Elizabeth Kier, Ronald Krebs, Anne Pitcher, Laurence Whitehead, and Nuffield College, Oxford University, for assistance with this project.

[1] See Walter 2002, 167; Stepan 1986, 82; Wood 2008, 54.
[2] My quantitative work has been done in collaboration with Raymond Hicks of Princeton University and will be available in a forthcoming manuscript titled "The Puzzle of Conflict Democracies." My larger project is an individually authored book provisionally titled *Democracy and the Legacies of War*.

than 10 to 1. Like Mansfield and Snyder, our research also finds little evidence that either international or internal war leads democracy to emerge.

That said, this particular chapter is not about democracy's emergence but about its durability. It focuses exclusively on how long a democracy lasts once its basic electoral institutions are in place. Why key decision-makers opt for democracy in the first place is obviously an important question, but this chapter focuses on what happens after that choice has been made. It compares countries in which the choice was made in peacetime with countries in which the choice was made during or shortly after armed conflict. Its subject thus complements Mansfield and Snyder's chapter but is decidedly different. Their concern is with whether the "processes triggered by war ... lead to true democratization." My concern is with electoral democracies (which may not have undergone "true democratization") and with the question of durability rather than emergence.

What explains the durability advantage? A proper answer requires in-depth case studies, immense amounts of historical evidence, and much more space for exposition than a single chapter allows. It also requires methods other than regression analysis. Regression analysis can tell us what correlates with durability but not about the causal mechanisms driving durability.[3] In any case, many important causal factors are not quantifiable, and the mix of mechanisms is likely to differ from country to country. Thus my purpose here is not to present a parsimonious causal theory but to explore one plausible explanation for the puzzle and the subsidiary hypotheses that led me to it. Stated simply, the explanation is that the durability advantage is rooted in the elements of armed conflict itself. By elements of armed conflict, I mean the aspects of armed conflict that shape its individual character, such as how and if the conflict ends, how combatants are organized and supported, and how the conflict and its democratic aftermath affect the strategic concerns of foreign powers. These elements vary from conflict to conflict, but when they take certain forms, they provide a foundation for key components of electoral democracy and thus, advantages that peacetime democracies might not enjoy. New democracies of any origin are advantaged by constraints on antidemocratic spoilers, by electorally viable political parties, and by leaders with strong incentives to participate in electoral competition. Ironically, armed conflict can increase the likelihood that these factors will emerge.

I explore this argument through the examination of six subsidiary hypotheses about conflict democracies. The first three involve constraints on anti-democratic spoilers generated by the way conflicts end. The last three involve potentially democratic parties and leaders and the domestic and international incentive structures generated by the armed conflict itself. In summary form, the hypotheses run as follows:

1) A decisive loss that allows a democratizing power to reshape national institutions can be the foundation for potent constraints on spoilers.

---

[3] Hall 2003.

2) A humiliating loss that chastens the military can be the foundation for potent constraints on spoilers.

3) A peace accord that restructures state institutions can be the foundation for potent constraints on spoilers.

4) Rebel armies with effective organizational structures and broad public support can be the foundation for viable political parties.

5) Rebel armies with effective organizations and broad-based support can be the source of "heroic" leaders who can win free elections and gain a vested interest in continued electoral competition.

6) The death and destruction intrinsic to armed conflict can attract a diverse range of foreign material and nonmaterial resources that provide incentives for the continuation of the new regime.

These advantages are either unavailable to peacetime democracies or available to a lesser degree.

Of course, the development of these advantages is not inevitable. (Little in politics is.) My list of hypotheses is far from exhaustive. The legacies of conflict are as varied and as complex as armed conflicts themselves. No country inherits the same legacies, and many countries struggle with legacies that make durable democracy impossible. That said, there are fairly consistent patterns of conflict-based institutional development that emerge across a broad range of countries. These legacies constitute the core of the durability advantage and the essence of the hypotheses I have summarized above.

I explore these legacies below in a three-part discussion. The first part sets out definitions, discusses methods, and situates the puzzle in the larger literature on the longevity of democratic regimes. The second section explores the argument summarized above and explains how certain elements of armed conflict leave legacies that are helpful to new democracies. In the third section, I speculate on how the processes described here are likely to be affected by the "war on terror" and then end with a brief and depressing reminder of how new democracies are disadvantaged by a history of armed struggle.

DEFINITIONS, METHODS, AND THE LARGER LITERATURE

This chapter focuses on *electoral democracies*, which I define as those political systems in which key leaders are chosen through competitive elections with universal suffrage.[4] This is the minimal threshold for democracy. Deeper democracies require much more than competitive elections, but since competitive elections are an essential part of any democratization project, the factors that maintain them are also worthy of our attention.

---

[4] I agree with the definition of democracy popularized by Philippe Schmitter and Terry Karl, and with Robert Joseph, who writes that a system is "democratic to the extent that it facilitates citizen self-rule, permits the broadest possible deliberation in determining public policy, and constitutionally guarantees all the freedoms necessary for open political competition." Schmitter and Karl 1991; Joseph 1999, 240.

The armed conflicts referred to in the text are (with few exceptions) those chronicled in the SIPRI Armed Conflict Data Set (ACDS). *Armed conflicts* are confrontations motivated by a dispute over the "control of government or territory," which take place "between the military forces of two or more governments" or between the military of "one government and at least one, organized and armed group" and which produce at least twenty-five "battle-related deaths in any single year." *Wars* are conflicts resulting in at least "1,000 battle-related deaths over the course of their existence." Lower-mortality conflicts are classified as *armed struggles*.[5] As my hypotheses make clear, I suspect that different sorts of conflicts leave different sorts of legacies, so the cases include civil wars, international wars, and combinations of the two.

I define a *postconflict democracy* as one that is formed during an armed conflict or within two years after the armed conflict formally ends. I include democracies emerging during a war (such as El Salvador) because they are so clearly affected by the conflict itself. I exclude democracies formed long after conflicts end (such as Spain in 1978), not because I believe the legacies of conflict are irrelevant in these cases, but because the passage of time lengthens the list of other factors that might be driving the associations of interest. I chose a two-year threshold to code the nature of each regime because this is the time it typically takes to set up national elections and signal a democratic regime change.[6]

My set of cases includes all regime changes that occurred between 1945 and 2001 and that produced an electoral democracy in a country with a population over 500,000. I confine the study to cases emerging after World War II because I am interested in democracy as a global phenomenon, and electoral democracies were found almost exclusively in Europe and a few white settler states before this period. Moreover, the data for some of my most important variables (such as foreign aid) are either unavailable or highly problematic if we go further back in time.

To qualify as a regime change producing an electoral democracy, a country must have a three-unit single-year increase in its Polity score that brings the score up to or above +6. The three-unit jump is used to capture the existence of a temporally identifiable regime change. Though I acknowledge, thanks to Munck and Verkuilen, that the Polity scoring system is far from ideal,[7] I have not found a better way to operationalize the transition to electoral democracy. In any case, since this cut-point is the "standard threshold" for "interpreting whether a country should be classified as democratic,"[8] it facilitates comparison with other research on democratic durability.

---

[5] These definitions, and the data for the quantitative work that follows, come from the ACDS. See Strand, Wilhelmsen, and Gleditsch 2002, esp. 2–3. We have collapsed two ACDS categories into one for our definition of war, merging cases in which 1,000 people were killed per year with cases in which 1,000 people were killed in total.

[6] Reilly 2004, 117.

[7] Munck and Verkuilen 2002, 11, 14, 26, 28.

[8] Howard and Roessler 2006, 368; Jaggers and Gurr 1995, 469–482. I recognize that scholars such as Epstein et al. (2006) use +8 as a cut-point in their attempt to highlight the difference between

In light of what the literature on democratic durability has taught us thus far, the relative longevity of conflict democracies is especially perplexing. There is broad consensus in the literature that democratic durability is positively associated with economic development.[9] Yet conflict democracies are, on average, poorer than peacetime democracies at the start.[10] There is also a fair amount of consensus in the literature that there is a connection between consolidation and various measures of "performance."[11] Yet conflict democracies are, on average, relatively poor performers: They do not grow faster than their peacetime counterparts, and their overall quality, measured in terms of civil and political liberties, is lower, both initially and over time.[12]

The durability puzzle is compounded if we consider it in historical perspective. We know that the conflict democracies that emerged in Europe in the interwar years did not enjoy longevity for the most part. Quite the contrary, six of the nine new regimes that qualified as conflict democracies collapsed.[13] This record must be seen in comparative context because all the other non-authoritarian regimes that emerged in Europe between 1918 and the start of World War II collapsed as well. Nevertheless, the dismal fate of conflict democracies after World War I suggests we should expect a dismal fate for democracies after World War II as well.

Yet, despite the pattern observed in the interwar years, and despite seemingly serious structural and performance disadvantages, conflict democracies formed after World War II were more likely to endure than their peacetime counterparts. Sorting the ninety-nine new democracies in our study into forty conflict democracies and fifty-nine peacetime democracies, Hicks and I found, through event history analysis, that the probability that a conflict democracy will last thirty years is about 90 percent, while the probability that a democracy that emerges during peacetime will last thirty years is about 75 percent. We also found that 18 percent of peacetime democracies fail within twelve years of their transition, while only 5 percent of conflict democracies share this fate.[14]

"partial democracies" and "full democracies," but "electoral democracies" may be "full" or "partial," depending on the case.

[9] Przeworski and Limongi 1993, 51–69; Przeworski et al. 1996, 39–55; Boix and Stokes 2003, 517–549.

[10] See Bermeo and Hicks forthcoming.

[11] Diamond 1999; Espinal, Hartlyn, and Morgan-Kelly 2006, 200–223; Jhee 2008, 362–388; Chu et al. 2008, 74–87.

[12] Bermeo and Hicks forthcoming.

[13] According to the Polity IV data set, Austria, Estonia, Finland, Germany, Latvia, and Poland qualify as conflict democracies that failed and Czechoslovakia, Ireland, and the Netherlands as conflict democracies that succeeded. It should be noted that detailed historical work classifies Finland as a success. See Capoccia 2007; Bermeo 2003a, 21–64. The other new regimes that failed during the interwar years were Bulgaria, Italy, Greece, Lithuania, Romania, Yugoslavia, Greece, and Spain. All but the last two of these never reached the +6 Polity threshold to be classified as electoral democracies. The new regimes in Greece and Spain reached the +6 threshold, but did so more than two years after armed conflict had ended.

[14] Bermeo and Hicks forthcoming.

EXPLAINING THE PUZZLE

So why are conflict democracies more durable? The question requires much more research, but we can start by dismissing a false lead. By itself, material aid from abroad is not the answer. There is no statistically significant relationship between durability and aggregate nonmilitary aid when we control for other variables. Aid directed specifically toward the promotion of democracy might help explain the puzzle, as I discuss below, but nonmilitary aid in the aggregate does not. Though nonmilitary foreign aid may help democracy endure in individual countries, and though foreign aid may be beneficial in a multitude of other ways, nonmilitary foreign aid has no independent, positive effect on democratic durability across our cases.

This fact merits our attention. The mass media are replete with references to the successful postwar democratization of Germany and Japan and to the role U.S. aid played in the process. But we must remember that the United States has given a great deal of nonmilitary aid to new democracies that failed. Pakistan (1956), South Korea (1960), Turkey (1960), and Haiti and Russia more recently are all cases in point. Most of these experiments lasted two years or less.[15] Looking beyond the most visible post–World War II success stories and at fifty years of history instead, we see that material aid – even a great deal of aid – does not, by itself, make a lasting democracy.

Lasting democracies require much more than material aid from foreign actors. They require institutions and incentives that discourage the forces that undermine democracy and encourage the forces that sustain democracy. Armed conflict can, under certain conditions, boost the likelihood that these institutions and incentives will emerge. The durability advantage derives from this fact. Analyzing precisely how armed conflicts produce the legacies that boost durability in individual countries requires a level of detail that this short chapter does not allow, but the examples below illustrate how legacies of conflict have worked to the advantage of new democracies in a broad range of cases.

Institutional Constraints on Spoilers

Institutional constraints on spoilers emerge after both international and internal conflicts, though the mechanisms differ across conflict types. The constraints that develop in the wake of defeat in international war appear especially powerful. Indeed, all of the conflict democracies that emerged in countries that lost a full-scale international war between 1946 and 2000 proved immune to breakdown.[16] These cases are listed in Table 4.1.

---

[15] The electoral democracies in South Korea, the Dominican Republic, and Russia lasted only one year, and Pakistan's lasted only two years.

[16] Electoral democracy emerged in Pakistan after international conflict on two occasions and then broke down (1973–1977 and 1988–1999), but the first case was an internal war over the independence of Bangladesh, which was internationalized when India intervened. The second

TABLE 4.1. *The Durability of Conflict Democracies Losing International Wars 1946–2000*

Involvement of Foreign Actors in Crafting Constraints	Country	Year Democracy Begins	Year Democracy Ends
HIGH	Japan	1952	Ongoing
	Germany	1949	Ongoing
	Austria	1946	Ongoing
	France	1946	Ongoing
	Italy	1948	Ongoing
	Argentina	1983	Ongoing
	Greece	1975	Ongoing
LOW	Portugal	1976	Ongoing

A variety of factors account for this extraordinary consistency, including the fact that each of these countries had some previous experience with party competition, but the constraints that emerged as a direct result of defeat in war were highly consequential. In each country, constraints developed in different ways. In Austria, Germany, and Japan, foreign elites played a dominant role. In France and Italy, both foreign and domestic forces were at play, while in Argentina, Greece, and Portugal, domestic actors controlled the shaping of constraints. Taken as a whole, the outcomes depicted in the table suggest the validity of our first two hypotheses.

H1: A Decisive Loss to a Democratizing Power Can Produce Constraints on Spoilers

Institutional constraints on democratic spoilers were highly consequential for the postwar democracies of Japan, Germany, and Austria. Each of these countries suffered a decisive loss to victors who were determined to establish a new electoral democracy in place of a defeated dictatorship, and as a consequence, ensured that the new electoral democracy would be protected from possible spoilers.

In Japan, the occupying powers dismantled the military, purged far-right militarist forces from civilian politics, neutralized Japan's Communist party, controlled the press,[17] and engaged in the "hands-on manipulation of the

---

was an international conflict with India on the Siachin Glacier in Kashmir, but this was not a full-scale war, and Pakistan was never declared the loser. See Ganguly 2001, 83–88; SIPRI 1988, 291.

[17] U.S. occupation forces engineered land reform and other egalitarian programs and promised free trade unions, but eventually prevented a general strike and then withdrew the right to strike from public employees. Labor failed to become an "equal partner in the sharing of 'democratic power'." Dower 1999, 554.

educational system and everyday culture."[18] Occupation and defeat left Japan with what John Dower aptly calls "democracy in a box," where "centrists and conservatives maintained firm hold on the levers of power."[19]

In Germany, antidemocratic forces were also tightly constrained. Political parties could not operate legally unless they were certified as democratic, strict press and media controls prevented antidemocratic forces from maintaining support,[20] and strict personnel policies ensured that "those who had been opposed to or were at least untainted by Nazism were firmly entrenched in power."[21]

Allied policy was less intrusive in Austria than in Germany, but ten years of occupation left antidemocratic forces there similarly disadvantaged.[22] The Allied Council had veto power over constitutional laws and had thirty-one days to examine the acceptability of all other legislation.[23] Press laws ensured that the "public order should not be disturbed,"[24] and, most importantly, an Allies-backed power-sharing agreement between the two largest democratic parties ensured that antidemocratic forces would be effectively shut out of power.[25]

In postwar France and Italy, U.S. (and British) forces were less obtrusive because domestic resistance forces were ready and eager to play the role themselves, but constraints were put in place nevertheless. In France, the constraints were probably weakest, but even there, thousands of citizens were prosecuted for collaboration, the Right lost its former control over the press, and figures who had aided Vichy were prevented from running for office.[26] In Italy, millions of dollars of covert U.S. aid for De Gasperi's anti-Communist campaign

---

[18] Ibid., 205–206, 558.

[19] Ibid., 561.

[20] Merritt 1995, 94.

[21] Ibid., 95. The whole political system was controlled; Otto Kircheimer (1961, 254) reminds us that the new political system was controlled by a "benevolent American overlord." For more on how the occupation constrained opposition to democracy, see Frye 1968, 679.

[22] The difference was rooted in the fact that Austria was invaded by Germany and thus considered a "liberated" country. The policy contrast was explicit in U.S. documents; see, for example, U.S. Forces in Austria 1947, 14.

[23] The Americans on the Allied Council maintained that if aid for Austria were to be forthcoming, "the Austrians should have a way of life of which Americans would approve." Barker 1973, 169.

[24] Ibid., 170.

[25] The two parties were the People's Party and the Socialists. They managed to shut the Communist party out of power despite the Soviet occupation of Vienna. Their power-sharing arrangement, known as the *proporz* system, was the product of both elite political learning and the "pressures of the occupation" (ibid., 164, 203). The fact that the Communist party won only four seats in Austria's first free election in 1947 made the task of the democratic parties easier.

[26] Micaud 1946, 293–296; Williams 1958, 192. It should be noted that these constraints were thought to be inadequate by parties of the Left and that they did not, in fact, affect the Left as much as in the Italian case. It should also be noted that the United States pursued policies to contain Charles de Gaulle, who was deemed a destabilizing force. See Kasitsky 2005, 110–125.

guaranteed that the Communist party would be kept out of government and bolstered centrist institutions of all sorts.[27] The United States was determined to reshape the vanquished countries, "both institutionally and intellectually," to ensure "politically and economically compatible national systems."[28]

Of course, loss in war and occupation do not in themselves guarantee the emergence of democracy. The case of contemporary Iraq is a tragic illustration. The defeat must be unambiguous, and the victor must have both the capacity and the commitment to establish democracy in the defeated state. This is why democracies were not established in occupied Korea or in the Philippines after World War II.[29] It also helps explain why the 1994 U.S. invasion failed to bring durable democracy to Haiti. The U.S. political elite was hostile to Haiti's ousted but freely elected leader, Jean-Bertrand Aristide, and deeply ambivalent about the merits of full democracy in the nation that had voted him into office.[30] Moreover, the occupying powers did not enjoy the autonomy that total victory brings. On the contrary, they failed to control, much less disarm, the lawless military and paramilitary forces that were terrifying the population, and they left "Haitian democracy vulnerable to its old adversaries."[31] The electoral democracy that was reinstated by the (very brief) occupation lasted only briefly itself, disintegrating into chaos in 1999. By themselves, neither loss in war nor even occupation guarantee long-lasting democracy, but a rout by an occupying force that genuinely seeks to establish democracy can boost durability and offer advantages unavailable to peace-time democracies.

H2: A Humiliating Loss that Chastens the Military Can Produce Constraints on Spoilers

Constraints on antidemocratic spoilers can emerge without foreign occupation in new democracies, notably where the armed forces have lost an adventurist war, meaning a war that was questioned within the military itself. When the "military as institution" perceives itself as harmed by a war brought on by the "military as government"[32] or by another authoritarian coalition, it is less likely to make itself available as a partner for coup coalitions after democracy is established.[33] This is a powerful constraint on potential spoilers. The

---

[27] Miller 1986, 229, 248; Kasitsky 2005.

[28] Berghahn 2006, 134–135. The impact of the Western victors was consequential in Italy and France as well, though constraints from domestic delegitimation were especially decisive in these cases. More recently, the presence of foreign peacekeepers has produced a number of constraints that explain the persistence of electoral democracy in Kosovo. See Tansey 2007, 129–150.

[29] Olsen 1991, 332.

[30] Mark Danner, "The Fall of the Prophet," *New York Review of Books*, December 2, 1993.

[31] Morley and McGillion 1997, 383.

[32] These terms are those of Alfred Stepan (1988) in his classic *Re-thinking Military Politics: Brazil and the Southern Cone.*

[33] My argument about the primacy of institutional interests dovetails with the argument about the military in Geddes 1999.

assembling of a new authoritarian coalition requires military elites who are willing either to govern directly or to lay down their lives for a civilian-run state. A wartime experience that traumatizes the military as an institution diminishes this willingness and thus decreases the probability of a new military-backed dictatorship. The probability of democracy enduring rises because few spoilers are willing to confront a country's official military apparatus head-on. The Portuguese, Greek, and Argentine cases exemplify this dynamic. In all three, military debacles made the armed forces unavailable as a dictatorial coalition partner and thereby helped make possible an effective constraint on spoilers.

In Portugal, the costs of the African colonial wars in the early 1970s rose so high that the military mounted a bloodless coup to put an end to them altogether. At the time of the 1974 coup, Portugal was fielding one of the three largest armies (per capita) in post–World War II history, but victory was nowhere in sight.[34] The middle-ranking military officers who were actually fighting were painfully aware that the futile wars had wreaked havoc with the military as an institution. By the mid-1960s, the once-prestigious military academy had more places than students. Its class of 1973 graduated only thirty officers. When the dictatorship decided to correct the shortfall by allowing conscripts into the officer corps, morale plummeted further. By the time of the coup, barbers in Angola's capital were earning more than military officers on active duty, and an estimated 75 percent of the officers serving in Africa had turned against the wars.[35]

After radical officers in two provisional governments attempted to enlist military support for a Communist or ultra-Left regime, a pro-democratic majority mobilized within the military and made it clear that the armed forces were not available for a coup coalition of the Left or the Right. A full 80 percent of regular army officers gave their written support to a public document calling for protection of the military as an institution and for the establishment of an electoral democracy.[36] Through the trauma of a hopeless war and the chaos of a radical military government, the "military as an institution"[37] had learned that its interests were best served by a European-style democratic government that would enable it to become a truly modern organization.[38]

Constraints on spoilers emerged from within the Greek military after the Ioannidis dictatorship launched a coup in Cyprus in 1974. The "deplorable condition" of the nation's soldiers "betrayed the dictatorship's neglect of the army's preparedness for battle" and thus exposed the military's inadequacies in the face of Turkish retaliation.[39] The military dictatorship had

---

[34] Costa Pinto 2001, 20.
[35] Porch 1977, 33.
[36] Maxwell 1995, 87; Porch 1977, 207.
[37] Stepan 2001, 127.
[38] For more details, see Bermeo 2007, 388–406.
[39] Veremis 1985, 37.

suffered from extremely low legitimacy since its seizure of power in 1967. It had traumatized the military as an institution when it purged some four hundred senior officers upon taking power, but its disastrous performance during the Cyprus crisis proved unbearable to the military hierarchy.[40] Facing an all-out war with Turkey, the Joint Chiefs openly condemned the junta's policies, signaled "the distancing of the armed forces from the disintegrating regime,"[41] and initiated the "immediate extrication" of the armed forces from government.[42] Interviews revealed that "the great failures of the dictatorship became lessons for the armed forces as officers saw the destructive consequences of military intervention." As one officer put it, "The armed forces in their totality now know of the tragic situations that come from the intervention of the army into politics ... [:] the damages to the nation and the damages to themselves."[43] Coupled with civilian elites, who also had rethought their position on dictatorship,[44] a critical mass of officers showed determination to "avoid any path that might bring the military back into the political arena."[45] The public sensed that, when it came to democracy, "no further deviation in any direction was likely to occur."[46]

The legitimacy crisis facing Argentina's military government in 1982 had parallels with that confronted by the Greek colonels. Ironically, the Argentine dictatorship also failed miserably in its attempt to use military adventurism to defuse domestic opposition.[47] The regime's humiliating defeat in the Malvinas War exacerbated divisions within the military itself and caused the regime to implode from internal schisms.[48] The armed forces came to realize that "it could not govern without subverting [its] own essence."[49] As the military retreated to the barracks, the axes of Argentine political life shifted away from the armed forces and trade unions toward Parliament and the political parties.[50] Argentine civil-military relations have not been without conflict in the nearly two decades since, but "the crushing defeat in the Malvinas War" caused "a fundamental restructuring of the armed forces,"[51] including the civilianization of military budgeting and the wholesale rewriting of the

---

[40] Danopoulos 1983, 485–506. The figure on the purges comes from Danopoulos, "Farewell to the Man on Horseback-Intervention and Civilian Rule in Greece," unpublished paper, as cited in Linz and Stepan 1996, 130.

[41] Diamandorous 1986, 157.

[42] Linz and Stepan 1996, 131.

[43] For more on this point, and an outstanding study of the Greek transition, see Karakatsanis 2001, 158.

[44] For evidence of the political learning of Constantine Karamanlis, the center-right political leader who restored Greek democracy, see ibid., 69–71.

[45] Larrabee 1981, 162.

[46] Woodhouse 1985, 172. There was a failed coup attempt in February 1975 orchestrated by Ioannides from prison, but it was easily foiled.

[47] Munck 1985, 85–93.

[48] See, for example, Fontana 1984, 35; Gomez and Viola 1984, 31.

[49] Ricci and Fitch 1990, 68.

[50] de Riz 1984, 119.

[51] Pion-Berlin 1997, 10.

nation's defense laws. By the end of the transition, it was clear that "neither the military's place in the chain of command ... nor the viability of the democratic regime was up for grabs."[52]

Though emerging on different continents in different decades, these three new democracies were each advantaged by the fact that their military establishments were no longer available for coup coalitions. This potent constraint on would-be spoilers was a direct outcome of a humiliating loss in an adventurist war. It thus appears that each of our hypotheses concerning democracies that emerge after defeat in international war may be correct. Both a decisive loss to a democratizing power and a humiliating loss that divides the military itself can be the foundation for potent constraints on spoilers.

H3: Peace Accords Can Produce Constraints on Spoilers

Though they often have no formal winners and losers, internal conflicts can produce institutional constraints on spoilers too. Peace accords are likely to be an effective vehicle for these constraints. As Jonas reminds us, "a peace negotiation is in the end a political settlement" concerning "*post*war political arrangements."[53] Their provisions often provide incentives for the cooperative behavior that democracy requires and often become the foundation of constitutions and central state legislation.[54]

Peace accords have embodied constraints that proved immensely helpful to the maintenance of electoral democracy in cases ranging from Colombia in the 1950s through a number of sub-Saharan countries in the 1990s.[55] The causal connection can be fully understood only through careful process-tracing, but Table 4.2 provides strong suggestive evidence that there is, indeed, a connection between peace accords and the durability of democracy.

Twelve of the twenty-two enduring conflict democracies emerging after internal wars began with peace accords, and an additional three formulated peace accords shortly after their founding elections. In sharp contrast, only one of the eight conflict democracies that collapsed between 1946 and 2001 was associated with a peace accord at all. Malaysia's new democracy negotiated a peace accord with the Communist party of Malaya in 1963. Yet this accord was brokered six years after Malaysia's regime change, and the conflict erupted again as soon as the accord was signed. In each of the other

---

[52] Ibid., 215.

[53] Jonas 2000, 10. Emphasis added

[54] Walter (2002) shows that the implementation of peace accords is heavily dependent on the role of third parties. See my sixth hypothesis for more on this.

[55] Costa Rica's civil war ended with the formal abolition of the Costa Rican Army in 1948. This well-known fact is often cited as one of the main reasons that the country's democracy avoided the dictatorships and wars afflicting its neighbors. This case verifies my general point about wars' legacies and democratic durability, but since the abolishment of the army took place in a constitutional assembly rather than through a peace accord, I do not include it in the discussion that follows. For more on Costa Rica, see Dunkerley 1985, 182–190; and Yashar 1997. For a superb contrast of Costa Rica and Nicaragua, see Cruz 2005.

TABLE 4.2. *Failed and Enduring Democracies Emerging from Internal Conflicts by Type of Conflict Termination*

	Peace Agreement or Party Pact		Ceasefire or Low Activity		Victory		Ongoing Conflicts[a]
	Before Democracy Begins	After Democracy Begins	Before Democracy Begins	After Democracy Begins	New Democracy Wins	New Democracy Loses	
Failed		Malaysia			Bangladesh (1972–1974)	Pakistan (1973–1977)	Russia (1992–1993)
					Haiti (1990–1991)		Sudan
					Russia (2000–Dagestan)[b]		Myanmar (BCP)
							Myanmar (Arakan)
							Russia (2000–Chechnya)[b]
Enduring	Colombia	El Salvador	Mexico (EPR)	Philippines (Mindanao)	India (Hyderabad)		Senegal
		India (CPI)	Moldova		Panama		Turkey
	Croatia	Indonesia (Aceh)			Paraguay		
	Guatemala	Philippines (HUK)					
	Indonesia (E. Timor)						
	Mali						
	Mexico (EZLN)						
	Mozambique						
	Namibia						
	Peru						
	South Africa						
	Slovenia						
	Yugoslavia						

[a] Only internal conflicts considered active either during the transition year or within two years prior were included. Any conflict that continued either through the entire democratic period or through 2000 is considered ongoing.

[b] Though Polity IV coded Russia as a democracy in 2000, country specialists dispute this coding.

conflict democracies that failed, violent conflict either never ended, or it ended through outright victory. Even a brief look at a selection of cases illustrates how peace accords and constraints on spoilers are connected.

Colombia's electoral democracy began in 1958 at the end of a civil war between Liberals and Conservatives, two multiclass parties that battled one another for nearly a decade causing some 160,000 deaths.[56] Uniting to oust a dictatorship led by General Rojas Pinilla, the parties' leaders brokered a series of pacts. These included a power-sharing arrangement that ensured the parties' hegemony[57] and excluded other parties from office unless they allied with one of the hegemonic groups.[58] The National Front that emerged from these accords ruled Colombia for two decades. Colombia was clearly only an electoral democracy, and a deeply troubled one at that, but it was one of the few states in South America that was not a dictatorship in the 1970s.

In El Salvador, the forging of peace accords took a full three years, and their implementation often proved problematic, but there, too, a new electoral democracy emerged with a set of institutions that could successfully constrain the spoilers of the past.[59] The military was purged, the security forces were disbanded, the judiciary gained independence, and a new electoral tribunal was set up to guarantee fair elections. A new ombudsman's office guaranteed an independent channel for citizen participation, and the new two-thirds legislative majority required for any major constitutional reform lowered the stakes of the national elections.[60] El Salvador's electoral democracy is certainly not without flaws, but the major parties of the Left and the Right have both won national elections and devolved power peacefully, even at the level of the presidency.[61]

Guatemala's thirty-six-year civil war gave rise to peace accords that constrained the historic spoilers of democracy too, though the changes were slower than those experienced in El Salvador. Constraints on the country's military, the long-time spoiler of Guatemalan democracy, were applied only piecemeal but have become fairly impressive.[62] The military police has been disbanded, and the notorious civil patrols are no longer sanctioned by the state.[63] The military budget has been reduced below the level decreed in the

---

[56] Eric Hobsbawm estimated that the parties' militias amounted to "the greatest armed mobilization of peasants in the recent history of the Western Hemisphere." See his "The Anatomy of Violence," *New Society*, April 11, 1963, as cited in Hartlyn 1989, 307.

[57] Hartlyn 1989, 307.

[58] Peeler 1992, 95.

[59] For a useful update on this case, see Whitehead et al. 2005. For a classic treatment of the transition, see Wood 2000.

[60] O'Shaughnessy and Dodson 1999.

[61] For a critical review of El Salvador's democracy, see Stahler-Sholk 1994.

[62] The military reform process began under President Alvaro Arzú in 1996, but was then delayed during the presidency of Alfonso Portillo and his ally, the ultraconservative, Rios Montt. Oscar Berger, who was elected president in November 2003, quickened the pace of reforms.

[63] Seligson 2005, 210–213.

peace accords, and the number of men in arms has dropped 65 percent. An additional five hundred officers have been forced to leave their positions,[64] and, though a 1996 amnesty protects most of those who committed human rights crimes during the civil war, henceforth military personnel accused of crimes will be subject to civilian justice. In June 2004, the military officially endorsed a new doctrine that reaffirmed its subordination to elected civilian authority.[65] Guatemala is far from being a consolidated democracy, but even its most knowledgeable critics find "little reason to doubt that electoral democracy is secure" there.[66] "The democratizing elements of both the negotiation process" and the "accords as signed" help to explain the regime's durability.[67]

The civil war in Mozambique gave rise to an extensive peace accord[68] that has contributed to the sustainability of electoral democracy in one of the poorest countries in the world. The General Peace Agreement (signed in Rome on October 4, 1992[69]) provided a range of safeguards based in part on lessons learned from the failed attempt to establish democracy in Angola. To guarantee that the country's first elections would be "free and fair" and that their outcome would not be challenged with violence, the agreement required the demobilization of all soldiers before the beginning of the electoral campaign.[70] It also guaranteed that a new national army would be formed under the guidance of generals from both of the warring groups (Renamo and Frelimo), with an equal number of soldiers from each.[71] The accord guaranteed basic freedoms and stated clearly that parties would only be legal if they "pursued democratic purposes" and promoted "objectives that were ... nontribal, nonseparatist, nonracial, nonethnic, and nonreligious."[72] Renamo and Frelimo officials would agree on lists of election observers,[73] and international agencies would provide funds to finance the activities of political parties.[74] The international funding of opposition parties continues today, and many of the provisions of the original accord have been written into Mozambican law. Democracy in Mozambique is still deeply troubled at the time of this writing, but, in the fifteen years that followed the signing of the peace accords,

---

[64] Ruhl 2004, 137–152. For a well-researched discussion of the delays in implementation, see Ruhl 2005, 55–85.

[65] Ruhl 2005.

[66] Seligson 2005.

[67] Jonas 2000, 10.

[68] USAID 1997.

[69] Ironically, the moving force behind the start of the accords negotiated between July 1991 and October 1992 was a little-known Catholic charity organization called the Sant'Egidio Community. Alden 1995, 104.

[70] The concern was to avoid the recent outcome in Angola where the side that lost the elections resumed the war in their aftermath. This involved 63,000 Frelimo troops and 20,000 Renamo troops. Alden 1995, 105, 107.

[71] General Peace Agreement for Mozambique October 1992, USIP Digital Collection, Protocol IV.

[72] Ibid., Protocol II.

[73] Ibid., Protocol V.

[74] Ibid., Protocol VII.

the country held three sets of competitive national elections and kept violent conflict in check. These are considerable achievements for a country where the annual per capita income barely tops $200.

Namibia provided a positive example for Mozambique some years before the latter's transition. In 1988 to 1989, a "long and bloody domestic war ... encouraged Namibia's political leaders to create an explicit pact" between liberationist South West African People's Organization (SWAPO) forces, their allies, and an amalgam of groups supported by the South African apartheid regime.[75] The turning point was the 1988 U.N.-brokered tripartite agreement that put an end to twenty-three years of fighting and mandated free and fair elections.[76] The agreement was decades in the making, but left several important advantages in its wake. First, it enabled Namibia's new democracy to emerge without militarized spoilers: warring domestic armies were demobilized, foreign forces were expelled, and a new Namibian defense force integrating former enemy armies in equal parts was established.[77] Second, the accords constrained spoilers of all sorts by lowering the level of risk that electoral democracy involved. This was done by explicitly integrating the peacemaking and constitution-making processes. Peacemakers managed, as a leading participant recalls, "to convince all the affected parties [including] SWAPO ... of the merits and indeed the necessity of a set of pre-agreed Constitutional Principles"[78] "in order to satisfy the concerns" of all involved.[79] After free elections were held, a constitutional assembly produced a pact-like document drawn up by all the political parties[80] and then adopted by consensus.[81] Miraculously, it contained the agreed-upon provisions. To protect the new regime from white backlash and decapitalization, the constitution guaranteed employment for existing civil servants, provided security of land title,[82] and forbade the "creation of criminal offences with retrospective effect."[83] To constrain spoilers of all sorts, the constitution

---

[75] Forrest 1992, 742; Gretchen Bauer 2001, 53.

[76] Consistent with the provisions of UNSCR 435/78, the Republic of South Africa and the People's Republic of Angola shall cooperate with the secretary-general to ensure the independence of Namibia through free and fair elections and shall abstain from any action that could prevent the execution of UNSCR 435/78. The parties shall respect the territorial integrity and inviolability of the borders of Namibia and shall ensure that their territories are not used by any state, organization, or person in connection with acts of war, aggression, or violence against the territorial integrity or inviolability of borders of Namibia or any other action which could prevent the execution of UNSCR 435/78, 1988.

[77] Howard 2002, 116–117.

[78] These are the words of the legal director of the U.N. special representative in Namibia. See Szasz 1994, 245.

[79] Ibid., 247.

[80] Lindeke 1995, 17.

[81] Howard 2002, 125.

[82] What it included, to be precise, was a provision that "no ancestral land claims would be honored" and no property would be seized without compensation. Civil service jobs were guaranteed as a part of "national reconciliation." Ibid., 125.

[83] U.N. Security Council Document S/15287 in Weiland and Braham 1994, 231–233.

endorsed a democratic government with a strong and independent judiciary, a two-thirds majority requirement for constitutional amendments, an ombudsman with a "very powerful control function," and rights provisions mirroring the Universal Declaration of Human Rights, which are both entrenched and nonderogable.[84] The peace accords led to a document that was "universally heralded as the most democratic on the continent," and even staunch critics of the regime conceded that SWAPO "gave every indication of wishing to abide by it."[85] Though democracy in Namibia today is seriously hampered by SWAPO's electoral hegemony,[86] its press "is considered one of the freest on the continent,"[87] the state has managed to hold three sets of national elections, and there "appears to be an eagerness on the part of many organizations to engage the state."[88]

The peace accords summarized above differed in content and implementation, but each left lasting legacies that help explain the persistence of electoral democracy. This discussion begs many questions, including how the structure of accords affects their success and why some accords are adhered to while others are not.[89] Nevertheless, it provides suggestive evidence that the third hypothesis is valid: Peace accords can yield potent constraints on spoilers. Carrie Manning's insights on Mozambique appear to apply elsewhere: The elements of peace accords "designed to build confidence and provide positive incentives for participation may turn out to be extremely important for the long-term survival of the system."[90]

Of course, democracies that emerge in peacetime can also construct institutions that constrain spoilers and bolster cooperation, but the process involves more time than many new democracies can afford and more institutional strength than many new democracies can muster. Peacetime democracies are also less likely to have international forces monitoring even the early adherence to their reforms. As the short-lived democratic experiments of South Korea (1960–1961), Argentina (1973–1976), and Ghana (1979–1981) illustrate, authoritarian coalitions can often be built up faster than constraining institutions.

---

[84] Szasz 1994, 252–253.

[85] Saul and Leys 1995, 200.

[86] Good 1997, 547–573.

[87] Freedom House 2005, 441.

[88] Bauer 2001, 40.

[89] Space constraints prevent a lengthy discussion of these issues here, but a preliminary analysis of the data provided in Hartzell and Hoodie 2003, 325–326, and the UCDP Peace Agreement Data Set suggests that there is no clear association between the nature of settlements and democratic success or failure. All five of the successful peace settlements summarized here contained some sort of power sharing (ibid.). Yet, economic and military power-sharing were also part of the peace accord in the failed case of Malaysia. The role of third-party enforcement is also inconclusive: There was no third-party guarantor in the cases of Malaysia, Colombia, and Guatemala, for example, but only the first case failed.

[90] Manning 2002, 64.

Parties, Leaders, Resources, and Incentives

Armed conflicts require organization. Long armed conflicts require durable organizations capable of amassing extensive material and human support.[91] These simple facts can give democracies emerging during and after sustained armed conflict a surprising advantage in providing the foundation for viable political parties, genuinely popular leaders, and effective resource networks.

H4: Broad-Based Rebel Armies Can Be the Foundation for Viable Political Parties

Rebel movements and political parties differ in important ways, but both require hierarchical organization and voluntary support. These similarities make the conversion of armed movements into parties substantially easier than starting political parties from scratch. The conversion process is difficult, and far from fail-safe,[92] but compared to trying to build large party organizations from a small group of notables or from a bounded identity-group, it has advantages. Since the absence of strong parties has long been identified as a major impediment to democratic durability, the availability of conflict-related institutional bases for parties is an important asset for a new democracy.[93]

A broad range of postconflict democracies contain viable political parties with deep roots in armed struggle. El Salvador's main parties were actually forged in the crucible of war itself.[94] War-related economic crises, international pressures, and political learning transformed the right-wing Nationalist Republican Alliance (ARENA) from the murderous arm of the landed oligarchy to a broad-based liberal party led by more "moderate elites" who were "tolerant of democratic norms."[95] Similar processes, culminating with an official demobilization in mid-December 1992, transformed the leftist Farabundo Martí National Liberation Front (FMLN) from a guerrilla movement to a political party capable of winning elections at various levels of government.[96]

Southern Africa provides us with three cases in which wars were the crucibles for strong political parties. In Namibia SWAPO was especially well situated to make the formal transition to electoral politics when Namibia's democracy took shape in the late 1980s. The U.N. General Assembly had recognized

[91] Weinstein 2007.
[92] Marina Ottaway (1991, 61–82) explains the difficulties of integrating liberation organizations with transitions to democracy. Carrie Manning (2008) has traced the conversion process in her comparative work on Bosnia, El Salvador, and Mozambique.
[93] Mainwaring and Scully 1995.
[94] Thomas Carothers properly points out that the key to success in El Salvador was the stalemated war, which forced pivotal actors to recognize that they could not destroy one another and would be better off "backing a strong party that would represent their interests in electoral politics." See Carothers 2006, 224–225.
[95] Wood 2005, 185–189. See McClintock 1998 for a helpful analysis of the FMLN. Though I have no space to discuss it, the Nicaraguan party system also has its roots in armed struggle. See Anderson and Dodd 2005, 297.
[96] Baloyra 1998, 17–19.

SWAPO as "the sole and authentic representative of the Namibian people" in 1976 and thus accorded the organization a prestige and legitimacy that no other Namibian political group could match.[97] As "a government-in-waiting for more than a decade,"[98] it had years to become known internationally and to polish its organizational skills. "Massive" aid from both the western and eastern blocs gave it significantly more resources than any other Southern African liberation movement.[99] It used these resources to organize the war, but also to organize huge settlements in Zambia and Angola as well as training programs throughout the world, honing its skills and nurturing its base, long before its first electoral challenges.[100] Internally, SWAPO was substantially more cohesive than parties in neighboring African countries "because of its origins as a liberation movement as opposed to a ... pressure group."[101] This internal discipline helped the party present a cohesive image to the electorate. Since the majority of the people came to "equate SWAPO with Namibia's independence,"[102] no one was surprised when the party garnered nearly 57 percent of the vote in the country's first free elections in 1990.[103]

In Mozambique, a colonial struggle and a sixteen-year civil war gave rise to two competing parties converted from guerrilla armies, Frelimo and Renamo. Frelimo, the larger and older party, was shaped by two wars: first, by its armed struggle with the Portuguese, running from 1964 to 1975, and then (after independence) by a brutal civil war with Renamo. The anticolonial war left Frelimo with a pantheon of ennobled freedom fighters who provided the party with a heroic aura and a pool of leaders who "remained essentially unchallenged" in the postindependence period.[104] The party "laid heavy emphasis on people's collective memory during the campaign," and since the "message that one should vote for Frelimo because it liberated the country still had relevance to people," this boosted party performance at the polls.[105] The civil war with Renamo gave Frelimo a convenient excuse for monopolistic rule. After over a dozen years in power and years of ruling "liberated zones" during colonialism, the party became an "effective organization" enveloping key actors. Many of these key actors were in the military, but the majority of civilian state personnel were Frelimo members as well.[106] Monopolistic control of state resources also smoothed Frelimo's transition from vanguard to machine politics when elections loomed. As soon as negotiations for the peace accords opened, the

---

[97] U.N. General Assembly Resolution 31/146, 1976. In 1973, the U.N. had recognized SWAPO as merely "the authentic representative."
[98] Lindeke 1995, 16.
[99] Dobell 1995, 172.
[100] Saul and Leys 1995, 198.
[101] von Doepp 2005, 79.
[102] Slatter 1994, 10.
[103] Bauer 2001, 42.
[104] Carbone 2005, 430.
[105] Harrison 1996, 27.
[106] Carbone 2005, 430.

party leadership began recruiting members. Between 1990 and 1991 alone, the party's membership rose 140 percent to half a million people.[107]

Renamo's history differed from Frelimo's in dramatic ways, but it, too, was advantaged by its wartime experience.[108] Despite its early association with the racist governments of Rhodesia and South Africa, and its notorious brutality during the civil war, Renamo eventually became known as a "protector of all those who had been penalized or marginalized under Frelimo's rule."[109] This meant rural communities in the center and north, traditional rulers everywhere, and religious forces of various sorts. Notwithstanding its many shortcomings, years of war had given Renamo deep "roots in large portions of the national territory" and many representatives in rural areas with traditional forms of authority.[110] The war's peace settlement gave Renamo a second weighty advantage – funding. Fourteen donors, committed to elections, contributed $18 million to establish what soon became known as the Renamo Trust Fund. That these funds were, indeed, a legacy of war is illustrated by the fact that eighteen other parties, which had never been armed, had to share $3 million of aid between them.[111]

Though Renamo's leader, Afonso Dhlakama, threatened to derail the creation of electoral democracy on several occasions,[112] the institutional and material resources produced by the postwar settlement were "necessary and sufficient" "to draw Renamo into the new political system."[113] Coupled with the support the party had won during years of civil war, these resources helped produce a surprisingly respectable showing at the polls. In the end, Dhlakama won 34 percent of the first presidential vote, and Renamo won elections in five of Mozambique's ten provinces.[114] Renamo has controlled approximately 45 percent of the seats in the legislature since Mozambique's democracy began.[115] Though the country's party system is unbalanced, Renamo has exhibited the capacity to mobilize effective protests in civil society,[116] and Dhlakama even came close to winning the presidency in 1999 with 47 percent of the vote. Though Renamo suffers from serious institutional weaknesses, it has "contributed to keeping all sections of society within the pluralist framework,"

---

[107] Simpson 1993, 331

[108] Manning 2004, 56.

[109] Carbone 2005, 424.

[110] Manning 1998, 188. The party was operating in ten of the country's twelve provinces by the early 1980s. Morgan 1990, 603–619.

[111] USAID 1997, 5; Alden 1995, 126.

[112] Alden 1995, 19–21.

[113] Manning 1998. Resources to strengthen political parties are still flowing into Mozambique. Weinstein 2002, 154.

[114] Significantly, Renamo won in the country's two most populous provinces, Nampula and Zambezia, where the majority ethnic group the Makua-Lomwe dominated, showing it had support beyond the Ndau people, who were heavily represented in the party's early supporters and leadership. Lloyd 1995, 155.

[115] Krennerich 1999, 645, 658.

[116] Carbone 2005, 434, 436; Manning 1998, 189.

and its presence helps explain why there is "no significant support for non-democratic alternatives to the multiparty regime."[117]

The long struggle against apartheid in Mozambique's neighbor, South Africa, left the African National Congress (ANC) with an enviable range of organizational resources when the country held its first free elections in 1994. Since its founding in 1912, the ANC had incorporated "a broad range of forces," and they grew even broader when civil society began to organize more intensively in the mid-1970s.[118] By 1994, ANC official documents were saying that "the constituency of the ANC is the entire South African society,"[119] and this was almost true. As the symbol of the antiapartheid struggle, the ANC enjoyed "automatic acceptance" "at home and abroad, escaping close scrutiny of its shortcomings."[120] Even before its most famous leaders emerged from prison and exile, the ANC's first legal rally drew some 70,000 people[121] – suggesting a support base that would either encompass or dwarf all others.[122] The movement's armed wing, Umkhonto we Sizwe ("Spear of the Nation"), had between 4,000 and 11,000 members, mostly in exile,[123] and its leader, Chris Hani, had a vibrant support base, especially among young men in the townships. When it came to actually formulating policy positions, the ANC's size and diversity were to prove problematic. This is why support for the ANC has been described as "broad but shallow,"[124] but the depth of the organization's support mattered less than its breadth at election time. The ANC won South Africa's first free elections with 63 percent of the vote, and the party has dominated the electoral scene ever since.[125] The party won its last national elections with 70 percent of the vote. The advantages of converting an armed liberation movement into a political party are well illustrated by the ANC.

The case of Israel suggests that the conversion advantage existed long before the third wave began and that it can affect parties of all sorts. In 1948, the militia led by Menachem Begin, and known as Irgun Tsvai Leumi, disbanded and became the core of the Herut (Freedom) Party. Though dwarfed electorally by Mapai (the precursor to the Labor Party), it became the second largest party in Israel by 1955 and later the largest party in the Likud.[126] Mapai,

---

[117] Carbone 2005, 434, 439.

[118] Prevost 2006, 163–181. Many were shocked when the ANC announced that armed struggle was over (167).

[119] ANC Strategy and Tactics 1994, section 8.7, as in Herbst 1997, 610.

[120] Ottaway 1991, 63.

[121] Johnson 2003, 321–340.

[122] Johnson (2003, 332) notes that membership in the South African Communist Party (SACP) dropped off quickly after the ANC transformed itself into a party, noting that nearly half the national leadership allowed their membership to lapse.

[123] Ottaway 1991, 70.

[124] Herbst 1997, 610.

[125] Alence 2004; Engel 1999, 817–842.

[126] Shlaim 1996, 281; Arian and Shamir 1983, 144. The party's symbol drew on its military roots. It was an arm with a rifle superimposed on a map including both sides of the Jordan River.

which led every government until Likud's victory in 1977, was also bolstered
by its experience with paramilitary activities. Long before independence, its
armed Haganah (Defense) organization fielded 10,000 mobilized soldiers plus
40,000 reservists. The military movement became a base for party activists
and an important source for party leaders, including Moshe Dayan, Yitzhak
Rabin, and Ariel Sharon.[127]

The relationship between the nature of organizations during and after conflict holds for the weak as well as the strong. Organizationally weak guerrilla
movements make for organizationally weak political parties after democratization.[128] In Guatemala, for example, war was not the stimulus for an effective
party system. Quite the contrary, as the nature of Guatemala's armed struggle
prevented the development of a strong party on either the left or the right.
The Guatemalan National Revolutionary Movement (URNG), an amalgam of
four different guerrilla movements that united uneasily under Cuban mentor-
ing in 1982, never succeeded in constructing an organizational structure or a
popular base comparable to that of the war-time FMLN.[129] It consequently
fared relatively poorly with Guatemalan voters when it converted itself into
a political party.[130] Facing fragmented and relatively weak opposition on the
left, Guatemala's right-wing parties have had less incentive to compromise
and unite. As a result, Guatemala has a level of party instability that is not
typical of other durable postconflict cases.[131] The organizations that emerge
in wartime are often mirrored in peacetime. The contrast between the fate
of Guatemala's URNG and the other, more popular parties emerging from
rebel movements highlights the point that it is not armed conflict per se that
explains the durability advantage. That advantage emerges only when the elements of armed conflict take certain forms.

Nevertheless, there does appear to be a strong positive association between
sustained internal war and strong parties. Many of the rebel groups that have
had the organizational capacity and appeal to wage full-scale wars have used
these capacities to their advantage in the electoral arena; their strength has
also encouraged competing parties to unite. Table 4.3 illustrates the point.
The electoral strength of the parties that win the founding legislative elections
in democracies emerging during or after internal war is significantly greater
than the electoral strength of winning parties in peacetime democracies. The
mean popular vote for winning parties in "internal war democracies" exceeds
that of peacetime democracies by 11 percentage points. The share of seats for

---

[127] Peretz and Doron 1997, 37–38.
[128] This point has been made eloquently by Michael Allison and applies to Honduras as well. See
Allison 2006, 137–164.
[129] Though the URNG joined a coalition of left-wing parties that won 12 percent of the vote in
1999, in 2003, it won only 4 percent of the vote in legislative elections, and its candidate for
president came in a humiliating sixth at the polls. For a discussion of the divided nature of
the URNG, see Ryan 1994, 34–36.
[130] Allison 2006.
[131] Carothers 2006, 224–225.

TABLE 4.3. *Winning Party: Peacetime and Conflict Democracies Compared[a]*

Results of Founding Legislative Elections

	Mean Percentage of Seats Won by Largest Party	Mean Percentage of Popular Vote Won by Largest Party
Internal War Democracies[b] (N = 53)[c]	61.48	52.12
Peacetime Democracies (N = 17)[d]	48.02	41.15
t-test	2.32*	2.78**

*p < .05; **p < .01

[a] All figures are for the lower chamber where two exist.

[b] Internal war democracies are those emerging from an internal conflict coded as a war in the SIPRI Armed Conflict Data Set, as opposed to smaller regional conflicts. Results for democracies emerging from conflicts other than internal wars are similar to those for peacetime democracies. The mean percentage of seats won by the largest party in these cases is 47.09 percent; the mean popular vote is 39.43 percent.

[c] Elections in Montenegro were held in 2001, outside our time period, and thus not included in these results. Including the case, the mean difference is still statistically significant for both variables.

[d] Reliable data were not available for the popular vote in Belarus 1995, South Korea 1961, Sudan 1958, and Turkey 1954.

winning parties in internal war democracies exceeds that of peacetime democracies by 13 percentage points. These are statistically significant differences.

These effects hold only for democracies emerging during or after internal war. The figures for other sorts of conflict democracies do not differ significantly from those of peacetime democracies. When internal wars involve rebel armies with effective organizations and broad public support, they provide the foundation for electorally strong political parties.

H5: Broad-Based Rebel Movements Can Be a Source of "Heroic" Leaders

The individuals who lead rebel organizations are often key actors in new democracies. Though successful rebel leaders do not always become successful politicians, certain conflict situations give rise to leaders who can make a successful transition to electoral politics. Where rebel leaders have run organizations in which political strategy is forged collectively, where they have gained administrative experience running occupied regions, where they have organized nonmilitary entities, and where they have gained a following through legitimate means, a successful transition to electoral politics is within reach.[132] Leadership is of critical importance to any organization's success,

[132] de Zeeuw 2008, 8–10.

and organizations that have successfully engaged in armed conflict are often led by especially inspirational figures. This means that regimes emerging from armed struggles with the qualities listed above have a ready pool of leaders who can be framed as "heroic" and who are viable democratic politicians once the choice for democracy has been made.

These leaders have emerged in a broad range of new democracies. ANC leader Nelson Mandela was "viewed as a figure of almost biblical stature" by the time he was released after 27 years in South African jails.[133] SWAPO leader Sam Nujoma was known as "the founding father of the nation" in Namibia before he began his campaign for president.[134] Joaquím Chissano was "liked better than his party" in Mozambique in part because he was a former Frelimo freedom fighter.[135] Xanana Gusmão "attained almost supernatural status" fighting the Indonesians for twenty-five years in East Timor and was characterized after independence as "the only unifying force among East Timor's leadership."[136] Other examples could be marshaled,[137] but the point is clear: New electoral democracies that emerge from long, violent struggles are often led by figures who played a heroic role in the struggle itself. This can be good for democratic durability. If the heroic figure commands the obedience of the armed forces, this is even better, for it both eliminates the possibility that the military will assault the regime and raises the costs of assaults for all actors outside the military.

Leaders of social movements during peacetime transitions can also take on a heroic hue and win elections, as the case of Lech Walesa in Poland illustrates. But the fact that Walesa did not manage to hold on to elected office is attributable, in part, to the fact that he had no disciplined, country-wide organization comparable to a converted rebel army. Solidarity succeeded in toppling Poland's authoritarian regime, but it lacked the discipline, the membership base, and the cohesive leadership that an enduring party requires. Walesa's inability to stay electorally competitive despite his heroic beginnings was due in part to the fact that both Solidarity and Polish democracy were born in peacetime.

Writing of liberation movements in the 1960s, Immanuel Wallerstein suggested that heroes and parties were like "a pair of surgical clamps," which could "hold the state together while the bonds of affection and legitimation grew."[138] History has shown us that healing states requires much more than the weight of charisma and the pressure of any single institution. It has also shown us that rebel heroes can use their power to create new political systems that are

---

[133] Blanton and Glad 1997, 565–590.
[134] Good 1997, 562.
[135] Bill Keller, "Mozambique Voting Today in First Election," *New York Times*, October 27, 1994.
[136] BBC News Profile: Xanana Gusmão. Gusmão was East Timor's president and was then chosen to prime minister.
[137] For the use of heroic imagery, see Arian 1998, 149.
[138] Ottaway 1991, 65, quoting Wallerstein.

not democratic. Leaders from Mao through Mugabe have done precisely this. Clearly, armed conflicts do not always produce democratic leaders. This is one of the reasons that armed conflicts do not produce democracy. Armed conflicts do, however, offer a proving ground and a ready public for leaders who choose to engage in electoral competition. Military and political campaigns differ in important ways, but those who manage to mobilize support and loyalty during armed struggle often develop a following that civilian political leaders in peacetime transitions cannot match. This is why so many conflict democracies have begun with the landslide victory of an electorally powerful party headed by a "heroic" figure. Even if they do not succeed in strengthening bonds of affection and legitimation, the fact that they can win fair elections and enjoy all the (material and nonmaterial) resources that this implies gives these leaders a vested interest in making sure that democracy endures.

Victors in the founding elections of peacetime democracies do not often have comparable popular, party, and military backing. Their risks of playing the electoral game are, therefore, greater, as is the probability of their defection. The etiology of democratic leadership after conflict clearly merits more research, but there is much evidence to suggest that the fifth hypothesis listed above has some validity: Armed struggle can be advantageous in producing heroic leaders who can win elections decisively and gain a vested interest in democratic durability.

H6: International Resources Can Contribute to Durability

Differential treatment by foreign actors constitutes a final factor that may explain the durability advantage. Conflict democracies benefit from access to two sets of foreign resources. The first are those emanating from a vast network of private and governmental postconflict assistance organizations. These groups have been active in varied forms and in various ways throughout the post–World War II period. They run the gamut from the agencies associated with the Marshall Plan, through the network of postconflict teams sponsored by the United Nations, through the multitude of nongovernmental organizations (NGOs) that flock to postconflict settings to undo the damage and to help ensure the peace. Conflict democracies attract more attention from abroad precisely because they have been the scene of violence and destruction. This attention can work to the advantage of electoral democracy's longevity.

The role of foreign actors in the preservation of conflict democracies merits much more attention than I can give it here. The transfer of norms through contact, the creation of social and human capital, the implications of having internationally connected actors bear witness to systemic threats, and the implications of their becoming victims of coercion themselves are not phenomena that lend themselves to summary analysis or to quantification. Yet, they are phenomena of undeniable consequence.[139] We need only recall how profoundly

---

[139] Dobbins (2003, 159) reports that aid per capita to postconflict regimes varies between 20 and 48 percent of GDP in the first two years after war.

the murder of six Jesuits affected the evolution of El Salvador's democracy after 1989 to appreciate the point.[140] Institutional links to powerful groups in powerful states can empower even those who lose their lives in struggle. This is why democratic spoilers so often frame foreigners as villains.[141]

A broad range of scholarship finds a strong, positive association between democratic durability and links to democratic actors abroad. Doyle and Sambanis highlight the positive association between democratic durability and U.N. peace-building operations.[142] Pevehouse finds a statistically significant relationship between the longevity of new democracies and their affiliation with democratic international associations.[143] Levitsky and Way illustrate how "linkage" to the West and the "emergence of a transnational infrastructure of organizations" raise "the external cost of openly autocratic rule."[144] To the extent that political leaders of conflict democracies are better linked to the West, and to the extent that their need for assistance has been raised by the legacies of conflict itself, they should be especially sensitive to these external costs and to what Levitsky and Way describe as the "new political conditionality." This, too, is an asset for durability.

In addition to better access to the (material and nonmaterial) resources of international organizations, conflict democracies enjoy greater access to targeted democracy assistance programs. Although foreign aid in the aggregate seems to have no significant effect on democratic durability, recent research suggests that aid targeted specifically toward democratic governance may, in fact, be effective. Finkel, Pérez-Liñan, and Seligson have found a significant association between democracy aid and democratization in general.[145] Kapstein and Converse have shown that targeted democracy aid "does seem to increase the likelihood that a young democracy will survive."[146] Because of data limitations, these conclusions apply only to the period after 1990 and only to aid from the United States. They also leave us with many questions. We do not know, for example, how much of the durability advantage this aid might explain. But we do know that conflict democracies receive significantly more democracy aid than peacetime democracies – in both the first full year of their existence and over time. Table 4.4 illustrates the point.

The multitude of aid programs and organizations that assist postconflict regimes today had few (if any) counterparts in interwar Europe.[147] Quite the contrary, as the focus on reparations and on crippling old enemies dwarfed concerns for the preservation of new democracies in the aftermath of World War I. Even Hitler's nomination to the chancellorship caused "no great

---

[140] U.S. aid to El Salvador's military was cancelled. Wade 2008, 38.
[141] The sad fact that foreigners do act like villains in some settings explains these behaviors too.
[142] Doyle and Sambanis 2000, 779.
[143] Pevehouse, 2005.
[144] Levitsky and Way 2010, 26–27.
[145] Finkel, Perez-Liñan, and Seligson 2008.
[146] Kapstein and Converse 2008, 124.
[147] Judt 1998.

TABLE 4.4. *U.S. Democracy Aid 1990–2004: Peacetime and Conflict Democracies Compared*[a]

	1st Year Average Democracy Aid	1st 5 Years Average Democracy Aid
Peacetime Democracies (N = 21)	$ 0.17	$ 0.24
Conflict Democracies (N = 18)	$ 0.82	$ 0.86
t-test	1.98[b]	3.61[c]

[a] Figures are aid per capita.
[b] Significant at the .05 level.
[c] Significant at the .01 level.
Source: USAID.

sensation" abroad.[148] This difference helps explain why conflict democracies fared so differently after the two world wars.

The fact that foreign actors behaved so differently in different time periods reminds us that foreign support for conflict democracies is contingent on strategic concerns. Not all conflict democracies attract the same resources from international actors, and not all of the actors within a conflict democracy are treated equally by the international community.

On this dimension, too, it is not armed conflict per se that explains the durability advantage, but particular elements of armed conflict. How a conflict and its democratic aftermath impact the strategic interests of powerful states is of key importance. If powerful established democracies (such as the United States) see the preservation of a particular conflict democracy as in their strategic interest, the probability of that democracy receiving positive attention rises. If powerful democracies see the preservation of a conflict democracy as threatening, the probability of positive attention declines. It is not coincidental that the durability advantage disappears for regimes emerging between 1956 and 1966 – at the height of the Cold War. Nor is it coincidental that throughout the time period studied, so many of the conflict democracies that failed were replaced by explicitly anti-Communist regimes. The durability advantage cannot be fully understood without taking international context into account.

The effects of links to international civil society and to international organizations more generally are neither constant nor wholly positive. Nor are they well understood. Yet, the evidence summarized above suggests the sixth hypothesis may have validity. Unique links to international actors give conflict democracies access to a range of nonmaterial and material resources unavailable to peacetime democracies. These links can affect incentive structures in consequential ways and in so doing help to keep electoral democracy alive.

[148] Craig 1978, 569; Bermeo 1994.

A CAUTIONARY CONCLUSION

Whether today's international context will help perpetuate the durability advantage remains an open question. Though neither international civil society nor international peace-building missions are likely to wither away, the "War on Terror" may become the policy priority that trumps all others. Conflict democracies with electorally viable "terrorist organizations" may lose any advantage they have over peacetime democracies. Movements with real or imagined links to terrorism may not be offered the incentives to become political parties.[149] This, in turn, may eliminate the conversion advantage altogether because many of the Islamist movements that are so politically suspect today are among the only movements in the post-Soviet world with the characteristics that facilitate conversion. With the fall of the Soviet Union and the end of the Cold War, the leftist movements that had these attributes in the past are vastly outnumbered (in nondemocratic states) by groups with no clear ideational foundation, chaotic leadership, and little genuine popular support. Mueller and others insist that "most" of today's armed conflict is waged by "thugs," "mercenaries," or "brigand gangs."[150] If this is true, and if the War on Terror discourages armed groups motivated by religion from converting to political parties, fewer conflict democracies will manifest the durability advantage, and it may disappear altogether.

It must be noted in closing that wars of any sort leave horrendous negative legacies and that the particular legacies discussed in this chapter are double-edged. They often lead to institutions that are durable but seriously deficient. Institutional constraints can be used to shut out effective opposition. Parties born of armies can grow into dominant-party regimes that stifle pluralism. The discipline that made for effective liberation struggles can silence political debate,[151] and the heroic leaders that led those struggles can personalize power and create unrestrained executives.[152] Finally, the foreign actors that offer the resources to rebuild a war-torn land can distort democracy by diverting the attention of the new democracy's political elite; the demands of donors may take precedence over the demands of the electorate. In sum, the legacies of armed conflict might explain not simply democratic durability but democratic deficiency as well.

How might the negative legacies of conflict be minimized? How pervasive are the more positive legacies discussed above? What determines their impact and longevity? This chapter knowingly raises many more questions than it answers. We still know remarkably little about the legacies of armed conflict, but their political importance is undeniable.

---

[149] This may have affected the RUF in Sierra Leone. Richards and Vincent 2008.

[150] Mueller 2004, 86; Gamba and Cornwell 2000, 157–172.

[151] Johnson 2003.

[152] Knowledgeable specialists noted the risk of big-man democracy as early as the mid-1990s. See Bratton and van de Walle 1997, 253. Nicaragua's Daniel Ortega seems to have fallen prey to this sort of opportunism. As his former vice president Sergio Ramirez put it, "Danielismo is a corruption of Sandinismo." Feinberg and Kurtz-Phelan 2006, 77.

PART II

WAR AND DEMOCRATIC PUBLICS

Reshaping Political Participation?

5

The Effects of War on Civil Society

Cross-National Evidence from World War II

Rieko Kage

Citizen participation in membership organizations, or civic engagement, is a crucial component of social capital, itself a key to an assortment of beneficial social outcomes, including economic growth,[1] better political performance,[2] more successful democratic consolidation,[3] and even better health and longer life expectancy.[4] These are undoubtedly important concerns for countries in times of peace, but they should be particularly pressing issues for societies seeking to recover from war.[5] Precisely for this reason, recent international efforts at peace-building and reconstruction have devoted substantial resources to the strengthening of indigenous civil societies.[6] But despite the importance of this question, few studies have considered, in a theoretically and empirically systematic fashion, the extent and manner in which war itself may have transformed civil society in post-conflict societies. Such an inquiry should yield important insights into how postwar civil societies may be rebuilt and/or fostered. This study attempts to take a step in that direction.

Earlier versions of this chapter were presented at the Annual Meeting of the American Political Science Association (2007, 2009); the Comparative Politics Workshop, Harvard University (2006); the annual meeting of the Japanese Political Science Association (2007); and the Japanese Association for Comparative Politics (2008). The author thanks the participants at these gatherings, as well as Margarita Estevez-Abe, Mary Alice Haddad, Jacques Hymans, Torben Iversen, Peter Katzenstein, Koji Kagotani, Koji Nakakita, Susan Pharr, Yasuo Tsuji, Sidney Verba, and Jong-Sung You, for their insightful comments. I also thank the Kobe YMCA for access to their archives and the Grant-in-Aid for Scientific Research, Japanese Ministry for Education, Culture, Sports, Science, and Technology, for its financial support.

[1] Fukuyama 1995.
[2] Putnam 1993.
[3] Diamond 1999; for a contrary view, see Encarnación 2006.
[4] Putnam 2000; Rose 2000.
[5] Kage 2010.
[6] See, for instance, Azimi et al. 2003.

What impact does war have on levels of civic engagement? Existing studies of participation generally lead us to expect a fall in civic engagement in the wake of defeat and no fall, or perhaps even a rise, in the wake of victory. There are two main perspectives in this literature: socioeconomic and social-psychological.

Socioeconomic perspectives suggest that defeat is often accompanied by extensive physical destruction, economic weakness, and individuals' loss of income. Moreover, war, especially when prolonged, often interrupts young people's formal education. And, as numerous studies have shown, income and education are the two key determinants of an individual's participation in politics and civil society.[7] Thus, defeated societies are likely to see a marked decline in levels of civic activity. Of course, victorious countries may also see declines in income and educational opportunities, but recovery is likely to be faster, and the extent of losses less severe, than in defeated countries. Victorious countries may also be able to compensate for the wartime loss of formal educational opportunities with postwar programs like the United States' G. I. Bill.[8] Such a luxury is usually not an option for defeated societies, at least in the immediate postwar context. Thus, the reasoning goes, war's negative effects on civic engagement are likely to be less severe in victorious countries than in defeated countries.

Social-psychological theories of participation also suggest that civic engagement is likely to rise in the wake of victory and to fall in the wake of defeat.[9] This claim rests on a hypothesized process of social learning. If a country is victorious in war, citizens learn that their wartime participation on the homefront or the battlefield has yielded tangible benefits, which in turn encourages them to continue to participate voluntarily after the war. Defeat, in contrast, is likely to lead citizens to believe that their wartime participation was futile, and they therefore withdraw from public life altogether once the war is over.

These existing perspectives focus especially on the macropolitical outcomes of wars. But in so doing, they give short shrift to the day-to-day reorientation of citizens' behavioral patterns that war, especially major war, can bring about. A fuller examination of war's processes as they are experienced by citizens is necessary. War, particularly major war, while unfortunate, may also present new opportunities for citizens to acquire the civic skills that are crucial for subsequent civic engagement. This chapter contends that mobilization during wartime may play a crucial role in elevating postwar levels of voluntary participation, *regardless* of whether the country emerged from the battlefield victorious or vanquished.

The chapter proceeds as follows. The next section lays out a theoretical framework that offers a new perspective on the relationship between war

---

[7] Verba, Schlozman, and Brady 1995; Brehm and Rahn 1997; Hall 1999; Oliver 2000.
[8] Mettler 2005.
[9] Skocpol et al. 2002.

and postwar levels of civic engagement. The third section tests the hypothesis, using cross-national quantitative analysis of the effects of World War II. Section four further probes the validity of the hypothesis through an in-depth case study of the revival of the Kobe YMCA in post–World War II Japan. The fifth section summarizes and concludes.

WAR, MOBILIZATION, AND CIVIL SOCIETY

This study argues that war greatly affects the trajectory of civil society via the mechanism of wartime mobilization. Mobilization, defined by the Merriam-Webster Dictionary as "the act of assembling and making ready for war duty," may take place in major wars at the warfront, the workplace, and/or the neighborhood. First, mobilization into the armed forces has generally involved the recruitment or conscription of many thousands of young males, and sometimes also females, usually roughly between the ages of eighteen and forty.[10] As wars intensify, mobilization can also extend to marginalized groups within society, such as ethnic minorities,[11] and to both older and younger age groups.

Mobilization of citizen-soldiers, however, represents only the tip of the iceberg of social mobilization for major wars. On the homefront, citizens are often mobilized into war-related work in the economy. As government demand for steel, aircraft, and other heavy production expands, workers are often shifted to war-related industries – for instance, from farms to factories. The conscription of young workers may also create demand for new workers – typically women and minorities – to enter the labor market.[12]

Third, and perhaps even more consequential for civic behavior, citizens are also mobilized at the neighborhood or community level. In what Skocpol et al. call "patriotic partnerships,"[13] voluntary associations have played a particularly important role in providing wartime services during the modern era, from recycling to food drives. For instance, numerous voluntary groups in the United States organized food drives during World Wars I and II; Oxfam, one of the best-known international nongovernmental organizations (NGOs) today, was founded in Britain in 1942 to provide relief in wartorn Europe.[14]

The effects of these movements of people out of their prewar routines go beyond their consequences for the state's military or economic power. Mobilization also involves a dramatic expansion of the public sphere. Citizens are transferred to "strategic" industries; jobs and tasks that had hitherto not been seen as serving the public good take on greater public meaning; and

---

[10] Flynn 1998.
[11] Krebs 2006.
[12] Donnelly 1999.
[13] Skocpol et al. 2002.
[14] Iriye 2002.

groups and individuals who had scarcely participated in the public sphere, particularly minorities, enter this growing public sphere, often for the first time. Whether citizens find themselves in the military, the factory, or the neighborhood bucket brigade, they inevitably come into contact with individuals, officials, and groups that they had not previously encountered and that they would not have encountered except for the war. Through these interactions, citizens acquire important communication skills, political and social awareness, organizational savvy, and the art of deliberation – in short, "civic skills."[15] Participating in the disbursement of rationed food, for instance, brings citizens into greater contact with their neighbors as well as government officials. In that capacity, they may need to negotiate various demands, giving them firsthand experience in civic engagement. Many of these lessons are transferable to postwar contexts.

Beyond social learning via wartime mobilization, societal actors are often given a greater voice in public affairs as war intensifies. War strengthens the state,[16] but it often strengthens society as well. The state's need to induce citizens into performing war-related services often leads it to give them greater access to decision making over the process of producing and delivering services. The British government, as well as private management, opened up new channels for labor unions to weigh in on issues of common concern during World War II.[17] The famously close consultative relationships between the postwar Japanese state and industries, as well as between labor and management, also have their roots in the war.[18]

This is not to say that all citizens welcome these new opportunities. Citizens may resent mobilization, and mobilization may strain the relationship between state and society. However, regardless of how they feel about wartime mobilization, many individuals may come gradually to embrace their new responsibilities, perhaps less out of a commitment to the war's objectives than to their fellow citizens. Scholars have often noted the close lifelong relationships forged among soldiers during wartime,[19] and such relationships can also be forged at the homefront.

This socializing effect of mobilization should be particularly strong among youth, in their "formative years" and thus more susceptible to external influences. Indeed, many studies have found participation during this period to be a strong predictor of participation during adulthood.[20] Wartime mobilization presents opportunities for the acquisition of civic skills that have lasting

---

[15] Verba, Schlozman, and Brady 1995.
[16] For instance, Tilly 1975.
[17] Donnelly 1999.
[18] Noguchi 1995.
[19] Elder and Clipp 1988.
[20] See, for instance, Verba, Schlozman, and Brady, 1995; Putnam 2000; Jennings 2002. In recent years, this finding has led to a heated debate over whether "required" public service programs in schools are desirable: see, for instance, Metz and Youniss 2003.

effects, facilitating individuals' participation in civic activities once the war has ended.[21] Individuals who experience intense mobilization as young adults should continue to participate at high levels throughout their lives, whether their country emerged from war victorious or vanquished.

In sum, mobilization during war, especially major war, presents citizens with opportunities for social learning that are typically not present during peacetime. Citizens, especially those who were young adults during wartime (youth cohorts), emerge from war equipped with various civic skills that remain with them over their lives. All else being equal, this should lead them to participate at substantially higher levels than their elders (immediately preceding cohorts) over their entire life course.

QUANTITATIVE ANALYSIS

Dependent Variable: War, Generational Cohorts, and Civic Engagement

Does war elevate participation among certain generational cohorts? To systematically answer this question, this section examines the effect of World War II on postwar civic engagement in thirteen industrialized countries.

Following much of the existing literature, this study operationalizes civic engagement as participation in membership associations.[22] Membership associations are those "groups in which people do things together as fellow members."[23] Nonmembership civic associations, such as nonprofit research institutes, were excluded since they do not measure the extent to which individual citizens are willing to engage in collective endeavors. For the same reason, associations with only corporate members, most typically industrial and/or business associations, were also excluded. In addition, professional associations were excluded if, as with the American Bar Association, membership is a requirement for practicing one's trade.

In assessing the effects of war on postwar civic engagement, one must compare prewar and postwar participation in membership associations across different countries. At present, however, reliable data on levels of civic engagement that span both the prewar and postwar periods are available only for the United States.[24]

This study, therefore, devises an alternative strategy. It leverages more recent surveys to gain information on the participatory behavior of citizens of different ages and thus with different formative experiences. It compares the participation in civic groups of individuals belonging to the immediate pre–World

---

[21] While society as a whole is likely to be impacted by mobilization, the marginal members of society, or those who are generally least likely to participate in civic affairs in times of peace – such as women, youth, or other minorities – may be likely to benefit the most from these new opportunities for participation. See, for instance, Braybon and Summerfield 1987.

[22] See, for instance, Skocpol et al. 2000; Andolina et al. 2003.

[23] Skocpol 2000, 34, fn.19.

[24] Skocpol et al. 2002.

War II cohort with those belonging to the cohort that came of age during the war. If the standard socioeconomic and social-psychological hypotheses are correct, then generational cohorts in countries that were victorious in World War II would exhibit markedly higher rates of participation throughout their lives than previous generational cohorts. Similarly, countries that experienced defeat in World War II would see declines in levels of participation from pre-war to wartime cohorts. If, however, my hypothesis is valid, then the wartime generation in more highly mobilized countries would participate at consistently higher rates throughout their lives than individuals in the immediately preceding cohort – regardless of whether their nation won or lost the war. In less mobilized countries, individuals who came of age around the war would participate at rates similar to those of individuals of the immediately preceding cohort, and this difference would manifest in contemporary surveys of political participation.

This is admittedly a second-best option: Events since World War II may have affected subsequent participation rates. But studies consistently find participation during youth to be a strong predictor of participation during adulthood.[25] Individuals who experienced intensive mobilization as young adults thus should continue to participate at high levels throughout their lives.

This study analyzes data from the World Values Survey (WVS) – waves 1981, 1990, and, when available, 1995–1997. Using three waves of surveys, each with identically worded questions, allows analysts to some degree to isolate cohort effects from life-cycle effects: that is, to distinguish the participatory behavior that is affected by a cohort's unique experiences from that driven by an individual's life cycle, such as entry into the workforce, beginning a family, or retirement. Countries were selected if high-quality data (i.e., few missing values) is available from at least two of the three WVS waves. Thirteen countries met this criterion: Belgium, Canada, Finland, France, Germany, Ireland, Italy, Japan, Netherlands, Sweden, Switzerland, United Kingdom, and the United States. This list includes all the major belligerents that either were already democratic or became democracies in the immediate postwar period, plus several neutrals, some of which also experienced extensive mobilization.

Following Arthur Schlesinger, Jr.'s definition of "generation,"[26] this study divides survey respondents into fifteen-year generational groupings: individuals who were born between 1906 and 1920 and those who were born between 1921 and 1935. The 1921–1935 cohort is particularly important because these are the individuals who were young enough, but not too young, to be molded for life through participation in wartime mobilization; at the end of World War II, these individuals were between 10 and 24 years old. This is also

---

[25] Verba, Schlozman, and Brady 1995; Jennings 2002.
[26] Schlesinger 1949.

TABLE 5.1. *Mean Number of Associational Memberships: Pre–World War II and World War II Cohorts*

	1911–1920 Cohort	1921–1935 Cohort	Percent Change
Belgium	0.69	0.79	114.94
Canada	1.02	1.18	115.69
Finland	1.96	2.20	112.24
France	0.39	0.52	133.33
Germany (West)	1.09	1.63	149.54
Ireland	0.62	0.73	117.74
Italy	0.30	0.31	103.33
Japan	0.38	0.61	160.53
Netherlands	1.39	1.44	103.60
Sweden	1.14	1.64	143.86
Switzerland	1.00	1.30	130.00
United Kingdom	0.86	1.23	143.02
United States	1.73	2.11	121.97
13-country mean	0.97	1.22	128.93

Sources: World Values Surveys 1981, 1990, 1995–1997.

almost identical to the "long civic generation" identified by Putnam.[27] For the 1906–1920 generation, respondents from the 1911–1920 cohort, rather than the 1906–1920 cohort, were used in order to exclude possible effects of World War I.

Table 5.1 compares the number of memberships in civic organizations by generational cohort. It shows that memberships in civic organizations rose across the board between the pre–World War II and the World War II cohorts among belligerents, regardless of whether they were victorious or defeated, as well as among neutrals. While there is considerable variation in the magnitude of the increase, war outcome does not appear to be the crucial explanatory variable. Japan and Germany show the largest gains, while Italy and Finland, two other defeated countries, are near the bottom. The United Kingdom, which emerged victorious, exhibits one of the largest jumps in participation between the two cohorts, but the United States, another victor, displays a much smaller increase. There is also substantial variation among neutrals: Sweden exhibits a rapid rise in civic engagement between the two cohorts, but Ireland, which also remained neutral, shows much less change.

Table 5.2 breaks down the figures further, controlling for age. It again shows a rise in membership between the pre–World War II and World War II generations as they reached the same age. West German respondents born between

[27] See Putnam 2000. Putnam refers to the "long civic generation" as those born before 1934. In order to isolate the effects of World War II, this study added a lower bound of 1921, following Schlesinger 1949.

TABLE 5.2. *Number of Associational Memberships at the Same Age Level: Pre–World War II and World War II Cohorts*

Country	Age 61–65		Difference (%)	Age 66–70		Difference (%)
	1911–1920	1921–1935		1911–1920	1921–1935	
Belgium	0.52	0.92	176.92	0.84	0.90	107.14
Canada	0.91	1.01	110.99	1.13	1.34	118.58
France	0.53	0.58	109.43	0.37	0.73	197.30
Germany (West)	0.68	1.90	279.41	1.03	1.98	192.23
Ireland	0.82	0.40	48.78	0.74	0.65	87.84
Italy	0.31	0.25	80.65	0.36	0.23	63.89
Japan	0.36	0.67	186.11	0.36	0.93	258.33
Netherlands	1.33	1.81	136.09	1.27	1.51	118.90
Sweden	1.24	2.03	163.71	0.86	1.67	194.19
Switzerland	.	1.42	.	0.63	2.61	414.29
United Kingdom	0.64	1.31	204.69	0.80	1.32	165.00
United States	1.46	2.15	147.26	1.18	2.83	239.83
13-country mean	0.80	1.26	157.50	0.88	1.48	168.18

Source: World Values Surveys 1981, 1990, 1995–1997, Table 2. Finland not shown due to small sample size (N = 8).

1911 and 1920 participated in an average of .68 associations at 61–65 years old, but those born between 1921 and 1935 participated in 1.90 groups, on average, at 61–65 years old. Even when one controls for age, the difference in memberships between the two cohorts persists. Across the thirteen countries under study, individuals born between 1911 and 1920 participated, on average, in .80 and .88 groups at ages 61–65 and 66–70, respectively, while those born between 1921 and 1935 were members of 1.26 and 1.48 groups at the same age. These are substantial increases. The differences in memberships as individuals in the two generational cohorts reached the ages of 61–65 and 66–70 were 157.50 percent and 168.18 percent, respectively. There was an across-the-board increase in levels of civic engagement between the 1911–1920 and 1921–1935 cohorts.

Index of Mobilization

Existing studies have operationalized mobilization, the key independent variable in this chapter, in at least two ways. Jaggers[28] uses the number of battle deaths. This, however, is problematic since the number of battle deaths is more likely to reflect the nature of warfare than levels of mobilization per se. Thus

---

[28] Jaggers 1992.

the United States experienced relatively moderate mobilization during World War II but incurred relatively high numbers of battle deaths owing to the particularly vicious nature of the Pacific War. Battle deaths also do not allow for mobilization in countries that remained neutral. Bennett and Stam[29] use a more sophisticated Correlates of War (COW) composite capabilities index, which combines measures for a country's share of total international military personnel, military expenditures, energy consumption, iron/steel production, total population, and urban population. This index is an improvement, since it captures mobilization on both the homefront and the warfront. The COW index, however, conflates the presumed effects of mobilization with mobilization itself. Iron/steel production, for instance, measures the effect of mobilization rather than mobilization per se; similarly for energy consumption. There is no necessary relationship between the number of mobilized workers or the extent of mobilization and the resulting levels of production. Cohen, for instance, notes that Japan's industrial production suffered during World War II despite large-scale mobilization because skilled workers were not exempt from conscription.[30]

This study instead focuses on the peak number of soldiers serving in the armed forces. This provides a useful measure not only of military mobilization, but also indirectly of civilian mobilization, since countries that mobilize heavily militarily should also mobilize intensively on the homefront. If more men are drafted into the armed forces, for instance, women would be more likely to leave the home to undertake tasks previously performed by men. Militaries may rely on manpower as opposed to technology to varying degrees, so this measure of overall mobilization is indirect. But using peak military mobilization as a proxy for overall mobilization is less problematic in the World War II cases, given the common time frame and the relative extremity of the threat.[31] In addition, since civic skills may be acquired gradually, it is important to include a measure of the duration of mobilization. I created an index of mobilization by multiplying the percentage of citizens who served in the armed forces at its peak by the number of years of wartime mobilization.[32]

The configuration of this index is shown in Table 5.3. Predictably the main belligerents – Germany, Japan, the United Kingdom – rank high on the index, but interestingly so do some neutrals, such as Switzerland and Sweden.

The basic relationship between the independent and dependent variables is plotted in Figure 5.1. At first glance, there does appear to be a rough correlation between countries' levels of mobilization and their differences in mean

---

[29] Bennett and Stam 1996.
[30] Cohen 1949, 271.
[31] This may be truer of wars such as World Wars I and II than more contemporary wars.
[32] Another measure of the extent of mobilization might be the total number of soldiers mobilized over the entire course of the war. Unfortunately, these data are often missing or questionable. Ellis 1993, 253–254.

TABLE 5.3. *Index of Wartime Mobilization*

	Population (in 1000s)	Peak Strength of Armed Forces (in 1000s)	Percent of Pop.	Length of Full-Scale Mobilization (years)	Mobilization Index: Peak Strength × Duration
Germany (West)	78,000	10,000	12.82	6	76.92
Switzerland	4,206	430	10.22	6	61.32
Japan	72,200	6,095	8.44	7	59.09
United Kingdom	47,500	4,683	9.86	5	49.29
Sweden	6,326	500	7.90	6	47.40
Italy	43,800	4,500	10.27	4	41.08
Finland	3,800	250	6.58	6	39.47
United States	129,200	12,364	9.57	4	38.28
Canada	11,100	780	7.03	4	28.12
France	42,000	5,000	11.90	2	23.80
Belgium	8,300	800	9.64	1	9.64
Netherlands	8,700	500	5.75	1	5.75
Ireland	2,940	20	0.68	5	3.40
13-country mean			8.51	4.38	37.20

Source: Ellis (1993).

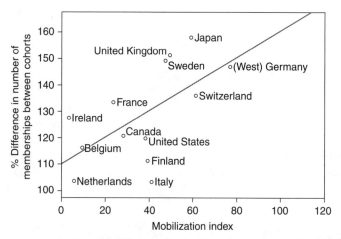

FIGURE 5.1. Percent difference in number of associational memberships between the 1911–1920 and 1921–1935 cohorts.
Source: Table 5.2 and World Values Surveys 1981, 1990, 1995–1997.

associational memberships between the prewar and wartime cohorts. A more systematic test of this relationship will be presented below.

Quantitative Analysis

The hypothesis was tested using beta-binomial regression analysis, controlling for education, income, gender, age, and survey year. The control variables were chosen on the basis of existing studies of voluntary participation.[33] The analyses use the beta-binomial model because of the nature of the dependent variable: the number of associational memberships per survey respondent. Associational membership is a binary variable – that is, one either is or is not a member. However, the dependent variable in this study is the sum of the associational memberships. Moreover, it is reasonable to assume that the probability of being a member is not constant across individuals; to the contrary, it is quite possible that others' participatory behavior would affect the decision to participate. The beta-binomial model is well suited for handling this kind of variation.[34]

The study tested two models. First, in order to test for the effects of mobilization, the study tested a model that includes the mobilization index and, since mobilization is likely to interact with cohort variables, a multiplicative interaction term between mobilization and the 1921–1935 cohort. The results are shown in Model 1 of Table 5.4.

Second, to test the validity of the alternative hypothesis that the outcome of war drives the postwar growth or decline of civic engagement, the variables for mobilization were replaced with variables for victory or defeat. Two dummy variables were created to measure victory (Britain, Canada, United States) and defeat (Finland, Germany, Italy, Japan). Other countries were either neutral or had ambiguous outcomes. Since the war outcome variables were expected to interact with cohort variables, two interaction variables were created (*victory*1921–1935 cohort, defeat*1921–1935 cohort*). The results of this regression are shown in Model 2 of Table 5.4.

In Model 1, the coefficient of the *mobilization*1921–1935 cohort* variable is significant at the $p \le .01$ level, as expected. In contrast, in Model 2, the coefficients for *victory*1921–1935 cohort* and *defeat*1921–1935 cohort* are not statistically significant, also as expected. This supports the proposition that levels of mobilization, rather than war outcome, shape postwar civic engagement.

Note that, unlike ordinary least squares (OLS) regression, the coefficients of beta-binomial regressions are neither linear nor immediately interpretable.[35] For this reason, I used the results of the beta-binomial regression in Model 1 to

---

[33] Verba, Schlozman, and Brady 1995; Brehm and Rahn 1997; Hall 1999; Oliver 2000.

[34] King 1989, 119–121; see also Cox and McCubbins 2005, esp. chap. 4.

[35] In all analyses, the overdispersion coefficient was significant at the $p \le .01$ level. This confirms the intuition that the probability of participation in voluntary associations is not constant across different individuals.

TABLE 5.4. *The Determinants of Associational Membership, Comparing the Mobilization Hypothesis (Model 1) and the Victory/Defeat Hypothesis (Model 2)*

	Model 1	Model 2
Education	0.045	0.037
	(0.000)***	(0.011)***
Income	0.040	0.030
	(0.022)*	(0.025)
Gender	-0.147	-0.153
	(0.048)***	(0.047)***
Age	0.009	0.009
	(0.001)***	(0.001)***
Survey Year (1990)	0.396	0.395
	(0.180)**	(0.188)**
Survey Year (1995)	0.980	1.057
	(0.180)***	(0.164)***
Mobilization	0.006	
	(0.003)**	
1911–1920 Cohort	-0.323	-0.335
	(0.033)***	(0.033)***
1921–1935 Cohort	-0.231	-0.205
	(0.033)***	(0.033)***
Mobilization*1921–1935 Cohort	0.002	
	(0.000)***	
Victory		0.112
		(0.214)
Defeat		0.053
		(0.219)
Victory*1921–1935 Cohort		0.045
		(0.047)
Defeat*1921–1935 Cohort		-0.034
		(0.064)
N	24418	24418
Number of Countries	13	13

Notes: Coefficients are beta-binomial maximum likelihood estimates, standard errors in parentheses. ***$p \leq .01$, **$p \leq .05$, *$p \leq .1$. Both models include country-specific intercepts (not shown).

simulate the predicted difference in the number of associational memberships between the 1911–1920 cohort and the 1921–1935 cohort, holding all control variables constant at their means. One thousand simulations were conducted. The results of this simulation are shown in Figure 5.2.

Figure 5.2 shows a clear difference in levels of civic engagement between the 1911–1920 cohort and the much more intensively mobilized 1921–1935 cohort. At the low end of mobilization, where the index of mobilization = 10, the 1921–1935 cohort is predicted to participate in an average of .10 more associations than the 1911–1920 cohort (standard error = .045), holding all other variables at

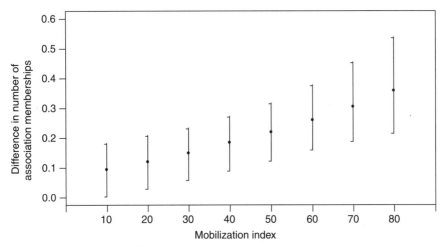

FIGURE 5.2. Predicted difference in number of associational memberships between 1911–1920 and 1921–1935 birth cohorts, by level of mobilization, on the basis of beta-binomial regression analysis.
Note: Calculated from 1,000 bootstrapped simulations. Line segments denote 95% confidence intervals.

their means. During World War II, countries such as Ireland, the Netherlands, and Belgium exhibited levels of mobilization of 10 or lower. At the high end of the spectrum, where the index of mobilization = 80, the 1921–1935 cohort is predicted to participate in an average of .36 more associations than the 1911–1920 cohort (standard error = .081), holding all other variables at their means. During World War II, Germany's mobilization was roughly at this level.

These differences are substantial. Across all countries, the 1911–1920 cohort participated in an average of .97 associations (standard error = .102). This means that even for the least mobilized countries (index of mobilization = 10), mobilization served to raise participation among succeeding cohorts by roughly 10 percent, while for the highest-mobilized countries (index of mobilization = 80), mobilization boosted participation by roughly 35 percent. Especially at the higher levels of mobilization, the magnitude of the mobilization-induced increase in participation is hardly negligible.

One potential complication is the Great Depression: The Depression may have lowered participation rates for pre–World War II cohorts. If this is the case, the wartime generation may have simply been returning to levels of participation that were normal by pre–Depression standards. In other words, war itself may not have caused the change in participation rates. The empirical evidence, however, does not support this view. Japan and Germany, both of which were highly mobilized, exhibit large differences in participation between the World War II–affected cohort and the immediately preceding cohort, but in those countries the Great Depression was not as deep or as long as in the United States. In short, there appears to be no clear-cut relationship between the relative severity of the Great Depression and the difference in levels of participation between the World War II generational cohort and the Great Depression cohort.

CASE STUDY: THE YMCA JAPAN

To trace the causal relationship between mobilization and postwar participation, the chapter now turns to the case of Japan during the decade immediately following World War II. For obvious reasons, this decade was most affected by defeat. Indeed, Japan's economy only took off after 1955. Because Japan was a defeated country, this should be an easy case for the conventional view that defeat suppresses civic engagement. Japan also incurred heavy levels of destruction. It lost almost 2.5 million soldiers and civilians.[36] It was particularly vulnerable to fire raids because most of its houses were built from wood and paper: more than 2 million private homes were destroyed by the end of the war, by far the highest figure among industrialized countries,[37] and this left an estimated 9 million individuals homeless.[38] At the same time, Japan was one of the most intensively mobilized countries during World War II, as shown in Table 5.3. Yet the rise of civic engagement in Japan began well before 1955.

This section tests the validity of my hypothesis through process-tracing of the revival of the Japanese YMCA in the city of Kobe. The Kobe YMCA represents a particularly illuminating case for the hypothesis presented in this chapter. Kobe was a major center of heavy industrial production, particularly in steel and shipbuilding, and this made the city a major target of U.S. bombing. It thus incurred especially heavy levels of destruction during World War II. Hyogo Prefecture, where the city of Kobe is located, suffered 3.49 deaths per 100,000 people, the fourth-highest number of deaths among all Japanese prefectures, following only Hiroshima, Nagasaki, and Tokyo.[39] As the major urban center in Hyogo Prefecture, most of these deaths were concentrated in the city of Kobe. In terms of destroyed buildings, Hyogo Prefecture ranked third, following Tokyo and Osaka, with 63.99 buildings destroyed per 100,000.[40] As a major manufacturing center, Kobe also had a relatively high level of mobilization compared to other cities in Japan. Therefore, a case study of Kobe can shed light on the relative merits of the mobilization and victory/defeat hypotheses. This study focuses on the Kobe YMCA in particular because of its unusually well-preserved records from the prewar and postwar periods and because, as an association with strong Christian ties, it was repressed by the Japanese regime during World War II. The combination of physical damage – the YMCA building was destroyed in a 1945 bombing

---

[36] Goralski 1981.
[37] Ibid.
[38] Dower 1999, 47–48.
[39] Calculated from Keizai Antei Honbu 1949, 279–281.
[40] Ibid., 344–345.

raid – as well as political repression during the war might lead one to expect that the YMCA's prospects for postwar membership growth were dim: This organization had taken substantial hits in a city that was particularly hurt in a country that was utterly defeated. Membership in the Kobe YMCA, however, which had hit a prewar peak of 735 members in 1937, stood at 2,395 by 1950, only five years after the war and still during the darkest years of Japan's postwar economy.

Did the Kobe YMCA revive and prosper so quickly in the postwar period because of positive externalities from Japan's wartime mobilization? It is hard to find evidence of individual citizens' motivations. But the hypothesis that mobilization during wartime drove postwar civic engagement generates a key prediction that where mobilization is intense, the postwar surge in participation should be largely *bottom-up*. That is, individuals who acquire various civic skills during wartime should be eager to continue to exercise those skills after the war, and thus the primary impetus for postwar participation should come from the citizens themselves, even in the absence of a major push by associational "entrepreneurs." Membership levels thus may increase rapidly even if wartime damage severely constrains the resources for recruitment. This is precisely what happened in the case of the Kobe YMCA. Of course, the bottom-up surge in interest may also encourage association leaders to be more ambitious in their plans for the future.

The rest of this chapter traces the processes through which the Kobe YMCA grew after the war by comparing the YMCA's experiences in the prewar, wartime, and postwar periods. It will pay special attention to how the experience of mobilization during wartime led to heightened grassroots enthusiasm for participation in the wake of war.

Prewar Period

The Kobe YMCA was founded in 1899. It was Japan's fifth-oldest YMCA, after Tokyo (1880), Osaka (1882), Yokohama (1884), and Sapporo (1897). It was founded by Christian missionaries who arrived in Kobe after the Meiji Restoration of 1868, in which Japan jettisoned its 200-year policy of closing off the country from foreign influences. Around this time, Kobe was a small town of about 20,000 people, miniscule compared to Tokyo, which had already passed the 3 million mark. But Kobe grew rapidly, and by the end of World War I, it had become the largest trading port in Japan as well as one of Japan's largest cities.[41]

The YMCA's prewar heyday came during the "Taisho Democracy" (1905–1932), the period of liberal rule in Japan before militarism set in. During this time, Japan saw the emergence of a broad spectrum of social and cultural movements. The Kobe YMCA thrived in this liberal climate. During this period,

[41] Kobe-shi n.d.

enrollment in its evening classes grew by roughly 20 percent every year.[42] It also housed Japan's first indoor gymnasium, where Japan's first basketball and volleyball games were played.[43] The Kobe YMCA Hall, completed in 1913, allowed for the expansion of the YMCA's activities, and the YMCA quickly became an important intellectual, cultural, and athletic center. The Hall provided the facilities for numerous lectures by leaders of labor and agricultural movements as well as by writers and artists.[44] While the Kobe YMCA itself was not particularly politically active, it played a key role in fostering various social movements, often providing physical space for lectures and rallies. This was especially important because few facilities could accommodate as many spectators as the YMCA Hall, which had a capacity of 1,200.[45] Toyohiko Kagawa, a major labor leader as well as consumer activist, frequently spoke at the Kobe YMCA and is said to have donated substantial sums.[46]

Wartime Mobilization in Kobe

Then came the war. According to one estimate, roughly 146,000 men were conscripted into military service between 1937 and 1945 from Hyogo Prefecture,[47] of which Kobe is the capital – that is, roughly 4.5 percent of the 1940 population or 8.8 percent of the 1940 male population. Reflecting Kobe's status as a major trading port as well as a major center of steel production, industrial mobilization rapidly accelerated.

Mobilization was also extensive at the community level. As with the rest of Japan, this mobilization occurred primarily through neighborhood associations.[48] As of 1942, there were an estimated 1,418 neighborhood associations in Kobe, with an average of 159 households per association.[49] The number of households per association ranged from 9 to 345,[50] indicating considerable variance in the associations' size. Neighborhood associations were further organized into smaller units, *tonari-gumi*, each of which had an average of 8 households; the number of households in the *tonari-gumi* ranged from 1 to 22.[51] These associations engaged in a broad range of war-related tasks, including savings drives, recycling drives, food rationing, and providing assistance to widows and/or the elderly. As the fall in imports reduced food supplies, these associations often taught families how to cook meals out of leaves and flowers.[52] As air raids on mainland Japan increased, neighborhood

[42] Kobe YMCA 100nenshi Hensanshitsu 1987, 163.
[43] Ochiai and Arii 1967, 122–123.
[44] Ibid., 154.
[45] Kobe YMCA 100nenshi Hensanshitsu 1981a, 20.
[46] Kobe YMCA 100nenshi Hensanshitsu 1981b, 7.
[47] Oe 1988.
[48] Kasza 1995.
[49] Kobe-shi 1965, 6.
[50] Ibid.
[51] Ibid., 7.
[52] Ibid., 14.

associations also organized fire drills. With the expansion in the associations' tasks, the city government hired 200 new administrative staff to work with the associations.[53] Subsidies for neighborhood associations surged from 300,000 yen in 1942 to 820,000 yen in 1944.[54] The strengthening of the state proceeded in tandem with the strengthening of society.

As the war intensified, mobilization covered more and more of the population. Even secondary school was suspended, and all students were mobilized into war-related work. While imposing hardships, mobilization also provided opportunities for socialization and the acquisition of civic skills, especially among the youth. Ken Zako, who grew up in Kobe during the war, recalls that when the children worked for the military, they would often receive one *anpan* [sweet bun] as a reward for the hard day's work. "What did we do with the *anpan*? We could have eaten it all by ourselves. But instead, we would bring it home carefully and share it equally with the others. We wanted to use the *anpan* as leverage to get more food from others in the future."[55] Young children were acquiring norms of generalized reciprocity. At the same time, civic engagement may breed less, not more, trust in government: "Even back then, we thought: What kind of military uses children to build their cannon bases? We quickly became very skeptical of the military's ability to defend us from attacking planes."[56]

The intensification of the war also led to stricter restrictions on voluntary activities, especially Christian-influenced movements, which were increasingly suspected of serving as spies for the Allies. This placed the YMCA in a difficult position. It could oppose the militarist regime and face persecution, or it could support the regime in the interest of organizational survival. The YMCA Japan chose the latter and provided a wide range of wartime services, from sending care packages to soldiers on the front lines to providing assistance to families where the breadwinner had been drafted. The YMCA's cooperation with the regime led to considerable criticism after the war.[57]

Despite its best efforts, however, the YMCA did not escape state repression during the war. As shown in Figure 5.3, membership levels declined steadily after 1937. *Kobe Seinen [Kobe Youth]*, the Kobe YMCA's newsletter, came under military censorship.[58] In September 1942, *Kobe Seinen* ceased publication on orders from authorities to conserve paper.[59] YMCA meetings were watched closely by the police.

After 1943, so many of the Kobe YMCA's officials and staff had been drafted that the YMCA's activities could no longer be sustained. The military had also been eyeing the YMCA building, and in the spring of 1944, the board

---

53 Ibid., 477.
54 Ibid.
55 Zako 1990, 66–67.
56 Ibid., 67.
57 Kobe YMCA 100nenshi Hensanshitsu 1987, 268.
58 Ibid., 285–286.
59 Kobe YMCA 1969, 26.

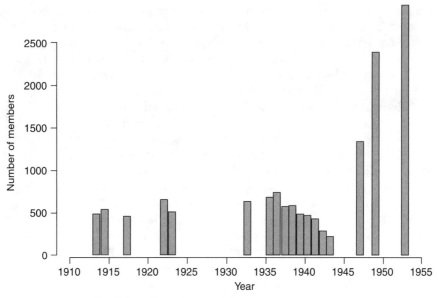

FIGURE 5.3. Membership in the Kobe YMCA, 1913–1954.
Source: Kobe YMCA (1987).

of directors agreed to rent it out for military use, effectively putting an end
to YMCA activities. One last board meeting was held in April 1945,[60] so that
the association's 1944 annual report could be submitted. The YMCA in Kobe
held out longer than in many other cities. In Kyoto, all recreational activities
had come to a virtual halt by 1942.[61] At the Osaka YMCA as well, all classes
were closed by December 1944. Seemingly the last straw, the Kobe YMCA
building was destroyed by fire raids in June 1945. In Kobe, however, the postwar revival of the YMCA was swift.

Postwar Revival

Leaders of the Kobe YMCA met for the first time after the war on October
28, 1945, two and a half months after the war's end. Since the YMCA building had been destroyed, the board assembled in Kobe Church, just across the
street from the former YMCA. Surviving minutes from these early meetings
indicate that the leaders never considered closing down the YMCA; rather,
they moved to reopen the Sunday schools the following spring and thereafter met monthly to prepare the group's revival.[62] However, a severe lack of
resources at the time hampered their revival efforts.

---

[60] Kobe YMCA n.d.
[61] Nomura 1975, 205.
[62] Kobe YMCA, internal documents.

Despite this, membership doubled every year, from 124 in 1945 to 240 in 1946 to 472 in 1947.[63] These numbers understate how many citizens took advantage of the YMCA's various activities. For instance, in 1946, English language classes resumed. The use of English had been banned during the war, and 2,454 students enrolled that first year.[64] Children's events attracted another 1,850,[65] 800 people participated in YMCA-sponsored Easter events, and 635 people participated in Bible-reading classes.[66]

Notably, the growth in membership began before systematic efforts at recruiting new members began, in the fall of 1947.[67] Even after the necessarily modest recruitment efforts did begin, the YMCA's recruitment far exceeded expectations; in 1948, 649 new members joined, many more than the target of 500.[68] In 1953, in a later recruitment drive that was part of a nationally organized one, the Kobe YMCA sought to recruit 400 more members, but brought in almost 1,300.[69]

As these figures suggest, the impetus for the postwar growth in participation appears to have been primarily bottom-up, rather than a result of top-down recruitment efforts. Aspiring members came of their own accord. As one member who joined the YMCA in the early postwar years recalls, "Young people who were starved for culture, recreation, or knowledge all flooded into the small quarters of the YMCA. In those days, we were both materially and spiritually impoverished, but the YMCA was seen as a place where personal relationships were very important."[70] Indeed, there is some evidence that the YMCA leadership did not welcome, and was even somewhat baffled by, this sudden surge. Suekane Tetsuo, a senior leader of the YMCA, noted in October 1947, "It is true that the number of members is growing rapidly. However, many of them seem to come to the YMCA without really knowing what the YMCA stands for. Some of the senior officers of the YMCA are quite concerned."[71]

This bottom-up surge in participation is consistent with my hypothesis that wartime mobilization drove civic engagement in the postwar period. Mobilization during war provided individuals like Ken Zako with opportunities for the acquisition of crucial civic skills. Once the war ended, citizens sought to continue to exercise those skills. Many individuals had been

[63] Kobe YMCA 100nenshi Hensanshitsu 1987, 323, 339.

[64] Ibid., 323.

[65] Ibid., 324.

[66] Kobe YMCA 1947, 2–3.

[67] Kobe YMCA 100nenshi Hensanshitsu 1987, 328.

[68] Kobe YMCA 1969, 29.

[69] YMCA Annual Report 1954. It is possible that the YMCA Kobe set modest recruitment targets that could be met with relative ease. However, other YMCAs were unable to meet their much more modest recruitment targets, suggesting that groups may not simply have set goals that they saw to be easily attainable. Moreover, the membership growth rates in the Kobe YMCA were indeed more rapid than in many other cities in Japan.

[70] Kobe YMCA 100nenshi Hensanshitsu 1987, 8.

[71] *Kirisutokyo Seinen*, 26.

conscripted or had been evacuated to other areas, but they returned with skills that made them eager to collaborate with others and to seek out new opportunities for participation. Moreover, the high demand for associational activities probably encouraged former group leaders to try to revive their organizations as quickly as they could once the war was over, even though some leaders resisted what they saw as overexpansion.

U.S. Occupation?

It may be useful to address an alternative hypothesis – that U.S. occupation policies crucially affected the growth of participation in the YMCA, and indeed, in Japan more generally. U.S. occupation forces imposed democracy on Japan, along with Germany, in the war's wake. The Supreme Commander, Allied Powers (SCAP) encouraged the growth of some associations while severely repressing others.[72] Labor unions, Christian groups, and the like were especially encouraged. Perhaps the growth of membership in the Kobe YMCA had less to do with mobilization and more to do with its favored status by the occupation as both a Western-oriented and Christian organization.

U.S. occupation policies did play an important role in shaping the evolution of civic engagement in postwar Japan. After all, the new constitutional provision for the freedom of association was a great relief to a YMCA that had been severely repressed during the war. Nevertheless, this does not provide the full, or even the most important, explanation for the puzzle at hand. A careful examination of the precise contours of SCAP's policies suggests that while they encouraged civic activities in some ways, their effects also can be overestimated.

Occupation policies toward voluntary associations in Japan took three forms: (a) the breakup of ultranationalist organizations; (b) the dissociation of the Japanese state from private associational activities, especially through the new Social Education Law; and (c) the (re-)training of associational leaders in democratic associational procedures, particularly in democratic deliberation.[73]

Should these policies be viewed as the main source of the growth of civic engagement in postwar Japan? First, clearly, breaking up "extremist" groups would not encourage participation but would rather suppress it, for all generational cohorts.[74] Second, SCAP's ban on public funding of private voluntary activities would also hardly be expected to help an organization get back on its feet. The YMCA did receive some financial assistance from its sister associations in the United States, but its postwar rise in membership was not due to lavishly funded recruitment drives.

---

[72] Kage 2003.

[73] Ibid.

[74] It might be possible that people previously engaged in ultranationalist groups would join the YMCA instead, but this seems unlikely, since there were still many associations that focused on traditional Japanese culture.

Third, it is also difficult to see a direct link between the democracy training programs and the rise in participation. The training programs served less as nonprofit management programs than as civics classes meant to instill democratic values and methods. As such, they focused heavily on abstract principles, such as democratic deliberation or the place of voluntary associations in a democratic society.[75] Little emphasis was placed on the more practical dimensions of operating a voluntary association, such as recruitment or financial management, which would be more directly related to organizational success.

SCAP's policies thus seem to be hardly connected with the postwar resurgence of the YMCA, except, of course, for the important general policy of freedom of association. Another possibility, however, is that SCAP conferred special legitimacy on Western and Christian groups and thus encouraged participation in them. There is no doubt that groups with Anglo-American roots, such as the Girl Scouts and the Rotary Club, gained in social status with the arrival of the occupation forces and that this was helpful for attracting members. But many could also have been turned off by the idea of joining groups that were deemed too close to the former enemy and present occupier. In the case of Japan, there is no evidence that citizens participated only in groups deemed to be legitimate by SCAP. A case in point is the neighborhood associations; although the occupation forces formally outlawed the associations in 1947, citizens of all ages continued to participate in them. Participation in judo also continued to rise into the 1950s, despite the fact that SCAP viewed it as promoting militaristic values and banned it from schools between 1945 and 1950. The YMCA is not an isolated case, but part of a general rising tide of civic engagement.

Liberal policies toward voluntary associations provide the space for civic activity to flourish, but this space must be filled by citizens themselves. Occupation authorities neither forced individuals to join associations nor brought organizations into being by fiat. A complete explanation for the rise of participation in postwar Japan must include the social conditions in which the occupation policies were implemented.

CONCLUSION

This chapter has argued that citizens' mobilization during wartime exerts a crucial impact on postwar civic engagement. This proposition was tested using both quantitative analysis of cross-national data and an in-depth case study of the YMCA in Kobe, Japan. The quantitative analyses showed that countries that saw more extensive mobilization during World War II saw greater differences in levels of civic engagement between the generational cohort that came of age around the war and its immediately preceding cohort, differences that persisted decades after the shooting ended. The

[75] Kage 2003; Trainor 1983, 259.

case of the Kobe YMCA illustrated how citizens' experiences during war-time led to a surge in postwar participation, despite high levels of war damage, diminished incomes, and reduced opportunities for formal educational advancement.

To what extent does this study yield insight into the effects of wars today? Full-scale mobilization has become rare, and some would even say unthinkable, among industrialized countries. This suggests that when countries do go to war today, as in the U.S. war in Iraq, the "mobilization premium" is likely to be more limited. For soldiers, however, recent studies still find evidence that military service leads to higher levels of civic engagement over the course of their lives. Based on a survey of African Americans, Ellison finds that military service and/or combat experience is a significant predictor of participation in "high-intensity" political activities, such as campaign activities or contacting officials, as opposed to "low-intensity" activities such as voting.[76] Ellison's study does not control for selection effects – that is, it is possible that the more civic-minded may have joined the military in the first place – but other studies that have such controls confirm Ellison's finding. In particular, Jennings and Markus report that individuals with military service in Vietnam participated in community or neighborhood affairs at substantially higher rates than those with no experience. In fact, individuals with longer service experience in Vietnam tend to exhibit higher levels of participation.[77] Drawing on a survey of Latino veterans, Leal argues that veterans, especially draftees, were not only more likely to vote in elections, whether presidential, congressional, or school board, compared to nonveterans, but they were also more likely to participate in rallies, sign petitions, and wear a button.[78] Thus, although the absence of full-scale mobilization among industrialized countries in recent years may limit the contemporary relevance of this chapter's finding, those who have been mobilized clearly follow the patterns it documents.

However, a fundamental change seems to have occurred in the nature of war over the last few decades. Conventional warfare, epitomized by World War II, has been replaced by counterinsurgency in places like Vietnam, Afghanistan, and Iraq. There is circumstantial evidence to suggest that this sort of wartime experience may be more likely to cause post-traumatic stress disorder (PTSD) than the conventional "band of brothers" warfare of World War II. Although surely not absent among World War II veterans, PTSD only became widely documented with Vietnam veterans. PTSD has also become prevalent among those who served in Afghanistan and Iraq, affecting between 12 and 20 percent of active-duty soldiers.[79] Psychological

---

[76] Ellison 1992.
[77] Jennings and Markus 1977, 195–196.
[78] Leal 1999.
[79] Hoge et al. 2004.

disorders like PTSD may be expected to depress participation rates.[80] How wartime socialization into civic skills and post-traumatic stress may interact to affect the types and levels of participation after service is an important question that merits further study.

Among developing countries, full-fledged war is less unusual. This analysis of World War II still yields insights into the impact of war on civic engagement in these societies. Since many countries in the developing world are not democratic but authoritarian, a key related issue in thinking about the effects of mobilization is whether it may have some bearing on postwar regime change. A lively debate has recently emerged on the extent to which vibrant civil societies may be a necessary precondition for successful democratization. Earlier studies argued that it was,[81] while more recent studies cast doubt on this claim.[82] This study suggests that large-scale wartime mobilization should propel a rise in civic engagement not only in democratic states, but also in states that were authoritarian during the war but then became democratic. The heightened civic activity may offer part of the explanation for the puzzle that Nancy Bermeo (Chapter 4) addresses, namely that new democracies founded after armed conflict tend to be more durable than democracies that emerge in peacetime. Further exploration of the relationship between war, civil society, and the success or failure of democratic transition poses a fruitful avenue for further research.

For reasons of data availability, this study did not explore whether civic engagement also rose in states that were authoritarian both during and after the war. But theoretically, the findings from this study should be applicable to such cases as well. As Elizabeth Kier points out (Chapter 7), the distinction between democratic and authoritarian regimes appears less important in thinking about mobilization than the relationship between state and society. The extent to which participation grows in authoritarian countries should depend at least in part on the policies that the state implements toward collective activities after war. If authoritarian countries mobilize extensively but then break up voluntary activities after war, even exceedingly high levels of wartime mobilization should not produce heightened postwar participation. This was precisely the case in the Communist regimes in the Soviet Union and Eastern Europe after World War II, and it could also be true of authoritarian regimes today.

Finally, to what extent does the case of World War II offer relevant lessons for understanding the impact of the modal type of war today, civil war? This is another subject for further research. Civil wars may be much more disruptive to a society's social fabric than international wars. But they may also foster civic skills via mobilization within ethnic or religious groups.

[80] Keane et al. 2006.
[81] Almond and Verba 1963; Inglehart 1988; Diamond 1999.
[82] See, for instance, Encarnación 2006.

Some preliminary evidence from Serbia, for instance, suggests that voluntary activities have indeed grown in the wake of the civil wars of the 1990s.[83] Similarly, rapid growth in the NGO sector has also been reported in postwar Cambodia.[84] But this is an empirical question that awaits further study.

[83] NGO Policy Group 2001.
[84] Persson 2003.

6

Veterans, Human Rights, and the Transformation of European Democracy

Jay Winter

The role of veterans in postwar political life is a subject in need of attention. The primary reason is the tendency of scholars to work from an American or from a German perspective to probe the political outlook and pressure of veterans groups over the last century. In that optic, veterans are overwhelmingly patriotic, conservative, or reactionary. Their experience of war or of preparation for war makes them authoritarian, illiberal, or natural supporters of right-wing or extreme-right-wing political parties and movements.[1]

What happens if we choose a different optic, a French one, and juxtapose it with the conventional view? In some respects, there is evidence of right-wing or extreme-right-wing tendencies among some French veterans, like Jean Marie Le Pen of the *Front National*, or the interwar *Croix de feu,* or among the Organisation de l'armée secrète (O.A.S.) assassins who tried and failed several times to kill Charles de Gaulle after his *volte face* on Algerian independence in 1959. But in other respects, French history provides a long and well-documented alternative narrative that today remains in the shadows. It tells a story of a different kind, that of a mass movement of pacifist veterans, millions of them, who from the 1870s to 1940, saw military service as the shield of the Republic.[2] It arises in the late nineteenth century in the cry of Jean Jaurès for *La nouvelle armée.* It moves to the left in revulsion over the anti-Republican and Catholic cabal to convict, imprison, and forget Colonel Dreyfus. It rails against the use of troops as strike-breakers, but virtually to a man answers the call-up of August 1, 1914, and fights to the bitter end. Contrary to their expectations, the authorities could not find and arrest thousands of "troublemakers" on the left who threatened to disrupt war mobilization. Why? Because they had already joined up.[3]

During the war itself, many of these men worked to create a veterans movement with two central objectives. The first was decent treatment for the

---

[1] The literature on veterans movements is vast. For a start, see Ward 1975.
[2] On this subject, the locus classicus is Prost 1977.
[3] Becker 1973.

wounded and a decent pension for the demobilized. The second was the abolition of war. Perhaps 60 percent of the roughly 8 million men who served in
French forces joined these organizations. These were not the voices of parliamentary politics, but of an extraparliamentary movement, the membership of
which came from small market towns and villages – what we call *La France
profonde*. Their voices were heard throughout the interwar years and beyond,
and while they were never univocal, they carried an unmistakable pacifist
message.[4]

In the short term, their cause failed miserably. Betrayed by their own illu-
sions, by their belief in reaching out to ex-servicemen in Italy and Germany,
even to Mussolini and Hitler themselves, they were left in 1940 with a taste as
of ashes. Their story is one of political bankruptcy, to be sure.

And yet that is not the end of the story. Out of the veterans movement
to outlaw war came another crusade, one privileging the rights of soldiers,
of the wounded and the unemployed, within the framework of human
rights. Drawing on elements of the French Revolutionary tradition and the
Universal Declarations of Human Rights of 1789 and 1793, French veterans created a new form of human rights message, one that arose out of the
catastrophe of World War II. The passage from the struggle for dignity in
and after one world war to an even more profound and long-lasting commitment to human rights after a second world war is the subject of this
chapter.

The defeat of interwar soldiers' pacifism was a prelude to their longer-term
victory. In the post-1945 period and beyond, a number of World War I veterans found ways to reconfigure successfully their message. There is a line that
connects the pacifist movement arising from World War I to the Universal
Declaration of Human Rights to the Helsinki Accords to Charter 77 to the
fall of the Berlin wall and the Soviet Union. It was not the work of one
man, but of many men and women, who affirmed that the defense of human
rights was the best way to preserve peace. Among this group of people, a
few individuals stand out. Eleanor Roosevelt and the Lebanese philosopher
and diplomat Charles Malik were among them. So was the Canadian international civil servant John Humphreys. But while all of them made essential contributions, one man's contribution must be acknowledged as unique.
That man was the French jurist, Resistance leader, and Nobel laureate René
Cassin. His role in launching the modern human rights movement was decisive. A profound theorist of state sovereignty, a consummate draftsman and
negotiator, he brought a determination and an optimism to the process of
amending international law to make human rights everyone's business. That
optimism was surprising, and to a degree paradoxical, since Cassin's convictions were forged in the suffering and bitterness of the two world wars. I
want to tell Cassin's story to show how the emergence of our current human
rights discourse came out of defeat, defiance, and transcendence.

---

[4] See Prost 1973.

Most accounts of today's international human rights regime locate its emergence as a response to the barbarities of the Nazi regime.[5] There is much truth in this assertion, but it is not the whole truth. In some respects, the core idea of human rights – that state sovereignty is not unlimited – emerged in response to World War I and provided a point of departure for those finally persuaded after 1945 that *raison d'état* is not and can never be the *ultima ratio* or the *prima ratio* of the international order. The message of this earlier human rights movement, driven by veterans organizations, is that Leviathan states that trample on the rights of their citizens are a threat to peace. Sooner or later they will trample on the territory of other states. Wherever and whenever state sovereignty is treated as an absolute, there lies a threat to the dignity of ordinary people and a threat to peace.

Consider this paradox. A war to defend territoriality in 1914–1918 in response to the Austrian invasion of Serbia and the German invasion of Belgium and France set in motion forces that, twenty-five years later, helped undermine the notion that territorial states are a law unto themselves. The resolution of the apparent contradiction is that total war created the conditions that brought into being an idea of limited state sovereignty, sovereignty limited by a human rights regime superior to national law. During World War II, this idea moved from the realm of the utopian to the realm of politics, in particular, the politics of retribution for Nazi crimes. The preparation, while the fighting was still going on, for war crimes trials and for a successor to the moribund League of Nations framed both innovations within a commitment to base the peace to come on a commitment to human rights. That commitment was embodied in the Charter of the United Nations and adumbrated in the Convention on Genocide and in the Universal Declaration of Human Rights approved by the United Nations assembled in Paris just over sixty years ago, on December 9–10, 1948.

This story has important implications for our understanding of the effects of war on democratic ideas and practices. The notion that soldiers have earned the right to speak with special authority about the nature of state power is not surprising. But what is less well known is that many veterans in different countries went beyond the conventional position that military service in time of war is an obligation of citizenship or a reflection of patriotism alone. Many people who served in the two world wars learned to look at the state in different ways, in Shakespeare's words, "when blood is their argument." Some pressed for the expansion of entitlements. Others turned against war and used their experience to help disseminate pacifist ideas.

Furthermore, not only did war prompt the political mobilization of veterans; it also broadened the space for contestation as these veterans introduced new elements into the political conversations, both domestic and transnational, that followed World War II. This was particularly true for veterans who had

---

[5] Glendon 2001.

fled from Nazi-occupied Europe, and who both had to assert the legitimacy of their visions of the future and plan for the time when they would return home and try to clear up the chaos and repair the damage the Nazis and their collaborators had done to the rule of law and to the lives of millions of their compatriots. A new international order to guarantee the peace required a new way of thinking about the linkages between state sovereignty and collective security. The old way of thinking had destroyed the League of Nations, on whose French delegation Cassin had sat for fourteen years, until he refused to go back to Geneva after his government had signed on to the Munich Agreement, effectively killing the League. World War II was the time to rethink the premises on which international relations rested.

Here is where the story of human rights intersects with pacifism. The conversion of the warfare state into the welfare state, promised by the Atlantic Charter and embedded in Allied war aims in World War II, was premised on the avoidance of war and the reduction of the significance of military expenditure and military power in the postwar international order. Economic aid and economic growth on a monumental scale were at the core of this transformation. But so was a new European commitment to human rights.

Over time the new European order linked notions of democracy with notions of human rights to produce a stunning transformation in the nature of the European state. "Where have all the soldiers gone?" is the title of James Sheehan's study of the history of Europe in the twentieth century.[6] The answer is that the states they served no longer exist in the same form. European states more and more provide for welfare, not warfare, and welfare is meaningless without a primary commitment to peace. The language of human rights expresses that commitment, and over time, it has come to represent an alternative path to the defense of democracy, one remote from American experience. To understand this European discourse, we need to appreciate how World War II provided veterans with access to critical debates about the nature of state power, something that they had lacked prior to the outbreak of war in 1939. They had failed to stop that war, but they could see the way to rectify some of the flaws that helped bring it about and that had prevented democratic states from resisting the Nazis in the 1930s.

Between 1945 and 1950, a new Council of Europe was born. Its most important acts were to draft the European Convention on Human Rights and to set up a European Court of Human Rights to oversee its implementation in the process of European reconstruction and recovery after the worst war in history. From 1950 on, countries wishing to join the European Union must sign the European Convention on Human Rights. Doing so truncates state sovereignty, since they agree to respect and observe the rulings of the European Court of Human Rights. Countries that sign take on additional responsibilities to restrict the role of the military in their countries' political life. Together

---

[6] Sheehan 2008.

these two developments – the increase in the significance of human rights and the diminution of the role of the military in politics – are the bedrock on which European democracy now rests. The story below shows how significant a role veterans played in this fundamental change in the nature of democratic institutions in Europe after the convulsions of the two world wars.

BEFORE 1933

How did veterans contribute to this set of events? I will tell this story in three parts. The first is located within the 1914–1918 conflict. The second is a feature of the interwar period. The third is an element of wartime resistance and postwar planning during and after World War II.

First the Great War. During the 1914–1918 conflict, and especially at the outset of the conflict, soldiers who bled for their country were maltreated in ways hard to believe today. Part of the source of their misery was military incompetence of the kind brought to light in the United States in 2007, in reports of neglect at Walter Reed Army Medical Center. No preparation, no forethought, nothing but callous bureaucratic ineptitude.

It is worth pausing for a moment to locate this problem in a longer timescale. When the Great War broke out in 1914, the International Red Cross was already fifty-five years old. Founded by Henri Dunant, who was horrified by the sight of wounded men left to suffer or die on the battlefield of Solferino in 1859, the Red Cross had created codes of conduct that gave to the wounded the right to be treated and cared for. These rights extended to prisoners of war as well, and were human rights. They did not arise out of citizenship or other affiliation. They were the property of all men. The code of conduct drawn up by Francis Lieber in 1863 for the Union armies was based on the same set of assumptions.

International humanitarian law emerged from the nineteenth-century battlefield. The laws of war were codified in the Geneva Convention of 1864 for the amelioration of the condition in armies in the field, and in the Hague Conventions of 1899 (Convention II) and 1907 (Convention IV). These conventions drew on earlier currents in the abolitionist movement to deepen a natural-law, human rights tradition. In this tradition, we have duties to the wounded not as a function of citizenship but as a matter of humanity.[7]

In World War I, this set of obligations was in place, but it did not apply to the wounded of your own side. Let me illustrate this point in the case of Cassin, who founded the French veterans movement to ensure that the wounded received decent treatment and later a decent pension from the state that sent them off to battle.

In August 1914, René Cassin was a twenty-six-year-old lawyer, born in Bayonne to a prominent Jewish family living in the southwest of the country. The outbreak of war found him in Paris, from which he immediately journeyed

7 Best 1980.

south to join the 311th Infantry Regiment in Aix.[8] In September, he was promoted to the rank of corporal and served near St. Mihiel. He remained in this sector, where on October 12, he was ordered to take a squad of sixteen men and advance toward a German strong point near Chauvencourt on the outskirts of St. Mihiel. German emplacements made such a probe suicidal. All sixteen men in his unit were hit by flanking fire from well-entrenched machine guns and artillery. He himself was hit in his side, his abdomen, and his left arm. He knew that a stomach wound was almost always fatal. Cassin refused evacuation, but told a passing soldier to inform their commander of the strength of the German positions in his sector. In addition he begged this man, Sergeant-Quartermaster Canestrier, to write to Cassin's father that he had died painlessly (which was a lie) and to send to his family a leather cigarette case, two gold pieces of 100 francs, and some small bills. Canestrier vanished, and so did Cassin's valuables.

Clearly Cassin thought he would never survive. He asked a priest if someone could say Hebrew prayers with him. The priest replied that his prayers were for everyone, and gave him the benefit of his company.[9] Somehow, Cassin got through the night, and was then handed over to the French army medical services.

The way these units were organized in the early days of the war almost killed him. The rule was that on mobilization you reported to your regiment, in whatever region you were assigned. After battle, you returned to *that* site, whether intact, wounded, or in a coffin. Cassin would not be treated in the northeast of France but in Provence, 600 kilometers away. He was sent by wagon and then by train south, and after a journey of ten days, arrived in the regiment's hospital in Antibes on the Mediterranean. There surgeons were astonished to see that he was still alive, despite the fact that his abdomen had been torn to shreds. Cassin had been wise enough to drink virtually nothing on the trip. They then told him that his case was critical and that they did not know if he would survive more than a few hours. That meant they did not have time to anesthetize him, but needed to operate immediately. This Cassin accepted, and somehow endured an hour under the surgeon's knife. He later said he was fortunate that the operation was on a less-than-sensitive part of his anatomy.

While in convalescence, he wrote the story of his service and framed it in terms of a conventional French patriot and a Jew. One of the Jewish men with whom he served had told him that a Jew had to be more courageous than others in order to evade accusations of cowardice. This bravery was Cassin's

---

[8] Paris, Archives Nationales. 382AP/1, Guerre 1914–1918, Souvenirs de la campagne 1914–1915. These memoirs were composed about a year after the outbreak of the war. Cassin wrote that they constituted a "Temoignage vécu, à l'histoire d'une campagne d'un regiment de ligne au cours de la guerre franco-allemande" [living testimony of the history of a company of an infantry regiment during the Franco-German war].

[9] 382AP/1, Guerre 1914–1918, Souvenirs de la campagne 1914–1915.

trademark. But for our purposes what is intriguing about his narrative is how laconic it is. He nowhere dwells on the hideousness of being wounded, of the incompetence of his own medical service, of the appalling cruelty inflicted on him by it. His train journey alone, holding his intestines in his stomach with great difficulty, is a middle passage that might have broken many other men. He saw and felt what battle was, and yet managed to frame his part in it without feeling that it had undermined his own identity.

The courage of his war service was palpable, but so was the miserable treatment he received. This was hardly exceptional among the wounded or among those disabled and discharged. What followed his convalescence was a fight not against the enemies of the French state, but against the callous, inhuman bureaucracy of the French state itself. Cassin worked tirelessly to assure that men who had been wounded in the service of their country would have a decent pension and that the orphans of the men who did not return would be given a start in their lives.[10] This work brought him up against recalcitrant and indifferent authorities. These rights were earned, not only by military service and the shedding of blood, but thereafter by harsh political struggle. French veterans, like others in Europe, were given their pensions grudgingly, not as a right but as a privilege, wrested from the hands of unfeeling administrators and the physicians who served them.

This struggle for natural justice for the lame, the halt, and the blind, for men who had answered their countries' call but then found that few were prepared to heed the voices of the wounded, created something new in European affairs – a pacifist veterans movement. The notion of soldier pacifists may seem like a contradiction in terms, but in interwar France it was not at all oxymoronic. French Republicans like Cassin saw it as their life's work to ensure that their sons would not have to enter *la boucherie* – the slaughterhouse – of modern warfare. They knew what it had been like and were determined that the young would be spared the fate they had suffered. In striking contrast to the myth of the war experience and to the lies about the nobility of armed conflict conjured up by the Nazis – veterans too – the French *ancien combattant* movement made war on war. On November 11, they marched to the war memorials in every tiny village; they did so in civilian dress and deliberately out of step. They had been civilians in uniform, and they bore a message to the young from their comrades who had died: War must never return.[11]

This political program was crippled from the start. The focus of the veterans movement in France was justice for their brethren and for the widows and orphans they had left behind. But their mission extended into the field of international relations as well, and that meant struggling with and through the League of Nations.

As a leader of the French veterans movement, Cassin had much to do with the International Labor Organization (ILO), headed by Albert Thomas, the

[10] 382AP/10 Anciens combattants.
[11] Agi 1980.

successor to Jean Jaurès, assassinated leader of the French Socialist party. This association, building on welfare work in munitions factories in wartime, was committed to ensuring the right to work of all those disabled in the war. On September 2, 1921, Cassin was present at an international veterans discussion of work for war invalids. The meeting was sponsored by the ILO in Geneva. Cassin represented the largest French veterans movement, *l'Union Fédérale*, with 2 million members, and it was at this venue that he and his colleagues met for the first time enemy veterans from the defeated Central Powers. Such contacts convinced Cassin that veterans had to work together with their former enemies and within the League of Nations if their voice was to be heard in international affairs.

Here is Cassin's point of entry into politics of a very peculiar kind. It was a kind of nonpolitical politics, filled with contradictions that ultimately destroyed it. Cassin was among a host of French veterans who felt that their vision was *above* politics. These were angry men, men who had formed what they termed the generation of fire, and were not prepared simply to let the old merry-go-round of politics go on its way. Politics was a word they used as an insult, and they played with it and mutated it into a host of venomous rhetorical forms, all filled with vitriol: *politicaille*, "*politicailler*," "*politicaillerie*," "*politicaillon*" – roughly translated as political scum, criminal rabble, wily, shady, scandal-ridden, little piggies at the trough, vulgar, partisan, blood-sucking shits. The vulgarity of this language is not to be missed: We are dealing with ex-soldiers here, and however high-minded their motives, their anger descended to the gutter where they believed their opponents, the politicians, were to be found.[12]

How to get around them without joining in their miserable game was an open question. Cassin refused the offer of a post in the Cabinet of Herriot who came to power as head of a left-center coalition in 1924. Instead, Cassin was glad to join the French delegation to the League of Nations as the representative of the veterans movement, as if that institution were free of all the faults of politics at home.

At the same time, he took the initiative in establishing an international veterans organization, CIAMAC, which met for the first time at Geneva in September 1926.[13] This body emerged from earlier discussions among veterans from both sides in the war, men who were committed to coming together to discuss matters of common interest. The German delegates from the *Reichsbund* affirmed their commitment to Republican values. They accepted the need to pay reparations and to contribute to the reconstruction of devastated regions, all as steps to reassure Allied ex-servicemen that they, too, wanted to preserve the peace. Italian, Polish, Austrian, and British delegates joined them and went on in later meetings to share information through the ILO on questions of pensions, work placement, and medical and orthopedic

[12] Prost 1973, passim.
[13] 382AP/10, Rapport de René Cassin à la Commission de la Paix sur la CIAMAC, 1931.

assistance for veterans. Belgian and Yugoslav veterans joined in these discussions. When the Dawes Plan regularized reparations payments, the political conditions were ripe for more formal discussions about the formation of an international organization of veterans associations. Initially eighty delegates from ten nations and twenty associations came to the inaugural meeting and committed themselves to working for the principle of mandatory arbitration of international conflicts. Here was a body unattached to national governments, able to speak out with the moral authority earned by military service and sacrifice.

Annual meetings were held in the later 1920s in Vienna, Berlin, Warsaw, and Paris. They had no difficulty in integrating German delegates, whose commitment to peace was unquestioned. It was harder to bring Soviet veterans to the table, since the war had been entirely eclipsed by the 1917 revolution.

This set of initiatives was part of the political culture surrounding the League of Nations. Veterans like Cassin argued that repairing the physical damage caused by the war was a first step toward repairing the moral damage it caused. Their task was political education at home and the lessening of enmity between former enemies. They were committed to making the League of Nations as powerful as possible an obstacle to war. That is why their distance from foreign offices was essential: These men spoke over the heads of governments to the millions of men and women whose lives and families had been disfigured by war. They spoke to youth who did not know what war was and urged them to join in their international crusade for peace.

Their main aim was what we have come to term moral rearmament. By that Cassin meant that those who knew war had to educate the public as to the horrors of violence and the absolute necessity to save the new generation from the catastrophe of another war. This could not be done within the boundaries of one country alone or solely among the victors. That is why he bypassed the more conservative Inter-allied Veterans Federation (FIDAC), which had no truck with the idea that German and Austrian veterans had to be brought into the conversation. Bridges had to be built, Cassin believed, but with prior agreement on certain clear principles about the way to preserve the peace.[14]

All these efforts were marked by both the strengths and the weaknesses of the League of Nations. Cassin's first speech was on international intellectual cooperation, and wearing his hat as a professor of civil law in Paris, he worked to transform the League of Nations from a forum for world peace into a quasi-juridical assembly.[15] One starting point in this effort was the construction of a center for international intellectual cooperation, an idea sponsored by Henri Bergson and the direct antecedent of United Nations Educational, Scientific and Cultural Organization (UNESCO). The midpoint was the construction of a protocol for the peaceful resolution of international disputes

[14] 382AP/10, Rapport de René Cassin à la Commission de la Paix sur la CIAMAC, 1931.
[15] 382AP/14 Cassin, Speech on disarmament to League of Nations, September 1929.

through arbitration. Once drafted and approved, the League would reach the endpoint, as a kind of high court of international justice, a tribunal, whose moral authority would rest in large part on the support of tens of millions of veterans, who knew a thing or two about war. "A world marked by the blood we shed would do well to accept the imprint of our ideas," he noted.[16]

Disarmament was one of them. Cassin served on the French delegation to the League of Nations for fourteen years, from 1924 to 1938, and much of his work in this body concerned arbitration and disarmament. "It isn't enough," he wrote in 1929, that veterans are represented at the League. What mattered more is that "in each nation burned by the war, organizations develop public opinion and that of youth to struggle against the mundane and the murderous language" of armaments and national defense. Only then can they "stand for the principles of Geneva: the defense of peace and security."[17]

It was during his service at Geneva that Cassin began to formulate notions that ultimately bore fruit in the Universal Declaration of Human Rights. In Geneva, Cassin had a front-row view of the fragility of an institution that challenged the supremacy of state sovereignty as a principle of international political order. He saw how entrenched were conventional approaches to unbridled state power as the *ultima ratio* of international affairs. No one could question his patriotism, but he had no time for what he termed "the ordinary obstinacy of old ideas which, in the name of the absolute sovereignty of states, flow directly into the construction of armaments, to the politics of prestige, and then to war."[18]

Cassin discerned that there was an immense gap between the thought of conventional nationalists like Clemenceau or Henry Cabot Lodge and the notions of those like Briand or Wilson, who were prepared to sacrifice some elements of state sovereignty to the League of Nations if that were the necessary price to erase war from the international political agenda. In the first round, Lodge won the argument, and older notions of state sovereignty prevailed. If a more robust League of Nations or any similar venture would ever succeed, it would do so only after a sea change had occurred in both academic and popular notions of the indivisible sovereignty of the state and of the power of the duly elected statesman, acting like a *"châtelain dans son château"* [master of his own domain].

Two major events led to the undermining or refashioning of this older definition of sovereignty. The first was the Nazi constitutional and lawful seizure of power in 1933; the second was the transformation of the French state in 1940 legally under Pétain and Laval. These episodes would open the door to a new kind of thinking on state sovereignty, and we will arrive at these developments in a moment. But for our purposes, it is important to note how

---

[16] Agi 1998, 54, 57.

[17] 382AP/14 League of Nations, La Xè assemblée vue par un ancien combattant, *Le Journal*, October 13, 1929.

[18] 382AP/14 League of Nations, Speech on disarmament, September 1929.

Cassin – among others – was active long before these two political earthquakes in the effort to provide an alternative view of state sovereignty. And that view ultimately bore fruit in the 1948 Universal Declaration of Human Rights.

Cassin made the argument explicit in the course of a series of lectures he gave in 1930 at the Academy of International Law in the Hague.[19] His title was "The new conception of domicile in the resolution of conflicts of law." His aim was to "desacralize" claims of state sovereignty. Only thereby, he believed, was it possible to create an environment in which the all-powerful state cannot by its own fiat and with impunity trample on the rights of the individual.

Before turning to the structure of the argument, it is useful to note the echoes of Cassin's earlier battles. He joined up in defense of a state whose meanness to the disabled men it had sent out to fight had to be resisted through a vigorous campaign originating in civil society. That struggle first for and then against the state is a stance to which Cassin returned throughout his life. It ensured that he would resist conventional views of political authority and state sovereignty and look to revise them in order to establish a just order.

In the Hague, he sketched out how such a new system might operate. To this end he juxtaposed the right of domicile to the right of citizenship and argued that each has merit as a basis of political rights.

The tie of nationality is not a primary or a unique bond among the members of a nation: there are other more elementary ones ... the home, the town, the city. It is precisely because the right of domicile rests on a universal and permanent fact, the concreteness of a place where one lives, a place where families reside, that it has been taken into consideration everywhere to determine the point of juridical attachment of persons and to order more or less completely the status of the individual.

Regimes change, but (with luck) domiciles remain. People remain attached to their homes whatever happens at the political level. This has always been the case among minorities and refugees, as long as they respect the laws of the land. The right of alien residence (while obeying the laws of a land) in a host nation is therefore based on the prior and superior force of domicile over nationality. One reflection of this principle, Cassin argued, is that married women in France could have more than one nationality; in deciding which applies, her domicile could be the point of reference. Cassin here cites explicitly the plight of over 1 million Russian and Armenian refugees whose personal status was thrown into doubt by war and revolution. Their standing, he insists, must be based on a right of domicile independent of nationality.

To Cassin, the choice between nationality and domicile had evolved over time. Throughout the later nineteenth century, in an era of state-building, those standing on claims of nationality grew in number. By the third decade of the twentieth century, most European states took this approach; in contrast, about the same number of people lived in states where domicile trumped

[19] Cassin 1930.

nationality. These were the Anglo-Saxon countries and Latin American states, in which immigration played a powerful role. Cassin's point is that it was time for the pendulum to move back toward the claims of domicile over nationality in a continent riven by powerful political and ideological quarrels exposed during the Great War. Jurisprudence had to follow events in order not to be overwhelmed by them.

The implications of the argument are far reaching. Domicile over nationality describes the bonds of the veterans of different countries who came together to work with Cassin in his international veterans organization. Domicile over nationality is the principal defense of vulnerable minorities stalked by powerful nationalist movements in states worried about their ethnic composition. Domicile over nationality helps correct the imbalance in then-current international law, "which confers to the sovereign nation a competence which is too exclusive, simplistic, and ill adapted to satisfy the complex needs of international life."[20] What is worse, despite having done its job well in the period of state formation, "the principle of nationality has exhausted its beneficial effects and has become a germ of doctrines destructive to the international community and oppressive to the individual." And finally, by privileging the concept of domicile over nationality, Cassin points the way to establishing the standing of the individual within international law itself. This same line of argument was adopted by the Institute of International Law in New York in October 1929, when it drafted a "Declaration of the international rights of man."[21]

Note the date of Cassin's disquisition. Three years before the Nazis came to power and used sovereign law to destroy every single trace of natural justice, Cassin constructed a powerful argument against the extremes of state sovereignty then still unrealized. How much more powerful then was his argument against the all-powerful state once that state under Hitler had made war, first on millions of its own citizens, and then on the rest of Europe.

AFTER 1933

Between 1933 and 1945, the balance between human rights and state power shifted radically. Nazi power and Nazi crimes – alongside those of Stalin – pushed to the limit the notion that a state is unconstrained in its treatment of its own citizens. And through the Italian invasion of Ethiopia in 1935, the Japanese rape of Nanking in 1937, the Nazi annexation of Austria in 1938, and the dismemberment and then destruction of Czechoslovakia in 1938 and 1939, the link between states' human rights abuses and their propensity to court the risk or the reality of war became evident for all who had eyes to see. The fascist assault on liberalism was an assault on the entire human rights tradition.

[20] Ibid., 771.
[21] Ibid., 770, directly citing this declaration.

And yet the international effort to translate the suffering of the men of 1914–1918 into a political barrier both against war and against the trampling of individual and minority rights failed miserably. It was not only that the League of Nations was hampered by its own structure and the weakness of a policy based on sanctions never carried out. It was also that the veterans movement itself tended to lose sight of the link between human rights and pacifism. In doing virtually anything to appease Italian and German aspirations, and in placing the need to avoid war above every other consideration, the international veterans movement broke apart. One wing moved toward the position that war was terrible but necessary. Another carried to the bitter end its belief that men like Hitler and Mussolini who had served in the Great War were men of peace who would step back from the precipice.

In April 1934, Cassin – now honorary president of the organization he helped found, the *Union Fédérale* – joined 450 members of CIAMAC on "Un voyage du souvenir et de l'amitié" to Italy. These men marched into the heart of Rome, where Cassin met them. There they were greeted by what the *Cahiers de l'Union Fédérale* called "toute Italie le plus noble et le plus sympathique qui vient de rendre les honneurs à la France Combattante" [the most noble and positive elements in the Italian nation who came to honor the French veterans]. Mussolini himself received the delegation, some of whom expressed a starry-eyed admiration of *Il Duce:* He spoke to them, so the *Cahiers* noted, in a "powerful and simple manner, giving the impression of the physical force of a worker or an athlete; poised and impatient for action, his thumbs in the pockets of his jacket … . His strength was in his gaze." He spoke in French and assured them of his solidarity, "as head of state, as a veteran, as an Italian, as a fascist." Later that day Cassin joined others in Vatican City, where they were met and greeted by Pope Pius XI.[22]

Why was Cassin there, and how did he stomach these empty gestures of solidarity? Italy was still a member of the League of Nations in 1934, though Germany had withdrawn the year before. To preserve the international character of CIAMAC, Cassin accepted this kind of diplomacy, well known to him from his years of service in the League of Nations. But after the Italian invasion of Ethiopia, after the dignified appeal of Haile Selassie for effective League sanctions, and after the failure of those sanctions, Cassin began to wonder whether his commitment to veterans internationalism was a mistake. The fact that after 1933 Germany was a pariah state was one thing; CIAMAC could not hope for help from German veterans groups any more. Besides, Hitler had taken Germany out of the League of Nations in 1933. But what of Italy? If the League could not act in the case of blatant aggression, and if the veterans movement (like the League) put its faith in solidarity with ex-soldiers

[22] Bernard Secret, "Un voyage du souvenir et de l'amitié," *Cahiers de l'Union Fédérale des Associations Francaises d'Anciens Combattants et de Victimes de la Guerre et des Jeunesses de l'Union Fédérale*, iv, 55 (April 15, 1934), 6–15.

before its commitment to human rights, then all that he had done for two decades in this field was futile.

Cassin was far from alone is seeing that war was both unimaginable, too terrible to contemplate, and yet just around the corner.[23] In 1936, he caught the tragedy of the moment in a testament he wrote before undergoing an operation, which, his doctors told him, might take his life. They were attempting to repair damage to his intestines caused by the wounds he had suffered in 1914. Thereafter Cassin had not passed a single day without pain. His condition had worsened in the mid-1930s and required major surgery. The envelope enclosing the note Cassin wrote before the operation is labeled: "Open only in the case of death. This is not a will."[24]

Instead this document is a political testament. While facing death, he returned to the moment in 1914 when he lay wounded on a battlefield in the east of France. He was proud of having served and of having been one of the founders of the French veterans movement. For him, the defense of human rights was part of his old soldier's pacifism. That commitment led not away from confronting fascism but toward that collision of fundamental values. And on that point, in 1936, he had had to part ways with his brethren. For them, peace came before everything. Not for Cassin. He knew that he was in the minority in the veterans movement and that, as such, his voice was more and more marginalized. "I will die without realizing my dreams," he wrote. The veterans movement had rallied "the peaceful aspirations of the masses," but at the price of opening "the door to the dictators, the warmongers, and those who prepare new massacres." I wonder, he mused, if the French people were being led to a new Sedan, a new military catastrophe. The press and the sordid assembly of politicians were preparing the ground. I face death, Cassin wrote, in full knowledge that my life has been futile, that I have not realized my potential in the law or in politics. "Before the grave, I will not draw back. I would have preferred to die for a reason, at the front or in combat." But that was not to be. His last words before going into surgery were, "Je veux vivre" [I want to live].[25]

What an extraordinary *cri de coeur*. Here was a man facing what he took to be the emptiness of his life's work. His twenty years of effort in the veterans movement had come to nothing. His colleagues had pushed him aside in their rush to appeasement. He hated war as much as any of them, but he would not sacrifice on the altar of appeasement his sense that fascism had to be stopped.

I know of no other document as eloquent as this one on the theme of how little we know of the full contours of our lives. Cassin survived the operation and began a life the shape of which he could not possibly have imagined at the time.

[23] Winter 2006, 118–134.
[24] 382AP/1, Note of January 19, 1936.
[25] Ibid.

He was right, though, about the impending catastrophe. In 1940, he watched the collapse of France from an office in the Ministry of Information. He realized that as an antifascist and a Jew, he was a marked man. He returned to his home in the south of France, paid his taxes, and decided to embark on an Australian troop ship to England. He never heard the call to arms of de Gaulle of June 18, 1940, but responded to it on arrival in London on June 29. He told de Gaulle that he was a veteran, founder of the veterans movement, and a Jew. He put himself, as a jurist and as a Frenchman, at the disposal of de Gaulle's embryonic movement. De Gaulle called him a godsend. Why? Because de Gaulle had thirty-six hours left to prepare a document for Churchill establishing his credentials and that of his movement, *France Libre*, as a French government in exile. Churchill was prepared to recognize and, of equal importance, to fund de Gaulle's movement if he could claim *de jure* status as the representative in exile of the French Republic. Cassin drew up the document that provided this crucial legitimation, later ratified on August 7, 1940, and the cornerstone of the French Resistance movement.[26]

The significance of this juridical service was of the highest importance, which de Gaulle recognized by making Cassin one of his ministers (or commissioners) in exile. Cassin had responsibility for education and justice, and sat on all the major committees of the French resistance movement in London. He represented de Gaulle on missions to Lebanon and to Africa, showing that the Republic was alive in its empire. He ran the central bureau of *France Libre* throughout the worst months of the Blitz.

Cassin was not a politician; everyone knew that. He was a professor and a jurist. But his standing as a jurist – professor of law in Paris and a world authority on civil law – and his work establishing the illegitimacy of Vichy made his name synonymous with the Republican cause.

Cassin's position as commissioner of justice opened the door to a new phase of his life. In 1941, in two meetings in St. James' Palace in London, one just before the invasion of the Soviet Union by Germany and one after the signing of the Atlantic Charter in August 1941, Cassin's life took another turn, one that led slowly but inexorably to the Universal Declaration of Human Rights.

The fact that he was there at all, among all the other exile delegates, was a great achievement. The delicacy of the French position was evident. Many countries, including the United States, still had diplomatic relations with France, which meant after June 1940 with Vichy. Free France was not a representative body, but rather the spirit of a representative body – the Chamber of Deputies – which had been dissolved without a referendum. Here was the core of the *coup d'état*. Vichy ruled by fiat and not by the will of the people. De Gaulle represented that will, then dispersed beyond the borders of France, but still intact nonetheless.

In June 1941, Hitler spoke of a new European order, one designed in Berlin. In London, the exiled governments of Europe joined the representatives of the

[26] 382AP/27 Diary entry, August 7–8, 1940.

British Empire and Dominions in St. James' Palace, and announced that there would be a new order, but not the one Hitler planned. It would be built on very different principles.

Those principles were drafted soon after in the Atlantic Charter. After the invasion of the Soviet Union, Churchill knew that his isolation had ended. To support him, Franklin Roosevelt met him off the North American coast, and the two men signed a document promising, after the defeat of Nazism, that their countries and their allies would build a welfare state in place of the warfare state. Remember that the United States was technically neutral; this document was virtually a declaration of war.

In mid-September a second Allied conference was held in St. James' Palace, and Cassin was there too. So were the representatives of the Soviet Union and other members of the alliance. There the subject of postwar war crimes trials was raised formally for the first time. Here the subject of the preparation for a new postwar international legal order incorporated not only war crimes trials, but also the construction of a new human rights regime over the ruins of Europe. The United Nations was to rest on such an approach to international affairs. Then and there, Cassin's commitment to human rights as a bulwark of peace became a facet of grand strategy.

From 1942 to 1944, Cassin worked on the construction of this new juridical order within the grand alliance against Hitler. In 1943, he became president of the Juridical Council of the French Resistance movement in Algiers, thereby ensuring the continuity of Republican law, and then returned to France, after liberation, to serve as vice-president (effectively the president) of the French *Conseil d'Etat*, the country's high administrative and constitutional court. From this point on, it is impossible to distinguish the contribution of Cassin the *ancient combatant* from Cassin the international diplomat to the construction of the new international order.

Three points, though, need to be emphasized. The first is that Cassin joined Eleanor Roosevelt, Charles Malik, John Humphreys, and others in the United Nations in drafting the Universal Declaration of Human Rights in 1945–1948. When the job was done, though, it was Cassin who made the final changes and read out the document to the United Nations assembled in Paris on December 10, 1948. There is no slight to the many people who supported Cassin's thinking and strategy to say that it was this one French jurist whose name was written all over the document, which he himself proclaimed in the country of his birth, a country that a few short years before had sentenced him to death in absentia for treason against the collaborationist state. Second, Cassin saw clearly that the opening of the Cold War made it impossible for the United Nations Commission on Human Rights to act with any coherent authority. Third, as a consequence, he transferred his efforts to create an institution higher than state sovereignty from the United Nations to the project of European unification. The European Convention on Human Rights, passed in 1950, had teeth: It was the document any country had to sign and respect in order to join the European community. It still is. To enforce the Convention, a new European Court of Human Rights was formed. In 1958, that court opened in Strasbourg, and Cassin was first vice-president (associate justice) and then in 1965, president (chief justice). On his retirement from that post in 1968 he was awarded the Nobel Peace Prize.

Let us consider a thought experiment of a relatively innocent kind. Consider Cassin on the dais in Oslo about to receive his Nobel Prize. Imagine for a moment that with him, at that place of honor on that evening, were millions of old soldiers, men who were pacifists of a special kind: men who had fought for their country and who knew what war was. Cassin's plea to defend human rights as a way to defend the peace was their plea. It became the cause of others after Cassin. It was at the heart of the Helsinki process in 1974, a process establishing the surveillance of the human rights situation in the Soviet Union as the prize for the legitimation of the western borders of that state. It was the plea of Charter 77 and of the host of organizations that undermined Soviet power by insisting on the inviolability of human rights. It was the plea of those who dismantled the Berlin wall and the Soviet empire behind it.

Cassin, who died in 1976, was not to know this extraordinary passage of the human rights project he helped to found. But he did know one part of it. Just a few months before his death, he asked his new wife, Ghislaine Maréchal, who was a film actress in the 1930s and a member of the Resistance in those dark days in London, to ensure that the text of one of his speeches would lie with him in his grave.[27] It was his salute to his brethren in the French army in 1914, who won the Battle of the Marne and who suffered with him in the autumn of the first year of the Great War. He delivered these moving words of commemoration on September 8, 1940, on the BBC, with the Luftwaffe literally over his head. In his address, he called his comrades of 1914 by name and added: "Yes, I still see you all."

I know you well, Captain Woignier, a Catholic from Lorraine with an ardent soul, whose eyes closed forever contemplating your native soil, and you, Vandendalle and Pellegrino, fearless and without fault, peaceful farmers whose blood was as red as your beautiful flowers. I remember you Garrus, humble laborer from the hills of the Var, poacher, free-thinker, volunteer for dangerous patrols, and you Magistrate Samata, who as a Jew refused to move to a less exposed position. Yes, I see you all, guys from Paris, the east, the south, Muslims from Algeria or Senegalese, who fought together with me on those days ... and whose bodies formed an immovable rampart in defense of France.[28]

It was men like these, Cassin asserted in 1940, who would achieve victory again.

Cassin was one of millions of men who never ceased to be *Ceux de '14, un ancien combattant de la grande guerre.* Everything he did, everything

[27] 382AP/181.
[28] 382AP/185.

he achieved, was an expression of that identity. He was a pacifist soldier, a Republican militant who all his life fought war even while waging it.

His legacies are many. In his last will and testament, he noted that while not ignoring the world as it is, he was conscious of his achievements, which in his view merited burial in the Pantheon, that secular cathedral honoring the great men of the Republic. In 1940 he had helped keep Republican France alive and united. Thereafter he knew that he had contributed to international law and above all to what he termed "a mystique of human rights" which had not been there before him.[29] That commitment to stand as a soldier of the right, that spirit arose during one war, informed a veterans movement that strove to avoid another, and then when war came anyway, these values helped Cassin and his brethren to fight and win yet again. Cassin died in 1976, but eleven years later, his casket was indeed interred in the Pantheon, next to Jean Moulin, the leader of the Resistance. And that was right and proper.

Cassin spent his life in a double quest: in search of peace and of the best means to defend human rights, in full knowledge of the link between the two. That message is with us still. His story is dramatic and worth telling in its own right. It has more than biographical significance since it describes a moment when a form of soldiers' pacifism became the pathway between a Europe armed to the teeth in 1914 and a Europe that has progressively moved away from the notion that the state is defined by its ability to wage war to another idea of the state: one located in the sense of its being a guardian of welfare and the rights of individuals as so important that they stand above *raison d'état* itself. Ironically, perhaps only soldiers and ex-soldiers, had the experience, the vision, and the moral authority to point the way toward the disarming of the state, or more precisely, the redefinition of the powers of the state, through the development of international law. For evidence of this, all you need to do is go to the old border between France and Germany at Strasbourg, where the European Court of Human Rights is situated. Pass by the International Institute of Human Rights established by René Cassin with the money he won with his Nobel Peace Prize. And then cross over by foot into Germany. Not a soldier, not a policeman in sight. Welcome to René Cassin's Europe.

---

[29] 382AP/181.

7

War and Reform

Gaining Labor's Compliance on the Homefront

Elizabeth Kier

How does the prosecution of war on the homefront affect postwar democratic politics and the likelihood for major reform? Wars cause death and destruction, but important political and social reforms often follow in their wake. At times it appears that the greater the destruction, the greater the growth of state power, and the greater the infringement on civil liberties, the more fundamental and far reaching the reforms. After World War I, Britain, Austria, and Belgium broadened the franchise and many countries granted political rights to women. World War II led to an even greater extension of political and social reforms. It is no accident that a historian would entitle her book *War Is Good for Babies and Other Young Children.*[1]

The mobilization of the homefront is critical to a state's ability to wield power in international politics, and this was especially true during the total wars of the twentieth century. As an American industrialist put it, total war "demands that the blood of the soldier be mingled with from three to five parts of the sweat of the man in the factories, mills, mines, and fields of the nation-in-arms."[2] Modern states cannot wage total war effectively without labor's cooperation. Industrial strikes are potentially as damaging to the war effort as military mutinies.

All states must increase economic productivity during war, but different states use different strategies with different results. Some states develop a harsh and punitive strategy to gain labor's compliance with the war effort. Other states gain labor's consent through increased wages and benefits. Still others rely on labor's identification with the state through calls to patriotism and promises of future rewards. Some states also appeal to labor's sense of what is "just" by equitably distributing wartime sacrifices and including

I thank Mike Desch, Ron Krebs, Jon Mercer, Joel Migdal, Sid Tarrow, and the anonymous reviewers for Cambridge University Press for their excellent suggestions and critiques. Thanks also to participants at a Peace Studies seminar at Cornell and at workshops at the University of Texas at Austin and the University of Washington.

[1] Dwork 1987.
[2] Cited in Harries 1997, 57.

labor's representatives in decision-making forums. I argue that these varied strategies influence labor's wartime development and are key to unraveling the link between war and reform. Wartime transformations in labor's power and preferences influence its ability to retain wartime gains and extract further reforms in peacetime. They help explain why wartime promises for a better future are sometimes realized, but oftentimes not.

By focusing on how mobilization for war restructures society, this chapter corrects the tendency to treat war as a temporary interruption of routine politics. It illustrates how wartime strategies to mobilize labor can fundamentally alter postwar politics. The link is not obvious, but, as I show, the consequences are profound: Mobilization strategies affect the state's ability to extract resources during the war and shape the type of society that emerges from that war. The process is critical to the restructuring of society and to the likelihood for postwar reform. Just as we search for the origins of war in the preceding years of peace, we should also consider how the origins of the domestic order may be found in the preceding war.

I first review alternative accounts of the link between war and reform that rely on egalitarianism, increases in state power, and wartime bargains. I then present my argument about the importance of mobilization strategies and illustrate it through case studies of Britain and Italy in World War I. These examples challenge three common assumptions: that military victory legitimizes the regime in power; that a robust civil society benefits democracy; and that the scale of war, and in particular the extent of civilian participation, determines postwar reform. The explanation for why Britain expanded its conception of social citizenship after World War I while Italy did not rests on *how* each state mobilized its economy, not the *intensity* of that effort. The Italian and British comparison also illustrates the importance of affective ties between state and society, why process is often as important as outcome, and why the origin and duration of wars can sometimes be found in their anticipated consequences.

WAR AND REFORM

Historians, sociologists, and political scientists offer three explanations for the link between war and reform. The first focuses on society. Scholars argue that mobilization creates strong norms of egalitarianism. As the Queen Mother declared after a bombing raid on Buckingham Palace, "At least I can now look the East Enders in the eye." This newfound sense that "we're all in the same boat" may lead to widespread support for democratic reform.[3] The second set of arguments focuses on the state. War *strengthens* the state (administratively and fiscally) so it is better equipped to implement reform. War also *enlightens* the state: Mobilization exposes chronic social problems,

[3] Bruce 1961.

or, as Peacock and Wiseman put it, war has an "inspection effect."[4] These state and society arguments are either apolitical or rely on a functional logic. There is a *granting* of reforms: from the rich to the poor, from the state to society. Or alternatively the state has increased its capacity to address newly exposed social ills. The beneficiaries of reform do not figure in these accounts, and there is no sense of political struggle despite the stakes involved in any significant reform effort.

The third, and more political, set of arguments combines state and society and recognizes the conflict inherent in any expansion of democratic citizenship. These "payback" arguments assume that the state strikes a bargain with civilians: Cooperate on the homefront and the battlefield, and you'll be repaid with postwar reform. Stanislaw Andreski's "military participation ratio" suggests that the greater the proportion of the population mobilized for war, the greater the leveling of social inequalities. Michael Mann points to a similar dynamic, and Charles Tilly famously argues that societal actors extract concessions during war.[5]

These "payback" arguments are good as far as they go. There is not just a granting of reform; there is some sense of conflict, of societal actors using leverage to force change. However, reform does not always follow war – even the most demanding wars – and "payback" arguments do not explain why. British participation in World War I was unprecedented and the promises were great, yet the payback was not. Many of the reforms instituted in the United States during World War I did not survive demobilization. We do not know if these wartime "bargains" have much to do with postwar reform and, if they do, how they work. Once the war ends and labor's leverage is gone, why would the bargain be fulfilled? During World War I, the head of Bethlehem Steel talked of a "New Age" and "a world for workers." Yet once the war ended, the National Association of Manufacturers sought to "liquidate labor's wartime achievements." Payback arguments leave unanswered the question of *how leverage in war translates into political power during peace.* We need to understand whether, when, and how wartime mobilization restructures societal actors so that they can retain reforms wrung during war and extract new ones in peacetime.

Mobilizing for Total War

During a total war, all states must maximize productivity without provoking labor unrest. Yet all states do not react similarly to this challenge; they adopt a range of strategies to mobilize their economies for war. I draw on Amitai Etzioni's typology of compliance in organizations, and on research on organizational justice, to classify these diverse approaches.

---

4 Peacock and Wiseman 1961; Titmuss 1958.
5 Andreski 1954; Mann 1993; Tilly 1993.

Etzioni argues that there are three forms of control in organizations: coercive, remunerative, and normative.[6] *Coercive* power relies on sanctions, or the use of pain and punishment, to gain compliance. Economic mobilization can be predominantly coercive. The example of Italy during World War I is especially striking: Industrial mobilization was turned over to military authorities and the state imposed a harsh military discipline in war-related firms. The second source of control is *remunerative,* in which states offer wages and fringe benefits to gain compliance. States often use material incentives to mobilize their economies for war. During World War I, the U.S. government required companies supplying army uniforms to pay minimum wages and maintain an eight-hour work day; this period also saw the first U.S. experimentation with public housing and health insurance. With coercive and remunerative power, compliance rests on external incentives.

In contrast, the third source of control – *normative* – relies on commitment and identification. It relocates individuals within a social world: Members of a normative organization identify with the organization and are committed to it. Normative power does not assume the absence of conflicts of interest, but it differs from the hierarchical control of coercive organizations and the contractual exchange of remunerative ones. Whereas members have a negative orientation toward a coercive organization and little emotional attachment to a remunerative one, those in a normative organization have a positive attachment to it. Normative power is an important strategy for economic mobilization. This is the realm of patriotism and moral commitment. Workers work not because they are punished if they don't or paid if they do, but because they identify with the state and its goals. Workers are called upon in their identity as German or British to contribute to the war effort.

Mobilization strategies also differ in the extent to which they incorporate issues of justice. The literature on organizational justice distinguishes two broad categories. The first is *procedural* justice, which is the fairness of the rules and procedures by which rewards are distributed. During wartime, labor is sometimes included in decision making: Woodrow Wilson encouraged firms to recognize unions during World War I, and Winston Churchill attached the minority Labour Party to his governing coalition during World War II. Yet in other cases, such as France during World War II, labor is excluded from the decisions that affect it. The second is *distributive* justice, which is the fairness of outcomes compared to what others receive. State policies to equitably distribute wartime sacrifices can vary radically: Churchill imposed a 100 percent tax rate on excess corporate profits, but Franklin Roosevelt's efforts to cap wartime salaries failed.

In summary, states use a variety of strategies to mobilize their economies for war. Labor can be punished, paid, or persuaded to contribute to the war effort, and some strategies appear more just than others. As I discuss below,

---

[6] Etzioni 1975.

these different strategies have profound effects on labor's wartime development and so the prospects for postwar reform.

Mobilization and Reform

Mobilization for war can transform postwar politics. It can restructure political actors and transform the links between them, altering social identities, shared definitions of what is possible and desirable, and the costs and benefits of joint action. And in the case of labor, the different strategies used to gain its participation in the war effort can transform what it wants and the resources at its disposal.

Mobilization politicizes labor regardless of the strategy chosen. The more the state intervenes in the economy – and even the most liberal states cast aside their economic principles during total war – the more labor will hold the state responsible for its fate.[7] However, the direction of this politicization depends on the strategy used. I expect coercive mobilizations to radicalize labor and encourage working-class solidarity. These hypotheses are adapted from arguments about how the character of the state shapes the working class: the more repressive state action, the more radical labor's demands.[8] They also reflect Etzioni's finding that coercion breeds workers' alienation from authority while simultaneously increasing their cohesion with each other. Suffering the same fate, members of coercive organizations rally with each other against the source of their repression. In contrast, I expect normative strategies to encourage reformist goals and promote working-class disunity.

The degree of procedural and distributive justice influences the evolution of labor's power and preferences. State policies that promote procedural justice have the most immediate effect: The recognition of union rights and labor's inclusion in governmental bodies increase labor's power. These actions are sometimes reversed after the war, but regardless of whether the increase in union membership endures, labor's participation in wartime decision making enhances its legitimacy as an actor in the formation of public policy.

The extent of procedural justice influences labor's attitude toward the state. Normative strategies capitalize on the nationalist fervor that war often ignites, but as casualties mount and sacrifices grow, war can test these affective ties between state and society. It is here that procedural justice becomes critical: The more that the state promotes labor's participation in economic and political forums, the more it can retain and reinforce labor's identification with the state and its belief in the state's good intentions. Organizational theorists find that the greater the perception of procedural justice, the deeper the commitment to, and trust in, the organization.[9] Perceptions of procedural

[7] Poole 1986, 70.
[8] Marks 1989.
[9] Cropanzano and Greenberg 1997.

injustice have the opposite effect: They breed alienation from, and distrust of, organizational authority. Mobilization strategies that exclude labor from decision making will not only do nothing to enhance labor's institutional power or its legitimacy as a representative of working-class interests, but they will also aggravate labor's affective ties to the state and fuel its suspicions about the intentions of state actors.

The perception of distributive justice shapes labor's attitudes. Researchers find that an individual's sense that others are not doing their part encourages dissatisfaction; I expect this reaction to be especially powerful during a total war.[10] Individuals often accept peacetime inequity as the result of an impersonal market, but total war politicizes injustice. State and society come together in what amounts to a single national firm for waging war and workers are exhorted to place collective goals above personal ones. They expect all members of the collectivity to do the same. As John Kenneth Galbraith noted during World War II, "no feature of this war has been more striking than the scrutiny that each economic group brings to bear on what the others are getting." Whereas evidence of profiteering is likely to fuel industrial unrest, the perception of shared sacrifice will encourage working-class support for state goals. As the British labor leader Ernest Bevin remarked in 1940, the 100 percent tax rate on corporate excess profits "will make Labour throw itself heart and soul into the war effort."[11]

Finally, the interactive effects of distributive and procedural justice influence labor preferences. Researchers have discovered a striking effect: Individuals react less negatively to bad outcomes when they perceive the procedures to be fair.[12] Labor will be dissatisfied if its wartime sacrifices are rewarded unfairly, but it is only when those unjust outcomes are coupled with unfair procedures that labor will become vengeful and challenge state authorities.

In short, the postwar labor movement often differs radically from its prewar organization, and these transformations in its power and preferences shape the nature of postwar politics and the potential for democratic reform. For example, one of the most influential approaches to the welfare state argues that strong reformist labor movements were critical to the emergence and growth of welfare states in Western nations.[13] These theorists acknowledge that the structural characteristics of a society do not determine labor's size or its goals, but they do not explore alternate sources. In particular, they do not examine how the pursuit of the national interest sometimes restructures labor so that it can better promote class interests. By examining how strategies to mobilize the homefront alter labor's power and preferences, this chapter addresses how leverage in war can translate into political power during peace.

[10] Greenberg and Cohen 1982.
[11] Quotes from Leff 1991, 1301, 1315.
[12] Brockner and Wisenfeld 1996.
[13] Korpi 1989.

ITALIAN AND BRITISH MOBILIZATION IN WORLD WAR I

Italy and Britain both faced unprecedented demands on the homefront and both emerged as victors from World War I. Yet they adopted radically different mobilization strategies with radically different results. Italy relied on coercion and Britain on normative and remunerative power. In neither case did labor emerge with full political, civil, and social rights, but explaining their divergent paths – one that led to the destruction of democracy and the other to its deepening – requires understanding how the strategies used to mobilize labor shaped its development and thus the prospect for reform.

Italy: Disciplining Labor

Soon after entering the war, Italy created a new bureaucracy, *Mobilitazione Industriale* (IM), to direct its industrial mobilization. Subordinated to the Ministry of War and headed by General Alfredo Dallolio, IM was organized into regional committees – chaired by admirals and generals – that implemented IM's provisions in war-related firms. The appointment of military officers to run IM signaled Italy's militarization of the working class: The state would use repression, not economic concessions or appeals to patriotism or a sense of justice, to force labor's participation in the war effort.

IM's provisions drastically altered labor's position in the firms under its supervision. Wages were frozen at prewar levels, strikes became illegal, and arbitration boards set wages and working conditions. Absences from work or job transfers were prohibited. The punishments for violating these provisions were harsh, determined by army officers, and they were not subject to appeal. Striking workers were punished under a military code that equated strikes with desertion, and absent workers could be charged with desertion and sent to the front. Workers merely suspected of union activity or political militancy often lost their draft exemptions, and disobedience to a superior civilian official was punished under the military code.[14] The Italian government also removed large regions from civilian jurisdiction. A rigid military penal code replaced the civil one, and the army had absolute power over any firm not under IM's jurisdiction. These "war zones" were initially in strategic border areas, but as concerns about social control grew, this designation expanded to cover most of northern Italy.[15]

As the war continued, and especially after the Russian Revolution and the disaster at Caporetto (where in October 1917 German and Austrian forces broke through the front line in northern Italy and routed the Italian army), Dallolio recognized that pure coercion was unsustainable. Some remuneration was necessary to separate the workers' economic demands from political ones. Dallolio introduced flexibility in wages, improved factory conditions, and

[14] Procacci 1989, 38; Tomassini 1990, 182–197.
[15] Tomassini 1991, 64–69.

created a temporary unemployment system for workers whose jobs were suspended due to raw material shortages. The state also began providing subsidies to soldiers' families and rationing primary foodstuffs.[16] However, this limited remuneration did not relieve the war's hardships. Inflation quickly erased the meager wages increases: By 1918, real wages had fallen to less than two-thirds of 1913 levels. Poverty and hunger reached critical levels in the cities teeming with new munitions workers and Italy's infant mortality rate rose, outpacing that of other European belligerents. The new factory standards were modest and sporadically enforced. Overcrowded factories, long hours, and intense work rhythms led to deteriorating conditions and skyrocketing accident rates. Even rationing and aid to soldiers' families had little effect; private charitable and patriotic groups dispensed this aid, which was irregular in large cities and absent outside them.[17]

Normative appeals played next to no role in Italian mobilization. Antonio Salandra, the premier of Italy's wartime government until June 1916, was uninterested in public opinion and never sought mass support. The military officers running IM developed some policies to promote morale, but private patriotic associations directed most of the state's propaganda. Even after Caporetto, the limited efforts were aimed at the middle class.[18] The absence of patriotic appeals probably made sense. Normative strategies rely on identification with the state, but a national consciousness had not developed in Italy. Historians concur that the *Risorgimento* did not fulfill the political aspirations of a people and that Italy's nascent democratic institutions had not created a national identity. "*La patria*," wrote Curzio Malaparte, "was a conception beyond their power of understanding."[19] Alone among the European belligerents, Italy entered the war without popular support. Giolittians, socialists, Catholics, workers, peasants, and a majority in parliament were staunchly neutralist. While German and French socialists reconciled their international ideals with national ones, the Italian worker agreed with the Socialist party that this war was for the *signori* (the gentlemen).[20]

The Italian state could have attempted to generate a sense of national identity through procedural justice, but labor was given little "voice" in wartime decision making. The "National Union" government included every party except the Socialists, management chose the labor "representatives" in IM's committees, and unions were excluded from IM's arbitration process. Dallolio eventually opened some decision-making bodies to labor: Beginning in mid-1917, union representatives sat in IM's Central Committee, some moderate unions were recognized, and worker commissions in factories were

---

[16] Procacci 1995, 15–22; Tomassini 1990, 189–190.

[17] Corner and Procacci 1997, 228; 142; Horowitz 1963, 142; Procaccci 1990, 157–163.

[18] Whittam 1975, 152–153; Procacci 1995, 11; Corner and Procacci 1997, 228; Tomassini 1990, 198.

[19] Quoted in Whittam 1975, 154; also see Lyttelton 2004, 3–5; Corner and Procacci 1997, 224.

[20] Seton-Watson 1967, 416, 436–449; Thayer 1964, 307–308.

legalized.[21] However, IM's reliance on coercion overwhelmed these limited efforts; labor lacked any real participation in decision making.

The Italian state also did little to promote distributive justice; it focused on controlling labor, not capital. State officials accepted the firms' prices without question and granted huge depreciation allowances and tax exemptions to firms engaged in war production. This system guaranteed high profits, but, with the working class suffering in the midst of a "national effort," it also provoked labor unrest. As Luigi Einaudi explained, "Every class ... had its own way of life, which changed very little from one year to the next; and each class considered the fact that its living standards were different from those of other classes to be perfectly normal. It was the war ... which led people to think about the idea of economic equity."[22] Yet the state did little as profiteers' conspicuous displays of wealth fed wartime industrial strife; it was only after the war that the state imposed a wealth tax and duty on war profits.

Italian labor's wartime experiences were unrelentingly negative. Industrial relations had reverted to the social control typical of the reactionary politics of the nineteenth century. In fact, Italy's coercive strategy more closely resembled its autocratic adversaries than its democratic allies; it often went beyond the policies adopted in Central Europe. Austrian women were never subjected to militarization, the German army was not present in firms, and German labor retained some job mobility. Even Dallolio's turn to some remunerative measures in 1917 did not supplant the harsh tactics; the repressive legislation was repeatedly tightened in response to labor unrest.[23]

Britain: Managing Manpower

Britain expected a quick victory and initially followed a "business as usual" strategy, but these traditional methods were inadequate. The army was short on material, and the factories lacked skilled labor. In June 1915, the government stripped the War Office of its authority over arms supply and appointed David Lloyd George the head of the Ministry of Munitions. This newly formed ministry ran Britain's industrial mobilization. It had broad powers, grew rapidly, and by the end of the war controlled critical areas of the economy. The army played no role in domestic administration and the civil servants in the Ministry of Munitions were sympathetic to moderate trade unionism.[24]

British policy focused on consent more than control, and it capitalized on labor's patriotism to pursue a normative strategy. British workers often saw themselves as part of a class or a local community, but they also had a sense of being part of a "concrete community" of the nation. As one historian put it,

[21] Galassi and Harrison, 2005, 285; Procacci 1989, 49; Tomassini 1990, 182–183.
[22] Quoted in Zamagni 1993, 390; Procacci 1990, 164; Tomassini 1991, 61.
[23] Procacci 1995, 10–15.
[24] Reid 1985, 63–69. A view of the British state as pursuing the national interest has largely displaced earlier historiography of a "servile state" serving the interests of capital.

"They believed in a Britain that was not necessarily the state. It was a Britain in which they had a stake. It was a Britain worth defending, whatever the sins of the government."[25] Although industrial conflict was rife in the summer of 1914 and everyone anticipated further unrest in the fall, British labor rallied to the flag when war was declared. The Labour Party and the major trade unions called for an industrial truce, the number of disputes declined sharply for the first six months of the war, and working-class volunteers from even the more militant unions flooded the British army. Miners enlisted at one of the highest rates and nearly a quarter of the munitions, metals, and shipbuilding workers had joined up by the following summer. Urban workers, even those from occupations with full employment, were enlisting at rates outpacing their rural counterparts. It was, as one historian remarked, "the greatest mass movement of modern British history."[26]

In March 1915 Lloyd George negotiated the Treasury Agreement with trade union officials and, following the "shell shortage" scandal in May, Parliament gave this voluntary agreement legislative force as the Munitions of War Act. This act, which was the most important legislation on British industrial relations during the war, contained three important provisions. First, strikes were forbidden and industrial disputes were to be referred to compulsory arbitration. Second, a system of "leaving certificates" limited labor mobility. Employers could hire workers from a war-related firm only with their previous employers' consent. Third, trade union practices were relaxed. This "dilution" allowed the breaking down of skilled craft procedures into simple operations that unskilled workers, many of them women, could perform. In exchange, the government promised labor that it would help secure the restoration of trade union practices when the war ended. Munitions tribunals were established to enforce these provisions.

Britain's reliance on normative power does not mean that labor was not restricted or that coercion was never used. Serious friction existed between labor and the government, and industrial unrest recurred. Many industrialists hoped the government would use the emergency situation to crush organized labor and the cabinet considered a coercive approach that would have severely weakened labor. That path was not taken, and the government was generally responsive to union pressure and reluctant to fully implement wartime provisions. When the miners of South Wales illegally struck in July 1915, Lloyd George conceded to most of their demands. Only a small fraction of strikers were convicted of breaking the law, and the fines paid for illegal actions were minimal. Official support for "dilution" was seen as the work of a repressive state, but historians have shown that its importance was exaggerated. The government's retraction of the leaving certificate best illustrates its preference for consent over control. This provision was one of the most coercive aspects of British policy, and, following negotiations with labor,

[25] Sibley 2005, 49–50, 68; Powell 2004, 58.
[26] Sibley 2005, 1–3, 47; Powell 2004, 61; Searle 2004, 800; Waites 1987, 186.

the government first amended and then abandoned what trade unionists had dubbed "The Slavery Act."[27]

The government's use of normative power developed as the war continued. Prime Minister Lloyd George restructured the program and in early 1917 created the Department (and later Ministry) of Information. It broadened its audience to the mass public and produced posters, pamphlets, and hundreds of propaganda films. Lloyd George himself enlisted numerous individuals, from Sylvia Pankhurst (a founder of the suffragette movement) to leaders of the Church of England, to go to the munitions factories and rally support for the war effort.[28]

The government's extensive use of procedural justice reinforced its normative strategy. Labor entered the war supportive of the state, and its inclusion in political and economic forums helped reinforce and maintain these ties as the war continued and hardship mounted. Beginning in May 1915, Asquith's coalition government included the Labour leader, Arthur Henderson, as president of the Board of Education and as an unofficial adviser on labor affairs. Lloyd George's government of national unity, formed in December 1916, went further and gave labor an unprecedented place at the table. Conservatives dominated the cabinet, but Henderson was one of only five members of the War Cabinet. Lloyd George also created new ministries in Shipping, Labour, and Pensions, and appointed Labour members of Parliament (MPs) to the latter two. Labor had wanted a Ministry of Labour since the 1890s and its creation, as with Labor's seat in the War Cabinet, was a potent symbol of labor's participation in official bodies. Lloyd George frequently consulted the leaders of key trade unions, government officials regularly discussed the implementation of industrial legislation with union leaders, and labor officials joined many industrial joint committees.[29]

The inclusion of labor had prewar precedents, but the depth of its involvement in official bodies at the local and national level was unparalleled. Lloyd George's description of Arthur Balfour's bewilderment at seeing "stalwart artisans ... on equal terms negotiating with the Government of this day" captures the novelty of labor's role. By 1916 labor leaders expected state officials to consult them about labor policies and by the armistice, the socialist reformers Sidney and Beatrice Webb could reasonably claim that, "Trade Unionism has ... won its recognition by Parliament and the Government, by law and by custom, as a separate element in the community, entitled to distinct recognition as a party of the social machinery of the State, its members being thus allowed to give not only their votes as citizens, but also their concurrence as an order or estate."[30] Labor had won power and recognition.

---

[27] Rubin 1987, 246–247; Reid 1985, 59, 66; Wrigley 1987b, 29–31.
[28] Wrigley 1976, 136; Searle 2004, 768.
[29] Wrigley 1987b, 44–46, 56, Wrigley 1976, 23.
[30] Lloyd George quoted in MacDonald 1976, 84; Webbs quoted in Wrigley 1982b, 80; Whiteside 1980, 873.

Although many British employers had bargained with unions prior to the war, many others had refused. The Ministry of Munitions' insistence on collective bargaining ended this resistance and increased labor's perception of procedural justice. Compulsory arbitration encouraged the spread of collective bargaining, and the government would grant contracts only to firms that recognized unions. Previously recalcitrant employers in engineering, coal mining, and port transportation were now sitting down with labor, and the shipping and railroad industries fully recognized unions during the war. The munitions tribunals consistently supported union rights. In a widely reported case, a tribunal ruled against an employer who had fired an iron molder for joining a union. The employee had signed a company statement renouncing union membership, but the tribunal decreed that the employer's actions were illegal. The Whitley Report in 1917 also led to the recognition of collective bargaining rights for many previously unorganized sectors, such as local and central government employees. Even labor in industries less critical to the war effort saw a growth in trade unions and collective bargaining.[31]

In contrast to Italy, Britain also recognized the importance of distributive justice. The Treasury Agreement (and later the Munitions Act) decreed that profits in munitions industries should be capped at 20 percent above the average of the two prewar years. Despite this initial effort, officials acknowledged that labor's charges of profiteering had merit. The employer tax rate was generous given the prewar boom and it applied only to war production, not coal or food, whose prices soared during the war. Many employers did exceedingly well. As one historian remarked, the excess profits tax "legitimized high profits rather than removed them." The failure to address further calls for shared sacrifice plagued British wartime industrial relations. Official reports repeatedly found that the feeling of distributive injustice, reflected in resentment over profiteering, fueled labor strife. Passage of the military service acts in 1916 also fed calls for "fair play" and support for a "Conscription of Riches" movement. The war was not labor's first encounter with injustice, but it was especially offensive given the rhetoric about a nation united in a collective struggle.[32]

Britain refined its normative strategy as the war continued, but it did not rely on patriotism alone. It also used remuneration to gain labor's compliance with the war effort. Working-class rents were frozen at prewar levels, munitions workers received unemployment insurance, and rationing and price controls were placed on food. Wartime legislation extended minimum-wage protection to a wider range of industries, and the government pioneered a cost-of-living sliding scale that spread to a broad section of industry. The Ministry

[31] Gospel 1987, 163; Wrigley 1976, 132; Rubin 1984, 323–324; Wrigley 1987c; Whiteside 1990, 114–116.
[32] Quoted in Searle 2004, 797; quoted in Wrigley 1976, 184; Waites 1987, 222; Wrigley 1987b, 31; Horne 1991, 54.

of Munitions also pioneered the spread of welfare provisions in war-related factories and attempted to create healthy workplaces through attention to heating, lighting, ventilation, and the provision of hot meals. Treasury controls were suspended, and firms could write off the cost of food, medical services, crèches, and recreational clubs against wartime taxation. The government also promoted maternal and infant welfare.[33]

The British working classes' aggregate income underscores the state's extensive use of remunerative power, especially in contrast to Italy. While Italian wages fell way below prewar levels, British wages kept pace with or outstripped inflation, and by the end of the war were roughly double their 1914 level. The gains were greatest at the lower end of the income scale: The wages of skilled workers often rose by less than the cost of living, but those of the semiskilled and unskilled kept pace with inflation. Indeed, one of the paradoxes of the war in Britain was that the carnage in the trenches accompanied a decline in mortality at home. While Italy's infant mortality rose to the highest in Europe, Britain's rate dropped steeply during the war. Caloric intake plummeted in Italian cities, but British workers improved their food consumption.[34]

Controls on rent, food, and liquor, as well as declining birth rates, helped to improve Britain's standard of living, but it was state involvement in wage negotiations that drove the biggest advances in welfare. Although employers were surprised by this new role for the state and dismayed that their preferences were often ignored, workers were relieved that they, for the most part, no longer lived in abject poverty.

TRANSFORMING LABOR'S POWER AND PREFERENCES

Mass mobilization for war ushered in new relationships between states and their societies. The Italian and British governments' involvement with labor influenced labor's development and the terms of postwar political debate. The prewar Giolittian regime had been officially neutral in industrial disputes, but the war radically altered this stance. The wartime Italian state regularly interacted with and directly disciplined labor. Labor had been unused to dealing with the state to protect its interests, and this new – and repressive – contact radicalized labor's demands, fueled its alienation from the state and created an unprecedented level of class solidarity. Wartime state intervention in the economy also politicized British labor, but London's reliance on patriotism and payoffs – its attempt to gain labor's consent and not just control it – generated a different response. Labor's preferences evolved, but remained moderate, its allegiance to the state endured, and working-class fragmentation persisted.

[33] Pugh 2002, 166–167; Searle 2004, 804, 816.
[34] Winter 1985a, 39; Winter 1985b, 213–248.

Italy's Radicalization

Italian mobilization for war transformed what had been troubled industrial relations with pockets of radical and syndicalist demands into a revolutionary situation. Italy's coercive strategy – the exceptional exploitation, the harsh and indiscriminate discipline, and the deteriorating working and living conditions – generated this new orientation. Throughout the country, calls for peace and revolution intensified, especially after the Russian Revolution and Caporetto. Thousands of militant workers in the industrial centers where the munitions factories were concentrated waited for the signal to "do as in Russia." As a prefect wrote in 1917, "They talk about the revolution as if it were something that could happen from one minute to the next." Some union leaders remained moderate, but they often took militant stances to retain their positions in the face of rising working-class militancy.[35]

This radicalization was not inevitable and it did not occur overnight. Early in the war, the Socialist party's postwar program was a typical basket of reformist demands: universal and direct suffrage, comprehensive social insurance, a minimum wage, and public works programs. Yet by the war's end, the state's punitive strategy had radicalized the party; the revolutionary wing captured 74 percent of the vote at the party's 1918 convention, with the reformist wing garnering just 13 percent. The "maximalists" rejected participation in government and announced that they sought a dictatorship of the proletariat; the following year, the party congress declared that "the proletariat must have recourse to violence for the conquest of power over the bourgeoisie."[36]

Italian labor also became increasingly alienated from the state. When the war began, few affective ties linked the working class to the state, but the regime's coercive strategy and its exclusion of labor from decision making transformed this neutral orientation into a highly charged and negative one. The intensity of labor's disaffection, especially in the war's later stages, is striking. Following the defeat at Caporetto, Austrian and German forces poured into Italy and occupied most of its northeast provinces. Rather than generating a sense of unity with the beleaguered Italian state – a typical reaction among European publics when their countries were invaded – Italian workers greeted this news with relief, hoping that the foreign occupation would bring a better government that would address their basic needs. Prefects around the country noted this sentiment, as did a journalist who reported that "in many areas they have prepared risotto and got drunk in order to celebrate the arrival of the Austrians in Italy – who have come ... to chop off the heads of the gentlemen who wanted the war, and then to help the poor." This alienation became so intense that rumors circulated that the

---

[35] Quoted in Procacci 1990, 148; Horowitz 1963, 136–141; Pernicone 1974, 207. The war also radicalized and strengthened the agrarian unions.

[36] Quoted in Smith 1969, 327; Horowitz 1963, 129–132.

state was using Italian babies to make salami. When the war ended, labor did not celebrate Italy's victory.[37]

Italian labor entered the war divided. Skilled workers in the munitions factories greeted the flood of unskilled labor with hostility; this new working class did not share their demands. Yet by war's end, the state faced a united front. This newfound solidarity emerged during a strike wave in the winter of 1916–1917 and became evident with the spread of egalitarian wage demands. Calls to decrease wage differentials increasingly replaced those targeted at protecting the status of skilled workers and joint action among different categories of workers became common. Italy's harsh mobilization strategy that hit all sectors of labor alike partially explains this reversal. But this newfound solidarity also stemmed from a particular feature of IM's repressive approach. Aiming to control labor more than gain its consent, IM tried to localize challenges to state power by requiring that cost-of-living demands be made on a factory-by-factory basis. This attempt to limit unrest to individual factories had an unintended consequence: By cutting the traditional interplant links between skilled workers and forcing workers within a factory to present a common set of demands, this regulation encouraged solidarity across skill levels.[38]

Italy's repressive strategy also altered labor's organizational power. It strengthened some aspects of it, restructured others, and generated support for the Socialist party. The factory council movement is the most well-known product of the war effort. Its particular form and nature grew directly out of IM regulations and especially IM's insistence on factory arbitration. Before the war, Italian employers had successfully resisted union representation within factories, but the war brought the state into the factory to resolve wage disputes. In the hopes of maintaining direct control, IM sidelined established unions and unofficially recognized the "internal commissions" that had spontaneously formed in response to IM regulations and the influx of new workers. These efforts backfired. These new bodies were the direct and necessary prelude to the most revolutionary labor challenge in the postwar period.[39] Not only had the coercive strategy radicalized labor and built working-class unity, but it had also encouraged the growth of a new organizational form that would be at the vanguard of revolutionary action.

Italy's mobilization contributed to two additional aspects of labor's power. First, it spurred a rapid expansion in trade union membership, both in the General Confederation of Labor (Italy's main trade union federation) and in the newly created Catholic union. Second, it generated much greater support for the Socialist party. Its membership quadrupled, and it became the largest

---

[37] Quoted in Corner and Procacci 1997, 230; Procacci 1990, 174–176. Procacci 1989, 51; Musso 1990, 238.

[38] Pernicone 1974, 205; Musso 1990, 232–238; Tomassini 1990, 195–199; Procacci 1989, 45, 52.

[39] Pernicone 1974, 206; Tomassini 1990, 194–196.

party in the first postwar elections. With the new Catholic party the second largest party in Parliament, the political regime of the prewar era was gone.[40]

Britain's Moderation

"Until August 1914," A.J.P. Taylor explains, "a sensible, law-abiding Englishman could pass through life and hardly notice the existence of the state, beyond the post office and the policeman."[41] Mobilization for war changed all that: The state now directly intervened in working-class life. The government's domination of economic activity challenged British labor's traditional separation of politics and economics. Problems once attributed to the market were now seen as problems to be solved by the state. Officials often spoke at local meetings, and workers knew that the state influenced wages, prices, and rents. As a member of the Boilermakers put it, "the prejudice of Trade unions against politics has hitherto held us back ... The events of the last three years have taken the scales from our eyes." In contrast to Italy, this politicization was not revolutionary. Activists calling for workers' control were a minority. Unlike in most European states, the war did not strengthen labor's left wing. A wave of unrest broke out after the armistice, but in contrast to Italy, where peace brought an explosion of blueprints for a new political and economic order, British industrial protest was reformist and focused on wages and working conditions. Even the calls for nationalization were more about better wages than a radical challenge to Britain's political economy.[42]

The growing support within the Labour Party for a moderate socialist position illustrates the evolution of labor's ideas. War collectivism had demonstrated an alternative to free enterprise, but the party's endorsement of socialism in 1918 was not a call for radical change. The party was committed to retaining labor's wartime gains and pursuing reform within the existing system, albeit with a greater state role. Most unionists concurred with industrialists that in peacetime, government involvement in industrial relations should be kept to a minimum.[43] The war created in labor expectations for using state power, but not for capturing it.

British labor was ambivalent about state power; it was not alienated from it. The working class remained patriotic and committed to the war effort. Cost-of-living protests in Italy often escalated into violent attacks on symbols of the state, such as public burnings of town property. British industrial unrest never assumed an antistate or antiwar tenor. The engineering strikes in 1917 illustrate the power of the shop stewards movement, but they also confirmed that even the militant sectors of British labor identified with state goals: Workers producing antisubmarine devices did not strike. And while Italian labor

---

[40] Seton-Watson 1967, 520–523; Pernicone 1974, 208; Smith 1969, 325.
[41] Taylor 1965, 1.
[42] Quoted in Degroot 1996, 317; also see Tanner 1990, 372–379; Waites 1987, 185, 207.
[43] Winter 1974.

welcomed news of its army's defeat at Caporetto, the German offensive in March 1918 generated an intensely patriotic reaction among British labor. Voluntary enlistments shot up, and even the most radical unionists discouraged strike action. The number of days lost to strikes fell off sharply after the German assault.[44]

Whereas Italy's repressive strategy created working-class solidarity, Britain's mobilization kept labor apart. Wartime wage increases for the unskilled and semiskilled increased labor homogeneity, but state policies did not generate worker solidarity. To the contrary, the erosion of wage differentials was the major grievance among skilled workers, skilled unions resisted closer ties with unskilled ones, and wartime strikes often sought to preserve preferential wages – a far cry from Italy's egalitarian demands. And though the inclusion of trade union officials in government bodies increased procedural justice, it also created tensions between the leadership and the rank-and-file and thus aggravated labor unity. It was only in those sectors of the union movement where its leaders refused to work with the government that unofficial rank-and-file movements did not arise.[45]

British mobilization also altered labor's power and the structure of industrial relations. Official endorsement of procedural justice made trade union recognition a foregone conclusion, compulsory arbitration encouraged workers to organize, and official support for war bonuses ensured that a union card was ever more attractive. As a consequence, union membership doubled between 1914 and 1920, and unionization reached low-paid clerical and unskilled workers.[46] Official arbitration also encouraged two contradictory trends in labor organization. On the one hand, it led to national wage bargaining and union amalgamation. Unlike Italy, which feared widespread unrest and thus negotiated at the factory level, Britain introduced national-level bargaining during the war, and this practice spread throughout the economy. On the other hand, "dilution" and labor leaders' cooperation with the government helped produce the shop stewards movement. Initially based in engineering, the struggle for job control in the workplace extended to other sectors of industry. Although only a minority of activists held radical beliefs and historians now argue that the movement's importance has been exaggerated, this new development strengthened labor organization within factories and divided labor against itself.[47]

Finally, although historians debate why the Labour Party replaced the Liberal Party after World War I, they agree that Labour emerged from war in a stronger position. The wartime experience split the Liberals and taught labor the importance of having representatives in Parliament and the potential

[44] Procacci 1989, 42; Stevenson 1990, 206; Waites 1987, 208, 323.

[45] Tanner 1990, 352–364; Wrigley 1976, 23; Wrigley 1987b, 28; Waites 1987, 132.

[46] Gospel 1987, 86; Turner 1992, 368; Wrigley 1987c, 71.

[47] Waites 1987, 213; Gospel 1987, 168–170; Whiteside 1990, 114; Wrigley 1987a, 3; Reid 1985, 57.

for statist policies. The rise in union membership also augmented the party's support, and its leaders' participation in government gave it credibility as a governing party.[48] The party's expectations were disappointed in the first postwar election in 1918, but it received more support than in prewar elections and formed the government in 1929.

POSTWAR REFORM

The immediate postwar periods in Italy and Britain were in many ways quite similar: expectations for reform were high, union membership skyrocketed, industrial unrest exploded, and most important, Italian and British labor achieved many long-sought reforms. In this sense, "payback" arguments appear right on target: Labor contributed to the war effort and was repaid afterward. However, within a few years and in both countries, most of these reforms vanished and many wartime promises went unfulfilled. These cases underline the difficulty of translating wartime power into durable postwar reform. They also illustrate how perceptions of justice can calm unrealized expectations (as in Britain), whereas perceptions of injustice can fuel alienation and undermine democratic consolidation (as in Italy).

Unleashed from wartime coercion and buoyed by massive increases in union membership, an unprecedented strike wave broke out in Italy in 1919. Fearing that resistance might provoke revolution, employers conceded to labor's demands. The metalworkers' union won an eight-hour work day, minimum wages, and paid vacations; these concessions soon spread to most of Italian industry. Labor also used its newfound power to recover the wartime drop in wages and to gain recognition of grievance committees in factories, which was a long-standing demand.[49] British labor was also in a strong position when the war ended and it also successfully pressed for better pay and improved working conditions. In 1919, for example, railroad workers achieved many of their postwar demands, including overtime pay, an eight-hour work day, and paid holidays. The engineering and shipbuilders union also negotiated a reduction in the work week to forty-eight hours, a settlement they declared "one of the greatest triumphs of British trade unionism." This practice became standard in British industry, and unemployment insurance – or the right to maintenance outside the Poor Law – was extended in 1920. Labor was also able to overcome employer opposition and hold the state to its promise to restore prewar customs for skilled workers.[50]

As similar as these outcomes appear, they are not what we think of when we consider the fate of Italian and British democracy after World War I. Explaining those divergent paths – the undermining of the fledgling Italian democracy and the deepening of the British one – is directly linked to how

---

[48] Turner 1992, 395–396; Reid 1985, 69.
[49] Horowitz 1963, 139–142; Pernicone 1974, 208; Seton-Watson 1967, 521.
[50] Quoted in Wrigley 1987c, 76–77; Horne 1991, 354.

each state mobilized its economy for war and the imprint those different strategies left on labor and postwar politics.

Within a few years of the armistice, Italian labor had lost its postwar gains and many of the prewar era as well. The state's mobilization strategy had created a radical and cohesive labor movement that had become increasingly alienated from and distrustful of the state. This revolutionary movement had gained concessions in the immediate postwar period, but the industrial conflict continued to escalate and reached a climax in 1920 with the ill-fated occupation of the metallurgic factories. The radicalization of the Italian Socialists also contributed to the collapse of government coalitions from 1918–1922. And in general, the revolutionary rhetoric and radical industrial and rural unrest sparked widespread fear among the middle and upper classes and provoked a counterrevolution. In October 1922, Mussolini marched on Rome. Within two years union membership sank to one-tenth of its 1920 peak. In an ironic twist on labor's fate, the fascist regime revived the wartime labor legislation and brought Dallolio back to implement it: Strikes were once again declared illegal, and employers' disciplinary power was greatly enhanced.[51]

The story of British reform is also a story of unrealized expectations. Many of the initial postwar gains were lost in the economic downtown in the 1920s and hopes for the nationalization of the mines and railroads were dashed. The extension of a national minimum wage, first set for munitions and agricultural workers during the war, was never implemented and educational reform was disappointing. But the most striking failure was in housing. The halt in construction and the deterioration of existing stock had produced a critical situation, which elicited promises of government reform. Yet the number of "Homes fit for Heroes" that were eventually built met neither the demand nor the expectations.[52] Excluded from government after the war ended, British labor was once again dependent on the vagaries of its market power and it lost most of its recent gains. It would take World War II and the Labour Party's electoral triumph to usher in full social citizenship for British workers.[53]

As disappointing as the post–World War I period was to British labor, the state's failure to deliver on its promises did not – in contrast to the Italian case – lead to an escalation of industrial conflict and the destruction of its parliamentary regime. Britain's reluctance to resort to coercion and its embrace of procedural justice had forestalled the growth of the radical industrial protest that bitterly polarized postwar Italian politics. When the armistice finally came, British labor remained committed to the state and to reformist goals. Labor's increased role in decision making during the war extended into postwar politics: British mobilization had strengthened labor's right to collective

---

[51] Corner and Procacci 1997, 236.
[52] Abrams 1963, 43–44; Lowe 1978, 283.
[53] Historians point to the 1921–1922 recession, conservative dominance in Parliament, Treasury's resurgence, and ideological resistance to state intervention to explain the failure of reform. Abrams 1963, Lowe 1978.

bargaining and the position of its political representatives, the Labour Party. British labor was not pleased that many of its postwar goals were unmet, but its perception of procedural justice helped prevent these negative outcomes from fueling anger at and resentment of state authority.

The same cannot be said of Italy. Excluded from almost all decision making, Italian labor did not accept the failure of postwar reform. It demonstrated the type of angry and vengeful behavior that often occurs when individuals simultaneously experience distributive and procedural injustice. Had Italy adopted a less punitive strategy, its nascent democracy might have survived. But Italy chose a coercive and unjust mobilization strategy that disastrously altered the terms of Italian political life.

It is important to note that not all was lost in the British case. Mobilization had translated into an important, if partial, step toward social citizenship. The sociologist T.H. Marshall first championed the idea that a minimum standard of welfare, regardless of an individual's market value, was one of the three sets of citizenship rights – political, civil, and social.[54] During the war, official cost-of-living indemnities fundamentally challenged the traditional basis of remuneration. For the first time, the state recognized that wages could be based on human needs and not on the value of the work done. And for the first time, official policy helped remove most workers from abject poverty. The differential between skilled and unskilled workers widened again after the slump of 1921, but the wartime improvement in the living standards of the worst off in British society survived the armistice.[55] This hardly approached a full-fledged welfare state, but it was an important step toward social citizenship. And it was coupled to a change in electoral rules that symbolized a broader conception of democratic citizenship: After 1918 – and again for the first time – the link between poverty and disenfranchisement was severed, as individuals on poor relief now remained on the voter rolls.

CONCLUSIONS

The hijacking of British labor's expectations for widespread reform and the destruction of the newly empowered Italian labor movement highlight the problems with standard explanations for why war leads to reform. All of the conditions that alternate accounts emphasize as linking war and reform were present: an unparalleled growth of state power, the exposure of chronic societal problems, and the widespread expectation (and government promises) that wartime sacrifices would be repaid with postwar reform. Indeed, to the extent that scale alone explains why war follows reform, these cases should be easy ones. Both Italy and Britain experienced unprecedented societal participation in the war effort; never before had these states asked so much from

---

[54] Marshall 1950.
[55] Spending on social services doubled from 4 percent in 1914 to 8 percent between the wars. Degroot 1996, 301–302, 330.

their citizens. Yet it was *how* the mobilization was implemented – the use of pain, payoffs, and persuasion – and not the *extent* of participation that was critical to labor's development and postwar reform.

Although there is no simple relationship between the scale of mobilization and subsequent reform, labor is more likely to benefit from mass-participation warfare than limited military engagements.[56] Labor's leverage is greatest during total wars: During World War I, Britain's unemployment was 0.7 percent. Indeed, a coda to the British case illustrates that high-threat environments can be labor's best ally. During the war, the British cabinet had planned to extend state intervention into peacetime to ensure a robust reconstruction. Policymakers assumed that Britain would be facing a powerful Germany, and they assumed that balancing German power would require an activist state. However, Germany's unexpected collapse in 1918 removed that threat and led to the reassertion of orthodox economic ideas and the return to a limited state ill-equipped to pursue widespread reform.[57]

Mass-mobilization warfare can help expand participation, but the patriotism that makes these wars possible can also be a double-edged sword. Affective ties between state and society were necessary for Britain's normative strategy, and labor was better off for being spared Italy's punitive approach. But the strength of labor's patriotism may also have kept it from taking full advantage of its wartime leverage. As the reaction to the German offensive in 1918 illustrates, British labor did not seize on the state's weakest moments to drive the best bargain. Beatrice Webb remarked that labor viewed assertive industrial action "as sordid and unpatriotic," and she worried that its leaders too readily succumbed to patriotic blackmail.[58] The immediate postwar British elections best capture this danger. Military victory had, in one historian's words, "brought a sharp recrudescence of the meanest forms of [British] working class chauvinism."[59] The Conservative party – the party most associated with the vigorous prosecution of the war but also the party most opposed to democratic reforms – reaped the benefits, as the newly enfranchised working class tended toward the Tories in 1918 and 1922. National pride trumped economic self-interest.

Focusing on affective ties between the state and society highlights an issue that is often lost in recent discussions about the difference democracy makes. David Lake argues, for example, that democracies are more likely to win their wars because consent is greatest when the public can punish a regime's rent-seeking behavior.[60] This view exaggerates the role of electoral incentives in generating consent. Italy's 1912 electoral law established virtual universal manhood suffrage; in 1914, 40 percent of British males were still

---

[56] Also see Centeno (Chapter 12) and Starr (Chapter 3), this volume.
[57] Wunderich 1939; Searle 2004, 801; Cline 1982, 158.
[58] Quoted in Tanner 1990, 361.
[59] Waites 1987, 233.
[60] Lake 1992, 24–37.

disenfranchised. Yet when World War I began, it was the British (and not the Italian) working class that rallied to the flag. Assuming that the only links between state and society are institutional obscures nationalism's critical role in generating public support. It also confuses which factors are most likely to enhance the credibility of a state's promises for a better future.[61] Whereas British labor accepted Lloyd George's assurances that the government would help restore trade union practices once the crisis passed, Italian labor distrusted its government's intentions and dismissed its claims for the future. For the Italians, only a new political order would realize their expectations. Both Italian and British labor had access to the voting booth – both could punish the regime for reneging on its promises – but only the latter identified with the state and trusted its assurances for the future.

This chapter also serves as a cautionary tale about the contribution of a robust civil society to democracy. Skocpol has alerted scholars to the role that war plays in the growth of civil society, and Kage's and Winter's essays (Chapters 5 and 6) in this volume illustrate how war can build civil societies that promote democracy.[62] Mobilization of the homefront enriches associational life, creating new forums for community involvement, connecting previously scattered individuals and groups, and heightening the perceived efficacy of civic engagement. After the war, British labor was more powerful, more connected, and more aware of the role that it could play in British democracy. But a newly vibrant civil society is not necessarily as productive of democracy as some neo-Tocquevilleans suggest. Just as the dense network of social interaction in Germany eased Hitler's rise to power,[63] the heightened political engagement in postwar Italy contributed to Mussolini's success. As in Britain, Italian mobilization generated a strong and politicized labor movement. But the intense and radical political engagement helped create the political space for a counterrevolution. The war had built another voluntary association that was decisive in Italian politics: the fascist movement. Led by veterans brought together by their war experience and their disillusionment with the liberal state, the *squadristi* (paramilitary groups) capitalized on the fear of revolution and gained support from mainstream sectors of Italian politics. Lacking strong political institutions to absorb and channel this activity, these waves of associationalism – both born of war – helped destabilize Italy's liberal regime and pave fascism's path to power.

Although this chapter explores how mobilization can broaden democratic citizenship, it suggests additional lessons that apply to democracies and non-democracies alike. The conventional wisdom suggests that military victory legitimizes the regime in power whereas defeat undermines it. Scholars find, for example, that defeated regimes are more often internally overthrown than

---

[61] Mercer 2005, 95–97.
[62] Skocpol et al. 2002.
[63] Berman 1997.

are victors.[64] However, the Italian and British cases again remind us that process is critical. It is not *whether* the state wins or loses, but *how* the war is fought. The process (or conduct during the war) was more important than the outcome (or victory or defeat in war). Italy was one of the victors of World War I, but the regime lost the battle for popular support. Italy's coercive strategy delegitimized the political order, and the Italian victory in 1918 could not resurrect the regime in labor's eyes. The majority of Italians greeted news of the armistice (and victory) with denunciations of the war and the sacrifices it entailed.[65] In contrast, Britain's wartime promotion of procedural justice – and the commitment to, and trust in, the government that it built – encouraged labor to see British victory as its triumph. Britain's mobilization strategy created bridges between state and society, and labor entered the postwar period committed to the existing political order.

In highlighting how war restructures society and sometimes deepens democracy, this chapter corrects a liberal tendency to focus on war's destructive effects. War diverts resources from social spending and often crushes civil liberties, but conservatives have long understood war's potential for reform. Bernard von Bulow warned that "history shows us that every great war is followed by a period of liberalism, since a people demand compensation for the sacrifices and effort war has entailed." An American put it more bluntly: "When the pot boils, the scum will arise." Reform does not always follow war, but our abhorrence of its destructive power should not blind us to its other effects. War really can be good for babies and young children not only because of the potential for reform, but paradoxically because of its anticipated effects. Policymakers who anticipate a link between war and reform may be reluctant to launch a war, fearing the changes it may bring. This fear of reform may also push policymakers to the peace table. In 1917 Lord Lansdowne urged London to negotiate with Germany. He worried that continuing the war might unleash democratizing forces (or, in his words, "spell ruin for the civilized order"), and he hoped that a peace settlement would short-circuit this process.[66] The cabinet rejected his proposal, but if this fear is common, the anticipated but unintended consequences of war may decrease both the likelihood of war and its duration.

---

[64] Bueno de Mesquita et al. 1992.
[65] Corner and Procacci 1997, 224.
[66] Quoted in Kaiser 1983, 456; quoted in Mann 1993, 152; Turner 1992, 129.

8

Spinning Mars

Democracy in Britain and the United States and the Economic Lessons of War

Mark R. Wilson

The largest wars of the modern era, which involved huge mobilizations of entire national economies as well as manpower, are often understood as having promoted social solidarity and a broader role for the state in guaranteeing welfare and economic equality. This view flourished in Britain in the 1950s, when social scientists, including Richard Titmuss and T. H. Marshall, suggested that the experience of all-out war promoted a sense of social interdependence that encouraged the expansion of citizenship and the welfare state. Although this understanding of the political consequences of war may no longer seem as compelling as it was a half-century ago, much of it is still accepted by historians of modern Europe.[1] Although more recent wars do not seem to have done as much to promote social democracy, this would not have surprised Titmuss and Marshall, since these have been more limited conflicts. We need to be careful, however, about assuming a direct relationship between the intensity of mobilization and the depth of social-democratic reform. To understand why, we need look no further than an important comparative case: Britain and the United States during and after World War II.

While mobilization for all-out war seems to have served as a catalyst for major social-democratic reforms in Britain and elsewhere, it did not have this effect in America. In the months and years after World War II, the United States saw little of the extension of universal social welfare provisions and the nationalization of large pieces of the economy that occurred across the Atlantic. After a stunning victory in the July 1945 elections, a new Labour government in Britain presided over the creation of a national health system, the expansion of unemployment insurance, and the nationalization of several large industries, including coal, rail transport, and steel. By 1949 about a fifth of the British economy was publicly owned. In the United States, little of

For their generous encouragement and many helpful suggestions, I thank Beth Kier and Ron Krebs, my fellow contributors to this volume, Paul Hanebrink, Peter Thorsheim, and two anonymous reviewers for Cambridge University Press.

[1] Jefferys 1987, 123; Lowe 1990, 155; Leff, 1991, 1316; Mazower 1999, 185–208, 298–300.

this occurred. In the 1946 midterm elections, Republicans retook control of Congress after demanding the quick end of remaining wartime controls and the creation of a postwar economy based on "free enterprise." (Important social benefits were extended to veterans via the G.I. Bill, but not to the population at large.) One should not overstate the contrast between British and American styles of postwar political economy, both of which by the early 1950s were characterized by a fiscal Keynesianism and unprecedented levels of peacetime taxes and government expenditures.[2] Nevertheless, there was in the years after World War II – and there remains – an important difference between domestic economic policies that champion public enterprise and other direct controls and those that eschew them. For anyone interested in past or present struggles over political economy and social-democratic reform, the contrasting record of American and British developments in the 1940s should remain of great interest.

Despite the subject's significance, the comparative literature on British and American war mobilization and economic policy remains thin and misleading. Even the best recent literature, including studies of rationing and price control and military-industrial relations, provides little comparative context.[3] Much of the comparative literature that does exist focuses on the development of Keynesian economic policy in the two countries.[4] Unfortunately, this literature, so impressive in certain ways, is weakened by a marked ignorance or misunderstanding of the efforts of the British and American states to reorganize industry for war production. Given that these were among the largest state-coordinated economic undertakings in all history, this is astonishing. To the extent that they consider the massive industrial mobilizations at all, these studies claim that there were significant differences in the level of central state control over war mobilization and that these differences help explain the contrasts in postwar political economy. "In the United States," Edwin Amenta and Theda Skocpol argue, "the weakness of most federal controls over the wartime economy made it likely that controls would not be converted into postwar reforms." Britain had "a command economy" during World War II, maintains Anthony Badger, while the United States used more voluntaristic methods. Most comparative studies, in other words, understand the differences in post-1945 economic policy to have been anticipated in the patterns of wartime mobilization, which themselves reflected long-standing differences in the two nations' political cultures and patterns of state formation.[5]

This chapter begins with an original comparative survey of the British and American industrial mobilizations for World War II, and it challenges the common assumption that Britain employed a more centralized, statist variety

[2] Tomlinson 1993; Katznelson and Pietrykowski 1991; Hooks 1991; Sparrow 2008.
[3] Zweiniger-Bargielowska 2000; Jacobs 2005; Koistinen 2004; Edgerton 2006.
[4] For example, Furner and Supple 1990.
[5] Amenta and Skocpol 1988; Badger 1997, 304. For one brief comparative account that is more compatible with the one presented in this chapter, see Leff 1991, 1314–1317.

of wartime economic management. In fact, the patterns of wartime economic mobilization in the two allies were quite similar overall; while British practices were more centralized and coercive in some areas, in other fields Americans used less voluntaristic, more bureaucratic methods of management. The greatest difference in the two national styles of industrial mobilization is not to be found in the level of centralization or voluntarism, but rather in the locus of formal state authority. Whereas Britain placed most significant powers over economic mobilization in the hands of new civilian-led ministries, in the United States much authority remained on the military side of the national state.

These comparative findings, which present the American wartime state as no less interventionist but more militarized than its British counterpart, enrich our understanding of the divergence of domestic economic policies in the postwar period. By 1945 many voters and policymakers in Britain accepted the Labour Party's claim that the war mobilization had shown that the state could be a competent economic manager. In the United States, by contrast, the 1946 midterm congressional elections suggested that business conservatives and Republican politicians, who defined any wartime increases in state capacity as temporary evils, had won the struggle over the economic lessons of the war.

These contrasting developments were shaped by the interaction between patterns of wartime mobilization, which were more militarized in the United States, and significant differences in the strength of the conservative opposition to social-democratic reform, which was far better organized and intense in the United States. Already energized by what they regarded as the excesses of the New Deal, American conservatives worked aggressively – through massive public relations campaigns, as well as in Congress and executive agencies – to prevent the war mobilization from fostering a permanent expansion of state intervention in the economy. The pattern of wartime economic mobilization strengthened their efforts in two important ways. First, the emergence in wartime of relatively large and powerful national bureaucracies helped to re-energize American conservatives and lend credence to their warnings in a way that a more decentralized, voluntaristic mobilization – which much of the comparative literature has mistakenly assumed to have taken place – would not have done. Second, the relatively militarized organization of American mobilization authority boosted the conservatives' cause. Military control over fundamental wartime economic tasks such as contracting made a difference, and not simply because military officers, military priorities, and military cultures were natural allies of corporate leaders and conservative politicians, as several historians have suggested.[6] The relatively high degree of military control also assisted conservatives by insulating the economic mobilization from democratic politics and by creating structures of public authority that, however massive and successful, were easy to dismiss as emergency expedients

[6] Waddell 2001; Koistinen 2004.

that should not extend beyond wartime. The relatively militarized American mobilization obscured the wartime achievements of public enterprise and made it more difficult for voters and prospective economic policymakers, even those on the political left, to envision models of state management in peacetime that did not entail unacceptable levels of coercion.

Although this chapter concentrates on just two nations during an extraordinarily large war that occurred over six decades ago, it also speaks to more general concerns. Perhaps most obviously, we continue to be interested in the origins of the marked divergence in British and American political economy and in the depth of the two nations' citizenship in the wake of World War II because it endured for decades afterward. This chapter, by showing that postwar economic policy was affected less by rational evaluations of the actual practice and results of war-fighting than by the outcomes of highly ideological discursive struggles over the war's lessons, suggests why it is so difficult to offer purely structural explanations of war's political effects. More broadly, this chapter speaks to the relationship between war and democracy, albeit in a way that requires a more expansive definition of democracy than one that focuses on elections and constitutions. The empowerment of common people and the responsiveness of government to popular concerns depend on how the state is organized and how economic resources are distributed. The quality of democracy is affected profoundly by, not isolated from, developments in the nation's political economy.

To draw meaningful lessons about war and democracy, we need to investigate the relationships among mobilization, domestic economic policy, and social citizenship. This chapter suggests that these relationships often cannot be explained adequately by considering macrolevel factors such as regime type or conflict intensity. More fruitful, at least in many cases, are approaches that consider the interaction between the development of material structures of social power and ongoing struggles over hegemonic language and ideas. The relatively militarized crystallization of state capacity in the United States seems to have been an important factor in national political development not only on its own, but because of the way it interacted during wartime with a conservative ideological offensive that was already underway on the eve of war. This interaction made an important contribution to a postwar political order in the United States that was much less committed than its British counterpart to public enterprise, social citizenship, and economic equality.

ANGLO-AMERICAN INDUSTRIAL MOBILIZATION DURING WORLD WAR II: A RECONSIDERATION

While British and American efforts to manage their national economies during World War II were hardly identical, the organization and reach of state control in the two countries were less different from what previous studies have suggested. While there were some areas of the war economy in which the British state adopted heavier, more centralized, or more direct controls than its American counterpart, this was hardly the universal rule. More striking and consistent, and more rarely noted, was that the United States concentrated far more of its mobilization authority in its military establishment.

In the fields of civilian labor and consumption, contemporary observers were struck by the depth of the British mobilization compared to its American counterpart, including the wider use of rationing, higher taxes, and the drafting of women into military or industrial service.[7] But fewer remember that there were also areas in which British practice was more voluntaristic and flexible. The British state, through the Ministry of Labour, had fuller powers over industrial manpower, including authority to prevent workers from leaving jobs and to prevent employers from hiring or firing without approval. But in practice, the Minister of Labour, Ernest Bevin (a prominent trade union official and Labour Party leader), avoided coercive approaches to the regulation of manpower.[8] Britain never attempted to cap wages, whereas the United States adopted a general wage freeze in mid-1942.[9] The British Food Ministry and Board of Trade controlled the prices of many goods and went further than the Americans in coordinating food production, rationing, and price control. But contemporary observers understood that the British approach to price control was more selective than the American "overall" approach.[10] By 1944 the Office of Price Administration (OPA) in the United States was setting 8 million individual prices in addition to controlling rents in 14 million dwellings.[11] In the critical areas of wage and price control, it was the United States, not Britain, that practiced more bureaucratic, rigid management of the war economy.

On the military side of the economy, British price and profit control seems to have cut deeper, but this was not because the British state developed a larger bureaucratic apparatus. If anything, the opposite was true. Both nations raised huge amounts of revenue from high excess-profit taxes on businesses, which reached rates of 100 percent in Britain and 95 percent in the United States; after credits for postwar refunds, the effective maximum rate in both nations was closer to 80 percent.[12] Overall, tax rates and rules kept the profits of British companies somewhat lower. So did the different expectations of British procurement authorities, which tried to set contract prices at levels that would allow an annual return to private capital of no more than 15 percent, while their American counterparts aimed at allowing roughly 10 percent profit on sales. In many industries, this meant that the standard profit allowance for

---

[7] Eldridge Haynes, "Report on Britain: War Production, Employment, and Future Prospects," *Harper's Magazine* 185 (October 1942): 509–517; Malcolm Muir, "Report on Britain: A Story of Grit and Production," *Newsweek* (December 28, 1942): 35–43.

[8] Middlemas 1979, 276–280; Howlett 1994, 24.

[9] "Wages and the War," London *Times* (August 4, 1942): 5.

[10] "American Survey: Wages Policy," *Economist* 143 (July 25, 1942): 106–107; "American Survey: Policing the Price Level," *Economist* 143 (August 15, 1942): 203–204; Keezer 1943.

[11] Brandis 1943, 130–132; Mills and Rockoff 1987; Bartels 1983; Jacobs 1997.

[12] Brandis 1943, 77; Murphy 1943, 74–75, 221; Thorndike 2005.

American contractors was double or triple that used in Britain.[13] However, despite this difference, American businessmen could credibly claim that they felt a much heavier state hand over wartime profits – in the form of the statutory renegotiation of prices on past and existing contracts, which affected several thousand prime contractors and subcontractors and cut corporate wartime profits by about a third.[14]

The renegotiation of contract prices was one of many fields in which the American wartime state operated through military, as opposed to civilian, organizations. Here, in the formal organization of the industrial mobilization effort, there was a significant difference between the two nations. While both Britain and the United States built relatively decentralized procurement systems, the Americans relied more heavily on military agencies. This reproduced arrangements that had prevailed during World War I, when Britain's giant civilian-controlled Ministry of Munitions created a vast network of government-owned, government-operated (GOGO) plants and government-owned, contractor-operated (GOCO) plants. This represented a significantly heavier state management of industrial mobilization than the much more limited coordinated activities carried out in the United States by the General Munitions Board and War Industries Board, which in many areas played second fiddle to the War and Navy Departments.[15] Although the Ministry of Munitions, disliked by the British military establishment, was eliminated in 1921, calls for its revival became louder in the mid-1930s, as public concerns about arms profiteering and militarism rose across the world.[16] Finally, in 1939, Britain established a Ministry of Supply (MoS), which re-established formal civilian authority over army procurement.

During World War II, many of these peacetime patterns continued, albeit in new forms. In both nations, procurement authority was divided among three major organizations, each of which handled one major field of war production: aircraft, ships, and army ordnance and equipment. In Britain, the MoS, the old Admiralty, and a new Ministry of Aircraft Production (MAP, established in 1940) controlled these areas. Starting in early 1942, the operations of these three major entities were coordinated, with a rather light hand, by a new Ministry of Production. This last body was created specifically to provide the British with a counterpart to the American War Production Board (WPB), which had been created a few weeks before.[17] Like its British counterpart, the WPB had little direct authority over procurement. In the United States, most of the important interfacing with industry – including the negotiation of contracts, specifications, troubleshooting, etc., – was done by

---

[13] Ashworth 1953, 87–90, 151–156; Tomlinson 1994, 141–142; Smith 1959, 296–298. This contrast in methods and margins continued well into the Cold War: see Fisher and Hall 1968.

[14] Smith 1959, 389; Wilson 2010.

[15] Hornby 1958, 3–7, 10, 26, 80–81; Wrigley 1982a; Cuff 1973; Gough 1997.

[16] Gordon 1988; Scott 1962, 241–256; Hornby 1958, 88; Anderson 1994.

[17] Postan 1952, 249–253.

military organizations. The Army Air Forces (AAF), then still part of the army establishment, directed aircraft procurement, and the Navy, in conjunction with Undersecretary of the Navy James Forrestal, handled its own procurement. Army procurement came to be coordinated in the Pentagon by a new Army Service Forces (ASF), but was largely handled by the existing technical services (such as Ordnance, Quartermaster, and Signal Corps), which divided procurement authority among regional districts.

Overall, while there were few differences in the concentration of formal authority over industrial mobilization between Britain and the United States, there was a clear contrast in the location of that authority: In Britain, it was housed in ministries led and staffed by civilians. What difference did this make, if any? To be sure, there is good reason to be wary of exaggerating the political consequences. In Britain, the MoS and MAP worked closely with the War Office and Air Ministry, which had formerly handled their functions; many of the same personnel supervised the industrial mobilization before and after the creation of the new ministries.[18] In the United States, when several leading Democrats in Congress called in the autumn of 1942 for a single civilian agency to take over all procurement and industrial mobilization functions, they said little about the potential political consequences of such a reform. Instead, they mostly argued that the reorganization of industrial mobilization authority was necessary to boost economic coordination and efficiency.[19]

But even if the difference between formal civilian and military control over procurement was limited in practice by informal authority, and even if its political consequences were seldom discussed in the 1940s (or since), the contrast is still important. By locating formal authority over industrial mobilization in civilian ministries, Britain connected the war economy more directly to party politics and democratic governance. The most obvious manifestation of this was the installation of Labour-left politicians in key mobilization posts. The wartime Labour Minister, Ernest Bevin, and the head of the Ministry of Aircraft Production for the second half of the war, Stafford Cripps, were prominent politicians on the left, who used their posts to promote new benefits for workers and more Labour participation in joint production boards in war factories.[20] Cripps, the vegetarian, teetotaling socialist who addressed workers as "comrades" in his speeches at war plants, had no counterpart in the American mobilization system. This was not simply because American business leaders succeeded in dominating the war economy by forging a conservative alliance with the military to oppose organized labor and New Deal liberals, as many historians have argued.[21] In fact, there were plenty of conservative businessmen at the top of the British mobilization system as well, including Lord

[18] Ibid., 272–274; Edgerton 2006; Scott and Hughes 1955, 294, 321.
[19] C. P. Trussell, "Congress Leaders Ask One-Man Rule of the Home Front," *New York Times* (November 16, 1942): 1; "Unified Control," *New York Times* (November 16, 1942): 18; Hooks 1991, 143–145.
[20] Tomlinson 1994, 143–144.
[21] Koistinen 2004; Waddell 2001.

Beaverbrook (a predecessor of Cripps at the MAP), Minister of Production Oliver Lyttleton, and, Minister of Supply Andrew Duncan. In Britain, however, the existence of civilian supply ministries directed by leading politicians made for a war economy that was more public and more politicized and thus – by most measures – more democratic. In the United States, where procurement authority remained in the military organizations (where it had rested for decades), the industrial mobilization effort was more thoroughly dominated by experts and professionals, including career military officers, business leaders, Wall Street bankers, lawyers, and accountants. While it is customary to characterize the American mobilization as dominated by business interests, it is equally correct to understand it as relatively professionalized and bureaucratic – and here again, contrary to common assumptions, more statist by many measures than its British counterpart.

While they differed in their distribution of formal authority over procurement, the two nations took very similar paths during the war years when it came to the balance of public and private enterprise. While their approaches differed somewhat from sector to sector, both nations built vast mixed military economies, in which not only massive public financing schemes but also large-scale government-owned and government-operated manufacturing enterprises complemented private sources of production. While the two nations' domestic economic policies would diverge significantly after 1945, during the war years both were dedicated to a mixed economy full of public ownership, regulation, and public-private partnerships.

Both the United States and Britain used massive amounts of public financing and public ownership of new war plants, both relied on the management of private enterprise in the massively expanded aircraft industry, and each used many GOGO and GOCO facilities as well purely private plants. During the interwar period, both nations flirted with creating substantial GOGO manufacturing capacities for aircraft, but both abandoned them after stiff opposition from private industry and some resistance from within the military establishment.[22] During (and immediately before) World War II, both nations spent huge sums on the building and equipping of new aircraft industry facilities.[23] Some of these plants remained government owned, but private firms operated nearly all of them.[24] Although the MAP nationalized two important suppliers in 1943, such actions were exceptional.[25] And they were not without parallels in the United States, where the Army and Navy temporarily seized some sixty private plants during the war.[26]

Outside the aircraft industry, both nations maintained major GOGO plants, but curiously they were overwhelmingly on the Army side in Britain

[22] Edgerton 1984, 247–279; Trimble 1986; Vander Meulen 1991.
[23] Ashworth 1953, 250; Holley 1964, 324.
[24] Hornby 1958, 383.
[25] Morgan 1987; Francis 1997, 70–71; Howlett 1995; Edgerton 1984, 259–271.
[26] Ohly 1999, 3, 313–320.

and on the Navy side in the United States. In both nations, the production of small arms and ammunition had long been handled by state armories and arsenals, supplemented in times of war by contractors. During World War II, as in World War I, a large proportion of British guns, small arms, powder, artillery ammunition, and small arms ammunition was made in state plants. By the early 1940s, the MoS was running 43 Royal Ordnance Factories with a total of some 300,000 employees, about 20 percent of all the people employed on all MoS orders.[27] From 1936 to 1945, the War Office and MoS spent £216.6 million on GOGO plants, nearly as much as the £339.6 million it invested in GOCO facilities and expansions to private plants.[28] In the United States, there was a relatively lower proportion of government-operated ordnance plants, but, as in Britain, government ownership of explosives and ammunition facilities was the rule.[29]

In contrast, the American state was far more directly involved in industrial production for the Navy. By the time of World War II, the Royal Dockyards, which in the nineteenth century had been building half of British warships, concentrated on refitting and repair.[30] The modest state-managed operations in naval shipbuilding in Britain paled in comparison to their counterpart in the United States, which – it is often forgotten – had never turned away from a mixed economy.[31] By any measure, the Navy's GOGO facilities made a huge contribution to the World War II fleet, even if one recognizes that contractors built many of the components in finished ships. By 1943 the U.S. navy yards employed 350,000 workers,[32] ten times as many as in the Royal Dockyards. This represented about a third of all American workers making warships.[33] As Aaron Friedberg has noted, the GOGO yards were an especially important source of larger ships and submarines.[34] While U.S. Navy yards built just 54 of 297 (18 percent) destroyers delivered to the Navy in 1940–1945,[35] they also built 7 of 10 (70 percent) new American battleships, 10 of 24 (42 percent) Essex-class aircraft carriers, and 98 of 226 (43 percent) new submarines.[36]

In sum, historians and social scientists have generally exaggerated the differences between the British and American styles of economic management during World War II. The wartime American state was not much more devoted, overall, to decentralized and voluntaristic methods, nor much less interventionist and far reaching in its dealings with private industry. One manifestation of this was the enormous amount of government-owned war

[27] Postan 1952, 424; Hornby 1958, 90.
[28] Ashworth 1953, 252.
[29] Smith 1959, 499–501; Thompson and Mayo 1960, 105.
[30] Hornby 1958, 9, 64–66; Postan 1952, 424; Ashworth 1953, 249.
[31] Weir 1993, 2–3; Friedberg 2000, 253.
[32] Friedberg 2000, 255.
[33] Davidson 1996, 56–61; Friedberg 2000, 255.
[34] Friedberg 2000, 255.
[35] Sparrow 1996, 221.
[36] Calculated from Silverstone 1965 and Silverstone 1987.

plants across the American landscape at war's end. Of the $27 billion invested in industrial facilities in the United States during World War II, the American state accounted directly for over two-thirds, or $18.5 billion, compared to about $4 billion in Britain. In 1945 the U.S. government owned a quarter of all manufacturing assets in the country.[37] The question of how to dispose of this massive quantity of public capital was part of a broader political dilemma: How would the all-out wartime economic mobilization influence postwar domestic policy? This question figured heavily in wartime and post-war politics in both the United States and Britain.

LEARNING DIFFERENT LESSONS FROM THE SAME WAR

The remarkable similarity in the British and American styles of industrial mobilization makes the divergence in the two nations' postwar economic policies all the more interesting, not least because it is difficult to attribute the difference to fundamental differences in state capacities, styles of political economy, and political cultures. How then was it possible that in Britain World War II seemed to serve as the midwife of social democracy, while in the United States, according to one historian, it "turned out to be the gravedigger of domestic economic and social reform"?[38]

Some might say that the explanation is obvious: Britain's Labour Party was far more committed to a social-democratic political economy than the regionally and ideologically divided Democratic party in the United States,[39] and when Labour won in 1945, it carried out many of its long-standing promises. This fact is important, especially insofar as it helps to explain why so little was done after Roosevelt's first term to expand the New Deal. But the existence of the Labour Party does not explain its victory in 1945, nor, more specifically, anything about how British and American voters and policymakers saw the lessons of World War II. These developments are better understood by comparing the fate of competing political discourses on both sides of the Atlantic: one insisting that the management of the war economy provided an important model for peacetime, and one that drew the opposite conclusion.

"Undoubtedly," one historian has written of Britain in the 1940s, "the political legitimacy of government intervention in the economy and in industry was enhanced by the perceived success of wartime intervention."[40] Such conclusions seem more than reasonable, given that the Labour Party's campaign leading up to its July 1945 electoral victory emphasized this interpretation. Its campaign manifesto, entitled *Let Us Face the Future*, called for the continuation of the egalitarian political economy of "fair shares" that wartime rationing and price and profit controls had created, and insisted that

---

[37] Ashworth 1953, 253; Sweeting 1994, 2, 247.
[38] Fraser 1991, 453.
[39] Katznelson, Geiger, and Kryder 1993.
[40] Morgan 1984, 23–24.

those controls must continue in order to avoid postwar economic chaos. Using the word "planning" repeatedly, the Labour platform also made it clear that the party was committed to the nationalization of several large pieces of the economy.[41] One of the important lessons of the war, Labour Party leaders told the British public, was that state control worked. "Labour does not believe in leaving our economy to chance," Bevin announced on the eve of the election. "During the war we have witnessed great developments, many of which can be turned to the advantage of the community in times of peace." Meanwhile, Cripps boasted of the "remarkable success" of wartime planning, organization, and controls.[42]

Britons closer to the political center expressed similar sentiments. From the beginning of the war, Labour promoted the idea that the war experience had proven the necessity of national planning and nationalization; if anything, the war moderated the ideas of Labour leaders, several of whom emerged from the war more amenable to indirect regulation of industry.[43] Meanwhile, the center of gravity of British public opinion moved closer to Labour's interpretation. By early 1942 Lyttleton, a Conservative, declared that in the future Britain should expand state planning, as well as competitive private enterprise.[44] By late 1944 the *Economist*, normally a champion of free markets, celebrated the success of state-led organization for war, arguing that "it will no longer be possible to argue that the British state is an incompetent instrument of social engineering."[45]

When Conservative politicians rejected this interpretation of the war's economic lessons, they met with widespread public criticism, followed by defeat at the polls. Like their counterparts in the United States, British conservatives sought to frame the war as a victory for free-market capitalism, which had proved itself superior to statist, totalitarian methods. Throughout the short campaign, Lord Beaverbrook, the former MAP chief and a close ally of Prime Minister Churchill, used his *Daily Express* newspaper to portray the Labour Party as the enemy of economic and political freedom. So did the Federation of British Industries (FBI), a leading business association, which equated economic controls with fascism and warned against a future of "doctrinaire socialism and bureaucratic control." In May 1945 Lord McGowan, the chairman of Imperial Chemical Industries (ICI) – a giant war contractor that was the counterpart to Du Pont in the United States – defended "free enterprise" as critical to the wartime achievements of his company and the British war effort, while warning against the expansion of "bureaucratic control." Days later, on June 4, Churchill gave his infamous "Gestapo" speech, in which

[41] Tomlinson 1994, 162; Brooke 1992, 314–315.
[42] Brooke 1992, 324–325; Taylor 1991, 22–23; Bryant 1997, 334–352; Clarke 2002, 376–385; Bullock 1967, 370.
[43] Taylor 1991, 8; Johnman 1991, 31; Brooke 1992, 231, 244; Mercer 1991, 75.
[44] "Shaping the Future," London *Times* (April 28, 1942): 5.
[45] "Lessons of Five Years," *Economist* 147 (December 9, 1944): 763–764.

he suggested that a Labour victory and subsequent imposition of a socialist economy would lead to a Nazi-like police state in Britain.[46]

In short, political rhetoric in wartime Britain, especially on the eve of the 1945 general elections, reflected the two leading parties' starkly different understandings of the economic lessons of the war mobilization and how to apply those lessons. Those who paid even the least attention to the campaign were well aware of the parties' divergent approaches to domestic economic policy. Especially in comparison to contemporary developments in the United States, Labour's victory in 1945 stands as a significant triumph for a vision of postwar political economy that promised to build on steps that had been taken in wartime.

In the United States, the struggle over postwar political economy had a very different result. By American standards, the sort of opposition of economic freedom and totalitarianism articulated in Churchill's "Gestapo" speech, which surprised and alienated much of the British public in June 1945, was familiar stuff. Unlike Britain, which had a wartime coalition government (and a decade without a general election), party competition and partisan electioneering continued in wartime America. Campaign rhetoric attacking bureaucracy and linking planning and public enterprise with totalitarianism may have been most successful in 1946, but, having been wielded widely by Republicans and conservative Democrats for much of the past decade, it was hardly new to the public. Furthermore, to a much greater extent than in Britain, American business associations and leaders had flooded the wartime media with "free-enterprise" rhetoric, which insisted that the war was being fought above all for economic liberty.

American labor leaders and progressive economists, like their counterparts in Britain, sought to turn the war emergency into an agent of reform. Among the most important manifestations of this were the so-called Reuther Plan and the reports of a federal government agency called the National Resources Planning Board (NRPB). Much discussed during the "defense period" of 1940–1941, the Reuther Plan – named for its creator, Walter Reuther, a leader of the United Automobile Workers (UAW) – called for organized labor to participate fully alongside business and government in the conversion of much of the auto industry to aircraft production. Meanwhile, the NRPB called in 1942–1943 for the creation of a postwar political economy that would provide the American people with an "economic bill of rights" – full employment, national health insurance, and other measures – similar to the social welfare benefits that the Beveridge Report promised in Britain.[47]

As the war went on, and as organized labor and other voices on the left continued to use the NRPB reports as models for a full-employment postwar

[46] Calder 1969, 574–578; Kandiah 1995; Johnman 1991, 42; "Company Meeting: Imperial Chemical Industries," London *Times* (May 25, 1945): 8; Herbert L. Matthews, "Eden Holds Up U.S. as Business Ideal," *New York Times* (June 28, 1945): 9.
[47] Fraser 1991, 506–508; Brinkley 1995; Lichtenstein 1995, 163–164.

economy, they did not overlook the implications of the huge stock of government-owned war plants. The NRPB itself had suggested that some of these
be managed after the war by "mixed corporations," in which the government would maintain a large stake in some industries it had built up during
the war.[48] Labor leaders were even more interested in the fate of government
plants. Reuther, for instance, promoted a reconversion plan in which the "vast
industrial empire of government-owned war plants," including the mam-
moth Ford-managed Willow Run bomber factory, would become part of a
giant new public works agency modeled on the New Deal's Tennessee Valley
Authority (TVA).[49] The challenge of reconversion "cannot be solved by hymns
to Free Enterprise or by efforts to turn back the clock to the halcyon days of
Harding," Reuther insisted just after V-J Day. Instead, the nation needed to
pursue "full production, full employment, and full distribution in a society
which has achieved economic democracy within the framework of political
democracy."[50] Other American labor leaders and New Deal liberals endorsed
Reuther's vision of a mixed, egalitarian postwar political economy.[51]

Although much in these proposals closely corresponded to Labour's
approach in Britain, all in all the Americans were less committed to state control. This was evident in the April 1945 "Charter for Labor and Management,"
agreed to by the American Federation of Labor (AFL), Congress of Industrial
Organizations (CIO), and U.S. Chamber of Commerce, which called for a full
employment postwar economy with a minimum of direct government controls.
Nationalization, the charter said explicitly, was to be avoided.[52] While one
source of this contrast between American and British labor was the oft-cited
historical weakness of socialism's appeal in American national politics, the
recent management of mobilization for World War II contributed as well.
American workers, more than their British counterparts, experienced the wartime state as an inflexible bureaucracy that froze their wages. Dissatisfaction
with the wage freeze administered by the National War Labor Board was
manifested most dramatically in the 1943 coal strikes led by John L. Lewis,
but it also contributed to a rash of wildcat strikes all over the country.[53] And
starting well before Pearl Harbor, the American state often used or threatened
to use the Army and Navy to intervene in labor-management conflicts. More
than their British counterparts, who were represented at the highest levels of
government by a Minister of Labour (Bevin) who refused to freeze wages,
American workers and their leaders faced a more militarized wartime state
with few officials drawn from the ranks of labor or the political left. The

[48] "Post-War Program," *New York Times* (March 11, 1943): 1, 12.
[49] "35,000,000 Jobless at War's End Seen," *New York Times* (September 23, 1943): 25;
Lichtenstein 1995, 222.
[50] "Reuther Challenges 'Our Fear of Abundance'," *New York Times* (September 16, 1945): SM5,
SM32–SM35.
[51] Lichtenstein 1989; Kersten 2006, 189–222.
[52] Fraser 1991, 563; Wall 2008, 130.
[53] Lichtenstein 1982; Zieger 1995, 169–170; Lichtenstein 1995, 226; Fraser 1991, 460–467.

British mobilization effort promoted public sympathy for state intervention, while the American effort eroded it.

Clearly, the very different relationships between labor and the state were an important factor in the divergent developments in America and Britain.[54] It is also easy to see how the existence of well-funded business public relations efforts in America may have made a difference. What was less obvious at the time, and remains obscure today, is how the more militarized structure of the industrial mobilization in America contributed to these differences in postwar political economy. The locus of state authority, which was a function of long-run institutional developments as well as wartime choices, affected public perceptions of the purposes and implications of the war effort. In the United States, the relatively militarized nature of wartime public enterprise may well have reinforced the idea, much favored by business conservatives, that any wartime expansion of the state must be understood as an emergency measure that – like the armies in the field – should be demobilized as quickly as possible at war's end. More obviously, the American military establishment was relatively free of the sort of progressive New Dealers who continued to populate other government departments and agencies. Although historians have overstated the conservatism of military authorities, there is no doubt that in the United States in the early 1940s, the civilian side of the state was more sympathetic to progressive political economy.[55] The long-run institutional trajectory that promoted military control of procurement, and not just short-run political choices, lessened the chances that the war mobilization would lead to a greatly expanded peacetime role for state enterprise.

The structure of wartime mobilization authority in the United States helped American conservatives set the terms of public discourse about economic policy – something they did with remarkable success. This was evident by the last months of the war, when a British observer was struck by the ubiquitous references, even among the most left-leaning American politicians and labor leaders, to the slogan "free enterprise."[56] While historians of the American business community's efforts to promote "free enterprise" have tended to focus on the early years of the Cold War, this campaign, which began in the 1930s as a reaction to the New Deal and the rise of industrial unionism,[57] became remarkably energetic during World War II. Indeed, business leaders and associations worked deliberately – and spent lavishly – to frame the war as a contest between totalitarianism and economic liberty. The lesson of an Allied victory, they insisted, would be a demonstration of the superiority of private enterprise over rigid governmental control. Although this interpretation fit

[54] Leff 1991, 1313–1317.

[55] Hooks 1991; Waddell 2001; Koistinen 2004.

[56] "Production Vital, Wallace Asserts," *New York Times* (March 18, 1944): 14; "American Survey: Free Enterprise," *Economist* 148 (March 31, 1945): 413–414; Fraser 1991, 509.

[57] Wall 2008, 48–62; Phillips-Fein 2009.

poorly with the realities of the industrial mobilization, it was nonetheless surprisingly successful in influencing American public discourse.

Before Pearl Harbor, important parts of the American business community launched a major effort to defend "free enterprise." One of the most important broadcasters of this message was the War Advertising Council (WAC), which had its origins in a large November 1941 business conference sponsored by the advertising industry. Conference organizers described the event as an effort to combat "those who would do away with the American system of free enterprise," something that had become an urgent necessity given the new global struggle of totalitarianism versus liberty. Weeks later, in early 1942, the WAC was born. By the end of the war, assisted by donations of advertising space and a favorable Treasury Department ruling that allowed companies large tax deductions for advertising expenditures, WAC had coordinated a series of pro-business public service campaigns that together were worth about 1 billion dollars.[58] Inside and outside the WAC campaign, this government-subsidized flood of business ads celebrated the achievements of American industry and free markets, which were credited with winning the war against a Nazi state that depended on social and economic controls. In a deliberate twist on President Franklin Roosevelt's rhetoric, American conservatives promoted the concept of a "fifth freedom" – business enterprise.[59]

As the wartime history of the WAC suggests, the pro-business lobby in the United States had large sums of money at its disposal, which allowed for a flood of print advertisements, radio programs, films, and the like. The tax rules on business advertising, mentioned above, meant that the U.S. government subsidized roughly three-quarters of the advertising outlays of many companies. No wonder, then, that expenditures on public relations ads seem to have jumped by a factor of seventeen between 1939 and 1943.[60] Meanwhile, there were a variety of other well-funded pro-business public relations efforts outside the WAC that spread the message that the war was being won by free enterprise. One of the best known of these was the campaign waged by the National Association of Manufacturers (NAM), a leading national business group, via its National Industrial Information Committee, which had annual budgets during the war years of about $1.5 million.[61] Its efforts were complemented by a variety of other groups, such as the American Economic Foundation, which was also funded by contributions from major American industrial corporations.[62] In Detroit, the automobile industry waged its own vigorous campaign, through the public relations department of the Automotive Council on War Production

[58] Griffith 1983, 390–391; Leff 1991, 1309–1310.
[59] Harris 1982; Griffith 1989; Fones-Wolf 1994, 26–28; Marchand 1998, 319–356.
[60] Marchand 1998, 320; Leff 1991, 1312.
[61] Workman 1998, 288–291; Fones-Wolf 1994; Henthorn 2006; Wall 2008, 128–129.
[62] George F. Dickie to J. Howard Pew, December 2, 1941, folder 1941, box 211, J. Howard Pew Personal Papers, accession 1634, Hagley Museum & Library.

(ACWP). Because the auto industry's war orders ran into the tens of billions of dollars, the dues the ACWP charged its members, an apparently modest 0.008 percent of net sales of war articles, added up to hundreds of thousands of dollars a year.[63]

Although we do not know enough about the resources available to various parties to offer precise figures, it seems clear that American free-enterprisers' financial resources exceeded those of their opponents, as well as their British counterparts. Organized labor in the United States, which enjoyed tremendous growth in union membership during the war, mounted vigorous political and public relations efforts of its own. But it seems to have been less successful than business in raising extra funds for this purpose. For example, the CIO's much celebrated political action committee, which helped the Democratic party in the 1944 elections, managed to get only 5 percent of the CIO's 4 million members to donate the one dollar it asked from them.[64] In Britain, there was simply less money to go around, and tax policy seems to have been less generous to private advertisers. There, the national government retained more direct control over communications, allowing private business interests to have less influence over wartime discourse. This pattern would continue into the postwar period.[65]

The American free-enterprise campaign was also taken up enthusiastically by the Republican party, which competed vigorously throughout the war to take control of Congress and the White House. This intense party competition contrasted with the situation in Britain, where the formation of a wartime coalition government muted open conflict. Well before Pearl Harbor, Republicans had warned the American public that any war effort might lead to a dangerous extension of state controls over society and the economy. As he joined the U.S. Senate in January 1939, for instance, Robert A. Taft of Ohio – who would quickly become one of the most influential Republicans in the country – warned that a war would likely create "a Socialist dictatorship" which would demand "the nationalization of all industry and all capital and all labor."[66] Although this never came close to happening, conservative politicians continued throughout the war to prevent permanent extensions of state control. After making impressive gains in the midterm elections in 1942, Republicans forged alliances with conservative Democrats to kill off several New Deal programs (including the NRPB) and began to resist state authority in several key areas of the mobilization effort, including taxation, labor law, and price and profit control. Well before the 1944 elections, in which he would challenge Roosevelt, New York Governor Thomas Dewey defined the Allied war effort as a defense of "free society."

---

[63] Correspondence on dues in folder General Motors Corp., etc., cabinet 8, drawer 2, box 2, ACWP Records, Detroit Public Library.

[64] Lichtenstein 1982, 175.

[65] Leff 1991, 1313–1317; Lowe 1990, 178–180; Wildy 1992.

[66] Patterson 1972, 200–201.

When the war was over, Dewey insisted, government must not continue to rule the economy.[67]

Perhaps the best measure of the success of the conservative campaign to define the war effort as a fight for free enterprise was the inroads it made among Democrats. Even left-leaning Democrats like Henry Wallace were using "free-enterprise" rhetoric at war's end, albeit in ways that did little more than repackage traditional populist, antimonopolist political economy. More impressive was the wartime conversion of centrist Democrats like Harry Truman. As chairman of the leading congressional committee watchdog over the industrial mobilization, Truman had been quite critical of American business, which – the committee's hearings and reports suggested in 1941–1942 – had evidently been slow to mobilize and quick to collude and profiteer. But by the latter part of the war, Truman and his committee had become more interested in celebrating the successes of American industry than in highlighting its deficiencies. The "astounding performance" of the American economy in wartime, the committee concluded in a March 1944 report, "exceeds anything of its kind ever achieved in the history of the world." This great success came mainly, Truman and his fellow senators now claimed, from the genius of private business firms and free markets. "Even in wartime," it explained, "it was the flow of private initiative that made possible the success of the war program." Looking ahead to demobilization, the committee explained that Americans should be wary of any effort to extend wartime controls past the end of the conflict. An expanded state, the committee concluded, "would be most unfortunate and contrary to the principles of democracy. The committee believes that we should have confidence in the operation of the free democracy for which the war is being fought."[68]

It is therefore not surprising that after Truman became president, his political rhetoric continued to reproduce the free-enterprise message. On August 9, 1945, a few hours after an atomic bomb exploded over Nagasaki, Truman informed the chairman of the War Production Board that during the reconversion process, "[e]very opportunity must be given to private business to exercise its ingenuity and forcefulness."[69] In January 1946, even as he called for a program of full employment and expanded Social Security (soon to be rebuffed by a coalition of Republicans and conservative Democrats), Truman described the economic reconversion process as "the challenging venture of a free enterprise economy making full and effective use of its rich resources and technical advances" – a venture that must not be managed by excessive federal controls. "On the contrary," the president explained, "the war has demonstrated how effectively we can organize our productive system and develop the potential abilities of our people by aiding the efforts of private enterprise."[70] From here it

[67] "Dewey Calls CIO to Post-War Risk," *New York Times* (October 31, 1943): 41.
[68] U.S. Senate 1944, 3, 16–18.
[69] Truman 1945, 200–201.
[70] Truman 1946, 39–40.

was a short step to Truman's remarkable address at Baylor University in March 1947, a sweeping manifesto for free trade that alienated social democrats in Britain and continental Europe. This speech offered a stunning reproduction of American conservatives' wartime efforts to promote a "fifth freedom" – outdoing that campaign, even, by dropping the half of FDR's "four freedoms" that called for the vanquishing of fear and want. In fact, there were now just three basic freedoms, Truman announced: "freedom of worship – freedom of speech – freedom of enterprise." Since the last of these "is part and parcel of what we call American," the United States would champion free enterprise abroad, as well as at home, during the Cold War.[71]

By endorsing an interpretation of the economic lessons of the war mobilization that conservatives had promoted since before Pearl Harbor, Truman left himself with a weak foundation for the political struggle over controls that would culminate in his party's crushing defeat in the 1946 midterm elections, when Republicans took control of Congress for the first time since 1930. While Truman frequently sided with progressives and organized labor in their efforts to pass a robust full employment bill and maintain price controls, he was defeated again and again by those who – taking Truman's own remarks about the lessons of the war to their logical conclusion – favored a more rapid dismantling of controls and a less regulated postwar economy. While some on the American left looked to Britain for inspiration, the business lobby, led by NAM, mounted a multimillion dollar campaign to dilute the full employment bill and kill the OPA. Even before the 1946 elections, legislators rolled back most wartime controls and rebuffed Truman's early efforts to expand the New Deal.[72]

While the success of the conservative interpretation of the economic lessons of the war was well established by early 1946, the Republican cause was further advanced by the passage of time. In contrast to the first postwar British general election, held before the end of the Pacific War, the first American postwar national poll took place over a year after V-J Day. Many U.S. citizens saw economic controls as desirable during a postwar transition period, but as the months passed, consumer resentment of controls increased. In the fall 1946 campaign, Republicans – running under the slogan, "Had Enough?" – railed against the continuation of wartime price controls, which earlier that very year had enjoyed widespread public support.[73]

Meanwhile, the emergence of a bitter Cold War against the Soviet Union bolstered Republican efforts to equate government bureaucracy, grown large under Democratic administrations during the Depression and World War II, with totalitarianism.[74] "Surely we are agreed," said Senator Kenneth Wherry, a Nebraska Republican, in an October 1946 speech in Chicago, "that our

[71] Truman 1947, 169–170; Mercer 1996, 145.
[72] Zieger 1995, 242–244; Fones-Wolf 1994, 34; Bell 2004, 4–9.
[73] Zweiniger-Bargielowska 2000; Jacobs 2005, 209–231.
[74] Patterson 1972, 313; Bell 2004, 32–34.

boys did not lay down their lives and pour out their blood to help America go totalitarian." And yet the American economy was still threatened, Wherry argued, by a minority of "economic planners and propagandists," who "took advantage of the war to... perpetuate themselves in power." Over the last decade, Wherry continued, there had been "107,138 executive orders, directives, grants, permissions, and prohibitions issued by the bureaucrats in Washington," which had only held back the American war effort, whose success came from the "liberty of the individual" and the "free economy."[75] Now it was time, Wherry said, to beat back the overreaching of the state. Three weeks later, the Republican triumph at the polls vindicated Wherry's vision.

Recent British historiography, seeking to correct earlier accounts that exaggerated the extent of political consensus in wartime and postwar Britain, has emphasized the Conservative party and the British business community's disinterest in accommodating Labour.[76] This work is less compelling when one adopts a comparative perspective. Contemporary observers had little doubt that British business associations were more politically moderate than their American counterparts, perhaps because the Blitz had infected them with the same dose of social solidarity that helped to make the British public so receptive to the Beveridge Report.[77] While the majority of Conservatives may have never abandoned the commitment to free enterprise that Churchill and Eden articulated during the 1945 campaign, a considerable number of them accepted – during as well as after the war – measures of nationalization and regulation that would have been anathema to virtually all of their counterparts in America. From an American perspective, Conservative moderates in the mid-1940s included not only leading reform "radicals" such as Quintin Hogg, but also more mainstream figures like Lyttleton.[78] The most prominent of the Conservative policy statements on postwar political economy, the Industrial Charter of 1947, managed to tout "free enterprise" and protest excessive government controls even as it accepted many of Labour's reforms, including the nationalization of several large industries.[79] The contemporary American equivalent of this Conservative position was closer to Truman than to a moderate Republican like Dewey.

While the war may have had little effect on the economic opinions of many British Conservatives, their efforts to influence public opinion did not come close to matching the intensity and stridency of their American counterparts until the late 1940s, after the Cold War had deepened, along with public resentment of continued controls.[80] As they contested the 1950 and

[75] Wherry 1946.
[76] Johnman 1991, 37–38; Mercer 1991, 72–73; Jones 1996; Jones 1999.
[77] Frank C. Hanighen, "The Shape of Things in Britain," *Harper's Magazine* 186 (December 1942): 11–19; Blank 1973, 31–46.
[78] "Enterprise," *Economist* (March 11, 1944): 335; Lyttleton 1962, 335.
[79] Singleton 1995, 21–23; Ball 1998, 105.
[80] Harris 1972.

1951 general elections, the two leading British parties continued to battle over rationing and price control, which Labour insisted were still necessary.[81] The Conservatives and British business associations, with the help of advice and funds from their American counterparts, now mounted a more aggressively antisocialist, libertarian public relations campaign. Going beyond their recent emphasis on building a "Property-Owning Democracy," British Conservatives now ridiculed the possibility of broadening nationalization, promising to "Set the People Free."[82] In the 1951 general election, five years after their American counterparts swept to victory, British Conservatives won a similar battle over the meaning and legacies of the World War II economy.

CONCLUSION

During a November 1945 visit to Washington, British Prime Minister Clement Attlee used an address to Congress to assure Americans that the recent Labour Party victory would not turn America's great wartime ally into an antagonist. The speech came at a moment of great uncertainty about the postwar world order, when many people on both sides of the Atlantic, watching developments such as the recent British election, wondered if the United States, despite its geopolitical power, might become an island of free-market capitalism in an increasingly socialistic world.[83] While Britain would diverge from the United States in the field of domestic economic policy, Attlee suggested, this difference grew out of a more fundamental similarity: the two nations' shared commitment to democracy. "In our internal policies," Attlee told the American legislators, "each will follow the course decided by the people's will. You will see us embarking on projects of nationalization, on wide, all-embracing schemes of social insurance designed to give security to the common man. We shall be working out a planned economy. You, it may be, will continue in your more individualistic methods."[84]

Although Attlee's words may have accurately characterized a real difference in British and American public opinion about economic policy at the end of World War II, they obscured as much as they revealed. The preferred economic policies of President Truman, Congress, and the American public in late 1945 were surely "more individualistic" in some important ways than those of the new Labour government, but Attlee's reference to continuity was misleading. American methods had not been any more libertarian during the

---

[81] Zweiniger-Bargielowska 2000, 206–234.

[82] Blank 1973, 64, 84–85; Rogow 1955, 139–142; Green 1997, 179–181; Jones 1999, 183; Singleton 1995, 24–25; Bell 2004, 162.

[83] Arthur Krock, "Labour Party's Sweep Raises Problems Here," *New York Times* (July 29, 1945): F3; "Mr. Truman's America," *New Statesman and Nation* 30 (September 1, 1945): 142; "Letter to America," *New Statesman and Nation* 30 (September 8, 1945): 155–156; William Hard, "What Britain's Labour Government Means to America," *Reader's Digest* 47 (October 1945), 3.

[84] Brooke 1995, 41.

Depression or during the recent industrial mobilization for World War II, which ranked as the largest economic crisis and the greatest economic project in all history. Furthermore, Attlee's invocation of the "people's will" obscured the degree to which recent and ongoing political struggles over the economic lessons of the war had influenced electoral results. In Britain, Labour had momentarily prevailed in these struggles by making a compelling case that one of the lessons of a victorious all-out mobilization was that the state could and should extend its social welfare guarantees to citizens and its controls over the domestic economy. In the United States, meanwhile, victory was more often attributed to free-market capitalism. As the former price controller and leading Cold War liberal economist John Kenneth Galbraith once explained, American wartime controllers like himself were resented, not without some justification, while "business spokesmen took credit for the superior industrial performance of the economy during the war." They succeeded remarkably in this project, according to Galbraith, with the result that victory was widely attributed to "the natural virtuosity of American enterprise and the American market system."[85]

As this chapter has suggested, while American and British political parties and interest groups promulgated selective, self-serving rhetorical framings of the war effort and its lessons, it was the American winners of this framing game who did more to distort the realities of the World War II industrial mobilization. While private enterprise had been a giant part of the successful mobilization projects in both nations, so, too, had public enterprise and a variety of robust state regulations and controls. Because the American side of this story has never been fully told, we have never appreciated how ludicrous is the "free-enterprise" interpretation of the American war effort. Indeed, by assuming a significant difference between the British and American war economies, historians and social scientists have participated in perpetuating the myths that disturbed Galbraith – myths that American conservatives deliberately generated, starting even before the United States entered the conflict. The relatively militarized structure of the wartime American state boosted the acceptance and longevity of these distortions, which obscured many dimensions of American state action altogether and suggested that others were legitimate only in the service of national emergency.

While the American conservatives' account of the workings of World War II distorted the truth, postwar developments did much to support their claims that governmental controls that might be necessary in wartime should not be applied to peacetime. This set them apart from Labour in Britain, as well as many left-leaning liberals in the United States. One of the latter, the prominent sociologist Robert Lynd, complained during the war, as he would after, that an aggressive pro-business propaganda campaign was "preventing us from learning the lessons of this war."[86] While Lynd was right to call attention to the power of the free-enterprise media blitz, the existence of that campaign did not necessarily mean it was entirely misguided. By the late 1940s, those sympathetic to the claims of American conservatives about the evils of excessive state regulation could point to developments in Britain and the United States that seemed to vindicate this position. By that time, the British public had tired of Labour's efforts to maintain wartime methods; it was clear to all that the American economy was much more prosperous than its British counterpart, even more than might be expected given their different wartime experiences and postwar circumstances. One American visitor dismayed by the low standard of living in postwar Britain was the actor Ronald Reagan, who recalled that his experiences there in the winter of 1948–1949 convinced him that government ownership was unworkable.[87] The Conservative victory in the 1951 general elections suggested that the British public, too, after six years of Labour policies, had become less willing to endorse the idea that the war effort presented a valuable model for the peacetime economy.

Over the longer run, the lessons promulgated by American conservatives in response to the threat of statism during World War II (and the New Deal before it) enjoyed even greater success. Starting in the late 1970s, Margaret Thatcher in Britain led a new push for privatization, undoing some of the structural and ideological foundations of a mixed political economy that Labour had created in the late 1940s and that had endured for three decades. As the twentieth century came to a close, many understood the end of the Cold War and the collapse of the Soviet Union as evidence of the superiority of a free-market approach to economic management that eschewed direct controls.

In the early twenty-first century, already well beyond the Cold War, we are increasingly sensitive to the costs of an entrenched American idiom of political economy that was shaped by the outcome of struggles over the lessons of World War II. National state power continues to be concentrated, to an extent that remains underappreciated, in a professional military establishment that is insulated from democratic pressures and that tends to be treated by voters and policymakers as outside the bounds of legitimate political contestation. Meanwhile, the antistatist, free-market discourse that was promoted by American conservatives during World War II has flourished. This free-enterprise idiom served as an important bulwark against excessive regulation, but it has also promoted a dangerously inflexible economic monoculture, in which state regulation and public enterprise have frequently been defined as out of bounds, even when they seem likely to achieve important results. One of the costs of this misunderstanding may be blindness to more effective solutions to serious economic, environmental, and strategic problems in our own

---

[86] "Big Business Held Halting Progress," *New York Times* (November 13, 1943): 14; Fones-Wolf 1994, 32.

[87] Kynaston 2007, 315.

day. Indeed, the recent responses of American political leaders to some of the greatest economic challenges since the era of the Great Depression and World War II suggest that their ideas about the uses of public authority are less wide-ranging and creative than those of their counterparts of the "greatest generation." This in itself represents a victory for the pro-business interpreters of the lessons of the industrial mobilization for World War II. Americans, at least, seem to have learned those lessons well enough to make it unlikely that even serious crises, whether they be wars or economic depressions, will cause any significant expansion of social democracy.

PART III

WAR AND DEMOCRATIC STATES

Government by the People or over the People?

9

International Conflict and the Constitutional Balance

Executive Authority after War

Ronald R. Krebs

In recent years, Americans witnessed assertions of presidential prerogative and a concerted effort to sideline Congress that were unequalled in the preceding three decades. Some hailed these developments, alongside increased government surveillance, as the price to be paid for a "War on Terror" whose effective prosecution required nimble governance. Others warned that Americans were, in this "long war," too swiftly relinquishing their hard-won freedoms and too readily acquiescing in the emasculation of the legislative branch. They feared that even if the United States should one day declare victory over terror – whatever that might mean – it might be too late to save the country's darkened soul.

This debate raised crucial questions. Do security-driven restrictions on liberty and expansions of executive authority become a new baseline, from which future crises compel further departures? Or are such measures rescinded, or at least substantially scaled back, once the emergency passes? Are both claims true, but only under certain conditions? What then is the likely staying power of post-9/11 initiatives? This chapter does not focus on developments in the United States since 2001, but they are a silent presence. And the concern is not only an American one: In the name of combating terrorism, countries around the world have extended detention without charge, limited speech, reduced government transparency, and hampered political opposition.

For very helpful comments on earlier drafts, the author is grateful to Gad Barzilai, Jim Burk, Mike Desch, David Edelstein, Piki Ish-Shalom, Sid Tarrow, and especially Beth Kier, as well as to participants in workshops at the University of Texas at Austin, the University of Washington, and the Hebrew University; to attendees of a panel at the 2009 annual meeting of the American Political Science Association; and to the anonymous readers for Cambridge University Press. For financial support of this research, the author thanks the Donald D. Harrington Faculty Fellowship at the University of Texas at Austin and the McKnight Foundation through the University of Minnesota.

In this chapter, I argue that, beyond the scale of war, how military operations are represented affects the fate of wartime measures expanding executive authority and contracting individual freedoms. Total wars call forth exceptional measures, but, because such wars are represented as departures from the norm, wartime steps reducing contestation have little long-run effect. Limited military ventures whose aims are cast as "restorative" are conducive to the normalization of wartime practices, while those missions framed in "transformative" terms facilitate a backlash that reworks the constitutional balance.

As a plausibility probe of the latter hypotheses, I examine one limited war of each sort and its implications for postwar politics. The Vietnam War was legitimated partly as a transformative venture to remake South Vietnam in America's image. The war gave rise to an assertive executive engaged in massive surveillance and political disruption. As the war's failure became clear, a perceived gap arose between the war's substantial costs at home (and abroad) and its lack of gains. Wartime measures were perceived as executive overstretch, and a resurgent Congress sought to rein in the president. In short, backlash against wartime executive authority. The French project in Algeria began as a transformative civilizing mission, but, under President Charles de Gaulle, it became a restorative venture – that is, a festering conflict from which France had to extricate itself to preserve its national unity and return to great power status. An unwinnable imperial war thereby became a winnable peace, and the result was general acceptance of the unparalleled and untrammeled power of the executive in the Fifth Republic, even after de Gaulle exited the political scene – in short, normalization of executive authority.

This chapter proceeds in five sections. First, I review the existing literature regarding the effects of international conflict on civil liberties and executive authority and identify its lacunae. Second, I lay out a theoretical framework that begins to fill those gaps. The next two sections assess the hypotheses in light of American and French wars in Vietnam and Algeria, respectively. The conclusion returns to the contemporary predicament, specifically the fate of the reborn imperial presidency after the Iraq War.

WAR AND CONTESTATION: OPTIMISTS, PESSIMISTS, AND SKEPTICS[1]

The health of a liberal democracy can be measured in part by the scope of and limits upon executive authority. When state power is exercised arbitrarily – that is, without the need for the public articulation of reasons legitimating actions taken for the sake of the commonweal – constitutionalism is under siege, and the regime occupies one end of the "contestation" continuum. Robert Dahl categorized regimes according to their location in a conceptual space defined

---

[1] This discussion draws on Krebs 2009.

by (1) *contestation*: the extent to which political opposition is sanctioned and protected, among those permitted to participate in governance, and (2) *participation*: the proportion of the population that can and does meaningfully engage in contestation, whatever its extent. Participation is often associated with the franchise, but that is only its most easily measured manifestation. Contestation is captured by the extent of civil liberties protections that nurture the formation and expression of opposition and by the scope of unchecked executive authority, which defines the boundaries of effective opposition. The greater the degree of contestation and the broader and deeper participation, the more a given regime approaches the liberal-democratic ideal.[2] Note that the expansion of the state and even of the executive, both of which have consistently grown in Europe and North America since the nineteenth century, are not inherently antiliberal developments: It is the expansion of executive institutions' *unchecked* power that constitutes a challenge to liberal democracy, not the spread of those institutions' reach per se.[3]

Scholars agree that security threats and war mobilization degrade contestation in the short run.[4] First, all manner of crises contribute to the expansion of unchecked executive authority. The tradition of "constitutional dictatorship" dates to the Roman Republic, and the view that the occasional need for speedy action may require strengthening the unified executive at the expense of the more divided and deliberative legislature has a distinguished lineage.[5] A second consequence is the diminution of civil liberties. In general, scholars have concluded that the more intense the threat, the more likely are substantial restrictions and the more broadly they fall. Many have observed that politically weak groups are common targets, since measures at their expense yield at least the illusion of security at seemingly low cost.

There is, however, less agreement about whether these measures endure. Optimists, pointing to the U.S. experience with political expression, argue that there is a silver lining to wartime restrictions, as progressive postwar social learning has led jurists and decision-makers to view the most oppressive steps as object lessons, not exemplars, and to embrace postwar steps to curb executive power, both in peacetime and in future wars.[6] Pessimists, in contrast, claim that war in particular and crisis in general cast a long shadow. They maintain that the exception has not been exceptional: temporary states of emergency have become permanent, emergency measures have been incorporated into ordinary law, authorities have employed emergency powers in everyday situations, and populations' civil liberties baselines have adjusted to these new realities.[7] Optimists see, and forecast, negative feedback (backlash), and pessimists, positive feedback (normalization). The normative stakes are

---

[2] Dahl 1971.
[3] For a more extensive discussion, see Chapter 1, this volume.
[4] Classic works in this vein include Hintze 1975; Lasswell 1941.
[5] Mansfield, Jr. 1989; Rossiter 1948.
[6] Rehnquist 1998; Stone 2004.
[7] Cole 2005 [2003]; Donohue 2008; Gross and Ní Aoláin 2006.

substantial: If contestation-reducing measures had no lasting negative effects, one might conclude that this was a tempest in society's teapot – albeit one costly for individuals – and if they had positive effects, one might paradoxically welcome them.

Framed as invariant generalizations, both accounts seem problematic. Optimists can identify instances in which crisis measures provoked a backlash, reining in the executive and protecting civil liberties, but they fail to engage with the pessimists' evidence. Moreover, the causal mechanism by which a postwar consensus emerges critical of wartime policy and protective of violated rights is never spelled out. Pessimists, however, also seem to overstate their case. If they were right, one would have expected a steady race toward the civil liberties bottom and the evisceration of constitutional government over the course of the twentieth century. But, for all its flaws, liberal democracy has proven resilient: Only the most radical critics see little difference between today's liberal and authoritarian regimes. Further, pessimists would expect "bleeding" across boundaries and domains to be regular and comprehensive, yet such bleeding is selective, episodic, and delimited. Neither optimists nor pessimists present a well-specified theory to answer what is arguably *the* critical question regarding the long-term effects of war on contestation: When does normalization, and when does a rights-protective backlash, follow?

A third perspective, however, concludes that "there just are no systematic trends in the history of civil liberties, no important ratchet-like mechanisms that cause repeated wars or emergencies to push civil liberties in one direction or another in any sustained fashion." Eric Posner and Adrian Vermeule suggest that "emergencies produce a cyclical pattern, in which civil liberties are restricted during emergency and then reinstated when the emergency passes."[8] If they are correct, the net effect of international conflict on contestation is nil. But these skeptics do not substantiate their claim. The more defensible inference is that the scope conditions for the optimists' and pessimists' accounts have not yet been established. Posner and Vermeule's correct observation that existing accounts lack well-specified mechanisms should serve as an invitation to theory-building, not a rejection of the enterprise.

REPRESENTING WAR: SOCIAL MEANING AND THE FATE OF CONTESTATION

"Bellicist" historical sociologists argue that major interstate wars have played a key role in state-building and democratization.[9] The adjective "major" is not incidental: In these accounts, the crucial variables are the scope of the threat and the scale of mobilization and warfare. It is normally presumed that the more intense the conflict, the greater its consequences. Rarely are

[8] Posner and Vermeule 2007, 149–150.
[9] Among others, Mann 1993; Tilly 1992.

more limited conflicts seen as producing political effects of note.[10] But to think that large effects are the product only of large causes is a fallacy, as social-science research informed by both complexity theory and path dependence has confirmed. System-altering wars often have been limited in their stakes, intensity, and duration, and large-scale wars have sometimes had limited consequences, certainly internationally and perhaps domestically too. While there is substantial research on the consequences of large-scale wars, that on limited wars is, well, limited.

Postwar political dynamics are undoubtedly shaped by the imprint wartime mobilization leaves on the power and interests of domestic actors, but they are also shaped by the social meaning of war. Even when wars do not levy great demands on populations, they must be legitimated, and those efforts may have lasting effects on the terrain of contestation. Scholars have previously noted that how adversaries and wars are framed can explain wartime patterns, specifically why certain freedoms are restricted and others preserved.[11] Extending that logic provides a way of bridging the differences among optimists, pessimists, and skeptics regarding the long-run relationship between international conflict and contestation. This approach brings war itself into the center of the conversation. It also has unexpected implications.

The conventional wisdom is that large-scale wars have the greatest domestic impact.[12] But from the perspective of contestation, what happens in large-scale war stays in large-scale war. Such wars are "total": Calling forth unusual levels of societal sacrifice and state extraction, they are normally cast explicitly as deviations from the norm.[13] Preparation for and engagement in large-scale war have justified exceptional executive authority in liberal states, and governments do not relinquish powers willingly. But the very terms in which leaders mobilize their populations provide societal actors with rhetorical resources they can deploy to prevent wartime measures' unwarranted extension, and thus, the powers that total wars bequeath come with a life span limited to the exceptional circumstances that gave rise to them. Large-scale wars, therefore, do not produce a "new normal": Even if deemed appropriate responses to the pressures of the moment, they are rolled back upon the war's conclusion.[14] Wartime executive power to manage the national economy appears to be an exception, as the rigors of postwar demobilization have often seemed to impose demands that permit executives to justify continued authority.

---

[10] But see Centeno 2002; Sparrow 2002.

[11] Scheppele 2003.

[12] An asymmetric war may be large-scale for one adversary but more limited for the other. Consider the Vietnam War, which required North Vietnam's "total" mobilization but remained limited for the United States. Wars, therefore, must be coded as total or limited for each adversary.

[13] On the nature of total war, see Imlay 2007, esp. 552–557.

[14] Space constraints prevent me from evaluating this hypothesis; I focus instead on the dynamics of limited wars.

Thus, the skeptics' conclusion that wars result in little long-run change in contestation seems most persuasive regarding large-scale war. Rossiter's classic narrative of British and French experiences in the world wars is largely consistent with this account. Wartime powers allowing authorities to detain citizens without charge and to prevent the publication of material deemed damaging to the war effort were swiftly rescinded. The transition to a peacetime economy, however, justified maintaining some emergency powers relating to economic affairs, such as prohibitions on labor's right to strike. Once the bright line between wartime and peacetime had been crossed, these powers could be – and were – retained, though they were used with decreasing frequency. The same pattern holds regarding America's total wars, the Civil War and World War II.[15]

Framed in less exceptional terms, limited wars can potentially pave the way for the conversion of wartime standards into peacetime practices. Normalization is not inevitable, however, for such wars vary in their stated ambitions. Some are "transformative" enterprises that promise to change the fundamental nature of either the international system or the adversary. Woodrow Wilson assured Americans that their sacrifices in World War I would revolutionize diplomacy and that the war would bring about a new, more transparent, more democratic, and more stable global order. Classic liberal imperialism was also rhetorically transformative, pledging to educate and uplift native populations; more recent imperial missions have promised to export democratic and capitalist institutions to authoritarian and economically backward countries. Some limited wars, however, are "restorative" missions that explicitly aim only to preserve or return the status quo. For the British, the Falklands War was a matter of returning British control to an overseas territory; the war did unseat the Argentine junta, but that was not its explicit goal. The 1991 Gulf War was a restorative limited war, waged to reinstate the al-Sabah family and contain Iraq, not install democracy in Kuwait and depose Saddam Hussein – though some of the war's backers undoubtedly harbored these visions. The war was not fought to bring President George H. W. Bush's "New World Order" into being; rather, the American-led global coalition was portrayed as a reflection of that order's emergence. Large-scale wars have also been legitimated in either restorative or transformative terms.[16] But these potentially important differences in the framing of these wars' missions do not have bearing on their "exceptional" nature, which is a more persistent feature of their rhetoric and which, I argued above, is crucial to postwar political dynamics.

Whether leaders legitimate limited military missions in largely transformative or restorative terms has two implications for postconflict politics. First,

---

[15] Rossiter 1948, 97–102, 165–172, 196–204; Stone 2004.

[16] Some argue (Imlay 2007, 554) that large-scale wars lean toward the transformative end of the spectrum, but this is not necessarily correct. Even in the world wars, combatants' representations of war aims differed.

it shapes the public's expectations regarding the postconflict world, and is therefore crucial to whether the conflict's conclusion brings satisfaction or disappointment, whether conflict-driven measures are perceived as warranted or not, and whether they are seen as having relevance to postconflict conditions. In liberal states, national leaders do not occupy the public sphere alone, and thus their portrait of the war's progress and prospects may not go unchallenged; but, in carrying the nation to war, they are primarily responsible for articulating the state's aims, and thus especially they establish the standards by which the public judges the war's outcome. Second, different forms of rhetorical mobilization render the gap between national ideals and institutions more or less salient, affecting whether the gap is tolerated or ignored and whether movements arise to eliminate it.[17]

Limited wars with explicitly transformative aims are unusually ambitious, and consequently they are particularly likely to result in unrealized aspirations and in a perceived disjuncture between the sacrifices war entails and the gains it brings: In short, transformative limited wars are likely to be seen as mistakes, if not failures. The U.S. intervention in World War I was crucial to the Allies' victory, but the prevailing reaction in the United States was not pride, but disillusion. Europeans' vengefulness at Versailles seemed to prove Wilson a dreamer and Washington's valedictory warning wise. Wilson's liberal-crusading rhetoric had established expectations so great that the war could not but appear a failure by their standards, and the measures that once seemed warranted now seemed less so. After Wilson's grand plans foundered, Progressives "rediscovered" civil liberties: They found the postwar Red Scare a hysterical overreaction, and moral campaigns at home, like Comstockery, were discredited.[18]

Transformative rhetoric brings national ideals into bold relief. To promise to transform the Other is to position the Self as superior, as worthy of leading such a project. Americans had long portrayed themselves as morally pure compared to corrupt Europeans, and this tradition legitimated U.S. participation in, in Wilson's words, this "final war for human liberty," this "opportunity for which [Americans] have sought to prepare themselves ... ever since the days when they set up a new nation in the high and honorable hope that it might[,] in all that it was and did[,] show mankind the way to

---

[17] This line of argument is inspired by Huntington 1981. Thanks to Aaron Rapport for suggesting I think about how my argument intersects with Huntington's.

[18] Starr 2004, 287 and generally chap. 3; Murphy 1979. As John Witt (2007, chap. 3) points out, this was less the rediscovery than the creation of "civil liberties" – a term that had not previously been part of the regular lexicon in its "disaggregated," plural form. Witt places prewar internationalism at the center of his account, but he ultimately reaffirms the importance of the war in fashioning a movement opposed to wartime measures and committed to the protection of civil liberties. The internationalist movement, which had taken on the civil liberties program to protect its core agenda, split asunder in the war's wake, while the movement for civil liberties advanced separate of any internationalist trappings. Thanks to Sid Tarrow for alerting me to Witt's work.

liberty."[19] Similarly, liberal imperialism went along, in the nineteenth century, with European confidence in the superiority of their civilization compared to the barbarians who required European tutelage.[20] Transformative rhetoric implicates identity: One cannot teach or serve as a model for the Other without articulated national ideals.

Trafficking in the liberal polity's central values, transformative rhetoric highlights the distance between those ideals and the reality of its political institutions. Such distance is inevitable, Samuel Huntington noted, because modern government rests on illiberal elements of hierarchy, arbitrary power, and secrecy.[21] Moreover, narrating the Self as superior invites not only self-congratulation, but muckraking: Liberal government does not suspend human nature, and corruption is ubiquitous. Wars, especially wars with grand aims that spark dissent at home, heighten the tension between liberal ideals and state power. The self-righteous logic of transformative war justifies not only redoubled efforts to surmount adversaries whose armed struggle confirms how desperately they require enlightenment, but also measures to suppress domestic critics who fail to grasp the national mission and who lack moral fiber. Transformative limited wars thus yield an executive that is secretive and shuttered and therefore prone to groupthink. In short, transformative rhetoric holds the polity to too high a standard, from which a fall is, if not inevitable, very likely. Huntington hypothesized that how people reacted to that distance was a function of the intensity of their belief in the ideals and the clarity of the gap, but he surprisingly did not see war as an important driver of either.[22] Yet wars framed in transformative terms boost popular commitment to national ideals, while, even more important, rendering both those ideals and the gap between ideals and institutions more salient.

The backlash after transformative limited war against existing structures of authority – in line with optimists' expectations – thus has two related sources. First, because transformative rhetoric sets so high a bar for success, such limited wars are often perceived as failures. The result is a chasm between the war's meager achievements (judged by its aims) and even the modest sacrifices it demands. That disjuncture gives rise to calls to reform the state institutions that pursued this misguided venture, from true believers in the war's transformative vision, as well as from political entrepreneurs who were skeptical from the start of the war's overt justification but who nevertheless see in the gap a strategic opportunity to further a reform agenda. The war's mobilizing transformative rhetoric precludes any defense that the war is merely a rational gamble gone awry and thus that deep reform is unnecessary. Second, transformative limited wars generate what Huntington called moments of "creedal

[19] "Address to a Joint Session of Congress on the Conditions of Peace," January 8, 1918; "Address to the Senate of the United States: 'A World League for Peace,'" January 22, 1917. Both in *Public Papers of the Presidents* (hereafter, *PPP*), www.presidency.ucsb.edu/ws/.
[20] Pitts 2005, 20–21 and passim.
[21] Huntington 1981, 39–41.
[22] Ibid., chaps. 4, 6.

passion," by inspiring movements to bring political institutions into line with liberal ideals. At such times, "existing structures of authority are called into question, democratic and egalitarian impulses are renewed, and political change – anticipated and unanticipated – occurs," exceeding mere revision of the domestic balance of power.[23]

Limited wars legitimated in restorative terms, in contrast, facilitate the normalization of which pessimists warn. Restorative rhetoric does not fan the flames of national ideals, leaving the gap between ideals and institutions less salient. Even as the war widens the gap between the liberal polity's ideals and its political institutions – as wars always do – the gap is not a resource that political entrepreneurs may profitably plumb, and incipient reform movements fail to gain traction, if they arise at all. Further, the restorative framing of the military mission sets the bar at a more achievable level, and if successful, the mission seems to confirm the wisdom of wartime measures. As a result, those practices and institutions that the pressures of war facilitated endure. De Gaulle's reframing of Algeria as a restorative mission, I will argue, helped consolidate unparalleled presidential authority in France by facilitating the casting of France's withdrawal from that festering conflict as a necessary step on the path to France's renaissance and thus paradoxically as a success. Finally, because limited wars do not entail massive mobilization, they often blur the line between wartime and peacetime, and successful measures are likely to seem reasonable in more peaceful times as well.[24] Thus, even as the Cold War's intensity moderated, it came to seem a permanent feature of the international landscape. Early Cold War contestation-diminishing measures in the United States were deepened and extended, and norms regarding fundamental liberties and the constitutional distribution of power were reshaped as the "imperial presidency" attained its apogee under Johnson and Nixon. Moreover, the restorative rhetoric of containing global Communism, which became the dominant U.S. goal by the mid-1950s as transformative rhetoric calling for the liberation of Soviet satellites waned, made all this possible – legitimating assertions of policy success, the need for constant vigilance, and illiberal measures' continued necessity.

LIMITED WAR AND THE IMPERIAL PRESIDENCY: A PLAUSIBILITY PROBE

Logic of Comparison

One might have expected the wars in Vietnam and Algeria to produce similar consequences in the United States and France. Both began as imperial ventures

---

[23] Ibid., 91.
[24] Legro (2005, 38) similarly suggests that when new policies are associated with success, they become the new orthodoxy, even if the desirable outcomes cannot be traced directly to them. See also Avant (Chapter 11), this volume.

in which the liberal metropole grandly sought to rebuild the uncivilized periphery in its image.[25] In both, the metropole's larger and technologically superior military confronted frustrating resistance by local irregulars. Both were costly wars, especially for the peripheral region where the conflict raged, but also for the metropole; however, they remained limited conflicts in terms of the metropole's mobilization. In both, the metropole's populace eventually turned against the war. Both ended in failure: France relinquished Algeria, and the United States abandoned South Vietnam. And both wars drove expansions of executive authority and suppression of political opponents. If anything, one might have expected more of a postwar reaction in France: The French commitment to Algeria vastly exceeded the U.S. commitment to Vietnam; the violence in Algeria manifested in France itself, while the less intense violence in the United States was only indirectly related to the war; and France became home to large numbers of Algerian immigrants and European colonist refugees, whereas the United States could seal itself off from subsequent events in South Vietnam.

Yet the postwar politics of the two countries were starkly different. The war in Vietnam prompted a reaction against the imperial presidency, while the war in Algeria led to a constitutional revolution that created a "republican monarch" with broad-based legitimacy. The wars' divergent paths with regard to executive authority, I argue, are rooted in how the metropoles' leaders articulated the wars' goals and thus shaped their social meaning.

Vietnam and the Backlash Against the Imperial Presidency

Histories of the Vietnam War and American democracy understandably focus on the Johnson and Nixon administrations' suppression of antiwar protest, deception of the public and Congress, and evasion of legislative constraints. More rarely is the war given its due for promoting contestation over the long run. By the time Arthur Schlesinger, Jr., published *The Imperial Presidency*,[26] however, the tide had already turned. Even before Watergate, Congress had begun to assert itself, and the revelations that came fast and furious in the mid-1970s consolidated a consensus that the interbranch distribution of power had become unbalanced. Congress augmented its capacity to monitor and constrain executive action, protected citizens from unwarranted government surveillance, reclaimed the power of the purse, bolstered its infrastructure for policy assessment, systematized and intensified oversight, and increased transparency. These reforms worked

---

[25] One might classify Algeria as a French civil war, since Algeria was administratively part of metropolitan France, unlike other French colonies. However, French discourse commonly distinguished between Algerians and French, and the former lacked fully equivalent citizenship rights, belying the notion that Algeria was as much France as the Île de France.

[26] Schlesinger, Jr. 1973.

at best imperfectly and sometimes, contrary to their intent, facilitated executive autonomy. Nevertheless, the postwar backlash against presidential power is as much a legacy of the Vietnam War as the wartime expansion of presidential power.

The outcome of the Vietnam War was unquestionably deeply disappointing to Americans, but it is less obvious why. If the war's purpose was halting the Communist advance and thereby preventing the dominoes from falling – a familiar restorative rhetoric – the conflict was not unambiguously a failure. In August 1966, alongside the U.S. commander in Vietnam, Lyndon Johnson announced that "a Communist military takeover in South Vietnam is no longer just improbable; as long as the United States and our brave allies are in the field, it is impossible."[27] Johnson regularly misled the American people on the war's progress and prospects, but this claim had merit: As long as U.S. forces were present in sufficient numbers, South Vietnam remained within the non-Communist orbit. The price would be high – nearly 60,000 Americans and several times as many South Vietnamese soldiers and civilians – but this limited goal was achieved. The United States *was* able to hold the line. Judged by such restorative standards, the military had not covered itself in glory, but it had avoided defeat.

If the gains seemed meager relative to the blood and treasure expended, it was because the Johnson administration had aimed for more: a stable, free, and prosperous South Vietnam that could anchor the U.S. security perimeter in Southeast Asia. In other words, this was a transformative mission, not merely a restorative one. When Johnson entered office, he warned his advisers against trying "to immediately transform ... [South Vietnam] into our image," but that caution fell by the wayside, as Southeast Asia became the testing ground for an international New Deal. As the country's political turmoil deepened, Johnson and his advisers embraced a vision of "pacification" through "development" and "nation-building." In Vietnam, the United States would demonstrate the validity of modernization theory and its universal path to the good life, and Vietnamese "hearts and minds" would follow. Vietnam would provide proof of the liberal dogma that economic and political development were mutually reinforcing. Johnson saw South Vietnam, in his biographer Robert Dallek's words, as a "remote, backward place dominated by squabbling factions unresponsive to political reason," and his aide Walt Rostow aimed to teach the Vietnamese "the great American traditions of compromise and consensus."[28] In short, Johnson and his advisers came to see political liberalization as the solution to Vietnam's woes. They called on Diem to "broaden" his government, adopt a lighter touch toward dissenting Buddhists, and compromise with domestic political opponents. In their eyes, a South Vietnam that was stable

---

[27] Remarks to the Press at the LBJ Ranch Following a Report on Vietnam by General Westmoreland, August 14, 1966, *PPP*.

[28] Dallek 1998, 99, 243, 284–285; Packenham 1973; Suri 2003, chap. 4.

and secure required that American practices, political and economic, take root in Vietnamese soil.[29] Senator J. William Fulbright decried all this as the "arrogance of empire."[30] Given such goals, the war *was* a failure. If the end was enduring security, which hinged in turn on political liberalization and economic progress, then the intervention in South Vietnam *had* been a disaster. Treading water against two-bit foes was not even a modest victory.

This transformative agenda was not bandied about only behind closed doors: From 1965 on, it was central to how the war was publicly legitimated. The goal in South Vietnam, Johnson regularly affirmed, was not merely holding off Communist aggression, but "lay[ing] the groundwork for meaningful and durable peace." This depended on "progress," on satisfying "people fiercely and justly reaching for the material fruits from the tree of modern knowledge." Sharing the secrets of modern industry, medicine, education, and agriculture and promoting socioeconomic equality were in America's security interests, but they also lay at the core of America's national mission, "commanded to us by the moral values of our civilization."[31] Johnson declared political reform – that is, democracy-building – "as important as the military battle itself." He hailed South Vietnam's new constitution as good news, not only for its own sake, but because "free political institutions are indispensable to the success of South Vietnam's long struggle against terror."[32] Promoting development and democracy constituted "the other war" in South Vietnam – intertwined with the military campaign and hardly secondary.[33] Johnson's grandiose vision extended beyond South Vietnam to the Third World as a whole. He exceeded Woodrow Wilson in his idealism: "Our destination is a world where the instinct for oppression has been vanquished in the heart of man. Given the means to work, to build, to teach, to heal, to nourish his family, man may yet achieve such a world." Asia was currently "torn by conflict, depressed by hunger, disease, and illiteracy, deprived of the means and the institutions that alone can offer hope to her people," and it was therefore "a source of turmoil and anxiety for nations beyond her borders, as well as those within." Peace depended

[29] Despite its other revisionist excesses, Moyar 2006 is persuasive on this score.
[30] Fulbright 1966.
[31] Address to Members of the Association of American Editorial Cartoonists: The Challenge of Human Need in Vietnam, May 13, 1965; Statement by the President Upon Announcing the Selection of a Task Force on the Health and Education Needs of the People, March 6, 1966 – *PPP*.
[32] Joint Statement Following Discussions in Honolulu with the Chief of State and the Prime Minister of Vietnam, February 8, 1966; Statement by the President on the New Constitution Adopted by the Constituent Assembly of the Republic of Vietnam, March 20, 1967 – *PPP*.
[33] Statement by the President on the Pacification and Development Programs in Vietnam, June 16, 1966; Remarks at a Press Briefing by David Lilienthal and Robert Komer, February 27, 1967 – *PPP*.

on American-led development projects, "for wherever men hunger and hate there can really be no peace."[34]

The representation of South Vietnam and other Third World nations as students eager to learn the secrets of development and democracy implied a portrait of their teacher, the United States, as the paragon of both. But the war widened the gap between America's liberal ideals and its political institutions by accelerating the growth of the unaccountable executive. Under the Vietnam War's pressure, Johnson and Nixon transformed the "presidency ascendant," in Schlesinger's phrase, into the "presidency rampant." Watergate was not only the product of Nixon's peculiarly paranoid personality. Nor was it the product only of long-term trends that had, over the preceding decades, bolstered and personalized the presidency.[35] It was also a product of Vietnam, of the surveillance, suppression, and secrecy that both administrations had embraced to silence antiwar protest in the streets and dissent in the establishment.

That the Vietnam War was unpopular was apparent virtually from the start. By 1966, reluctantly expressed doubts among elites had become full-throated, though they often focused on strategic and tactical choices. Protest on college campuses featured a mix of idealism (spurred by the war's transformative rhetoric against the U.S. military's unjust methods) and self-interest (against the draft). The Johnson administration was extraordinarily touchy about moral critique. "Distress at the amount of suffering being visited on the noncombatants in Vietnam, South and North," was, according to a Defense Department memo, among the chief reasons for the war's unpopularity, and "the picture of the world's greatest superpower killing or seriously injuring 1,000 noncombatants a week, while trying to pound a tiny backward nation into submission on an issue whose merits are hotly disputed, is not a pretty one."[36] Official sensitivity to this line of criticism far exceeded the dissenters' paltry popular support: The brutality of counterinsurgency operations troubled few Americans, who displayed little sympathy for the victims and presumed that misdeeds, even if true, were isolated incidents.[37] Yet the Johnson administration recognized that moral critique undercut the war's transformative justification and its underlying image of American moral superiority and that the gap between the war's legitimating rhetoric and the U.S. armed forces' behavior on the ground mobilized campus protest.[38] And both the Johnson and Nixon administrations, rightly or wrongly, firmly believed that campus protest marked the leading edge of mass popular opposition to the U.S. military presence in South Vietnam.[39]

---

[34] Special Message to the Congress Recommending Approval of U.S. Participation as a Member Nation in the Asian Development Bank, January 18, 1966; Remarks to the American Alumni Council: United States Asian Policy, July 12, 1966 – *PPP.*

[35] But see Crenson and Ginsberg 2007; Lowi 1985.

[36] Wells 1994, 152, 155–156, and passim.

[37] Engelhardt 1995, 215–227.

[38] Suri 2003, esp. 162–163.

[39] For many examples, see Wells 1994; Small 1988.

The war's unpopularity, actual and anticipated, prompted the White House to shield it from outside interference – at the cost of individual liberties and executive accountability. These well-known measures can be briefly reviewed. First, both presidents misled Congress and the public about the pace and extent of military escalation and about the war's progress. Second, both administrations *openly* hid information, invoking broad interpretations of "executive privilege" and thereby weakening Congress' and civil society's capacity to monitor the war. Third, as Congress became a greater obstacle, presidents developed the institutional capacity to evade legislative oversight. They rapidly increased the size of the White House staff and extended its portfolio; they also increasingly employed nonlegislative instruments to shape policy. Fourth, the antiwar movement became the target of extensive government surveillance and infiltration. Wiretapping rules were relaxed and even rescinded, records ransacked or stolen, mail intercepted. Both administrations tried to discredit antiwar forces by red-baiting, depicting the domestic howl as aiding the enemy, and painting all protesters as hooligans; establishment critics were the "radical militants'" dupes, if not their willing collaborators. The obvious purpose was to chill political dissent – that is, the lifeblood of democracy and the essence of contestation.

Finally, the imperial presidency extended its reach beyond foreign affairs. Before Vietnam, presidential "impoundment" was rare and limited: Presidents occasionally refused to spend monies Congress had appropriated, but usually small amounts and usually only to delay (rather than permanently prevent) expenditures. To control the runaway deficit, however, Johnson increased the scale and independence of presidential impoundment – at first on his own initiative, then with Congress' blessing. Congress also empowered Nixon, but his impoundments went beyond what it had authorized. Moreover, he asserted that it was an inherent presidential power, impounded immense sums by historical standards, and used impoundment to further his political agenda.[40] Nixon characteristically took impoundment to an extreme, but it was fundamentally the war that made possible and drove this arrogation of power: It exacerbated U.S. budgetary and economic challenges, and it poisoned executive-legislative relations.

The dynamics of the Vietnam War transformed the usual gap between the operation of America's liberal institutions and the nation's self-image into a yawning chasm, and the transformative legitimating rhetoric made this gap a focus of political contest. The result was a backlash, led by Congress, against presidential power. Measures once justified by wartime exigencies seemed like executive overreach, not warranted expediencies, let alone necessary permanent adjustments in the constitutional order. The imperial presidency was not the creation of Richard Nixon or a reflection of his paranoia and ambition. Even Schlesinger, who reserved special venom for Nixon, recognized that Nixon had merely "stripped away the fig leaves which [Johnson]] had

[40] Fisher 1975, chaps. 7–8.

draped over his assertion of unilateral presidential power"; Nixon was simply "carrying the imperial presidency toward its ultimate form."[41] Congress' efforts to rein in the presidency struck roots deeper than Watergate: "Watergate, or no Watergate, a war would still have occurred between Nixon and Congress. Both sides had geared up for a constitutional struggle before anything was known about the Watergate affair."[42] And Watergate was itself part of Vietnam's legacy. It was, as John Dean told the Senate investigative committee, "an inevitable outgrowth" of the administration's "excessive concern over the political impact of demonstrators" and its "insatiable appetite for political intelligence."[43]

Nixon threw down the gauntlet, but Congress had already begun to wake from its Cold War slumber. In the late 1960s, special congressional committees learned how little Congress knew and discovered how derelict it had been. Senator Stuart Symington chaired perhaps the most famous of these committees, revealing a pattern of executive practice that it summarized as "maximize commitment in secret discussions with foreign governments; then minimize the risk of commitments in statements made to the American public."[44] The nonbinding National Commitments Resolution, passed in 1969 over the Nixon administration's opposition, expressed the sense of the Senate that the United States should make no future international commitments without congressional consent. The Case Act (1972) required the secretary of state to submit to the Senate within 60 days the final text of any international executive agreement. First proposed in 1970, the War Powers Resolution was passed in 1973 over Nixon's veto. Its flaws, clear at the time, have become clearer since, but it was a signal effort to re-establish congressional control over military affairs. Over the course of the decade Congress passed several laws – including notably the Hughes-Ryan Amendments (1974) requiring the White House to inform Congress of covert operations – that sought to curb an out-of-control presidency that had embroiled the United States in Vietnam.[45]

While Congress' efforts to reassert itself in matters of war and peace dominate the memory of this era, it also sought to refashion the constitutional balance in more fundamental ways. It passed laws promoting government openness (the 1974 Privacy Act, the 1976 Government in the Sunshine Act, the 1978 Presidential Records Act). It reworked the Freedom of Information Act to ease access and to permit judicial review of executive claims to secrecy. It responded to the Supreme Court's call for statutory guidance on surveillance of foreign powers or agents. It limited its capacity to delegate authority: It repealed the Emergency Detention Act and passed a National

[41] Schlesinger, Jr. 1973, 187, 255.
[42] Milkis and Nelson 2008, 348.
[43] Wells 1994, 549.
[44] Quoted in Schlesinger, Jr. 1973, 206. See also Johnson 2006, chap. 5.
[45] Sundquist 1981, chaps. 9–10.

Emergencies Act that terminated all standing emergencies, set a two-year limit on future declarations of emergency, and permitted emergencies' early termination. It bolstered its oversight powers: It created Senate-confirmed inspectors-general in all executive departments and agencies and protected them from presidential punishment; it increasingly employed the "legislative veto" (even after the Supreme Court declared the device unconstitutional in 1983); and it established permanent Select Committees on Intelligence and formal reporting requirements for covert operations. Finally, it limited presidential impoundment.[46]

Congress also augmented its capacity to monitor implementation and craft innovative policy. It expanded the Congressional Research Service, transformed the Government Accounting Office from an auditing agency into a think tank charged with assessing policy effectiveness, created the Office of Technology Assessment, and established the Congressional Budget Office. Committee staffs were dramatically expanded, permitting independent vetting of bills. As James Sundquist concludes, albeit far too triumphantly, especially with hindsight, "By the end of the decade [of the 1970s], the resources at the call of the Congress for policy analysis and development had in many critical areas the capacity to compete effectively with, and serve as a check on, those of the executive branch itself."[47]

In the past, Congress had been deferential to the executive while war raged, but then, when the cannons fell silent, rejected presidential initiatives, serving notice that it was still relevant.[48] These regular postwar revisions of the "political balance," however, were markedly different from congressional action in the wake of both the Civil and Vietnam Wars. In those cases, Congress awoke to revise the more enduring "constitutional balance," ushering in congressional government after 1865 and striking a blow at the imperial presidency in the 1970s.[49] Some dismiss the period after Vietnam as a momentary setback for presidential power: The pendulum swung back under Ronald Reagan and especially George W. Bush.[50] If former President Gerald Ford in 1980 saw the presidency as "imperiled," no longer imperial, many more were skeptical that Congress' resurgence would last.[51] The skeptics' prognostications proved partly correct, but they underestimated the durability of post-Vietnam reforms. A determined executive cannot be entirely shackled, but the system also works over the long run: Efforts to defy Congress' will and circumvent its authority are eventually revealed, and the Iran-Contra shenanigans became a cautionary tale of executive officials run amok, not the exemplar of presidential stewardship. Congressional monitoring has its limits, as the run-up to

---

[46] Rudalevige 2005, chap. 4; Sundquist 1981, chaps. 11–12.
[47] Berkowitz 2006, chap. 5, esp. 87–99; Sundquist 1981, 368, and generally chap. 13.
[48] Crenson and Ginsberg 2007, chap. 6; Schlesinger, Jr. 1973, 68 and passim.
[49] For this distinction, see Schlesinger 1973, vii. Curiously, after introducing these concepts, Schlesinger subsequently hardly returns to them.
[50] Crenson and Ginsberg 2007; Rudalevige 2005.
[51] Davis 1980, especially the essay by Dodd.

the 2003 Iraq War clearly showed, but Congress' institutional capacity still vastly exceeds that of the 1960s, and that alone confines ambitious executives, at least some of the time.[52] It is revealing that two decades later champions of presidential power believed the presidency still to be "fettered" by post-Vietnam reforms, and that perception underlay their eagerness to reshape the constitutional balance after 9/11.[53]

The backlash against extensive executive authority in the 1970s cannot be explained simply by the excesses of Nixon or by wartime measures that objectively cut too deeply into America's democracy. The transformative terms in which presidents legitimated intervention in Vietnam account for the perception of the war as a clear failure, of a wide gulf between America's democratic promise and its illiberal reality, and of an imperial, and not merely appropriately empowered, presidency. Stanley Hoffmann observed, not long after the Vietnam War, that its domino-theory justification was politically necessary but strategically costly: On the one hand, "if we ... confessed the meagerness of our interests in Vietnam, then we were doomed to lose, for our adversary's interests were literally unlimited and far more vital than ours," but, on the other hand, "we weakened our credibility by asserting that our failure to do the impossible in Vietnam affected our capabilities to do the possible and necessary elsewhere."[54] The war's even more grandiose rhetoric, legitimating America's intervention on the grounds of Vietnamese nation-building, was similarly necessary and perhaps even more costly.

Algeria and the Consolidation of France's Imperial Presidency

The French experience with defeat in a limited imperial war did not produce a powerful backlash against wartime measures expanding executive authority and restricting civil liberties. Just the opposite. The Fifth Republic, which replaced France's parliamentary regime with a semipresidential one, was created and elaborated in Algeria's shadow, much like the U.S. imperial presidency had taken shape in the shadow of the Cold War and especially the Vietnam War. But in contrast to the U.S. experience after Vietnam, the period immediately following decolonization witnessed the consolidation of presidential authority, not its retrenchment, and for over three decades there was little questioning of repressive wartime measures, whether employed in Algeria or metropolitan France. Algeria did not result in anything like the post-Vietnam dismantling of the imperial presidency in the United States. Whereas Vietnam marked the demise of America's "victory culture"[55] and ushered in a national crisis of confidence, the French withdrawal from Algeria was imagined as a victory, a sign of France's capacity to adjust to the times and to recognize what

---

[52] Howell and Pevehouse 2007; Lindsay 1994.
[53] Crovitz and Rabkin 1989; Gellman 2008; Savage 2007.
[54] Hoffmann 1978, 24, 26.
[55] Engelhardt 1995.

was inevitable, even if painful.[56] Under de Gaulle's rhetorical leadership – his was a "government by words," in a French journalist's felicitous phrase[57] – most French saw extricating the nation from this festering and futile conflict as necessary to facilitate the country's "renewal" and "renovation" at home and to "restore" its "grandeur" abroad. Although de Gaulle, once returned to office in 1958, initially portrayed the French mission in Algeria in classic liberal imperial terms, by 1961, he had reframed the war as a hindrance to France's destiny, to the rebuilding that had commenced when the Resistance arose to defend the nation during its darkest days. In short, de Gaulle redefined French objectives in Algeria: The goal was no longer to remain so as to "transform" Algeria into a modern, civilized nation, but to leave so as to "restore" France to its rightful international status and to preserve French national unity and domestic tranquility. De Gaulle's restorative rhetoric, in the terms of this chapter's theoretical framework, thereby turned weakness into strength, failure into victory, and wartime measures into the peacetime baseline.

French colonialism in Algeria had long been legitimated in liberal imperial – that is, transformative – terms. The French saw theirs as a *mission civilisatrice*, a civilizing mission to transmit Western insights and practices to the benighted residents of Algeria, among other locales. The war was fought to advance these ideals and thus the interests of Algerians, properly understood.[58] De Gaulle himself did not believe that Algeria could ever be fully integrated: Trying to make Algeria's Arabs into Frenchmen was, he thought, like trying to "combine oil and vinegar. Shake the bottle. After a minute, they separate again. Arabs are Arabs, French are French."[59] But for two years after taking office, he nevertheless gave voice to the imperial vision. He declared it France's "great political, economic, social, and cultural task ... to transform Algeria, to deliver its inhabitants from fear and poverty, and to ensure their liberty and dignity." Even after he embraced Algerian self-determination in September 1959, this rhetoric persisted: Self-determination would follow only after "a prolonged period of restored peace" so that Algeria could "achieve the necessary progress in the political, economic, social, educational, and other fields." He challenged "Algerians of all communities" to "take part in this transformation which is going to make Algeria a land of men who are free, dignified, proud, and prosperous."[60]

At the same time, de Gaulle often spoke generally in restorative terms of France's "resurgence," "regeneration," "rejuvenation," "renovation," and "renewal." A vote for the new constitution, he declared in September 1958, would be "proof that our country is regaining its unity and, by the same

---

[56] See, generally, Shepard 2006.
[57] Quoted in Berstein 1993, 30.
[58] Gildea 2002, chap. 1.
[59] Shepard 2006, 77.
[60] de Gaulle 1964, 17, 71, 65.

token, its opportunity for grandeur." He credited his regime with "restoring our country to its rank in the world." De Gaulle's vision was by no means passive: He saw the France of the Third and Fourth Republics as hardly worth preserving, and he believed France had to become "a new country ... in step with her time." But what was needed was restoration, not transformation. For de Gaulle, France's rejuvenation entailed her reclaiming the mantle of greatness that was both her past and her future.[61]

Over time, de Gaulle linked this restorative vision to Algeria, or more accurately, to withdrawal from that "bottomless quagmire."[62] "The future of this people is blocked," he declared as early as 1960, "so long as the Algerian problem remains unsolved." Prior to the popular referendum the next year on Algerian self-determination, de Gaulle went on television three times to address the nation, and he began the first two appeals with long discourses on all that France had done and all it still must do to regain its proper place in the world; with that restorative context established, he then proceeded to make the case for his proposal. By 1961, those implicit connections between de Gaulle's restorative vision and withdrawal from Algeria had become explicit. This restorative mission – "to remake the State, maintain ... national unity, rebuild our power, restore our position in the world, [and] pursue our task overseas through a necessary decolonization" – had begun in June 1940, had been suspended after the war, and had then resumed in 1958, and it now depended on leaving Algeria. "This gigantic renovation," not Algeria's transformation, "must be France's major concern and principal ambition." Algeria was, in de Gaulle's view, no longer the jewel of the French empire, but merely an obstacle "in the march of the French nation toward power and prosperity and the re-establishment of her international position."[63]

De Gaulle thus redefined what was at stake in Algeria and how success or failure would be measured. Withdrawal from Algeria, despite the mass exodus of the *pieds-noirs*, could now be remembered as a victory celebrating de Gaulle's daring.[64] With de Gaulle painting the withdrawal as the price to be paid for France's restoration, at home and abroad, France avoided the crisis that afflicted the United States after Vietnam. Failure in Vietnam generated a popular perception of a United States adrift, but de Gaulle, without denigrating France's imperial past, insisted that it was the festering crisis in Algeria that indicated that France had lost its way. Withdrawal allowed France to find its footing: Under de Gaulle's leadership, "France lost an empire," Richard Vinen nicely observes, "and found a role."[65]

France found a new political system as well. If Charles de Gaulle was the father of the Fifth Republic, the Algerian war was its midwife. His vision of

[61] Ibid.,16, 65, 80, 131.
[62] de Gaulle 1971, 45.
[63] de Gaulle 1964, 71, 104–110, 127, 134, 155. See similarly de Gaulle 1971, 45, 69, 74.
[64] Shepard 2006, 11.
[65] Vinen 1996, 172.

a republican presidentialist politics had seemingly been strangled in its crib after World War II, rebuffed in favor of a return to a strong parliamentary regime. But the Fourth Republic was soon paralyzed by the sort of factionalism that had pervaded the Third. A temporary unity coalesced to make possible France's departure from Indochina, but such decisiveness evaded Fourth Republic leaders when it came to Algeria. A threatened military coup brought de Gaulle back to power, and he then supervised the adoption of a new constitution with a strong president. De Gaulle sold the new arrangement as laying the foundation for long-term French renewal but also as empowering him to address the exigency of the moment. Scholars universally agree: no Algerian crisis, no Fifth Republic.[66]

The president's formal constitutional powers were few but important – expansive emergency authority, the right to dissolve parliament and call new elections, the power to appoint the prime minister, and a substantial executive role in legislative processes. The constitutional text alone seemed to promise a regime that did not depart radically from France's parliamentary traditions, at least once de Gaulle had left the scene. De Gaulle, however, expanded presidential power in practice and secured those changes so that his less exceptional successors would enjoy the same prerogatives.[67] The festering crisis in Algeria was crucial in allowing him to strengthen the presidency beyond what the new constitution authorized. As long as France remained in Algeria, "the coalition parties often snarled, sometimes barked, but never bit."[68]

The year 1958 thus marked not the founding of the Fifth Republic, but the *beginning* of its founding. Over the next four years, de Gaulle cemented presidential leadership of the executive, limited the scope of prime ministerial autonomy, transformed the government from a policymaking body into an executor of presidential directives, established a "reserved domain" of foreign and defense policy in which the president exercised exclusive authority, shrank parliamentary oversight, and set the precedent for presidential dismissal of overly independent prime ministers.[69] De Gaulle also made extensive use of his constitutional right to conduct public referenda, keeping attention fixed on the presidency as the source of policy initiatives. The sum total of the French president's formal and informal powers came to exceed even those of his American counterpart. As David Bell observes, "the Fifth Republic presidency, precisely because it has no substantive constitutional backing, is an act of political self-levitation with few parallels in modern Western Europe."[70] Perhaps most important, however, was the 1962 reform authorizing the president's direct election. Direct election

---

[66] Sa'adah 2003, chap. 3; Vinen 1996, chap. 7.
[67] Andrews 1982, chap. 1; Bell 2000, chap. 1; Berstein 1993, chap. 1.
[68] Machin 1993, 123.
[69] Andrews 1982; Bell 2000, chap. 1; Berstein 1993, chap. 3.
[70] Bell 2000, 10. See also Raymond 2000.

was, de Gaulle understood, crucial for legitimizing presidents who lacked his mythic status, though it undercut his vision of the president as above partisan politics.

Once the basic parameters of an Algerian settlement had emerged, long-suppressed partisan resentments resurfaced, but the expected backlash in favor of a more open and less president-centered regime never materialized. There was even little public criticism of the president's control over the broadcast media, which had so advantaged de Gaulle. In fact, "by the mid-1960s," Bell notes, "presidential supremacy had come to seem the norm in Fifth Republic politics."[71] While the left complained about de Gaulle's Bonapartist tendencies, the opposition failed to unify around the rollback of presidential authority. The eruption of 1968 created an opening for institutional reform, and that was François Mitterrand's intention. But de Gaulle's theatrics reaffirmed the public's faith in presidential leadership, and the overwhelming Gaullist triumph in the ensuing parliamentary elections squashed any plans for a new parliamentary republic.

The so-called republican monarchy thrived after de Gaulle stepped down. The next presidential election revolved primarily around the nature of the presidency, with the Gaullist Georges Pompidou promising continued extra-constitutional presidential dynamism, and with his centrist opponent calling for a return to the constitutionally mandated president-as-arbiter. Pompidou's victory suggested no fundamental mass dissatisfaction with presidential supremacy.[72] The rhetorical and programmatic assertiveness of Pompidou's prime minister, Jacques Chaban-Delmas, combined with Pompidou's own lack of flair, allowed Chaban-Delmas to seize the public stage, and apparent differences between the two fueled fears of "diarchy." But Chaban-Delmas was himself committed to presidential preeminence, and the prime minister succeeded only as long as Pompidou shared his agenda.[73] When Pompidou cared enough, he reined in his reformist prime minister, and when Chaban-Delmas overstepped, appearing to root his authority in parliament's confidence rather than the president's, Pompidou replaced him with a less independent figure and thereby reaffirmed the president's primacy. In fact, Pompidou was more intrusive in government than de Gaulle had ever been, to the point that all policy domains became fair game for presidential leadership. It is only a slight exaggeration to credit Pompidou with being the Fifth Republic's second Founding Father: "If the Fifth Republic, owing to the General's exceptional personality, was an elective and temporary monarchy at the time of Charles de Gaulle, it was Pompidou who made the regime permanent through his use of the institutions of power."[74] On the whole, despite some liberalization, presidential authority was maintained and even extended under Valéry Giscard

---

[71] Bell 2000, 56.
[72] Ibid., 100–101; Berstein and Rioux 2000, chap. 1.
[73] Berstein and Rioux 2000, chap. 2. For a contrasting interpretation, see Bell 2000, 108–118.
[74] Berstein and Rioux 2000, 94.

d'Estaing.[75] By the time Mitterrand became president, this one-time fervent critic of presidential power had been converted into its defender: With more than a touch of Gallic irony, he admitted in 1981 that "the institutions were not designed with me in mind, but they suit me."[76]

The expansion of executive authority to which the Algerian War had helped give birth survived the war's end and continued to grow: de Gaulle's republican monarchy – the French version of the American imperial presidency – became the "new normal." His legitimation of withdrawal in restorative terms made this outcome possible: It set a test that the new institutions could pass with flying colors. France could negotiate a successful conclusion to Algeria only because, de Gaulle claimed, "stability, effectiveness, and balance of powers have replaced, as if by magic, the chronic confusion and perpetual crises that paralyzed the system of yesterday." In short, during the events of the past four years, de Gaulle declared in 1962, the Fifth Republic's Constitution "had proved itself."[77]

The 1962 debate over the direct election of the presidency suggests that the French people agreed. The proposal was immensely popular, and de Gaulle linked the fate of his restorative vision to the country's political institutions. The crises of the Third and Fourth Republics were, he argued, the product of a politics dominated by corrupt parties shuttered by parochialism and narrow ambition. For France to continue on her path to grandeur would require that her new institutions be sustained and even extended. "No one really doubts," de Gaulle asserted, "that our country would quickly find itself flung into the abyss if, by some misfortune, we delivered it over once again to the sterile and ridiculous games of the past." He enjoyed the nation's confidence implicitly, but his successors will not have "been given the same national distinction by past events." Only direct election could confer legitimacy on them, and only it could ensure "that our Republic may continue to have a good chance of remaining strong, effective, and popular despite the evils of our divisions."[78] Although the entire non-Gaullist political world joined forces to defeat the proposal, the opposition did not challenge the core of de Gaulle's argument, which it presumably thought unassailable. It was instead forced into weak procedural arguments regarding the illegality of amending the constitution by referendum. The voluble and sometimes strident opposition simply reinforced de Gaulle's point. "To refuse to extend the franchise for the presidential election appeared to be perverse," Bell notes. It seemed "to confirm the Gaullist accusation that the political class conspired against the public to the detriment of the national interest and of natural justice."[79]

The political paralysis that accompanied the Algerian crisis made greater executive authority inevitable, but there was nothing inevitable about its

[75] Bell 2000, chap. 7.
[76] Hayward 1993, 35.
[77] de Gaulle 1964, 190.
[78] Ibid., 191–192.
[79] Bell 2000, 54.

postwar normalization. To an outside observer, there was little reason for the French to take pride in the outcome: France had lost a territory that it had occupied for 130 years, that it considered part of the metropole, and that many colonists called home. "Algeria," de Gaulle accurately wrote later, "assumed an importance in our national life beyond comparison with that of any other of our dependencies."[80] Why would the French accept as normal the constitutional balance that had effectuated the painful end? Yet presidentialism was consolidated, and de Gaulle's restorative legitimation of the withdrawal from Algeria was crucial. Had he continued to adhere to the transformative colonial project, one could well imagine a postwar backlash against the republican monarchy, akin to that in the United States after Vietnam.

CONCLUSION

Optimists, pessimists, and skeptics about the long-run effects of war on contestation – on unchecked executive authority and civil liberties – each seem to have grasped a partial truth. This chapter has tried to unravel some of war's complexity by distinguishing military conflicts on the basis of how their purposes are represented. The skeptics' narrative, I have argued, may hold for total wars, the pessimists' for limited restorative conflicts, and the optimists' for limited transformative conflicts. If this chapter's claims yield general explanatory leverage, our reaction to crisis measures should be tempered by the discursive context. But this chapter should not be read as implying that citizens during total or transformative limited wars should be anything less than vigilant. There is nothing automatic in these processes.

As for our contemporary predicament, one might infer that I should be sanguine that the pretensions of the Bush administration will get their comeuppance. Iraq was a transformative limited war, legitimated in part on the basis of an imagined virtuous domino effect in which the toppling of one brutal regime and its replacement with a thriving democracy would be followed by similar creative destruction across the Middle East. The failure of the Iraq War when judged by this standard, over six years on, might serve as the basis for a backlash against Vice-President Dick Cheney's efforts to amass power in the White House.

Yet it is hard to sustain much confidence as revelations that might have consolidated domestic discontent have been swamped in the news cycle – by developments in Iraq and Afghanistan (good and bad), by the mortgage industry scandals, and by the global economic crisis. It is hard to sustain optimism when Congress has been unable to muster the votes or the will to challenge the executive branch. The Iraq War has not triggered a backlash against the new imperial presidency in part because the larger War on Terror still informs how many think, or at least talk, about the current security environment. While President Barack Obama has generally avoided the poisonous phrase

[80] de Gaulle 1971, 40.

itself, he has, in his first year in office, often reproduced crucial elements of the narrative underlying the "Global War on Terror" – among others, a portrait of the United States as a blameless victim on 9/11, of the 9/11 attacks as a turning point in global politics, of America's enemies as an undifferentiated mass of transnational terrorists. Not surprisingly, then, many of his administration's policies in this domain have been marked more by continuity than change.[81] Thanks especially to Democratic critics, the War on Terror, into which the Bush administration had initially tightly bound the Iraq War, has been disentangled from that less popular adventure and has survived – if not unscathed, then in reasonably good health. As long as Americans continue to believe they are engaged in a War on Terror, or at least as long as they pay rhetorical fealty to it, neither the constitutional balance nor the state of civil liberties is likely to be substantially redressed. That is the battleground on which the future of American democracy rests.

[81] Jack Goldsmith aptly summarizes the first months of the Obama administration's counterterrorism policy: "The new administration has copied most of the Bush program, has expanded some of it, and has narrowed only a bit. Almost all of the Obama changes have been at the level of packaging, argumentation, symbol, and rhetoric." Goldsmith, "The Cheney Fallacy," *The New Republic*, May 19, 2009.

10

Claims and Capacity

War, National Policing Institutions, and Democracy

Daniel Kryder

The formation of democratic states requires the reconciliation of two potentially antithetical processes: the construction of authoritative institutions and the development of modes of democratic participation. These two processes are, in practice, thoroughly intertwined, both conceptually, since state institutions are never fully separable from social interests, and causally, since social forces expressed through democratic mechanisms powerfully shape the state, even as authorities invent, alter, and channel social forces and their political organizations and behavior. One of the important ways that states affect democratic contestation is by policing the speech and actions of challenger groups – those that authorities identify as representing extreme and illegitimate ideologies. Wars affect these relationships in complex ways, by activating new or stronger forms of collective action, for example. This chapter focuses on one aspect of this larger developmental syndrome: Do wars generally augment state authority – here conceptualized as requiring both ideational claims and institutional capacity – in ways that affect the scope, practice, or quality of democracy?

The analysis is based on the assumption that police agencies, by their actions and inactions, enable legitimate and prohibit illegitimate social, civic, and political behavior. Scholars normally posit that wars favor institution-builders, including those building police agencies. Although the United States has enjoyed a secure geopolitical position compared to European nation-states, numerous large wars have still led to the construction of new executive powers and agencies. In emergencies, the public rallies to support the president, in part because of the executive's structural advantages in a crisis: It is a unitary actor and can act with dispatch, and it is able legitimately to gather and

Research for this chapter was supported by the Gordon Center for American Public Policy at Brandeis University. For excellent research assistance, I wish to thank Melissa Prosky and Timothy McCarty. I also sincerely appreciate the insightful and careful comments on this chapter made by the volume's editors, Elizabeth Kier and Ronald R. Krebs, who also deserve my thanks for organizing this volume and marshalling it to completion. Thanks also go to Gary Marx and two anonymous reviewers for their helpful advice.

control scarce information. Congress, in turn, grows more deferential, given the political risks of opposing the "rally." The Supreme Court also generally acts on the presumption that the president is pursuing the nation's interests until facts prove otherwise. Through such well-documented mechanisms, war privileges presidential definitions of internal security and empowers presidents to claim new powers to regulate, among other things, the terms of democratic citizenship and the nature of democratic participation. In this view, shared by both the state-making and civil liberties literatures, war enables authorities to constrain democratic contestation, broadly conceived. During World War I, Congress, at the urging of President Woodrow Wilson, passed the Espionage Act of 1917, which criminalized any intent to convey information that interfered with the American mobilization or promoted disloyalty. Indeed, antimilitarists invented what would become the American Civil Liberties Union – if not the modern sense of "civil liberties" itself – as a response to several such initiatives in surveillance and policing, and provided legal assistance to conscientious objectors and others prosecuted under repressive wartime statutes.

Scholars of American civil liberties, rightly concerned with the precise extent of these liberties, have produced a deep literature on the historical evolution of court doctrines concerning the constitutionality of authorities' claims to new powers. But the civil libertarians' focus is too narrow, just as the state-building literature's reach is too broad – for we know next to nothing about how such claims relate to the construction or expansion of the institutions necessary to execute such claims, particularly surveillance and policing institutions. Have wars, as we would expect, propelled the development of centralized policing institutions at the core of the Weberian state to regulate the speech and organizational efforts of political challengers and in doing so to shape the boundaries and quality of American democracy?

This chapter addresses the relationship between war and federal policing institutions in America over the long term. A fuller account of how war expands or contracts centralized state power – and broadens or contains democratic contestation – requires us to consider whether new claims of state authority truly go hand in hand with growth in the institutional capacity available to enforce them. The effect of war – or other causes – on new state claims and especially capacity must be studied empirically and comparatively over time.

Despite our expectation that war builds states, and presumably a state's coercive apparatus, histories of U.S. federal agencies with substantial policing responsibilities suggest that while war inspired new presidential claims, it did not necessarily build corresponding institutions. Periods of growth in the institutional capacity of federal police agencies more often stemmed from domestic reform movements unrelated to war. This is not to say that war did not affect democratic contestation in the United States, but rather that America's wars generally did not create or augment formal federal police agencies with substantial power to regulate political contestation, in contrast to the effects of war in some other Western democracies. In the United States, war-makers responded to unruly groups during wartime by, in an ad hoc fashion, assembling and reorienting numerous fragmented and overlapping federal and local agencies, rather than by constructing durable, centralized institutions. Authorities gained greater capacity to constrain political contestation and stabilize American democracy by mobilizing and exploiting the social and political power of civic groups. The chapter concludes with a brief examination of an alternative path of police development. German institutions from the late nineteenth to the mid-twentieth centuries, although more thoroughly centralized and insulated from social forces – that is, more "statist" – helped generate social and political conflict through excessive force and eventually lost control of ideologically polarized parties in the streets of Berlin. German police forces, rooted in an imperial army, both profited from and propelled the polity toward war.

By contrast, American presidents have always ruled with relatively spare and fragmented federal police institutions, and efforts to develop more unified and powerful agencies engage a fundamental obstacle. The Founders detested centralized authority, and their Constitution reserved the power to maintain domestic order, barring emergencies, to the states. Thus, in the first century of the republic, the executive enforced laws through extant, relatively capacious federal agencies such as the Post Office and the Army, for there were no other options. Federal efforts also involved local governmental and civic actors, more so in the past than today. A review of the circumstances leading to arrests in famous civil liberties cases suggests that at times of declared need, the president relied on the regular Army, state and local agencies, and even civilians for police work.

Consider the investigative process that brought the radical Charles Schenck to the attention of authorities, as recounted by Post Office Inspector Wynne in the appellate brief:

Q. During August of this year [1917] did you receive a complaint concerning the mailing of a particular circular?

A. Yes, on August 27th, of this – we received a number of complaints of people who mailed their complaints in, addressed to the Postoffice [sic] Inspector, and other people came in person and brought their letters that they had received through the mails[,] and the letter contained a circular which I have here and they complained as to the receipt of it.

* * * * *

Q. What did you do after you received that circular?

A. The same time, or about the same time, on the same day, I also received complaint from various postoffice station superintendents in Philadelphia that a great number of these letters were being mailed through their station. I directed them to hold the letters from mailing and send them into my office, and I received that pack of letters there, and there are some six hundred of them, I think, as I counted them.

Q. Then what was your next action?

A. The matter was then submitted to the United States Attorney and by his direction,
a search warrant was issued for the headquarters of the Socialist Party at 1326
Arch Street as it appeared on this circular.

Wynn believed that the mailer had violated the Espionage Act of 1917.
Although this episode is one of the most important examples of federal authorities' constraining an individual's civil liberties in twentieth century American
jurisprudence, it reveals a paper-thin federal police capacity.[1]

Scholarship on the courts and the Constitution generally conceptualizes
"powers" as the executive's claims of new warrants to survey, police, and
punish those individuals and organizations that challenge a war effort, for
example, or threaten the nation's security. The scholar's task is essentially the
same as the jurist's, to evaluate the reasonableness of the president's claim that
expanded powers are necessary to regulate certain challengers in the democracy. Is the Constitution "a law for rulers and people, equally in war and in
peace, and covers with the shield of its protection all classes of men, at all
times, and under all circumstances," as Justice David Davis argued in *Ex
Parte Milligan* in 1866? Or shall we judge a president by different standards
during emergencies, as Justice Oliver Wendell Holmes suggested in *Schenck*?
Principles dominate the scholarship on, for example, civil liberties in wartime,
at the cost of ignoring capacity – that is, the agencies, resources, and personnel
available to enforce new principles.[2] Interpretations of legitimate power are
analytically and practically distinct from institutions of enforcement. Both
are necessary components of authority, and principles lacking capacity can be
empty threats or promises.[3]

The capacities of enforcement institutions have evolved separately from
presidential claims to power. Unfortunately, the account of police capacity
in Supreme Court opinions, if present at all, is typically perfunctory, for such
facts are generally believed to be irrelevant to the principles engaged by a civil
liberties case.[4] But a consideration of several crucial cases shows how wartime

---

[1] Both of the Japanese internment cases, *Korematsu v. U.S.* and *Hirabayashi v. U.S.*, involved
a young American citizen of Japanese descent who refused to comply with orders to submit
to curfews and checkpoints. Each individual was arrested and convicted, and the Supreme
Court upheld both convictions. But their arrests could not have differed more. Hirabayashi
detailed his own crimes in a letter he presented to an FBI agent, while Korematsu assumed
a pseudonym, altered his draft card, and even attempted plastic surgery in order to evade
capture. Local police, acting on a tip, arrested him. Neither man owed his arrest to a robust
central state police capacity. Frank L. Walters, Brief for Petitioner, *Hirabayashi v. US* 320 US
81 (1943).

[2] Richard Neustadt made this distinction in Neustadt 1990.

[3] According to Richard Bensel, for example, Reconstruction "combined almost absolute political authority with grossly inadequate material force ... Formal grants of repressive authority
to military commanders was cheap. Enforcement was expensive. The end result was a slow
starvation of the Reconstruction project." Bensel 1990, 380–381.

[4] While the cases that reached the Supreme Court were not isolated incidents, we lack reliable
measures of the number of people affected by campaigns of intimidation. Such measures are

executives seeking to regulate democratic contestation have drawn on, activated, and temporarily patched together a variety of enforcement agencies over time.

Ex Parte Milligan 71 US 2 (1866).[5] During the Civil War, when Lambdin P. Milligan of Indiana helped organize groups of Confederate sympathizers, "military agents" followed and monitored him.[6] On October 5, 1864, military police acting on the orders of the Military Commandant of Indiana, under the authority granted to him by the suspension of habeas corpus by President Lincoln, arrested Milligan and charged him with conspiracy, inciting insurrection, and other crimes.

Ex Parte McCardle 74 US 506 (Wall.) (1868). William McCardle, a Confederate propagandist of Mississippi, was arrested by military police by order of the commander of the Fourth Military District. He was to be tried in a military commission for writing and editing "offensive articles" for the *Vicksburg Times*, which he edited.[7]

Schenck v. US 249 US 47 (1919). When Charles Schenck, a member of the Philadelphia Socialist Party, mailed leaflets to draftees on August 20, 1917, urging them to resist the draft, the missives contained the address of the local Socialist Party. A Post Office inspector, acting on complaints from citizens, directed inspection superintendents to withhold such letters from the mail and submitted the matter to a U.S. attorney, who secured a warrant to search the headquarters. Local police raided the office and arrested Schenck and another official.[8]

Abrams v. US 250 US 616 (1919). Jacob Abrams and four other immigrant anarchists printed leaflets urging workers to strike if the United States intervened in the Russian Revolution. They dropped the leaflets from windows in New York City on August 22, 1918. Civilians brought numerous copies to the police, and pointed out the buildings from which the leaflets had fallen; newspapers also reported on the circulars. Detectives from the army's Military Intelligence Division apprehended Hyman Roansky at his workplace, from which he had dropped the leaflets. Roansky provided the names of the anarchists who had written the leaflet.[9]

Gitlow v. NY 268 US 652 (1925). Benjamin Gitlow, a member of the Communist Labor Party, published a "Left Wing Manifesto" in *Revolutionary Age* on July 5, 1919, which brought him to the attention

---

another product of capacity. Robert Murray reports that over 1,400 persons were arrested for offenses such as syndicalism and sedition during the Red Scare; 300 eventually went to prison. Murray 1955, 234.

[5] Unless otherwise noted, all general information on the cases comes from the text of the opinions themselves.

[6] Irons 1999, 187–188.

[7] W. L. Sharkey, Brief For Petitioner. *Ex Parte McCardle* 74 US 506 (1868).

[8] Henry Gibbons, Brief for Petitioner. *Schenck v. US* 249 US 47 (1919).

[9] Irons 1990, 276–277.

of the Lusk Committee.[10] On November 8, when he addressed a Latvian
club in Manhattan to celebrate the Russian Revolution, some fifty
"police, detectives, and operatives" arrested him in the name of the Lusk
Committee.[11] He was charged under the Criminal Anarchy Act.

Whitney v. California 274 US 357 (1927). A member of the Communist
Labor Party of California, Charlotte Anita Whitney spoke at the
Oakland Center of the California Civic League on November 28,
1919. The local police commissioner allowed the event, cautioning that
seditious remarks would not be tolerated. A police inspector and an
operative of the Department of Justice in Oakland attended the speech
and arrested her as she left the building.[12] She was prosecuted under that
state's Criminal Syndicalism Act.

Ex Parte Quirin 317 US 1 (1942). In 1942, eight German-born American
citizens working for the German military arrived on American soil via
submarine for the purpose of sabotage or espionage. FBI agents captured
all eight – four in New York City and four in Chicago – and transferred
them to the custody of the provost marshal of the Military District of
Washington. Imprisoned there, President Franklin Roosevelt ordered that
they "be tried before a military tribunal under the Articles of War."

Dennis v. US 341 US 494 (1951). In July 1948, twelve leaders of the
Communist party were indicted in U.S. District Court under the Smith
Act. It is not clear from the case materials who arrested them.

Hamdi v. Rumsfeld 542 US 507 (2004). The family of Yasir Salim Hamdi,
a U.S. citizen born in Louisiana, moved to Saudi Arabia when he was
young. In 2001 he was living in Afghanistan and was captured by members of the Northern Alliance and delivered to U.S. military custody.
Detained and interrogated in Afghanistan, the U.S. military moved him
to Guantanamo Bay in January 2002. In April 2002, having learned that
Hamdi was a U.S. citizen, authorities transferred him to naval brigs in
Virginia and then South Carolina.

Hamdan v. Rumsfeld 548 US 507 (2006). Salim Ahmed Hamdan, a citizen
of Yemen and Osama bin Laden's former chauffeur, was captured by
indigenous militia forces in Afghanistan in 2001, delivered to U.S. forces
in exchange for a bounty, and transferred to Guantanamo Bay in 2002.[13]
The Supreme Court determined that Hamdan and five Guantanamo
detainees were subject to trial by military commission.

[10] The New York State Legislature created the Lusk Committee, or the Joint Legislative
Committee to Investigate Seditious Activities, in 1919 to investigate those suspected of promoting the overthrow of the American government. The committee raided organizations'
offices, gathered and examined documents, and infiltrated meetings, assisting in the arrest of
thousands, subpoenaing witnesses for hearings, and generating national publicity. The committee's work ended in April 1920.
[11] Gitlow 1940, 60.
[12] Richmond 1942, 90–99.
[13] Charles Swift, Brief for Petitioner, *Hamdan v. Rumsfeld* 548 U.S. 507 (2006).

While these classic cases reveal little about the arresting agencies involved, patterns nevertheless emerge. As *Milligan* and *Schenck* suggest, cases in the nineteenth and early twentieth centuries generally involved public behaviors and thus civilian reporting. A very spare enforcement apparatus sufficed when prohibited activities involved the public distribution of printed matter, published, mailed, or dropped from a window; such work requires neither professional expertise nor capacity. In the absence of specialized institutional capacity, the Army served as a surrogate police agency, and civilians and local law enforcement agencies also mobilized to serve broad and vague presidential claims so that these civilian and local agents at times informally augmented presidential capacity. Countless instances of political suppression did not involve police action at all, involving instead public and covert threats and harassment by state and civic actors. During World War I, "repression by state governments operated largely through the threat of prosecution; reported appeals are remarkably few, and in over half of these the convictions were reversed."[14] Some efforts relied explicitly on civic groups rather than police. The American Protective League, a private association backed by the Justice Department, had by June 1917 units in 600 cities and a membership of nearly 100,000.[15] This group inspected mail, infiltrated suspected groups, and recorded speeches by dissidents, all without official sanction.

The question of capacity may be obscured by the fact that, like the American state more generally, policing has been relatively decentralized and disorganized, and often augmented by formal and informal civic groups.[16] Indeed, in many of the cases prior to the "War on Terror," the president was wholly absent.[17] Such patterns of enforcement were in turn part of the explanation for institutional nondevelopment; the voluntary participation of temporary and informal adjunct or auxiliary police forces sufficed, impeding permanent institutional change. In such cases, new institutional capacity generally failed to accrue. But authority did accrue in federal agencies charged with important

---

[14] *Yale Law Journal* 1942, 811.

[15] Irons 1999, 266.

[16] The U.S. executive maximizes limited capacity by using intelligence data about the activities of groups as evidence against particular defendants. In *Dennis v. U.S.* and in *Yates v U.S.*, the government argued that evidence of membership in the Communist party was grounds for finding the accused guilty of organizing to overthrow the U.S. government. Despite the Court's rejection of this logic in *Yates*, the government employed it again, unsuccessfully, a half-century later in *Hamdan*, when only two of thirteen paragraphs mentioned the accused.

[17] J. Edgar Hoover, for example, took independent initiative without the involvement of several presidents. Andrew Jackson's declaration of martial law in New Orleans in 1814, the first instance of a serious infringement of habeas rights, did not result from a claim to authority by President James Madison (Warshauer 2006, 8). Likewise, the curtailment of civil liberties during World War I resulted from President Wilson's "carelessness in failing to restrain repression, rather than his instigating of it" (Murphy 1979, 22). This contrasts with President George W. Bush's hands-on approach to many War on Terror cases, including his personal designation of Hamdan as an enemy combatant.

policing responsibilities, and institutional histories, across war and peacetime, illustrate the mechanisms driving their development. This chapter analyzes three agencies – the Post Office, the Bureau of Alcohol, Tobacco and Firearms, and the Marshals Service.[18] What accounts for changes in their institutional capacity over time: war, or some other recurrent factor?

These cases deserve attention for two reasons: First, their histories extend back through the nineteenth century, allowing for an examination of institutional development over the long term, and second, these agencies were always capable of arrest, rather than merely investigation. Neither quality obtains in the case of the FBI. Still, the history of this agency largely mirrors the three examined here. War, especially World War II, was an important impetus to the FBI's development, but so were domestic factors, namely social movements and the expansion of central state authority in the nation's economy. The original Bureau of Investigation, formed in 1908, derived its jurisdiction from the Interstate Commerce Act of 1887, and its first investigations related to the movement to pass "The White Slave Traffic Act," or Mann Act of 1910. It became the FBI in 1935, and the next year, FDR authorized the agency to investigate fascist and Communist groups as threats to American security. World War II helped reshape the FBI's mission to include subversion, sabotage, draft evasion, and espionage conducted by German, Italian, and Japanese nationals. As a result, the total number of FBI employees rose from 7,400 to over 13,000 by the end of 1943. Throughout his reign, J. Edgar Hoover pursued his obsession with the threat he perceived from the American left, ranging from the Communist party of the United States of America, to union organizers and American liberals of various stripes. During the 1950s and 1960s, FBI officials investigated civil rights leaders, and its counterintelligence program (COINTELPRO) sought to investigate and disrupt disfavored political organizations within the United States. Concerns for internal security during hot and cold wars were indeed important causes of institutional growth, but war can account for only part of the expansion of the agency's mission. As with the FBI, factors other than war appear to have contributed to the institutional development of policing in the Post Office, the Bureau of Alcohol, Tobacco, Firearms and Explosives, and the Marshals Service.

POSTAL POLICING

Although the U.S. Postal Service is not typically considered a significant source of federal police capacity, postal inspectors were among the republic's first policemen and retain important federal law enforcement capacity today.[19] An 1801 executive order authorized the postmaster general to hire

---

[18] The fact that reformers repeatedly changed these agencies' names – and their locations in the federal bureaucracy – is an indication of the contested nature of national police powers over time.

[19] Wilson 1951, 145.

special agents, and Congress authorized hiring five temporary agents in the 1810 Post Office Establishment Act. While their primary responsibilities concerned internal security and administrative competence, once the practice of sending money through the mail became more common, these special agents shifted their work toward preventing and investigating theft.[20] As in the Army, the Post Office police were not a specialized force; the duties of special agents were ill defined, somewhat by design. Instructed to "correct and report to the Department any irregularities ... as well as to arrest mail depredators," they traveled in plain clothes and were "a secret detective force of great value."[21]

Such agents remained a small segmented force. By 1821, the capital offense of mail theft was more common, but the Post Office employed only eight special agents. Congress hesitated to employ permanent agents for fear of increasing the power of the postmaster general. In 1830, the postmaster general established the Office of Instruction and Mail Depredation. Six years later, Congress reorganized the Post Office Department and authorized the regular employment of special agents. The renamed Office of Inspection gained a larger budget to inspect postmasters' records, inspect the mails, and make arrests. The special agents' discretionary power immediately caused problems, and for thirty years, they were involved in numerous scandals and acts of political corruption, eliciting suspicion in Congress and in the public. Although mail theft continued to rise, the Office of Inspection employed only sixteen special agents in 1860. This number tripled during the war, and the new staff performed mostly "war-related duties such as monitoring the Union postal system for Confederate disruptions."[22]

The first serious cases of wartime censorship of mail occurred during the Civil War, as President Lincoln and the State and War Departments all expressed concern about the dangers of seditious mail or strategic information being mailed to traitors. On July 12, 1861, Postmaster General Montgomery Blair discontinued mail delivery to the Confederacy, and agents intercepted and opened all mail arriving in the Union from Southern states. Blair claimed a duty to "prevent seditious matter from reaching the enemy" and to prevent instigators from using the mail to assist the rebellion. He thus denied the use of the mails to newspapers he deemed "traitorous."[23] Blair, with the assistance of Secretary of State William Seward, declared twelve newspapers unmailable, pointing out that the Post Office was not interfering with these papers' right to publish, just their privilege to be mailed.[24]

The Post Office quickly ceded control of seditious mail to the military. In 1862, the War Department assumed control of newspaper censorship,

[20] Fowler 1977, 17; Fuller 1972, 240.
[21] Leech 1976, 59; Leech 1879.
[22] Carpenter 2001, 71; Fuller 1972, 242–247.
[23] Fowler 1977, 43–45.
[24] U.S. Senate, 582–584; *New York Times*, December 3, 1861, as cited in Fowler 1977, 48.

and Secretary of War Edwin Stanton urged the postmaster general to more aggressively censor newspapers. After the War Department seized telegraph lines, Blair ordered the censoring of all means of communicating military news, directing postmasters to notify publishers that they could not publish any fact that had been excluded from telegraph reports; any paper disregarding this order was to be excluded from the mails. Requests to censor papers began to come from military commanders, and the number of papers excluded from the mail increased exponentially. In early 1863, Congress began to demand greater oversight over the actions of the Post Office in determining sedition in the press. But the War Department handled most censorship, which went far beyond merely excluding papers from the mail. By 1864, when the postmaster general abolished the Office of Inspection – in part due to the creation of the money order system – and Blair was pressured to resign, the military could censor as much as it needed on its own.[25] Even though the Civil War initially boosted the number of inspectors, it did not introduce greater police capacity into the Post Office. Just the opposite: It reduced that agency's policing capacity and shifted authority away from it.

Postal inspection capacity developed in the early 1870s with the rise of Anthony Comstock and his crusade against obscenity. Special agents would no longer focus only on preventing mail theft.[26] Comstock quickly rose to fame as the head of the New York Society for the Suppression of Vice, and in 1871 and 1872, Congress passed two Comstock Laws. The more famous second law declared nonmailable "every obscene, lewd, or lascivious book, pamphlet, picture, paper, print or other publication of an indecent character, and every article or thing designed or intended for the prevention of conception or procuring of abortion," and deemed guilty of a misdemeanor any person who knowingly mailed such material.[27] To enforce these laws, the Post Office in 1875 renamed the Office of Inspection as the Division of Post Office Inspectors and Mail Depredations.[28] Comstock himself became a postal inspector. Postal officials led or founded the dominant antivice societies in the 1880s, and inspectors investigated crimes that were in no way related to the mail, "including the provision of abortion, the manufacture of contraceptive devices, the display of paintings of nudes by barroom owners, pickpocketing, and even alleged indecent exposures." Though controversial, these vice-suppression campaigns were wildly successful, and in the last decades of the nineteenth century, Congress expanded the powers of postal inspectors by declaring more and more material unmailable. The Supreme Court consistently upheld the postmaster general's authority to enforce these laws

[25] Fowler 1977, 49–54.

[26] Carpenter 2001, 84.

[27] "An Act for the Suppression of Trade in, and Circulation of, Obscene Literature and Articles of Immoral Use," 28 U.S. Stat. 598, passed March 3, 1873, as cited in Fowler 1977, 63; and Carpenter 2001, 84.

[28] Fuller 1972, 256.

as he saw fit.[29] The Comstock movement generated significant institutional development, as the number of postal inspectors quintupled, from about 20 during Reconstruction to 100 by 1897.[30] This boost in institutional capacity prepared the Postal Inspection Service for more controversial and more political policing actions to come.

The first modern attempt to draft postal inspectors into political work occurred in 1906, when President Theodore Roosevelt sought the help of the Post Office in suppressing anarchist and socialist writings. In 1908, the Senate amended the definition of indecent to "include matter of a character tending to incite arson, murder, or assassination."[31] Despite this authorization, the Postal Service took no action to suppress radical publications, and in the years leading up to World War I, the postmaster general rarely used his new authority to censor mail. Still, institutional capacity grew dramatically, "from 100 [inspectors] in 1897 (on a budget of $300,000) to 390 in 1912 (with [a budget of] more than $1 million)."[32] Inspectors' authority was virtually unlimited over internal affairs and mail censorship, although the targets of censorship remained guided by Comstockery.[33]

If the antiobscenity movement created both the mission and the capacity to pursue political surveillance through mail inspectors, World War I provided the impetus to execute such authority. In June 1917, Congress passed the Espionage Act, which outlawed mailing items of a seditious, treasonable, or anarchic character, granting wide discretion to the postmaster general. In October 1917, the Trading with the Enemy Act now allowed the Post Office to censor all mail to or from foreign countries. With these clear authorizations, Postmaster General Albert Burleson zealously pursued political censorship. Throughout the war, the agency censored, shut down, or denied second-class mailing privileges to numerous socialist and anarchist papers.[34]

But, again, it would be domestic social reformers rather than war-makers who would build these institutions. More than any other peacetime episode up to that point in American history, Prohibition prompted the development of federal police capacities, including postal inspectors, who monitored, in cooperation with the Prohibition Bureau, the use of the mails to distribute liquor or narcotics or fraudulent advertisements of intoxicants.[35] The Post Office not only buttressed federal Prohibition enforcement, but also various state-level efforts. Since the Constitution reserved many welfare protection tasks to the states, "the use of the postal clause was the most effective method

[29] Fowler 1977, 73–91. In the only major case limiting postal inspectors' power, the Court ruled in *Swearingen v. United States* 161 U.S. 446 (1896) that obscenity laws pertained only to matters of sexual impurity.

[30] Carpenter 2001, 86–87.

[31] Post Office Appropriation Bill, 35 *Stat* 416, as cited in Fowler 1977, 99.

[32] Carpenter 2001, 106.

[33] Fuller 1972, 267–273; Fowler 1977, 92–108; Carpenter 2001, 102–112.

[34] Fowler 1977, 110–112, 115–116.

[35] Sawyer 1932, 25.

because the Supreme Court had time and time again declared that Congress' power over the postal system was subject to few constitutional restrictions."[36] As Congress expanded its authority through its use of the taxing power and the commerce clause, it turned to postal inspectors to enforce federal laws, putting them in the company of the Bureaus of Investigation, Customs, and Prohibition, and the Secret Service. Although untrained for police work, "more than one-third" of the inspectors' work was at the time "pure criminal investigation."[37]

World War II extended the postmaster general's policing powers. In December 1941, the First War Powers Act established the Office of Censorship and authorized the postmaster general to censor mail to and from foreign countries. By 1944, the office had detained nearly 500,000 pieces of mail. Postmaster General Frank Walker again denied second-class mailing privileges to subversive papers, though not with the same zeal as had his predecessor.[38] Unlike earlier wartime practices, papers were not censored merely for publishing in a foreign language. After the war, officials reinstated most of the targeted periodicals' privileges, and in 1946, the Post Office discontinued the practice of confiscating unregistered propaganda from foreign agents. With the outbreak of the Korean War, the office reinstated the practice, this time in secret. Congress continually attempted to ban Communist propaganda, and while these efforts failed, this did not prevent the Post Office from restricting the flow of such mail.[39] During the Korean War, the government estimated that it seized fifteen million pieces of mail annually.[40] While wartime caused successive reorientations of the Post Office's work toward surveillance, it did not result in durable increases in institutional capacity.

The power and authority to censor mail finally waned in the 1960s. On March 17, 1961, President John F. Kennedy issued an executive order discontinuing the interception of Communist propaganda, restricting the authority of the postmaster general and postal inspectors to censor mail.[41] Congress fought back in October 1962, reinstating by statute the practice of intercepting mail deemed Communist propaganda by the secretary of the treasury.[42] Finally, in May 1965, the Supreme Court ruled in *Lamont v. Postmaster General* that the practice was unconstitutional.[43] The decision not only strictly limited the censoring powers of Congress and the Post Office, but it was one of the first cases in which the Court struck down an act of Congress on First Amendment grounds.[44] Decades of increasing postal inspection authority thus ended.

---

[36] Fowler 1977, 126.
[37] Langeluttig 1929, 41–54, 50–51.
[38] Fowler 1977, 146–147.
[39] Schwartz and Paul 1959, 621–666.
[40] Postmaster General, *Annual Report,* 1959, 94, as cited in Fowler 1977, 151–152.
[41] Fowler 1977, 153.
[42] Ibid., 158.
[43] *Lamont v. Postmaster General* 381 US 301 (1965).
[44] *New York Times,* May 31, 1965, as cited in Fowler 1977, 159.

By 1969, the Post Office Department was in financial ruin and organizationally dysfunctional. President Richard Nixon planned to turn it into a professionally run, nonprofit government corporation. The Postal Reorganization Act of 1970 renamed the agency the Postal Service, effectively depoliticized it, and strictly limited Congress' role in directing it.[45] Throughout the 1970s, both the Supreme Court and the Postal Service board of governors worked to lift restrictions on many forms of previously unmailable matter, including pornographic literature and radical political texts, and the policing role of the Post Office further withered. In July 2002, the organization demonstrated its relatively newfound political independence, displaying an unprecedented professionalism when President George W. Bush proposed a Terrorism Information and Prevention System (TIPS) as part of his Citizen Corps initiative. This was to be "a nationwide program to help thousands of American truck drivers, letter carriers, train conductors, ship captains, and utility workers report potential terrorist activity."[46] The Department of Justice expected letter carriers to serve as program agents, but the postmaster general quickly announced that the service would not participate.[47] This rejection helped doom TIPS.[48] The record of the Post Office suggests that while wars generate new presidential claims, social movements generate new capacities.

BUREAU OF ALCOHOL, TOBACCO, FIREARMS, AND EXPLOSIVES

The confusion surrounding the origins of the Bureau of Alcohol, Tobacco, Firearms, and Explosives (ATFE) reflects the uncertain and unstable institutional standing of the agency over time. Its founding is commonly traced to Congress' March 1863 decision to authorize the Treasury Department to hire three detectives to pursue tax evaders, especially whiskey gangs.[49] Although the Bureau of Internal Revenue was successful breaking whiskey rings, arresting moonshiners, and pursuing various excise tax evaders, its detective force did not begin to resemble the present-day ATFE until Prohibition, when responsibility for enforcing the Volstead Act fell to the Treasury Department. Again, it was not war, but a domestic morals movement – Prohibition – that drove exponential growth in this agency. Congress expanded its corps of agents to 1,550 and paid them a respectable $45 dollars per week, more than twice the salary of a Philadelphia policeman. Despite this institutional growth, Prohibition was a notorious law enforcement disaster, as corruption, inexperience, and

---

[45] Fowler 1977, 187–188, 198.

[46] Office of Homeland Security 2002, 12.

[47] *Grand Rapids Press*, July 18, 2002.

[48] Williams 2007.

[49] Moore 2001, 17, 134. Although this seems to point to the formative effects of war, some argue that the ATFE originated in 1791 with the first alcohol excise taxes, and others use the date of the creation of the Bureau of Internal Revenue's Prohibition Unit in 1919. Vizzard 1997, 2.

the overwhelming scope of the task made enforcement hopeless, even after the Bureau of Prohibition moved to the Justice Department in 1930.[50]

After the repeal of Prohibition, the agency returned to the Bureau of Internal Revenue as the Alcohol Tax Unit (ATU), where it focused its efforts on eliminating bootlegging and securing revenue from legal liquor operations. In 1951, the ATU gained jurisdiction over tobacco tax laws and was renamed the Alcohol and Tobacco Tax Division (ATTD).[51] Seizures peaked in 1956, and bootlegging prosecutions reached an apex in 1963, when 5,500 defendants faced liquor charges.[52] As bootlegging became less of a concern – by 1979 bootlegging defendants numbered only 75 – the ATTD found itself without much work until the passage of the Gun Control Act of 1968. That act was the product not of the Vietnam War, but of the government's desire to gain better control of illegitimate and illicit social behavior. Legislators believed that federal authority was necessary to control rampant handgun violence by prohibiting certain individuals from owning guns and by licensing firms engaged in the interstate trade of guns.[53] Between 1968 and 1972, the agency doubled its number of enforcement agents, while shifting its mission to firearms and assuming jurisdiction over explosives.

The new foci required retraining the entire enforcement staff, for these new responsibilities required new expertise. The new mission exacerbated conflicts between the agency and the IRS, leading to its placement as an independent bureau within the Treasury Department as the Bureau of Alcohol, Tobacco, and Firearms. Though many agencies revel in their newfound freedom when given bureau status, this transition proved difficult, for it resulted from the IRS's desire to shed the bureau. The new bureau failed to attract committed professionals, and its creation did not form a constituency in Congress. It was poorly organized, lacked relevant expertise, and in effect competed with the IRS for funds.[54] The ATF also faced a formidable political foe in the National Rifle Association (NRA). Whereas the legal liquor industry had been an ally of the ATF against bootleggers, the NRA opposed the passage or enforcement of gun laws. Lacking the institutional or political power to counteract pressure from the NRA, the ATF faced repeated political attacks, including the continual threat of bureaucratic reorganization "because of its apparent vulnerability and its lack of a well-defined, specialized enforcement mission." In May 1981, the Reagan White House made good on campaign promises to NRA members to kill the ATF, and it recommended abolishing the bureau and folding it into the IRS.[55] The Treasury Department proposed

---

[50] Moore 2001, 17–30.
[51] Vizzard 1997, 2; Moore 2001, 372–373.
[52] Vizzard 1997, 3; Moore 2001, 63.
[53] Pub. L. No. 90–618, 82 Stat. 1213. The same could be said of the relatively ineffectual 1934 National Firearms Act and the 1938 Federal Firearms Act, regulating and taxing the transfer of certain "gangster guns" across state lines.
[54] Vizzard 1997, 37, 13.
[55] Ibid., 77–78; Moore 2001, 237.

that it instead merge with the Secret Service, but Congress rejected this plan in the face of opposition from the insurance industry, the alcoholic beverage industry, and state liquor control agencies.[56] The ATF found itself diminished in both budget and political support.

Another constant source of political tension for the ATF has been its work suppressing domestic insurgency groups. Though critics of the ATF often claim that it has targeted particular political ideologies, it has investigated with equal seriousness left-wing groups such as the Weather Underground and the Black Panthers and right-wing groups such as the Ku Klux Klan and the Minute Men.[57] Because right-wing groups have tended to be more militant – and thus more likely to stockpile illegal weaponry – they have been a more prominent and constant focus. Labeling such groups domestic terrorist organizations and aggressively investigating weapons violations did not win the ATF many friends on the left or the right. Critics have accused the government of using weapons violations as a proxy for political suppression. This tension came to a head with the most infamous incidents in ATF history: Ruby Ridge and Waco. In each case, and especially in Waco, the ATF received the brunt of the criticism.[58] This was partially due to its institutional vulnerability, as the ATF, unlike the FBI or the Marshals, was still without a significant popular or congressional constituency.[59] Waco left the ATF arguably more damaged than it had been following the attempt to destroy it or merge it in the early 1980s.[60] But September 11, 2001, solved this problem of purpose, as the stature and import of all federal domestic police forces grew dramatically. The Homeland Security Act of 2002 transferred the ATF from the Treasury Department to the Department of Justice.[61] The act also created the Alcohol and Tobacco Tax and Trade Bureau, which remained in the Treasury and pursued revenue collection responsibilities. This split freed the ATF to focus on law enforcement, eliminating a bifurcation present in the organization's mission from the start. In sum, war played a minor role in the development of this enforcement agency. Most of its gains in capacity resulted from domestic reform movements seeking to control disfavored group and individual behavior.

---

[56] Vizzard 1997, 81.

[57] Moore 2001, 93–107; 231–233; Vizzard 1997, 121.

[58] Although the ATF suffered the bulk of the political and public relations damage from the debacles at Ruby Ridge and Waco, it was only the first agency on the scene. The U.S. Marshals Service and the FBI surrounded the Weavers' home at Ruby Ridge, and an FBI sniper shot Randy Weaver, Kevin Harris, and Vicki Weaver, who was killed. It was the FBI that shot teargas into the Waco compound, precipitating the fire that killed most of the Branch Davidian members. Vizzard 1997, 1552–1588; Moore 2001, 285–307.

[59] Vizzard 1997, 161, 205, 156. The ATF's enforcement of firearms laws lacked any legitimacy to NRA members, and to others the raid was "an unacceptable repression of religion"; civil libertarians and radical libertarians object to the government's use of coercive force.

[60] Vizzard 1997, 213; Moore 2001, 323.

[61] Pub. L. No. 107–296, 116 Stat. 2135, Title XI, Sec. 1111.

U.S. MARSHALS SERVICE

Unlike the ATFE or the Post Office, the U.S. Marshals Service has undergone relatively few institutional changes.[62] In the early days of the Republic, marshals functioned as enforcement agents for all three branches of government, but over time, their authority and responsibilities have become circumscribed as the federal bureaucracy has grown and developed more specialized enforcement agencies. The U.S. Marshals Service was the federal police force that mobilized to address new problems and then handed them off to new, more specialized agencies.

The creation of the offices of U.S. Marshal and Deputy Marshal was one of the first acts of Congress, through the United States Judiciary Act of 1789.[63] The act created the federal judiciary, established the original judicial districts, and ordered the appointment of one marshal, along with an unspecified number of deputies, for each district. At this time, the marshals primarily assisted the federal courts, serving subpoenas, summonses, writs, and warrants, and arresting and handling all prisoners. They also paid the fees and expenses of court clerks, U.S. attorneys, jurors, and witnesses; rented courtrooms and jail space; and hired bailiffs, criers and janitors. Congress and the president quickly recognized the marshals' usefulness. Lacking specific duties and jurisdictions, marshals have been available to perform all manner of administrative and law enforcement duties for the federal government. They conducted the national census through 1870, distributed presidential proclamations, collected statistical information on commerce, collected federal employee names for the national register, and performed other routine tasks.[64] Their work in numerous arenas is in part due to their position as an institutional bridge between the executive and judicial branches. Presidents appoint marshals to serve a particular judicial district.[65]

The marshals manned the front lines of federal law enforcement in the early decades of the Republic. They helped put down whiskey rebellions in Pennsylvania, registered aliens and censored mail during the War of 1812, investigated and arrested counterfeiters, guarded borders, and enforced neutrality laws against radicals engaged in struggles for Canadian and Mexican independence. In antebellum America, the marshals were responsible for enforcing the Fugitive Slave Law and the ban on the African slave trade, dual responsibilities that made them no friends in the North or the South.[66] Throughout Reconstruction, marshals were the primary civilian agents of the federal government in the South. Charged with upholding the newly granted voting rights of black men and overseeing Reconstruction reforms, marshals

[62] Moore 1991, 7.
[63] 1 Stat. 73 (1789); 28 U.S.C § 561.
[64] Calhoun 1990, 3.
[65] Ibid., 15.
[66] Ibid., 25–195; Goldstein 1991, 33–139; Sommer 1993, 8–79.

clashed with Southern whites and the Klu Klux Klan (KKK) throughout Reconstruction. Most famously, in the late nineteenth century, marshals helped stabilize the Western territories, which were governed by federal law until they developed local agencies of authority; as territories became states, marshals receded further.[67] Various nineteenth-century challenges clarified the need for new federal law enforcement agencies at the expense of the marshals. Until the Civil War, marshals were the primary agents charged with enforcing laws against counterfeiting. By 1865, Congress determined that the crime required more attention and created the Secret Service under the authority of the Treasury Department. Similarly, the new Bureau of the Census took over the job of counting Americans in 1880. Although such institutional growth freed the marshals to focus on other tasks, it also significantly reduced their power and prestige.[68]

In the early decades of the twentieth century, as the U.S. West developed local political institutions, marshals assumed leadership roles in two major federal law enforcement initiatives: strike-breaking and Prohibition. Though striking itself rarely involved a federal offense, marshals assumed the authority to oppose striking railroad workers because of the supposed interruption of the mails and interstate commerce. Treasury Department agents generally led Prohibition investigations, but marshals made federal arrests and seized breweries and vehicles and other equipment used by bootleggers. During World War I, the Department of Justice charged the marshals with registering and monitoring German nationals. Since Bureau of Investigation agents lacked the power to arrest suspects, marshals also made all federal arrests of suspected traitors and seditionists.[69] But again, it was not war but domestic lawlessness and social movements that have caused this agency to grow in power and size.

While postal inspectors and the ATF flourished in the early twentieth century, the marshals saw their power and prominence decline almost to the point of irrelevance. Tax investigators, postal inspectors, Prohibition agents, the Border Patrol, and the Bureau of Prisons all now enforced various federal laws previously the domain of marshals. The most significant setback for their authority was the creation of the Bureau of Investigation (BOI). Unlike the marshals, the BOI was a centralized federal investigative force under the authority of the Department of Justice. By 1934, Bureau of Investigation Special Agents gained arrest powers, usurping the power of the nation's oldest federal police force and relegating the marshals to serving process and overseeing the daily business of federal courts. In response to their diminished role, the marshals

---

[67] Calhoun 1990, 107–119, 143–171, 209–211; Goldstein 1991, 55–141; Sommer 1993, 40–62.
[68] Calhoun 1990, 63, 19, 231. By 1937, the Justice Department, for example, had established six new divisions to enforce new federal laws and regulations: claims by and against the government (1870), trade and commerce (1903), customs (1909), public lands (1910), internal revenue (1919), and crimes (1919). Of these, only internal revenue can be associated with war, among other founding factors.
[69] Calhoun 1990, 201–215, 223–227, 243.

began a slow process of bureaucratization, including the professionalization of deputies in the late 1930s in response to chronic corruption problems.[70] The second wave of institutional reform began in 1956, with the creation of the Executive Office for U.S. Marshals under the supervision of the deputy attorney general. Beginning with the Supreme Court's 1954 decision in *Brown v. Board of Education*, which declared public school segregation unconstitutional, the marshals developed into a federal enforcement adjunct to the civil rights movement, as the latter sought the legal and institutional means to dismantle segregation. For a decade, the marshals manned the front lines of the black freedom struggle, securing, for example, James Meredith's enrollment at the University of Mississippi after helping suppress a violent crowd of racists, occupying the campus with over 500 deputies, and guarding the new student for his first year there.[71]

In 1969, the Executive Office was renamed the United States Marshal Service, and in 1973, Attorney General William Kleindienst gave the Marshal Service bureau status, which brought a considerable degree of independent power to its administration and its missions.[72] In a rare instance of securing authority from another federal agency, the Service gained from the FBI responsibility for federal fugitives in 1979, and this has become the central focus of marshal activity. In 2005, marshals began teaming with state and local police forces for Operation FALCON (Federal and Local Cops Organized Nationally). Since repeated due to its success, this operation is a week-long intensive dragnet for fugitives of all stripes.[73] Again, war was not a recurrent cause of state-building expressed through the Marshals Service. To take the most important example, domestic political forces rather than international engagement caused this agency to assume its historic role in enforcing full citizenship rights for African Americans.

If war builds states, and if a core aspect of state formation is coercive capacity, this mechanism has worked in a convoluted way in the United States. Three compatible tendencies characterize the American system of policing. First, the United States was originally, and remains, constitutionally averse to developing centralized institutional capacity for policing. Second, because of this, American policing exemplifies the fragmentation of American institutional authority more generally. Policing is diversified functionally, belonging to various specialized bureaucracies that captured various tasks as federal criminal jurisdictions expanded over time. It spreads spatially, across the states, and spans vertically, up and down the federal hierarchy, from cities and counties to the central state. Third, due to these obstacles to centralized police development, authorities facing challenging internal security or criminal threats by necessity patched together temporary responses, either through

[70] Ibid., 235–238, 249; James and Lawson 1999, 115–131.
[71] Calhoun 1990, 257, 260–276.
[72] Ibid., 290–293, 314.
[73] U.S. Marshals Service 2009.

trying to coordinate the responses of various agencies or offloading some of these agencies' work to civic groups. Wars helped police-builders by promoting new executive claims. Domestic forces like moralistic social movements and economic regulators have generated most of the gains in institutional capacity.

These political mechanisms have affected American democracy in complex ways. First, at the level of party competition, the combination and convergence of new claims and capacities have worked to narrow the range of competitive ideologies that groups have brought to bear on democratic contestation in the United States. Second, the way officials often accomplished this, through a peculiar pattern of engaging civic actors and organizations in the president's surveillance and policing projects – America's long-running experiment in "community policing" – not only developed temporary capacity to compensate for the relative statelessness of the federal bureaucracy, but also helped foster and embed loyalties to "acceptable" American ideologies and practices inside local communities and civic organizations. In doing so, the loosely coordinated responses of federal policing agencies to internal threats have helped stabilize mass attitudes and party competition through trying domestic and international crises. As we will see in the next section, in Germany by comparison, a relatively militant, insulated and centralized police force, paradoxically, proved unable to contain conflict between and impose order on ideologically polarized parties and groups.

THE GERMAN EXPERIENCE

Rather than narrow and contain the ideologies and organizations of extreme or illegitimate regime challengers, police can also open a political system to challengers and exacerbate social and political conflict. In Germany, by contrast with the United States, national police agencies emerged from a nineteenth-century imperial and absolutist army, and offer an illustration of how an authoritarian political system rooted in war-making followed a different path of police development, which in turn powerfully shaped its nation's levels and forms of contestation. In Germany, a more militant policing tradition gained substantial institutional strength from successive wars. The increasingly centralized and professionalized institutions that resulted stoked political instability and helped pave the way for the seizure of national power by antidemocratic forces. In this case, war more clearly made the state, and policing agencies in particular, and fatally affected democratic contestation.

The current German constitution and national culture strictly separate police from military forces. These postwar strictures aim to prevent a recurrence of the fusion of the regular police and the regular military that increasingly characterized German state formation through the 1940s. Like other Western nation-states developing police forces, Germany drew organizational models, a professional ethos, and personnel from the military. Until 1848 a 1,300-man military constabulary, organized by the War Ministry but administered by civil authorities, patrolled the countryside. The army often deployed to supplement these forces in crises, creating widespread resentment that helped to fuel the Revolution of 1848. Authorities defeated this insurrection by supplementing their forces with civil guards (*Burgerwehren*), but disbanded these forces once the crisis passed. As a direct consequence of 1848, the monarchy, concerned especially with disorder in Berlin, agreed to create a well-funded and well-staffed royal Prussian state police, or *Schutzmannschaft*, for the capital, providing the city's first regular patrols. The capital city consumed more than half of the national police budget. In other important cities, also, the crown appointed loyal royal officers to direct local forces. Tight budgets caused the monarchy to return many such forces to local control, and through the late nineteenth-century state police forces controlled more and more jurisdictions.[74]

In the 1850s, nine years of army service qualified one to serve as a patrolman in most cities, including Berlin. Prussian elites preferred such men, who presumably offered discipline and experience in the exercise of authority, over unreliable working men. Policemen were subject to the same kinds of discipline and punishment as in the army, and such recruitment patterns sustained a deserved reputation for brutality. Police officers expected to retain their status and separate rank, maintaining an exaggerated obedience to a military code of honor; officers were extremely sensitive to and anxious about those recruits drawn from and living among the urban working class, and officials zealously quashed the efforts of patrolmen to organize.[75] The monarchy's police officials insisted on a highly militarized force, and the police assumed patrol functions unattended to by the army and service functions for the army, including occupying territories with language specialists during the Wars of Unification and surveying political organizations and members. Their most important role, the pacification of domestic unrest, promised faster and more flexible responses, and separated the army from dispiriting clashes with the citizenry. Still, local police forces were chronically underfunded, and they often shrank from all but the most trivial confrontations. In important ways, therefore, German cities were underpoliced. After the battle with the Ruhr coal miners in 1887, spending increased, and state and regional authorities improved planning for the movement of local police and gendarmerie. By 1907, Berlin had a police officer for every 354 inhabitants, comparable to staffing levels in London and Paris. Generally reluctant to arm relatively unreliable city men, local officials became more willing when such units confronted socialist or anarchist strikers and marchers, and they sought new and less provocative means of crowd control to replace deadly force, including rubber truncheons, tear-gas, dogs, and fire hoses.

Police forces also gained new responsibilities – crime prevention, traffic management, and record-keeping – for which the military model was less

---

[74] Spencer 1985, 305–306.
[75] Ibid., 308–310.

relevant, and local agencies began to discard poorly paid and trained night watchmen and pursue their own profession's skills, identity, and funding. New, specialized divisions like plainclothesmen as well as regular patrolmen received specialized tasks and training. An academy in Berlin opened in 1883, and other cities followed suit, often creating regional training associations. Still the military remained the overarching model for the police. The survival of Prussia's militarized police force into the twentieth century "reflected both the prestige of the army and the government's preoccupation with defense against internal enemies."[76]

Germany's interwar democracy now arrayed itself against – or alongside – a police force made by war. Visitors were astonished at the heavy police presence on the streets of Berlin in the 1920s; the uniformed police used massive displays of force to deter political protest. The Weimar Republic's police "stood at the center of nearly every significant activity in the city."[77] Four primary divisions comprised Berlin's police in the twenties: the security police (*Schutzpolizei* or *Schupo*); the criminal police (*Kriminalpolizei* or *Kripo*); the administrative police (*Verwaltungspolizei*); and the political police (*Abteilung I*). The first two were the most important to the daily lives of locals. The *Schupo*, which replaced the *Schutzmannschaft*, was the first line of defense for the republican government, since opposition forces tended to act openly and noisily in streets, with parades, public meetings, and brawls with opponents. The *Schupo* deployed about 16,000 uniformed patrolmen in 1920, about twice as many as its precursor. This new force was younger than the old constabulary even though every man spent six years in militarized barracks training for street battles. After joining local duty units in his seventh year, he trained continually for emergency deployments in the streets.

Starting in the late 1920s, street fights between Communists and Nazis tested the loyalty of this force, and social groups seeking advantage on the ground and in politics analyzed police behavior for favoritism. The police sought to assume a neutral stance, but by practicing "passive nonintervention" in 1932 and 1933 they in effect facilitated fascist unrest. The *Schupo*'s indifference to the political survival of the republic was crucial. Its leaders inherited a conservative Wilhemine ethos forged during the 1918 Revolution; lacking democratic convictions and fearful of a new civil war, police elites attended more to discipline than to instilling tolerance for political opinions. With the monarchy discredited and overturned, the public deeply distrusted holdovers from that order. The reconstituted police sought citizens' support by celebrating their many decades of professional experience, hoping to "command respect only on the basis of their longevity, in other words on their merit during past periods of absolute and autocratic government."[78]

---

[76] Ibid., 313.
[77] Liang 1969, 159. On the role police have played in stabilizing modern regimes as they have competed in the international arena, see Liang 1992.
[78] Liang 1969, 162–165.

Knowing that the police had failed both to defend the Hohenzollern regime in 1918 and to promote the transition to democracy, police leaders focused on technical efficiency. Recruits were prized for their physical fitness rather than for their "political maturity." Ill-prepared for the academy's lectures on democracy and policy, patrolmen "preferred to be told where the enemy stood." Free to express their political views and to carry private party literature into police barracks, *Schupo* faced few internal investigators. All of these factors reinforced an orientation toward the conservative ideals of order and discipline, and repeated confrontations with unbending Marxist youth tended to solidify this stance. When the Nazis arrived, many policemen welcomed them as allies, and the Nazis were careful not to alienate them; the *Sturmabteilung* chose not to resist the *Schupo* when they stepped into their street brawls, for example. Praising the street cop for his courage and determination, they focused their subversion on police superiors and administrators, gaining the silent approval of many policemen.[79] Most officers in the "*Schupo* and the *Kripo* quietly accepted the coming of the Third Reich. What misgivings they had after 1933 centered on the question of their professional future in the face of the powerful *Schutzschaffen* and *Gestapo*."[80]

In 1932, the police, as did most Germans, generally accepted the Reich's supercession of the republican government without complaint. When reactionary Chancellor Franz von Papen deposed the Social Democratic government of Prussia in July 1932, the personnel and the role of the political police changed, but its institutional structure remained unaltered. When appointed Chancellor of the Reich on January 30, 1933, Hitler "sought to capture as quickly as possible the most important civil power, [that is,] the Prussian police with its 50,000 men – and, not least, its political police." The Nazis completed the unification of all states' political police forces in 1936 with the passage of a third set of police Gestapo regulations and the appointment of Himmler as Reichsfurher SS and Chief of the German Police in the Reich Ministry of the Interior.[81] The growth and consolidation of national police agencies in the 1930s resulted from the fact that the Nazi regime combined elements of a domestic reform movement with a mobilization for war, using both new claims and new capacities to build and centralize executive power.

CONCLUSION

Those interested in the effects of war on democratic contestation must consider the full range of possible ways to conceptualize causes, intervening variables, and outcomes. This chapter highlights the ways policing institutions may mediate the effect of war on the boundaries of legitimate political competition. By tracing the history of federal enforcement agencies, the chapter hopes

---

[79] Ibid., 166–170.
[80] Ibid., 172.
[81] Graf 1987, 423–425.

to broaden our empirical knowledge of "war effects." The chief executor and enforcer of law under the U.S. Constitution, the president has pursued such tasks at a disadvantage compared to chiefs of state, with traditions of royal armies and the relatively centralized police systems that followed from them. But over time federal institutions and personnel have grown more capacious and more differentiated across a range of police functions. In contrast to a centralized and militant German force, American authorities often embedded their operations and missions within civilian and civic organizations. The state-building literature posits that just as states make war, war makes states, including, presumably, those policing institutions at the core of the state's coercive apparatus. But it appears that, at least in the American experience, war accounts for only part of the growth of central state police capacity. If police agencies, by their actions and inactions, enable legitimate and prohibit illegitimate social, civic, and political behavior, the United States and Germany provide contrasting cases of war's effects on democracy. In the former, war appears not to have been a primary cause of police institutionalization. In the latter, war not only helped build the police; the militarized force that resulted helped steer the polity toward a fascist regime, which eventually sought a new, merciless war.

Additional research might examine how particular wartime opponents or war-fighting strategies have shaped police institution-building in the United States and elsewhere. First, to what extent has the enemy established a presence within the home territory, or does it remain garrisoned abroad? Second, how completely can the security threat be removed? The Nazis, for example, for all their evil might, established a miniscule presence on American territory and were effectively terminated in 1945. Such an external threat would likely cause relatively little lasting institutional development in an opponent's home territory. International Communism, by contrast, ensconced itself in America and in Germany, and proved to be an enduring opposing ideology. Such a threat is likely to produce more lasting institutional change.

This research locates local police within a broad and differentiated grid that includes superior forces "above" it at the state and federal levels, a civilian population of varying and uncertain loyalties "below" it, and potentially cooperative private firms and parallel city, county, and state forces to all sides. Thus, one demanding measure of legitimacy is not just rates of law breaking or of law-challenging acts but citizens' willingness to participate in enforcement activities of the local or central state. Even the least professional police force has training that differentiates it from social forces and interests. But such trained men were never large enough in number, particularly in a polity as lightly policed as the United States. Thus, policing demands collaboration and cooperation on the part of citizens. Claims and capacities, for all their differences, have much in common. They both accumulate as well as shed prior meanings and capacities, but at different rates and according to different political processes. If previously tested principles based on prior constitutional conflicts provide a framework for resolving new controversies, so do previously tested institutional arrangements survive, on their own terms, providing a new repertoire of available enforcement agencies, resources, and personnel, even if their budgets shrink in peacetime.[82] Thus, each war emergency occurs in a "precedent-capacity context" set by prior emergencies. It is by considering claims in the context of capacity that we can measure the evolution of executive power as a product of war. Policing may be the core of the state, but in the Unites States, it has been a molten rather than a hard core.

[82] See, for example, Higgs 1989.

11

War, Recruitment Systems, and Democracy

Deborah Avant

War is an exogenous shock – allowing opportunities for vast changes in the political landscape or solidifying changes underway. War played a significant role as a catalyst that moved France (and then other countries in Europe) toward citizen armies in the nineteenth century. This was an important military change, but it also proved important for democracy. The citizen army as a recruitment practice in democracies both reflected democratic principles and was supportive of democratic practices. War, however, was also important in pushing the United States (joined by Britain and other European states) toward a vast privatization of military and security services in the 1990s, something that is increasingly affecting policy options in the Western world. These changes are far less supportive of democratic practices in the United States and may lay permissive conditions for undemocratic policies in states more broadly. In each of these change episodes, war not only served as a catalyst, but also as a screening device. The perception that the new citizen army contributed to French victory in the Napoleonic Wars strengthened the belief that citizen armies were more effective and aided their spread, and the perception that privatized military force has been effective has similarly made it an attractive solution to short-handed militaries around the globe.

In what follows, I first outline my general approach and then examine the politics of both cases. I focus on how war's catalytic developments were understood and used to create the political momentum necessary for change. I then examine the relationship between the political movement for change, the resulting systems of military mobilization, and particular democratic practices and policies.

Thanks to Beth Kier, Ron Krebs, the participants in the workshops "The Politics of Peace and the Consequences of War" (University of Texas at Austin, May 6–7, 2007) and "War and Democracy: The Domestic Political Consequences of International Conflict" (University of Washington, May 2–3, 2008), and the reviewers and editors at Cambridge University Press for useful comments.

INSTITUTIONAL ANALYSIS AND WAR'S CATALYTIC EFFECT

Institutional analyses that focus on how an individual's identity and interests are defined, and how individuals aggregate to form social groupings, provide the logic for this argument.[1] Structural or functional demands provide, at most, general framing conditions.[2] The processes that lead individuals to see themselves a part of one institutional framework rather than another are the key to understanding the institutional environment and individual choices.

Large, socially disruptive events like war can be seen as a product of institutional processes at some level, but the event itself also acts as a shock that disrupts prevailing institutional arrangements. The impact of war can propel leaders and their followers toward new paths and allow those with an interest in change an opportunity to mobilize new coalitions around their ideas. The resulting change can vary from moderate shifts in organizational arrangements (such as the reorganization of U.S. forces and their relationship to the executive and Congress after World War II) to revolutionary changes in mobilization strategies and the logic under which "civilian" and "military" are understood. Among these revolutionary effects has been the shift toward – and then away from – citizen armies. War played a catalytic role in both stories. And both shifts have had important consequences for democracy.

Though war often acts as a catalyst, it is rarely determining. What path leaders choose is crucial to whether and how war affects democracy. The choice of path depends on ideas prevalent in the political discourse and the coalitions that endorse, resist, or are indifferent to them.[3] Ideas define the range of issues a new policy is likely to encompass and the alternatives that are considered progressive. The Enlightenment ideas prominent in the period before the French Revolution, for instance, suggested a number of important issues about how polities should prepare for war.[4] Military writings from the late eighteenth century are filled with plans for reform that draw on these ideas.[5] It is also true, though, that many paths were consistent with these ideas. Some of these suggested the revolutionary change in recruitment that was ultimately undertaken, while others promised more modest change. When ideas suggest a variety of potential policies, which solutions are tried depends on political coalitions. Those policies that dominant coalitions embrace (or at least are indifferent to) are most likely to move forward. Those that dominant coalitions resist generally remain moribund.[6]

Not only can war open a space for change; it also functions as a screening device – indicating what solutions are relatively effective. This is not to suggest

[1] North 1990; Knight 1992; Ruggie 1998b.
[2] Avant 2000.
[3] Garrett and Weingast 1993; Avant 2000.
[4] Bien 1979.
[5] Shanahan 1945.
[6] Avant 2000.

that what works is obvious. Success is shaped by perceptual prisms as well as objective factors.[7] It is also possible to "construct" perceptions of success or failure. Nonetheless, whether institutional changes are perceived as successful is important. Perceived success can solidify new institutions, while perceived failure can undermine them and keep leaders looking for new options.[8]

Finally, in keeping with a path-dependent approach, once set, the impact of change should be long-term rather than subject to reversion.[9] When early success reinforces the path, revolutionary changes should be expected to continue even in the wake of changes in structural demands or functional needs. Another strong shock, accompanied by new ideas and new mobilizations, should be necessary to redirect or reverse the impact.

WAR AND THE RISE OF PRO-DEMOCRATIC RECRUITMENT

Napoleonic France and the Citizen Army

The eighteenth century was a period of flux, with vast material changes (population growth leading to territorial expansion among many states) and increased interest in Enlightenment ideas (natural law, reason, and progress) throughout Europe.[10] Prominent explanations of the rise of citizen armies give primacy to either material or ideational change. The material changes did not require citizen armies, though, and neither did Enlightenment ideas.[11] A turn to citizen armies was one of many different paths that could have been taken in response to material changes in the spirit of Enlightenment ideas.

War was a key factor in spurring attention to change. Though all European countries experienced flux, it was France that first incorporated new ideas into the structure of its military, and it did so in response to its participation in the Seven Years War. Reformers such as Jacques Antoine Hippolyte (Comte de Guibert), Pierre Joseph Bourcet, and Louis-Alexander Bertheir argued for the need to rationalize French forces according to modern ideas, and reforms were undertaken in technical arenas (mapping, road-building, and the standardization of artillery), recruitment (enlistment of soldiers for fixed terms and pay, and an end to the purchase of commissions), promotions (based on public and uniform rules reflecting concern with merit) and organization (the army was reorganized into divisions). These reforms were adopted prior to the French Revolution and were possible because the dominant coalition (a heterogeneous mix of old nobles and newly rich who shared few preferences

---

[7] Johnson and Tierney 2006.

[8] Avant 2000.

[9] The logic of path dependency can work through the mechanisms economists point out – material sunk costs – or those sociologists point out – social "scripts" – or both. For an economic argument, see North 1991. For a sociological argument, see DiMaggio and Powell 1991. For arguments that draw on both, see Sugden 1986; Avant 2000, 2005.

[10] McNeill 1982; Cassirer 1951; Brinton 1967; Hazard 1954; Cobban 1960; Meinecke 1972.

[11] Avant 2000.

on military reforms) was indifferent to their effects. The one issue on which
the dominant forces felt strongly – the officer corps – was the one issue on
which they successfully resisted reform. Thus, the reforms that were enacted
were in keeping with the Enlightenment's focus on rationalism and merit,
but they did not revolutionize the relationship between the people and their
state.[12]

The leaders of the French Revolution were also steeped in Enlightenment
ideas, but paid greater attention to these ideas' democratic components: the
inalienable rights of man and the role of the common man as a citizen in his
polity. They rallied support for their cause, in part, with cries to democratize
the officer corps and had significant support from those officers more sensitive
to this issue.[13] The revolutionaries chose to employ an army of citizens both
because it reflected their democratic ideals and because it was an expedient
way to generate a force against the French state. After the Revolution, the new
dominant coalition carried its ideas to the continued reform of the French
military and married the pre-Revolution reforms to the more democratic
Enlightenment ideas: The officer corps was radically democratized, and it was
declared that only a citizen army was consistent with the rights of man and
the rights of citizenship.[14]

It is the citizen army that we remember as the major innovation of this
era rather than the pre-Revolution reforms. This change was solidified and
became the focal point we remember because it was perceived to be successful. Regardless of its impact on military effectiveness (there is much evidence
that France's initial victories in the Napoleonic Wars were more attributable
to the reforms undertaken before the Revolution than citizen armies, per se),
France's early victories were perceived as a testament to the effectiveness of
citizen soldiers.[15] There is evidence of myth-making on the part of revolutionaries to foster this idea. Though this occurred from the start of the Revolution,
it was particularly apparent as Napoleon rose through the ranks and relied
more heavily on military success to justify his authority. The argument that
the citizen army was a successful fighting tool allowed Napoleon to foster his
connection to the Revolution.[16]

The success was noticed not only in France, but also by reform-minded officers in the Prussian military and, after perceived Prussian success, beyond.[17]
Though the spread of citizen armies across Europe was influenced by the
interaction between ideas and coalitions in each country, their perceived effectiveness elevated their appeal and enhanced the persuasiveness and power of
their proponents.[18]

[12] Black 1994.
[13] Kennett 1967.
[14] Ibid.
[15] Blanning 1996; Paret 1992.
[16] Blanning 1996.
[17] Paret 1992.
[18] Avant 2000.

Military Mobilization and Democracy

The idea that citizenship should be connected with military service is intertwined with Enlightenment notions about the social contract and underlies what many have called "republican" theories of democracy.[19] Within this broad consensus, however, there are different arguments about the ideal form of military service. Kant, for instance, while seeing military service as fundamental to republican government, argued that any manpower system should be voluntary and that a militia-based system was most appropriate for a republic. Standing armies, he argued, precipitate fear and offensive action. Also, he claimed that "to pay men to kill or to be killed seems to entail using them as mere machines and tools in the hand of another (the state), and this is hardly compatible with the rights of mankind in our own person. But the periodic and voluntary military exercises of citizens who thereby secure themselves and their country against foreign aggression are entirely different."[20] This perspective downplays the need for professionalism to generate military effectiveness and evinces considerable faith in voluntary individual decisions to generate collective benefits.[21]

Alexis de Tocqueville, though, worried that "men living in democratic times seldom choose military service" and thus claimed that democracies would soon resort to conscription out of necessity alone.[22] He argued that universal service is not only necessary but also desirable to democracies. Because it appeals to and imposes the same burdens on the entire political community, it both distributes obligations fairly and ties government policy most closely to the political community as a whole. Furthermore, this system does the most to infuse civilian values, the habits of the nation, and public opinion with the forces of a democracy. To the degree that the pacifying effects of a democratic government on foreign policy are connected with the cost of war being borne by the population at large, conscription would seem to engender the most pacific behavior.

The requirements of freedom implied by liberalism have posed considerable tension with ideas of equity – and duty – in thinking about the relation between citizenship and military service. Free will, inalienable individual rights, and the ability of citizens to check the state imply a suspicion of duty. Though the tension has periodically led military mobilization policies to generate fierce political debates within some democratic states,[23] it also made possible much of what we recognize as the democratic relationship between

[19] Rousseau 1978; Burk 2002; Paret 1992; Giddens 1985.
[20] Kant 1949, 432.
[21] It is thus consistent with what is described by Albert Hirschman as the "Doux-commerce Thesis" in which societies where the market assumed a central role produced not only greater wealth, but also greater civility among men – making them more honest, reliable, orderly, and disciplined. Hirschman 1982.
[22] de Tocqueville 1945, 228.
[23] Cohen 1985.

the military and the state: a military of citizens, committed to merit and effectiveness, and subject to the control of civilian leaders who are, in turn, subject to the will of the population.

The citizen army had important consequences for democratic practices in democracies. It blended the logic of merit, honor in military professionalism, and the duties of citizens to the state with the liberal commitment to free choice, willing commitment to political entities, and the duties of the state to abide by citizen wishes.[24] A military mobilization strategy based on its citizenry has played an important role in both limiting the power of democratic states vis-à-vis their citizens and enhancing their power vis-à-vis other states by strengthening public responsibility and patriotism.[25] Both the concept of a citizen and the relationship of the citizen to the state have been closely associated with the rise of the state and particularly the democratic state.[26] Military service has been seen as both instilling and reflecting an ethic of public responsibility and individual involvement with and attachment to the state.[27] In his prominent argument about the rise of the nation-state, Giddens claims that the connection between the nation-state and democracy "implies acceptance of the obligations of military service."[28]

There are logical reasons why a stronger connection between citizenship and military service could generate greater support for attributes of democratic practice, particularly its institutional features. Imagine a continuum ranging from universal conscription at one extreme – where some segment of citizens is obligated to serve in a hierarchically organized military – through a voluntary force in the middle – where rules govern the terms of service for those who opt to enlist in the hierarchically organized military – to purely market contracts at the other extreme – where leaders contract for services and where companies rather than governments recruit not only from one state but from wherever they can find the necessary skills.

In a democracy, a system of compulsory service involves citizens in the foreign policy of the state in a very direct way. The fact that citizens are obligated to give up their time, if not their lives, in service to the country's goals should increase the stake of citizens in those goals. It should ensure that citizens show an active interest in the policies of their government – including the rules by which they are conscripted. As Margaret Levi has demonstrated, citizens are more likely to comply with conscription policies that they see as fair.[29]

The ability of the government's policies to have an impact on citizens' lives should also prompt legislators to demand (and play) an active role in foreign policy in order to better serve their constituents. An engaged public and

[24] Rousseau 1978.
[25] Starr Chapter 3, this volume; Burk 2002.
[26] Andreski 1954; Tilly 1992; Giddens 1985; Mann 1986; Porter 1994.
[27] Giddens 1985; Burk 2002.
[28] Giddens 1985, 233.
[29] Levi 1997.

legislature should also increase the demand for – and supply of – transparency regarding foreign policy. By, in a sense, forcing interest in foreign policy, conscription should make it more likely that citizens play the role they need to in order to ensure the health of the democracy. If democratic foreign policy outcomes require a particular level of engagement by the citizenry to uphold democratic practices, obligatory service helps generate that level of engagement.[30]

There is evidence to support this claim. Eliot Cohen's argument that small wars "require" professional volunteer armies rather than armies based on conscription is partly based on this logic. Cohen claims that small, peripheral wars, which are not key to a country's survival, incite greater domestic protest when they are fought with conscript armies. In the experience of Great Britain and the United States, he says, "an unfettered press and a powerful and independent legislature have publicized and criticized the prosecution of far-flung military commitments."[31] This, along with the constraints of public opinion, led both countries to do better with professional armies than conscript armies in this kind of war. Cohen suggests that the United States was more successful in the Philippines because its volunteer force "precluded some of the violent domestic protest that accompanied the Vietnam War by avoiding any kind of conscription."[32] Though Cohen's larger point is somewhat critical of democratic processes – and his advice is to avoid them to a degree by using professional forces –his argument supports the claim that conscript armies promote these processes.

Another piece of empirical support is found by Vasquez. One of the central arguments about public involvement in foreign affairs is that the public will be more sensitive to casualties if it is likely to bear them. In keeping with this, Vasquez finds that democracies with conscription suffer fewer casualties (presumably because they are more sensitive to them) than those with volunteer forces.[33]

This is not to argue that citizen armies lead to or are in any way a sufficient condition for democracy. In the nineteenth century, citizen armies were adopted by very nondemocratic states such as Prussia, as well as democratic states such as Britain. Throughout the nineteenth and twentieth centuries, states generally relied on citizen armies, whether they were democracies or not. A citizen army in no way guarantees the expansion of democratic practices in authoritarian states.

In democratic polities, however, a mobilization strategy that relies on a citizen army should promote key democratic practices. As indicated above, some have argued that conscription ensures citizen interest in foreign policy and demand for practices to ensure the government is accountable to the

[30] Henderson 2006.
[31] Cohen 1985, 87.
[32] Ibid., 97.
[33] Vasquez 2005.

public. Even when popular demand leads to bellicosity, which as Angel Miguel
Centeno (Chapter 12) points out is not uncommon, a natural check is provided if the same citizens pay in blood for these adventures.

Even a volunteer army that relies on a relationship between military service
and citizenship – such as the model that dominates in the United States –
should provide demands for information and accountability, albeit to a lower
extent. The general connection between citizenship and military service can
support democracy in other ways as well. As Krebs has argued, military service
has often been an avenue for minorities to gain citizenship or greater citizen
rights.[34] Yet, a volunteer army that becomes highly professionalized and sees
itself as separate from and superior to the society that it serves should lead
to less respect for democratic practices. This was evident in France toward
the latter half of the nineteenth century and was arguably responsible for
the Dreyfus affair. Critics of U.S. military professionalism in the 1990s also
voiced concerns about this kind of practice.[35]

If a citizen army is supportive of democratic practices, movement away
from a citizen army may lead to less democratic practices.[36] One could argue
that a voluntary structure of service – where only a segment of the population is linked to the most extreme costs of foreign policy – should chip away
at the demand by legislative institutions for a check on policy and by citizens
for transparency, and should make securing public consent to use force easier.
This is the gist of Cohen's argument. A market-based system, however, should
remove even more support for democratic checks on the use of force. In a
market-based system, in which the deployed are not necessarily citizens and
military "service" is really just a job (albeit a dangerous one), the stake of
governmental institutions and the public in a conflict should be further weakened. This should reduce the level of concern and thus demand for input into
and information about the government's foreign policy – and thus provide the
weakest support for democratic practices.

In the next section, I look at exactly this sort of change. I first examine how
the end of the Cold War and the peace missions of the 1990s were catalysts
that induced a turn away from a citizen army in the United States. I then compare the effect of using private security forces versus military forces in the war
in Iraq on constitutionalism, transparency, and public consent.

WAR AND THE DECLINE OF PRO-DEMOCRATIC RECRUITMENT:
POST–COLD WAR UNITED STATES

War, both the Cold War's end and the peace missions of the 1990s, was an
important catalyst in the move toward privatization. The Cold War ended in

[34] Krebs 2006.
[35] Kohn 1994; Ricks 1997.
[36] Joanne Gowa's (1995) argument about the prospect for the capture of democratic governments by interested subgroups follows this logic.

the midst of simmering material changes associated with globalization and a liberal ideational milieu that held both privatization and multilateralist elements. The Cold War's end was thought likely to usher in a less threatening world – as indicated by the prevailing belief in a "peace dividend" and the downsizing of U.S. forces. At the same time, however, the market pressures, technology, and social change associated with a globalizing world created new demands, and the end of the superpower rivalry – combined with the way it ended: the triumph of the United States and the liberal model – emboldened many to push for intervention to support liberal values. In the context of globalization, the end of the Cold War produced contradictory political expectations in the United States: one for a smaller military force, and another for a force that could intervene more.

Liberal ideas suggested two different responses to these pressures. The first was joining with the forces of other nations via multilateralism. In the immediate wake of the Cold War, some argued that reaching new security goals required greater capacity for multilateral security organizations, and many predicted the growth and strengthening of multilateral institutions. The possibility that the United Nations (UN) should be arranged to provide security tools (such as peace enforcement) for this new world was debated – as was the possibility that North Atlantic Treaty Organization (NATO) or other regional security organizations might be strengthened to do the same. Funding, activism, and research on multilateral organizations like the UN, NATO, the European Union (EU), and the Organization for Security and Cooperation in Europe (OSCE) took off in the 1990s.[37]

Prevailing ideas about the benefits of privatization, however, suggested an alternative response to the demands engendered by globalization.[38] Arguing that governments generated massive inefficiencies and financing them required incentive-sapping levels of taxation and inflationary budget deficits, conservatives looked to the market for solutions to new material demands.[39] Initially, these ideas were associated with the powerful conservative coalitions in the United States and Britain in the 1980s, but the collapse of the Soviet bloc, the ensuing privatization of state-owned industries across Europe, and the endorsement of these principles by international financial institutions such as the International Monetary Fund (IMF) and the World Bank led privatization to be endorsed much more widely. Privatization has been associated with comparative advantage and competition, leading to efficient and effective market responses and contrasted with staid, expensive, and backward-looking bureaucratic responses.[40]

The appeal of privatization ideas both led people to see private alternatives as obvious and affected the growth of private supply for a wide

---

[37] Goldgeier and McFaul 1992; Ruggie 1993; Duffield 1994–1995; Ruggie 1998a; Wallender 2000.
[38] Pirie 1985; Donahue 1989.
[39] Pierson 1994.
[40] Feigenbaum et al. 1998.

variety of services – including military services. For instance, in the United States, revisions to the Office of Management and Budget circular A-76 *required* competition from the private sector for noncore governmental services.[41] The increasing enforcement of this requirement encouraged the development of new companies. The retired American military officers who founded Military Professional Resources, Inc. (MPRI) – the company that burst on the scene when it was credited with the training responsible for the Croatians' rout of Serbians in 1995 – saw this trend as a chance to capitalize on their skills and connections to profit by supplying services to the U.S. military.[42]

These two approaches were not antithetical – indeed both were tried simultaneously in the 1990s. Multilateral solutions, though, encountered a number of difficulties. The UN experimented with peace enforcement missions in Somalia, Bosnia, and Rwanda, but was beset with problems.[43] The operational issues could potentially be overcome, but the political issues that underlie them have proved more daunting. All may agree that *something* should be done in a particular instance, but generating agreement on what that something is has been difficult. In this context, the UN has been increasingly seen in the same framework as government bureaucracies – only worse, unresponsive, expensive, *and* unaccountable.[44] Under President George W. Bush, frustrations with the UN only grew.[45] Even within institutions such as NATO, agreement on whether and how to intervene have been hard to reach. This was an issue in Bosnia and then in Kosovo.[46] Other regional organizations, particularly in Africa, have manifested greater problems with operational capacity, legitimacy, and agreement.[47]

The private sector provided an alternative tool, and one that was seen as at least moderately successful. As contingency after contingency stretched U.S. forces in the 1990s, private security companies provided escape valves: a civilian police force for Haiti; military training for Croatia and then Bosnia; observers, technicians, and support staff in the Balkans generally; and the U.S. army's increasing reliance on private logistics support through its Logistics Civil Augmentation Program (LOGCAP)– to name just a few. Some even argued that private mobilization could make multilateral solutions more

[41] http://www.whitehouse.gov/omb/circulars/a076.pdf (accessed April 2003).
[42] Interview with Ed Soyster, April 12, 1999.
[43] Brahimi 2000.
[44] Ironically, some suggestions for improving UN missions involve the use of PSCs to train potential UN forces and perhaps provide some of the command and control that advocates of privatization believe would solve some UN problems.
[45] In his speech to the UN on September 12, 2002, then President Bush warned the UN of irrelevance if it did not act to enforce the resolutions of the Security Council. For more discussion of the relationship between the United States and the UN during George W. Bush's presidency, see Bolton 2007.
[46] Daalder and O'Hanlon 2000; Clark 2001.
[47] Howe 2001.

effective, and the private sector played a role in virtually every multilateral mission.

The extent of U.S. reliance on the private sector to mobilize for conflict became dramatically apparent in Iraq. Taking action without a UN mandate, the United States was able to generate little support from other countries. Its "coalition of the willing" amounted to roughly 25,595 troops from 32 countries at its peak.[48] By contrast, the number of contractors in Iraq in the spring of 2007 amounted to somewhere between 130,000 and 180,000 personnel from an undisclosed number of countries – a number that matched or exceeded the number of U.S. troops in Iraq.[49]

Privatized Security and Democracy

One of the reasons private forces are seen as a workable way to mobilize – in contrast with multilateral forces – is that they are relatively easy to deploy. As policy wonks in Washington, DC put it, using the private sector can avoid the "political costs" of mobilization. This is often taken to be a benefit to U.S. security. Private forces can be sent to meet a wide variety of threats in a wide variety of circumstances, even in instances when political will may be lacking. But this benefit of private mobilization also threatens to erode the processes that citizen armies have reinforced – the demand for checks and balances and transparency, the connection between citizenship and military service, and the activation of the public interest and awareness of foreign affairs. Mobilizing via the market may avoid the democratic benefits as well as the political costs of citizen armies.

An examination of the U.S. experience in Iraq – where two mobilization strategies, one based on voluntary citizens and the other on market contracts, work concurrently – provides a chance to compare the way in which these different mobilizations support democratic processes. Though in practice these work together and feed into one another, below I look separately at how the different mobilizations affect three particular democratic processes: constitutionalism, transparency, and public consent.

Mobilizing forces via contract changes the constitutional balance. It gives vast advantages to the executive branch and significantly erodes the power of Congress. The executive branch also dominates military information and oversight, but Congress has several avenues of influence – over military personnel, over funds for the military, over the structure of the service branches and the processes by which the military does its business, and over the deployment of U.S. troops.[50] Congressional authority over personnel ranges

---

[48] Joshua Partlow, "List of 'Willing' U.S. Allies Shrinks Steadily in Iraq," *Washington Post* December 8, 2007.

[49] Christian T. Miller, "Contractors Outnumber Troops in Iraq," *Los Angeles Times,* July 4, 2007.

[50] Koh 1990; Brandon 2003; Treanor 1997; Michaels 2004.

from limiting the size of the military to regulating and restricting how soldiers can be deployed and structuring chains of command and approving promotions.[51] Congressional appropriations frequently include restrictions on the use of military force. Among the most important tools at Congress' disposal is its ability to structure incentives within the services – requirements for entry, criteria for promotion, and so on.[52] Finally, as a consequence of the War Powers Resolution, the president must consult Congress and seek its approval to deploy U.S. military forces in conflict zones.[53] This set of tools provides Congress with numerous means of swaying military policy.[54]

These tools are less useful for controlling contractors. Congress retains its power of the purse, but it is more difficult to use this authority to direct the internal workings of private security companies (PSCs), such as decisions about whom to hire for particular tasks. The recent experience in Iraq has demonstrated that copies of contracts are hard for Congress to obtain and contracts for security services can be routed through the federal bureaucracy (via the Interior or Commerce Department, for instance) in ways that mask their military impact.[55] All of this makes it difficult for the legislative branch to affect either the internal processes of private firms or the terms on which the executive branch contracts with them.[56]

In addition, though Congress must authorize the deployment of uniformed troops, it need not authorize – or even know about – the deployment of private contractors, and this is true no matter what kind of service is provided. Congressional authorization matters. Witness the controversy and debate about President George W. Bush's 20,000-troop surge in early 2007. Contrast that with the invisible mobilization of a much larger surge of private soldiers as the insurgency heated up in the spring of 2004. The number of contractors deployed on behalf of the war effort by the United States in Iraq rivals the number of troops, without any authorization action by Congress.[57]

If Congress puts a ceiling on the number of troops, the executive branch can use contractors to evade that ceiling. When Congress caps the number of contractors, PSCs can use more third-party nationals. Indeed, this

---

[51] Avant 1994; Michaels 2004.

[52] Moe 1990.

[53] Auerswald and Cowhey 1997; Michaels 2004.

[54] Hammond 1961; Huntington 1961; Avant 1994.

[55] Prison interrogators at Abu Ghraib were hired through a Department of Interior contract (Robert O'Harrow, Jr. and Ellen McCarthy, "Private Sector Has Firm Role in the Pentagon," *Washington Post*, June 9, 2004).

[56] This is a common feature of contracting in general. See Donahue 1989; Guttman and Willner 1976; Guttman 2003.

[57] The military census of contractors in spring 2007 in Iraq showed 138,000. T. Christian Miller reported in the *Los Angeles Times* during the summer that the number did not include security contracts with the State Department and United States Agency for International Development (USAID) and thus reported that the actual number should be 180,000. At that point, there were 168,000 U.S. troops in Iraq. See Miller 2007.

maneuver was taken to avoid congressional restrictions on the number of military advisers and military contractors authorized under Plan Columbia in 2001.[58]

PSCs can facilitate "foreign policy by proxy" – where the United States merely licenses a commercial exchange between a foreign country and a private security company, allowing the exchange of military training but without any official U.S. involvement. Within the last fifteen years, these kinds of contracts have become common, and private trainers have gone to Croatia, Equatorial Guinea, Nigeria, Poland, and Uzbekistan, among many more.[59] This arrangement can hide information about U.S. training as well as avoid controversy that might accompany training by U.S. troops.

Once contractors are deployed, it is harder for Congress to oversee their use. Many reporting mechanisms to Congress contain no data about individual contracts, individual companies, or even if a particular mission is accomplished via troops, a mix of troops and contractors, or simply contractors.[60] Without this information, it is difficult or impossible for Congress to evaluate the performance of different companies or the policy ends they serve.

Congress has taken some steps to gain greater control over contractors in Iraq in response to outcry over several egregious events. For instance, after four Blackwater personnel were killed and mutilated in Fallujah in March 2004, and then CACI and Titan contractors were implicated in the abuses at Abu Ghraib prison, Congress required the Pentagon to keep count of the number of private personnel in Iraq, plugged one obvious legal loophole that prevented the prosecution of contractors alleged to have committed abuses at the prison, and issued several other instructions to bring contractors under tighter control. Thus far, however, the impact of these steps – though generally positive – has not changed the imbalance. Individual members of Congress, such as (then) Senators Barack Obama (D-IL) and Jim Webb (D-VA), and Representatives Jan Schakowsky (D-IL) and Henry Waxman (D-CA), became interested in the issue and proposed additional legislation in the Senate and House of Representatives, respectively.[61] The Obama administration has pledged to further control contractors and make the process surrounding

---

[58] Lumpe 2002.

[59] Avant 2005.

[60] Lumpe 2002.

[61] See S. 674 (Obama) "Transparency and Accountability in Military and Security Contracting Act of 2007"; S. 1547 (Levin) "National Defense Authorization Act for FY2008"; H. R. 369 (Price) "Transparency and Accountability in Military and Security Contracting Act of 2007"; H. R. 528 (Lynch) "Iraq Contracting Fraud Review Act of 2007"; H. R. 663 (Blumenauer) "New Direction for Iraq Act of 2007"; H. R. 897 (Schakowsky) "Iraq and Afghanistan Contractor Sunshine Act"; H. R. 1581 (Lantos) "Iraq Reconstruction Improvement Act of 2007"; H. R. 1585 (Skelton) "National Defense Authorization Act for FY2008"; H. R. 2740 (Price) "MEJA Expansion and Enforcement Act of 2007"; H. R. 97 (Murphy, Patrick) "Providing for Operation Iraqi Freedom Cost Accountability." See summaries of each in Elsea and Serafino 2007, 33–36.

them more transparent. Congressional control over private security, however, still pales beside its control over military forces.

It is not clear whether Congress always wants control over contractors. With little constituent knowledge about the role of PSCs in Iraq, many in Congress may feel little need to say much about it.[62] Indeed, Congress has been less likely to weigh in on the use of private security than troops. Note that the debate over bringing "our troops" home did not mention a word about what to do with the nearly equal number of private security contractors. Regardless of whether Congress wants to control contractors, though, if Congress cannot exercise its constitutional check, its impact as a veto point declines. Thus, as of now, privatizing military services has reduced the veto points through which policy must travel and thereby the impact of constitutionalism on U.S. foreign policy.

Using private security in Iraq is also much less transparent than the use of troops. News coverage of private security is minimal compared with coverage of troop activities. This may seem surprising in the wake of what seemed like a flood of articles on Blackwater and other contractors following the September 16, 2007, shootout in a Baghdad square. Even in the immediate days after the Baghdad shootout, though, the intense media spotlight on Blackwater generated fewer articles than those on U.S. troops. From the beginning of the war through the first quarter of 2007, for every one article that mentions private security forces, a private security firm, or any other reference to contractors or mercenaries in the *New York Times*, there are forty-seven that mention U.S. soldiers or troops.[63] This includes the wave of coverage that followed the dramatic killings of Blackwater personnel in Fallujah in 2004 and the implication of CACI and Titan employees in the abuses at Abu Ghraib.

Information about private security is much less accessible to the public and the press. There is no one central place to find out about the activities of private contractors in Iraq. While reporters can easily find out the numbers of troops and military deaths, the numbers of contractors and contractor deaths are hard to determine. Indeed, the Pentagon does not keep track of private security deaths, and it is only through insurance claims that we even know that more than 1,000 contractors have been killed. We do not know the names of the private security personnel who have died, and they are not part of media coverage such as the *The News Hour with Jim Lehrer*'s "honor roll." Finally, access to information on contracts between the U.S. government and private security firms is limited. Freedom of Information Act requests are frequently denied on the grounds that the contracts are with private companies and thus contain proprietary information.

[62] This is common. See Blechman 1990; Auerswald and Cowhey 1997.
[63] Avant and Sigelman 2010.

Some of the logic of the connection between citizenship, military service, and democracy might lead one to expect that even if the public knew of private security in Iraq, their reaction would be muted given the fact that the people working for the private sector are working of their own choice and often are not U.S. citizens. Evidence suggests, however, that is not the case.

In a recent experiment, Americans tended to view the motivations of soldiers and private security personnel differently. Soldiers were thought to be motivated primarily by patriotism, while private soldiers were seen as motivated primarily by monetary gain. These differences in perceived motivation, though, did not affect how Americans felt about the deaths. People reported feeling just as sad and angry about private security deaths in Iraq as they did about the deaths of regular U.S. soldiers. Nor was there any significant difference between support for and evaluation of the Iraq War between those who read news of private soldier deaths and those who read about soldier deaths.[64]

In follow-up interviews, respondents said that though they believed private soldiers were motivated by money, they did not necessarily mean greed, but also desperation. Many felt that private soldiers must need money badly to take such dangerous jobs. Some claimed that they would feel even angrier if non-American private soldiers had died because a foreigner must be even more desperate for money to fight for the United States in Iraq. They also expressed concern that the U.S. government was taking advantage of these individuals' great need. In response to questions about whether they might feel differently about the death of a soldier, a private soldier, or a foreign private soldier, though, the vast majority of interviewees said no. Their most common reaction to this question was "a death is a death."

It is possible that this surprising absence of difference in empathy for soldiers versus private soldiers was a product of the experiment and interview format, but obituary coverage of soldiers and private soldiers in local newspapers suggests otherwise. Pairs of articles – one soldier and one private soldier (generally within a month of each other) – that told of individual deaths in the *Plain Dealer* (Cleveland, Ohio), the *Saint Louis Post-Dispatch*, the *Denver Post*, and the *Oregonian* depicted similarly sympathetic portraits of soldiers and private soldiers.

Even though Americans see the motivations of private security personnel as more monetary than patriotic, people feel just as sad about their deaths and also express some feeling that their government is just as responsible for their deaths as it would be for members of the U.S. military. The experiment suggests that Americans' feelings about the war and its human costs are not tied to whether those costs are born by people who serve voluntarily or even whether they are U.S. citizens. Just as Americans have been shown to be increasingly

---

[64] The experiment was conducted through (National Science Foundation (NSF)-funded) Time-Sharing Experiments in the Social Sciences. Avant and Sigelman 2010.

sensitive to civilian casualties of whatever nationality, they are also sensitive to casualties on behalf of those fighting for the U.S. government – be they public, private, or even foreign private. Americans feel connected to the human costs of war no matter who bears them.

This finding is troubling in what it says about the current state of democracy in the United States, but it also suggests an avenue through which democratic practices might reassert themselves. The U.S. public feels concern over and responsibility for private security personnel. If Americans knew more about the role of PSCs, they would likely demand greater accountability from their leaders. With little information about it, though, and minimal Congressional involvement, it is hard for Americans to act on this responsibility.

One might argue that the effects of mobilizing through the market on democratic processes are no different from the effects of using clandestine organizations. This is true. And others have documented the degree to which the use of clandestine tools that avoid democratic processes also opens the prospect for U.S. foreign policy to operate outside democratic expectations.[65] The use of private security personnel to supplement military mobilization simply adds another tool of this sort – but one with significant potential capacity – as the numbers deployed in Iraq suggest.

Can Market Forces Support Democracy?

The demand for market-based mobilization in the United States is unlikely to ebb. The security challenges posed by a globalized world has led to goals – some requiring the use of military force – on both sides of the political spectrum that do not fit easily with the kind of national interest around which the public is easily mobilized. It is because private security can be easily mobilized to respond to this kind of issue that it is viewed as effective. Ironically, then, innovations that attempt to revive veto points or force public attention are seen as restricting the flexibility and effectiveness of this new tool. The very features that lead private forces to be viewed as effective are those that undermine the likelihood that they will support democratic processes within the nation-state.

Democracy – and citizenship for that matter – need not work only within the nation-state. There is a growing body of theory supposing ways in which democracy and citizenship might work at a transnational, regional, or even global level. Competitive Federalism and Cosmopolitan Republicanism are two visions of how this may unfold.[66] Within the Competitive Federalism model, efforts to create standards for private security professionals; to increase

---

[65] Forsythe 1992.
[66] For the former, see Harmes 2006. For the latter, see Beck 2000; Habermas 1999; Held 1995. For an application of these principles to private security, see Krahmann 2010.

transparency about their efforts; and to use a variety of local, national, regional, and nonstate bodies to hold different parts of their behavior accountable can all be seen as attempts to exert democratic control over private forces by enhancing the capacities of various consumers. Increasing the ability to democratically control private security is not the same, though, as increasing the degree to which forces mobilized through the market enhance or support the democratic processes of governance. One might infer from this vision rather weak support for democratic processes that could result in a minimalist form of democracy.[67]

The Cosmopolitan Republican model emphasizes the bases on which citizens of the world might identify with one another as members of the same community, feel obliged to contribute to that community, and feel connected to losses that community might suffer. The cosmopolitan soldier is one that works on behalf of cosmopolitan norms, according to common standards and training in transnational military units aimed at reducing the use of violence. In the Cosmopolitan Republican model, the use of violence is seen as a breach of law rather than a military issue of confronting an existential threat. Generally, this model is seen to be based on an aggregation of nation-states with conscript armies in pursuit of cosmopolitan peacekeeping missions.[68]

Many are skeptical that market-based mobilization could support such ideals. While this skepticism may be warranted, the responses of those Americans in the experiment mentioned above suggests that people may identify with deaths in pursuit of public policy as fellow citizens, whether those who die are mobilized via the market or not. If this suggestion is borne out, the mechanisms proposed by Competitive Federalists may also be tools that support democratic processes – at least in a modest way.

CONCLUSION

War's impact on mobilization policy worked in similar ways in the eighteenth century and at the end of the twentieth century, but with a different impact on democracy. War acted as an exogenous shock and then a screening device in each instance, but its effect on democracy depended on how that shock interacted with prominent ideas and political coalitions. Combined with ideas about the connection between citizens and the state and a pragmatic desire to mount a military challenge to the old regime, war led French revolutionaries to introduce a connection between citizenship and military service based on mutual obligation. When the citizen army was perceived to be successful, it worked to support democratic ideals and democratic processes within nation-states. Combined with privatization ideas and a desire to meet post–Cold War

---

[67] See Bermeo (Chapter 4) for a similar argument in a different context.
[68] Krahmann 2010.

global challenges with a smaller force, war led American presidents to rely on market mobilization as a way to do more with less. When seen to be more successful than its alternatives, market-based mobilization has thus far generally undermined democratic processes in the United States. War's impact on the character of polities thus follows similar patterns but with widely divergent implications for democracy.

12

Concluding Reflections

What Wars Do

Miguel Angel Centeno

What do wars do? They obviously kill and destroy, but ever since Weber and Hintze, if not before, we have known that they do much more.[1] These authors noted the centrality of war and military organization for the political, social, and economic development of the broadly defined "West." More recently, Charles Tilly has argued that without war, the contemporary state would be unimaginable.[2] The authors in this volume have sought to establish a more precise position: that there exists a positive link between war and democracy.

Such an argument seems paradoxical on many levels. Given our general positive view of democracy, how can it arise from the squalidness, violence, and injustice of war? Given the chaos and destruction that accompanies conflict, how can it produce something as dependent on rules as democracy? And yet the historical evidence does indicate a link.

Proponents of the war-democracy axis often rely on broad correlation rather than direct causation. Simply put, in certain periods and in certain places there were a lot of wars, and afterward there were more democracies than before. Small-*n* studies allow a better handle on how the specific policies that accompanied a country being at war later led to more progressive measures in one sphere or another. Even rigorous statistical testing does not falsify the claim, but merely suggests that the relationship may be more complex than some attest.

But the arguments always have some causal ambiguity. Are the exchanges that make democratic rule possible directly related to war or only spuriously associated with it? Does any conflict at any time have this effect, or only do some wars, at some times, and in some places help produce democracy? Does the simple size of the conflict (as measured in deaths, perhaps) matter, or is what counts the extent to which the populace becomes involved? If only some wars make democracies, can we really speak of a general rule, or only

This chapter is dedicated to the memory of Charles Tilly.

[1] Hintze 1975; Weber 1978.
[2] Tilly 1975; 1985; 1992.

a regionally and historically defined phenomenon? How long does it take for war to produce these effects? Finally, is war a necessary or a sufficient factor in establishing, bolstering, or extending democratic rule?

The preceding chapters all make valuable contributions to answering these questions. By way of conclusion, this chapter discusses how the "war effect" plays different roles in supporting the constituent parts or stages of democracy as defined by T. H. Marshall.[3] Rather than arguing that war supports or does not support the establishment of democratic rule in general, we need to ask about its role in producing and/or defending civil or constitutional rights, political and electoral rights, and social rights. Such a strategy will allow for more rigorous and concrete analysis of the proposed causal links. In the second part of the chapter, I propose that the creation of what Benedict Anderson calls an "imagined community"[4] is the central mechanism through which war supports democracy in its various aspects. This link is largely neglected in the contributions to this volume and needs much more attention. I then discuss the problem of geographical and historical specificity of the "war effect" and conclude with some thoughts on the implications for democracy of the transformation of what we may call the "Western Way of War."[5]

WAR AND RIGHTS

While the assertion that war and democracy are linked (in both causal directions) is often cited, much less attention has been paid to the specific aspects of democracy that war actually supports. What is the specific way in which war helps (or retards) the development of civil, political, and social rights?

The foundational right in a democracy is that which recognizes the basic autonomy and inviolability of the individual. Civil rights protect that status by assuring constraints on state actions regarding the life or property of a citizen. How does war affect this? It does so in both negative and positive ways.

As Ronald R. Krebs (Chapter 9) notes, war can have very different effects on the concentration of power inside a regime and how that power is exercised. In some scenarios, wars can have very detrimental effects on civil liberties. Wars provide "emergencies" during which legal rights are perceived as possibly unnecessary and even dangerous luxuries. The suppression of basic civil rights has often accompanied wars: freedom of speech is limited, the constraints on government are weakened, and individuals are required to give up some of their "negative freedom" to the collective needs of the endangered whole. In these instances, wars are prone to creating what Paul Starr (Chapter 3), following Harold Lasswell, calls "garrison states." As Daniel Kryder (Chapter 10) demonstrates, perceptions of imminent danger help determine basic policing capacity.

[3] Marshall 1950.
[4] Anderson 2006.
[5] Hanson 2000.

The appeal of such draconian policies is considerable. In the wake of 9/11, and considerably after, it was a brave and rare American public figure who warned about the dangers of giving federal and executive authorities too much power. Even eight years later, debate continues about the extent to which a democracy must "relax" its rules in order to protect itself. The notion that torture might "save lives" (no matter how empirically falsifiable) had (and has) adherents, as did (and does) the notion that constitutional guarantees should not serve as obstacles to strategy.

In the absence of dissenting views and with a constant flow of propaganda, states at war can create public atmospheres so consumed with fear of or loathing for an enemy that active suppression may even become redundant. *1984*'s Winston Smith might be well aware of the lies of dictatorial rule, but he still succumbed to the power of the "two minute hate":

The horrible thing about the Two Minutes Hate was not that one was obliged to act a part, but that it was impossible to avoid joining in. Within thirty seconds any pretense was always unnecessary. A hideous ecstasy of fear and vindictiveness, a desire to kill, to torture, to smash faces in with a sledge hammer, seemed to flow through the whole group of people like an electric current, turning one even against one's will into a grimacing, screaming lunatic.[6]

Similar experiences can be found in more democratic societies enraged with their enemies. Wars have the capacity to turn us all into lunatics and to convince us that only the state can protect us from the horrifying foe.[7] The consequences of this form of patriotic euphoria are evident and sinister.

In these cases, it is precisely democratic rule that may drive us into the arms of authoritarian temptation. There is a long tradition that blames democratic institutions and practices for such unnecessary measures during wartime. It is popular demands for protection and revenge that may lead governments to repressive policies they would not take on their own.[8] It is the call of the crowd for blood, rather than the tyranny of leaders, that presents the greatest danger. If the enemy is "foreign" or different enough, the simple drawing of the distinction between the threat and the victims can actually produce euphoric expressions of belonging. The most obvious rub, of course, comes from giving anyone the right to label whomever as an enemy; if they come for them today in the "Black Maria," when do they come for me?

Obviously, the effect of this fear sometimes dissipates in the postwar period. In fact, as Krebs notes, the excesses of war often can turn into the lessons that help us better protect our rights. "Permanent states of war," however, are not unknown. A variety of regimes justify the continuing limitation on individual freedoms by either claiming that the enemy remains undefeated, or by pulling ever-new terrors from the political magicians' hat. This is particularly tempting

---

[6] Orwell 1990, 14.
[7] Or simply do silly things, like rename French fries as "freedom fries."
[8] Ackerman 2006. Thanks to Sidney Tarrow for introducing me to some of these arguments.

in cases where the enemy remains unseen and where the fights are more about ideas than about resources. Most of our analyses of the relationship between war and democracy have dealt with relatively simple, territorial struggles with clear front lines and assumed homefront support. Struggles characterized by either significant domestic dissent or "hidden" enemies may produce very different politically institutionalized outcomes. In the case of Latin America, the "national security" doctrine of the 1960s and 1970s, with its emphasis on internal threats, was a corrosive force on regional democracies.

More optimistically, there are much more institutional contributions of war to civil rights than the simple setting of negative examples. First, we must consider the oft-cited exchange between states and (potential) soldiers.[9] This can be played out in many ways, but essentially involves citizens (even if the term is used anachronistically) demanding some rights in exchange for their participation in war. This participation need not necessarily involve violence. Arguably the most important instances of such an exchange have involved groups of citizens agreeing to provide financing in order to pay for the tools of war. Whether asking for blood or specie, states have often had to "pay" in order to "play" at war. In this way, war serves as the historical process through which subjects are transformed into citizens.

The grant of citizenship has often been historically linked to military necessities. The concept of the citizen-soldier was born in classical Greece and Rome, and advances in rights can often be traced to strategic needs. (Similarly, the decline of rights can also be traced to the development of military alternatives. So, for example, the professionalization of the Roman army undermined the link between service and citizenship). Similar exchanges have been a mainstay of the rise of the constitutional state in Britain and the institution of a militia in various parts of the world. Such contracts between states and populaces are not solely historical artifacts. Today in the United States, for example, programs offer "expedited citizenship" through military service.[10]

In some cases, the relationship between citizenship and military service is less that of a bargain between soldier and state than the product of simple strategic competition between rivals. In such cases, governments might compete to see which can promise or deliver more to its citizens, or they may seek to defend their international reputation. For example, the argument has been made that the competition for global legitimacy during the Cold War forced the federal government to support a broader civil rights agenda than might have otherwise been the case.[11] While war has often been associated with the elevation of civil rights for previously persecuted minorities, the institution of

---

[9] Turner and Hamilton 1994.

[10] Lee and Wasem 2003.

[11] Dudziak 2000. The prototypical concern was that a diplomat from a newly independent African country (also being courted by the USSR) would be denied service at a roadside restaurant in Maryland.

military service may conversely serve as a bulwark of ingrained power. Ethnic minorities may be excluded from the military for fear that their loyalties may be in question. Or military service may be used to legitimize a hierarchical ordering of society. The resistance of the samurai to the Meiji reforms, for example, was in part based on their awareness that these would elevate previously detestable peasants into potential soldiers.[12] Similarly, one could trace many of the gender- or sex-based barriers to full citizenship to the historical male monopoly on military service.

What of voting and war? The complex relationship between electoral democracy and the military, between the polling booth and the barracks, has been the subject of the most study, and Edward D. Mansfield and Jack Snyder's contribution to this volume (Chapter 2) provides a rigorous foundation for future discussion. When we include the entire globe of democracies, there appears to be a weak relationship between suffrage and conflict, or between war and democracy.

We ought not to be surprised that electoral rights are much more complicated and historically contingent than what we may call civil liberties or even citizenship. Electoral democracy requires both that people be allowed to vote and that their vote actually mean something for political decision making. The relationship between war and the political import of election results is, therefore, harder to unravel than a simple one-time exchange.

A key historical step here, as Deborah Avant (Chapter 11) notes, is the creation of mass armies, where the nobility no longer fights merely supported by a rabble, but where the nation as a whole is called to arms. For some, this represents an ideal of citizens voluntarily serving a republic and therefore establishing their ownership of it. For others, it is the mechanism of conscription, which following the logic of the discussion on civil rights, triggers the exchange exemplified in a Swedish folk saying: "One soldier, one rifle, one vote."[13] In this process, each individual willing to risk his life (and again the gender specificity is important) is paid off by the state with a promise of suffrage.

Conversely, wars can elicit states of emergency where elections need to be postponed, as Mayor Giuliani hinted in the aftermath of 9/11. In the same way that "emergency powers" required by war can lead to the trampling of civil rights, military crises may be seen as prohibiting the political expenses of electioneering. Wars also potentially limit suffrage by forcing the creation of "grand coalitions" that not only obscure political differences, but also retain power through an agreed deferment of elections, as was the case with the British War Cabinet of World War II.

There is also the tricky historical question of causal order. Which really comes first, the soldier or the citizen? Do mass armies produce mass citizenship, or do already massified polities produce mass armies? Avant notes that,

---

[12] Turnbull 2006.
[13] Ben-Eliezer 1995.

prior to the French Revolution, the concept of a conscript army was already making headway. Conscription regimes in places like Tsarist Russia certainly did not lead to greater political rights. (Except, of course, in that when the army had enough of the slaughter in 1917, the armed population could force a regime change.) It would appear that the notion of a participating citizen must already exist for conscription to translate into democracy. Conscription is, therefore, perhaps best thought of as a critical political stimulus to speed up an already ongoing process. We do not have enough historical detail on these questions. What is needed is detailed research that carefully documents the process through which conscription evolved from an obligation imposed on the most miserable of subjects ("the scum of the earth" in Wellington's phrase) to the expected duty of the free citizen. We know, for example, of Machiavelli's approval of "citizen armies" as opposed to the mercenary variety in the sixteenth century, but how did this relate to the domestic politics of the Italian city-states?

Moreover, suffrage does not mean democracy. Even if war plays a significant role in expanding voting rights, there is no reason to believe that these votes will have any meaning. Totalitarian regimes have considerable expertise in managing rituals of popular participation where the regime receives overwhelming support. "Perfect dictatorships," such as pre-2000 Mexico, can even have relatively free elections with little hope for regime change. How do elections become actually relevant, and what is the role of war, if any, in that process?

Nancy Bermeo (Chapter 4) comes closest to proposing specific conditions through which military conflict can promote democratic government. Her findings seem to indicate that military defeat is sometimes a driver of democratic reform (but no guarantee, as many cases in interwar Europe attest). Yet note that at the core of this effect there is no necessarily *military* component. It is the public failure of a regime to accomplish some goal that delegitimizes authoritarian rule enough to provide an opportunity for democracy. Such delegitimation could come from an economic crisis or a simple failure to perform adequately. Rather than *war* making democracy, we might better speak of *failure* doing so. Note, however, that similar failures can also lead to the collapse of democratic regimes.

The final aspect to take into consideration when defining the relationship between war and voting is that other supposed child of war, state development. For democracy to be established in any meaningful way, the state has to have enough capacity not just to run an election, but also to make its results mean something in policy terms. As Charles Tilly argued, the very process of demanding and defending rights was part of the give and take of state-making in the first place. Wars have been cited as producing both states and democracies, but the order of their creation might be critical. It may be that for a functioning democracy, one needs two wars: one to create a state, the next to make it democratic. Efforts to do the latter without the former may lead to failure and a return to simpler authoritarian rule.

Does democracy assist the development of what Marshall called social rights? Rieko Kage (Chapter 5) analyzes the basis for this argument: War does promote social mobilization and teaches a broader array of citizens "civic skills," which can then potentially be used to promote their interests. Moreover, as in the case of civil and electoral rights, the need for popular support by the state during wartime provides a key incentive for social spending (or at least the promise thereof). In this instance, instead of being "bribed" by a vote or recognition of citizenship, political subjects are offered state assistance in one form or another.

As Elizabeth Kier (Chapter 7) documents, war forces the state to both grow and redistribute. In the best cases, these strategies produce a broad legitimation of both the regime and socially progressive policies. This is particularly true in "mass" or "total" wars in which the population is required to make significant sacrifices and where these need to be politically "purchased." Yet there are no guarantees. The wrong kind of approaches to resource mobilization can lead to the rejection of the status quo by particular segments, as in Italy. Or, the measures taken can be seen as exceptional and not really challenging the politico-economic structures, as in the United States. Mark R. Wilson (Chapter 8) demonstrates that the perception of what happened during a war is also critical, as different forms of economic intervention may be recognized and celebrated, or not. Here it is good to recall Avant's point regarding the relationship between perceived success of military innovation and political change. Defeats can begin something of a vicious circle: Failure at wars may undermine both state legitimacy and the very infrastructure necessary to provide reasons to be loyal to the state.

In many instances, mobilization did not lead to democracy. Combinations of effective propaganda and coercion can produce significant popular support for military victory with no democratic institutional legacies. The totalitarian regimes of World War II mobilized their masses with the same fervor, and arguably as effectively, as the democracies. While we are now aware of subcurrents of discontent in Japan and Germany, for example, both regimes enjoyed significant popular support until the very end of the war. Success in war can forgive many political sins; witness Argentine reaction to the early stages of the Malvinas War when the widely despised generals enjoyed a brief honeymoon. Note, moreover, that the negotiation between state and populaces need not imply institutionalized social rights, much less welfare states. Populations may bargain for schools and hospitals, but also settle for bread and circuses.

Wars do produce a new subgroup in a population that enjoys a specific legitimacy and whose claims many governments are reluctant to ignore: veterans.[14] These groups not only enjoy a special symbolic status; they are also both more organized and better trained than other possible mass claimants. But

---

[14] Skocpol 1995. But note how little work there actually is on veterans and their political roles. See the discussion in Diamant 2009.

even in this instance, the demands of veterans are not enough to guarantee an expansion of social provisions. The U.S. military itself was willing to suppress demands when the Bonus Army of World War I veterans marched in 1932. Even with the post–Gulf War celebration of the military and the reminders of the sacrifice made by the men and women within it, funding for their health and education encounters significant obstacles. Moreover, while veterans may demand more welfare provisions, conversely they may demand a more conservative social order, as was the case with the *Heimwher* or the *Freikrops* of interwar Germany.

Yet another way that war may lead to greater social rights is through the instrumental use of welfare policies to produce better soldiers or simply more loyal citizens.[15] In the most basic version of such a policy, welfare policies can assure that recruits arrive at the barracks relatively healthy and literate. As warfare became massified, the ability of any state to produce large numbers of soldiers immediately ready to assume their roles, or at least to be trained, became ever more important. In this instance, institutions that assure a healthier and better-educated potential reserve for military duty provide significant advantages, and those states that have developed them may be positively selected.[16] Similarly, the ability of a state to count on a loyal population to support militaristic adventures often depends on its ability to deliver services. Both motivations, for example, appear to have played major roles in the development of the German welfare state under Bismarck.[17]

In more contemporary settings, war also seems to be the exceptional case whereby classic liberals or, in American parlance, economic conservatives, are willing to suspend their commitment to absolute individuality and encourage the development of collective goods. The sacrifice of the few thereby legitimizes better state provisions for the care of the many. Again, as in the discussion regarding civil rights above, note that such willingness to place collective interests or responsibilities ahead of individual autonomy may actually be detrimental to democracy.

Wars can, however, also limit the fiscal capacity of the state to address social ills. Certainly LBJ was concerned that demanding too much to pay for Vietnam would derail the creation of the Great Society. More recently, the Reagan defense build-ups, combined with lower taxes, provided much less fiscal wiggle room for any expansion of social services. Yet, recent work has challenged the alleged choice between "guns *or* butter" which still defines large elements of policy discussions. According to this developing view, it is imperative to recognize the welfare functions of the military itself.[18] Social assistance for military families, veterans' benefits, and educational supports

---

[15] For a broad discussion of this relationship, see Mann 1992; Giddens 1985.

[16] In a contemporary example, the dearth and physical conditions of recruits into the Russian military has focused that state's attention on the failure of public welfare provisions.

[17] War can accomplish a similar welfare function after its conclusion. See Mettler 2005.

[18] Rabinowitz 2008; Gifford 2006.

make the military a leading social service provider in the United States. The extent to which these services then lead to a broader welfare isomorphism needs to be better analyzed.[19]

The findings of the chapters in this volume indicate that war has a potentially important role to play in the development of democracy, but it is certainly not necessary or sufficient, and may even contribute to developments antithetical to democracy. As Starr notes, wars may be catalytic moments, but the outcome of transformations are far from certain. Instead of perhaps too broad a claim about the causal relationship between conflict and democracy, the chapters provide a more detailed view of the wake of war: states with more *potential* interventionist capacity, and citizenry with a greater *potential* claim for voice. The next step has to be to ask what makes these potentialities real.

WAR AND THE IMAGINED COMMUNITY

Describing the aftermath of an Athenian naval battle toward the end of the Peloponnesian War, Barry Strauss nicely evokes the spirit often associated with war:

For a brief moment they were all Athenians. On an afternoon in September 406 B.C., the city of Athens achieved a unity that usually eluded it. It was imperfect unity, with no women and only a small percentage of Athenian men present – less than one percent. Yet those men represented a cross-section of Athens' male population. They ranged from the richest to the poorest, from cavalier to knave, from representatives of families so old that they seemed to have sprung from the Attic soil itself to immigrants from obscure villages somewhere in Thrace or Sicily. As a group they comprised citizens, metics (resident aliens), foreign mercenaries, and slaves. They spanned the ranks of the Athenian military, from horsemen to hoplites (infantrymen), from deck-soldiers to rowers, from the home guard to scouts. On this afternoon, men who normally would have scorned each other became brothers. They extended their hands to each other, literally, because they had to hold on for dear life.[20]

This passage exemplifies that oft-cited claim that wars make "brothers" of us all (again, the gender/sexual identity question is an important one for democratic suffrage). The centrality of war in nation-making was recognized by the German idealists of the nineteenth century. Herder defined the origins of the German folk in the battle of the Teutoburg Forest, Fichte celebrated the spirit of Jena, and Hegel compared war to an ocean wind purifying the health of the people from the "corruption" of perpetual peace. The great historian of war, Michael Howard, claims that for much of nineteenth-century Europe, "war was the necessary dialectic in the evolution of nations."[21] Georg Simmel could

---

[19] The one policy that has received the most attention is the smaller black-white test gap and the generally higher educational achievement of students in Department of Defense schools on military bases.

[20] Strauss 2004.

[21] Howard 1992, 39.

celebrate the start of World War I as an opportunity to consolidate national sentiment and cohesion: "[T]he war heralded a purging in the Augean stables of the urbanized money cultures of the West, rooting out all that was ephemeral, superfluous, excessive, and inessential in the experience of life."[22]

More recently, in part as a reaction to the too-quickly accepted notion of what we may call an "Ambroasian spirit," there has been rigorous questioning of the extent to which wars do create nations.[23] As Jay Winter (Chapter 6) argues, wars can lead to what might even be called antinationalist or certainly antibellicist movements. The "Vietnam syndrome" is an obvious example, and we may expect something similar following Iraq. Yet I would argue that there is fairly clear evidence for war making a strong contribution to, not necessarily a state-centered nationalism, but a less institutionally coherent, united, if imagined, community.

Without that sense of community, the democratizing potential of war is nil. Why? Because war creates the social foundation necessary for the subsequent interactions between war and democracy to play out. Without the existing sense of a "nation," war does not encourage greater popular participation. Many of the classic liberal notions of democracy and the state, beginning in Greece, but more explicitly with the English tradition of Hobbes and Locke, assume the prior existence of a mutually accepted *polis* whose members recognize communal interests and identities. Democracy involves the elaboration of agreements regarding future political decisions. Such political pacts must remain vague and require considerable amounts of trust to be viable. Without such a sense of trust, doubts as to the enforceability of contracts and the willingness of others to live with its consequences would undermine the potential for social agreements. Without that pre-existing union, the exchanges described above would not lead to the Marshallian process of ever-accruing rights, but to a form of political free-for-all where each member or subcommunity sought to protect and expand its position vis-à-vis all others. War, by defining a clear boundary around the community, makes it possible for it to even consider governing itself.

The contrast of "us" and "them" is never clearer than in war. Regions, which had preserved their identities, can merge into a single group, at least temporarily.[24] The best indicator of this is precisely how veterans groups recognize each other's legitimacy even across national boundaries. But most of the time, those who are suffering through a war do not recognize their fellow victims across a political divide. Rather they seek to partner in new ways with those whom they see a common bond, be it ethnic, geographic, political, or

---

[22] Harrington 2005, 64.

[23] Stephen Ambrose was a well-known exponent of the special community created by war; for example, see 1992. Paul Fussell has been one of the strongest critics of such a romantic image of war, but even when criticizing, he admits to how war does create some sense of shared purpose. See his 2003. For an interesting revisionist analysis of the communitarian effect of war, see Bourke 2000.

[24] Colley 1994.

ideological. Wars provide opportunities for the elaboration of rituals of sacrifice and reciprocity, which arguably are the foundations of social life.[25]

This is the sense of unity that Dankwart Rustow claimed was an essential part of the foundation for democratic rule.[26] It is a unity born out of shared struggle, a sense of danger, and the euphoric celebration of community. This sense of oneness can then translate into a recognition of the less fortunate in the society as worthy of assistance (they are, after all, our "brothers and sisters at arms"), it can serve to expand suffrage ("there are no racists in the foxholes"), and it may also provide the basis for the recognition of minimal civil rights that all in the community can share.

The sense of community often fostered by war is the critical link separating armies of slaves and conscripts from that of soldiers and citizens. For example, one does not have to buy into Greek chauvinism to note the clear distinction between the hoplites, patently aware of their identity as citizens of a *polis*, and the cowed mass of the Persian army linked only through the common subjecthood to the king. We can thus see the contribution of war to democracy taking two paths: First, it encourages the kinds of negotiations and exchanges between state and populace described above, and, second, it provides the underlying social capital possibly required for these processes to be successful.

This spirit of commonality need not be triumphant. War monuments, the architectural expression of this unity, have gone from the celebratory (Arc de Triomphe in Paris, the Wellington Arch in London) to the commemoratory (the Cenotaph in London or the Vietnam War Memorial in Washington, DC). The culture of defeat, however, also contains the germ of reactionary responses. Yet, no matter the emotion they seek to elicit, all of these serve to recognize a shared identity and are used to habitually remind the population of such.[27] The particular suffering involved in civil wars may actually create bonds across ideological or ethnic divisions through the commitment of "never again," be it in nineteenth-century United States or twentieth-century Spain.

A final way in which war creates community is by literally bringing together populations long isolated from each other. While many of the European armies well into the twentieth century would rely on locally defined regiments, the identity basis of these dissipated as wars progressed and units became less regional and more national. This is true not just of Europe. Scholars of the Mexican Revolution have noted, for example, that being transported from North to South and back again was often the only time the peasant soldiers saw the country that was "theirs." In the case of the United States, boot camp was (and in some ways remains) a place where different members of the society could meet. The differences being gulfed could be based on class

[25] Papilloud 2004.
[26] Rustow 1970.
[27] Winter 1995.

(especially important in both world wars in almost all countries) or ethnicity (exemplified for the United States by the Hollywood cliché of the Italian from Chicago, the Jew from Brooklyn, the cowboy from Oklahoma, and the Ivy Leaguer from Connecticut, meeting on their way to war. After the mid-1960s, the urban black kid would join them). These meetings fostered not just a set of shared identities, but also may have contributed to the creation of a common language and even culture.[28]

Even if we accept the powerful effect of war, it is worthwhile noting that the cohesive potential of war is also highly dependent on the antebellum state of social relations, as noted above. Lewis Coser wonderfully contrasts the British and French responses to the onrush of war in 1940.[29] In the first case, the Nazi threat increased social cohesion, but in the latter, pressures led not to unity, but to defeat. The pressures of war can make a "happy national family" ever stronger, but it can finish with the destruction of those ready to break apart.

We should not forget, moreover, that inclusiveness, if and when it comes, is defined by exclusion. *We* are the same because *they* are different from *us*. Boundaries both keep *us* together and *them* apart. It is this sense of exclusive community, even more than the institutional basis of territoriality, which might make notions of transnational citizenship so difficult to achieve. War is an important part of the construction of this community, but in the absence of collective enemies that serve to underscore what we share, how to create a democratic unity on a non-national basis?[30]

There is perhaps no better example of the "Janus-faced" nature of war, on the one hand welcoming its citizens and on the other seeking to crush others against walls, than the Athenians in Thucydides. On the one hand, Pericles can claim:

It is true that we are called a democracy, for the administration is in the hands of the many and not of the few ... There is no exclusiveness in our public life, and in our private business we are not suspicious of one another, nor angry with our neighbor if he does what he likes; we do not put on sour looks at him which, though harmless, are not pleasant.[31]

On the other hand, some pages later, the Athenians can speak to the Melians with nothing but threats and disdain prior to their destruction of the city:

For ourselves, we shall not trouble you with specious pretences ... since you know as well as we do that right, as the world goes, is only in question between equals in power, while the strong do what they can and the weak suffer what they must.[32]

---

[28] The military as "school of the nation" has a long intellectual history. For a very interesting dissenting view, see Krebs 2004.

[29] Coser 1956, 93–94.

[30] Borrowing from J.H. Elliott's notion of a "composite monarchy" in sixteenth-century Europe, we might wish to analyze the possibility of a "composite democracy."

[31] Thucydides. Book 2.34–46.

[32] Thucydides. Book 5.85–113.

So citizens of democracies may look after one another, but also be willing to bully any of those they do not recognize as equals.

If war produces democracy, does it, in turn, produce peace? If there has been much written on war and democracy, it cannot compare with the massive literature on the so-called democratic peace.[33] It is true that democracies seem to be reluctant to fight each other, and it is possible that this reluctance stems from the power of the populace to punish belligerent politicians. Yet, democracies also seem quite willing and able to fight non-democracies. Sometimes these fights are bathed in the glow of a crusade for freedom, other times not. What is particularly interesting here is that in many cases it is popular demands that drive war, as in the various calls to teach someone or other a lesson or to simply "take what should be ours." Fear of a populace frustrated by an early peace or simply fear of appearing weak may motivate politicians as much as fearing the pacifist vote. For example, we will long debate the extent to which democratic mechanisms braked or fueled the American invasion of Iraq.

Starr reverses the question of war and democracy and wonders how and when democracies fight. Do democracies fight in different ways than do other types of regimes? Thucydides did not believe that democratic regimes would perform as well as more authoritarian counterparts and fairly explicitly laid the blame for the eventual Athenian defeat on the *hoi polloi*. And yet, the historical record is surprising in that, particularly in wars requiring the highest levels of social mobilization, democracies perform well. Moreover, their forms of victory seem better at assuring postbellic peace. This is a very promising line of research that will require scholars to go further than the standard measures of bellic behavior. We need, for example, analyses of battalion and smaller unit behavior and the extent to which differences across militaries can be explained by regime variables. There is no question that some armies have held together better and fought more tenaciously than others; would citizen participation help explain this?[34]

In many ways, these two sides of democracy, peaceful and bellic, are the paradox that Winter documents for his protagonist, René Cassin. How can notions of decency and humanity be made to apply universally, no matter the political identity? Note, for example, how the notion of basic human rights developed much more easily in the face of a totalitarian threat during the Cold War than in the post-1989 environment where economic considerations have been included. It seems easier to feel for others' suffering and to be willing to fight against it when there is a common bond (or the perception of one) between victim and observer. In this regard, it is interesting that a common theme in such contemporary "Earth is in danger" films such as *Independence Day* or *The Day After Tomorrow* is the creation of planet-wide unity. Perhaps

---

[33] Russett 1993.

[34] My thanks to Jay Lyall of Yale University for suggesting this question. He is in the process of answering it with a very interesting new work.

only in the face of such a "planetary emergency" will we develop a non-national sense of an imagined community.

No matter the import of bellic cohesion, it is also worthwhile noting that the same mechanism that produces social unity can also lead to centralization of power and to an increase in nondemocratic governance. Over and above threats to civil liberties discussed above, the unification brought on by war can lead to the suppression of dissenting views and the imposition of a single model for being a patriot. Lewis Coser warns, "Groups which are engaged in continued struggle tend to lay claim on the total personality involvement of their members ... [and] are unlikely to tolerate more than limited departures from the group unity."[35]

BEYOND THE MODERN ATLANTIC

How universal are these legacies of war? The literature on the social effects of war seems to be based on a relatively small number of cases: Napoleonic France, Bismarckian Germany, Meiji Japan, interwar Britain, and post–Civil War United States. This geographical and temporal sampling is partly the reason why scholarship on war and democracy can find so much historical support, and yet fail the statistical significance test when applied to a broader group of cases. For example, the literature on the democratic peace still seems mired in debates on whether it is purely a European and postwar phenomenon or whether we can identify structural links between regime type and international behavior. We need to expand the sampling frame of our scholarship on war if we are to discover truly generalizable principles.[36]

What seems to be the evidence for the effect of war and democracy outside of the usual suspects? The literature on the political and social effects of war first neglects many of the European cases outside of the preferred circle. Spain, for example, was engaged in wars almost continuously from the mid-sixteenth century through 1815 and yet, the resulting states, whether Hapsburg, Bourbon, or "Liberal," were infamous for their inefficacy. The Balkans were at war almost continuously, whether with one of the great powers or with each other, from the mid-nineteenth century through 1945, and yet strong states, much less democratic regimes, failed to develop. Perhaps the most surprising missing case is that of Russia, whose experience of conflict from 1914 through 1945 probably cost nearly 40 million dead. How did that experience shape Soviet society?

The cases of the Middle East are also relatively understudied.[37] The colonial and postcolonial struggles of Algeria and Egypt, for example, did not produce strong democracies, nor has the constant state of war with Israel done much for its neighbors. The Iran-Iraq War arguably did produce more potent (if

---

[35] Coser *op. cit.*, p. 153.
[36] Taylor and Botea 2008; Soiffer 2008.
[37] Waldner 1999; Miller 2007.

authoritarian) states, but ones also run by either small thuggish cliques or a *sui genesis* alliance of clerics, soldier zealots, and small businessmen. The case of Israel seems to confirm many of the claims made for war and the creation of both a deep democracy and a strong sense of nationhood. Note, however, than even in this case, the unity among Israelis facing external enemies has not trumped the deeper ethnic loyalties and identifications of Jews and Arabs. Nor has it guaranteed the rights of Arab veterans.

South Asia provides an excellent and yet barely used laboratory for testing the relative importance of war for democracy. Both India and Pakistan inherited parts of the Raj army. They both faced potentially disastrous wars with clearly demarcated others (each other!). Yet, the contrast between Pakistan and India could not be greater in terms of those two classic institutional legacies of war: state capacity and democracy. We need scholarship to explore how whatever these legacies might have been were dissipated in Pakistan or strengthened in India.

Outside of the Japanese case, the effect of war in the creation of the East Asian economic miracles has also been unappreciated.[38] We know that expenditures of the Vietnam War helped spur initial growth in some of these economies, but what about their own conflicts? One of the most incredible transformations in contemporary history was that of the Kuomintang from the corrupt and ineffective institution prior to 1949 to the (still corrupt, but much more effective) overseer of Taiwanese development. What role did the trauma of the defeat to the Communists play in the reform of the Kuomintang? Similar arguments could be made about the South Korean regime frightened by its easy collapse during the Korean War. Fear of both Communism and isolation from Malaysia arguably created war-like conditions for Singapore. As in South Asia, counterexamples also abound, as the experience of World War II and later local insurgencies did not create a strong or democratic state in the Philippines, nor did the equivalents do so in Indonesia.

Interestingly, African and Latin American wars and their state-building consequences have received the most attention.[39] In both cases, the absence of wars or of the "right" kind of wars has been noted as an important potential factor in the construction of states, or the lack thereof. Even here, however, exceptional cases like Chile and South Africa and the possible contribution of war to their political development have been understudied.

The sampling bias also includes a preference for some wars and not for others. The number of studies on the political and social consequences of the Franco-Prussian War would fill a not-so small library. The attention paid to the Russo-Japanese War might fill a shelf.

The Eurocentric perspective on war also applies to discussions of the future of conflict. Books such as James Sheehan's *Where Have All the Soldiers Gone?*, and many of the chapters in this volume, speak with assurance about the end

---

[38] Woo-Cumings 1999.
[39] Herbst 2000; Centeno 2002.

of war. If Sheehan is at least explicit that he is speaking of Western Europe, many other commentators are not. Yet, for large parts of the world, war, and even "total war," is not a thing of the past. India and Pakistan maintain fortified frontiers, Iran and Iraq fought something of a copy of the World War I Western front only twenty years ago, the Chinese military thinks geopolitically of challenges to the North and West as well as control of the South China Sea. The Great Lakes region in Africa has witnessed a poor man's version of geomilitary competition, and the Brazilian army does not take control of the Amazon for granted. For many of these countries, war is not only *not* a thing of the past; it is arguably a path toward a greater future. What do the scholars of war have to say to them?

One other problem with the "sampling" of war studies is the inadequate attention paid to differentiating between forms of warfare. Influenced in part by the availability of the Correlates of War data set, we have learned to speak of war as simply those conflicts rated as such by the number of participants involved. Yet, it would make sense to disaggregate war types. For example, "wars between equals," as in the classic cases of intra-European wars, should be treated differently than colonial wars. The role played in social and political development of occupation duties, as opposed to wars truly ending in decisive battle, also need to be defined and distinguished. (We can imagine that occupation duties would have corrosive elements on the democratic formation or political attitudes of veterans, for example).

A call for a broader set of comparisons is not simply the product of an inclusion fetish or of simply the desire to create ever more analytical categories for their own sake. The strange fact that Europe produced arguably the bloodiest centuries in history *and* the most progressive and democratic states deserves recognition, but also demands a broader comparative perspective. That the two aspects of European history are linked seems obvious, but what the precise mechanism may be and how these may be duplicated (hopefully with less blood) are not.

THE END OF WAR?

The last half-century has witnessed a dramatic change in the role of warfare in the daily political, social, and economic lives of the developed societies in North America and Europe. What are the implications of this for democracy?

Several of the chapters in this volume have addressed this question, with special attention to the implication for political life of the "War on Terror." Let us begin by analyzing what has happened to the kinds of war that most scholars argue did lead to democratic reforms.

The more functionalist reading of Marx sees capitalism as a product of the steam engine. Similarly, the military may be seen as a product of the relevant technology (from the long bow to the atom bomb). Thus, the "mass-reserve" army of the nineteenth and twentieth centuries was partly a product of the transformation of weapons from rifling to the machine gun. As many have argued, the mass production of weapons and their increasing lethality both undermined the aristocratic claim to military privilege and allowed the military to become ever more inclusive.[40] In a classic dialectical shift, however, the development of ever more destructive technology led to the creation of weapons that made these reserve armies impractical and even dangerous. Thus, the possibility of a classic "Western War" between the rich became ever less likely, especially after 1989.

The "West," however, did maintain a monopoly over such instruments, and when new powers made the mistake of challenging it in the military arena, the established order was able to use it in an incredibly destructive fashion. Thus, the stupidity or insanity of Saddam Hussein in challenging the United States to fight a World War II tank war led to his own annihilation.

Nevertheless, the West could not claim a monopoly on more "democratic" aspects of the new technology. Biological and nuclear weapons are potentially the ideal "weapons of the weak" in that, while requiring sophisticated technology, they can be produced by even the most destitute of states (as in the case of North Korea). The very complexity and interconnections of contemporary life also makes the rich societies much more vulnerable to the strategies available to the less developed. The "War on Terror" is particularly challenging, as the enemy is not even another state, but a much more elusive network of potential combatants.

The changes in technology and in the definition of the enemy made it possible, and even imperative, to do away with mass conscription. The capacity of the killing machines was such that one needed fewer men-at-arms to kill an equivalent number of the enemy. Moreover, the technology required so much training that a drafted recruit would only begin to become useful around the time his enlistment ended. These changes made it possible for the wishes of both the professional military and the burgeoning middle class to be satisfied: A professional (and in some cases privatized) military fit perfectly with the political and technological transformation of the "West." The new form of threat makes the old-style military even less practical. How is a mass army to deal with an enemy whose identity might be unknown and whose presence might be distributed across thousands of miles?

Will the new form of war change the relationship of conflict with democracy? Again, explicitly limiting ourselves to the developed countries that have experienced this transition, the answer has to be yes. Consider the links discussed above. The "exchange" mechanism of rights for service clearly breaks down when only a relative (and socially segregated few) can claim that they have served. When veterans are no longer part of the masses, but simply another interest group, the "back and forth" between state and populace is much less consequential.

---

[40] There is the ongoing debate about the existence of a "military revolution." For perhaps the most technologically driven analysis, see McNeil 1982.

More ominously, the segregation of military service also breaks down the positive contribution that war can make to the creation and maintenance of the imagined community. In the United States, the perception and reality of who has served since the Vietnam War has fed a class- and even region-based sense of an *intranational* them and us. The unpopularity of the Iraq War has made discussions of who serves politically charged.[41] The oft-cited difference in discipline, demeanor, and success of those with military background has also served to highlight the supposed "decadence" of the average civilian. The hagiographic worship of the "warrior" in contemporary American political rhetoric is potentially dangerous, no matter how well deserved such attention and praise may be.[42]

Finally, the very nature of the new form of war represents a much more intense potential threat to civil liberties. In a war where the identity and plans of the enemy are the key unknowns, the temptation to favor one side of the balance between safety and liberty is great. The "War on Terror" risks all the dangers associated with threats to democracy from war, while providing few of its benefits. The potential to manipulate an ever constant, yet secretive, threat from those with whom we (supposedly) share so few values is both obvious and immense. The ease with which the threat of war can and has been used to distinguish between "degrees of Americaness" should give us considerable pause.

This is not to say that democracy is under imminent threat. The long-term legacies of war discussed above are deep and institutionalized in laws and practices. Yet, in nations where ethnic identity is less and less homogenous, the absence of the cohesion of the "national" wars of the nineteenth and twentieth centuries will leave a significant hole in a political fabric. Such communities, constantly fed rhetoric of menace and xenophobia, may be far too willing to sacrifice liberties in order to feel safer in a dangerous world.

---

[41] Yet the demographics of military service and even being in Iraq certainly are not that of the aristocratic and racist state often depicted. The decades-long African American over-representation in the Army has been reduced, and whites are marginally more likely to serve in Iraq. The upper class is notable in its absence, but the recruits come more from the storied middle than the bottom. The most difficult demographic issue may actually be regional, with the South and rural areas in general over-represented. See Segal and Wechsler Segal 2004.

[42] The tone of recent "video-ads" for the National Guard, for example, could be troubling: http://nationalguardwarrior.com/. See Segal and Wechsler Segal 2004.

References

Abrams, Philip. 1963. The Failure of Social Reform: 1918–1920. *Past & Present* 24 (1): 43–64.

Acemoglu, Daron, and James A. Robinson. 2006. *Economic Origins of Dictatorship and Democracy*. Cambridge, UK: Cambridge University Press.

Ackerman, Bruce. 2006. *Before the Next Attack: Preserving Civil Liberties in an Age of Terrorism*. New Haven, CT: Yale University Press.

Agi, Marc. 1980. *De l'idée d'universalité comme fondatrice du concept des droits de l'homme d'après la vie et l'oeuvre de René Cassin*. Doctoral thesis, University of Nice, December 10, 1979. Antibes: Éditions Alp'azur.

——1998. *René Cassin, 1887–1976: Prix Nobel de la Paix*. Paris: Perrin.

Albert, Bill. 1988. *South America and the First World War: The Impact of the War on Brazil, Argentina, Peru, and Chile*. Cambridge, UK: Cambridge University Press.

Alden, Chris. 1995. The UN and the Resolution of Conflict in Mozambique. *Journal of Modern African Studies* 33 (1): 103–128.

Alence, Rod. 2004. South Africa after Apartheid: The First Decade. *Journal of Democracy* 15 (3): 78–92.

Allison, Michael. 2006. The Transition from Armed Opposition to Electoral Opposition in Central America. *Latin American Politics and Society* 48 (4): 137–164.

Almond, Gabriel, and Sidney Verba. 1963. *The Civic Culture: Political Attitudes and Democracy in Five Countries*. Princeton, NJ: Princeton University Press.

Ambrose, Stephen. 1992. *Band of Brothers, E Company, 506th Regiment, 101st Airborne: From Normandy to Hitler's Eagle's Nest*. New York, NY: Simon & Schuster.

Amenta, Edwin, and Theda Skocpol. 1988. Redefining the New Deal: World War II and the Development of Social Provision in the United States. In *The Politics of Social Policy in the United States*, edited by Margaret Weir, Ann Shorla Orloff, and Theda Skocpol, 81–122. Princeton, NJ: Princeton University Press.

Anderson, Benedict. 2006. *Imagined Communities*. London: Verso.

Anderson, David G. 1994. British Rearmament and the "Merchants of Death": The 1935–36 Royal Commission on the Manufacture of and Trade in Armaments. *Journal of Contemporary History* 29 (1): 5–37.

Anderson, Leslie, and Lawrence Dodd. 2005. *Learning Democracy: Citizen Engagement and Electoral Choice in Nicaragua, 1990–2001*. Chicago, IL: University of Chicago Press.

Anderson, Olive. 1967. *A Liberal State at War: English Politics and Economics during the Crimean War*. New York, NY: Macmillan.

Andolina, Molly W., Krista Jenkins, Cliff Zukin, and Scott Keeter. 2003. Habits from Home, Lessons from School: Influences on Youth Civic Engagement. *PS: Political Science and Politics* 36 (2): 275–280.

Andreski, Stanislav. 1954. *Military Organization and Society*. Berkeley, CA: University of California Press.

Andrews, William G. 1982. *Presidential Government in Gaullist France: A Study of Executive-Legislative Relations, 1958–1974*. Albany, NY: SUNY Press.

Arian, Asher. 1998. *The Second Republic: Politics in Israel*. Chatham, NY: Chatham House Publishers.

Arian, Asher, and Michal Shamir. 1983. The Primarily Political Functions of the Left-Right Continuum. *Comparative Politics* 15 (2): 139–158.

Ashworth, William S. 1953. *Contracts and Finance*. London: Her Majesty's Stationery Office.

Auerswald, David, and Peter Cowhey. 1997. Ballotbox Diplomacy: The War Powers Resolution and the Use of Force. *International Studies Quarterly* 41 (3): 505–528.

Avant, Deborah. 1994. *Political Institution and Military Change: Lessons from Peripheral Wars*. Ithaca, NY: Cornell University Press.

——2000. From Mercenary to Citizen Armies: Explaining Change in the Practice of War. *International Organization* 54 (1): 441–472.

——2005. *The Market for Force: The Consequences of Privatizing Security*. Cambridge, UK: Cambridge University Press.

Avant, Deborah, and Lee Sigelman. 2010. What Does Private Security Mean for Democracy? Lesson from the U.S. in Iraq (with implications for Afghanistan). *Security Studies* 19(2).

Azimi, Nassrine, Matt Fuller, and Hiroko Nakayama, eds. 2003. *Post-Conflict Reconstruction in Japan, Republic of Korea, Cambodia, East Timor, and Afghanistan*. New York, NY and Geneva: United Nations.

Bacevich, Andrew J. 2007. Warrior Politics. *Atlantic Monthly* 299 (4): 25–26.

Badger, Anthony. 1997. State Capacity in Britain and America in the 1930s. In *Britain and America: Studies in Comparative History, 1760–1970*, edited by David Englander, 295–306. New Haven, CT: Yale University Press.

Bailey, Michael, and David Braybrooke. 2003. Robert A. Dahl's Philosophy of Democracy Exhibited in his Essays. *Annual Review of Political Science* 6: 99–118.

Ball, Stuart, ed. 1998. *The Conservative Party since 1945*. Manchester: Manchester University Press.

Baloyra, Enrique. 1998. El Salvador: From Reactionary Despotism to Partidocracia. In *Postconflict Elections, Democratization, and International Assistance*, edited by Krishna Kumar, 15–38. Boulder, CO: Lynne Rienner.

Barbalet, J. M. 1988. *Citizenship: Rights, Struggle, and Class Inequality*. Minneapolis, MN: University of Minnesota Press.

Barker, Elizabeth. 1973. *Austria 1918–1972*. London: Macmillan.

Barnett, Michael N. 1992. *Confronting the Costs of War: Military Power, State, and Society in Egypt and Israel*. Princeton, NJ: Princeton University Press.

Bartels, Andrew H. 1983. The Office of Price Administration and the Legacy of the New Deal. *Public Historian* 5 (3): 5–29.

Bauer, Gretchen. 2001. Namibia in the First Decade of Independence: How Democratic? *Journal of Southern African Studies* 27 (1): 33–55.

Beck, Nathaniel, Jonathan N. Katz, and Richard Tucker. 1998. Taking Time Seriously: Time-Series-Cross-Section Analysis with a Binary Dependent Variable. *American Journal of Political Science* 42 (4): 1260–1288.

Beck, Ulrich. 2000. The Cosmopolitan Perspective: Sociology in the Second Age of Modernity. *British Journal of Sociology* 51 (1): 79–105.

Becker, Jean-Jacques. 1973. *Le carnet B: les pouvoirs publics et l'antimilitarisme avant la guerre de 1914*. Paris: Klincksieck.

Bell, David S. 2000. *Presidential Power in Fifth Republic France*. Oxford: Berg.

Bell, Jonathan. 2004. *The Liberal State on Trial: The Cold War and American Politics in the Truman Years*. New York, NY: Columbia University Press.

Ben-Eliezer, Uri. 1995. A Nation-In-Arms: State, Nation, and Militarism in Israel's First Years. *Comparative Studies in Society and History* 37 (2): 264–285.

Bennett, D. Scott, and Allan C. Stam III. 1996. The Duration of Interstate Wars, 1816–1985. *American Political Science Review* 90 (2): 239–257.

Bensel, Richard. 1990. *Yankee Leviathan: The Origins of Central State Authority in America, 1859–1877*. Cambridge, UK: Cambridge University Press.

Berghahn, Volker. 2006. *Europe in the Era of the Two World Wars: From Militarism and Genocide to Civil Society, 1900–1950*. Princeton, NJ: Princeton University Press.

Berkowitz, Edward D. 2006. *Something Happened: A Political and Cultural Overview of the Seventies*. New York, NY: Columbia University Press.

Berman, Sheri. 1997. Civil Society and the Collapse of the Weimar Republic. *World Politics* 49 (3): 401–429.

Bermeo, Nancy. 1994. Democracy in Europe. *Daedalus* 123 (2): 159–178.

——2003a. *Ordinary People in Extraordinary Times: The Citizenry and the Breakdown of Democracy*. Princeton, NJ: Princeton University Press.

——2003b. What the Democratization Literature Says – or Doesn't Say – About Postwar Democratization. *Global Governance* 9 (2): 159–177.

——2007. War and Democratization: Lessons from the Portuguese Experience. *Democratization* 14 (3): 388–406.

Bermeo, Nancy, and Raymond Hicks. Forthcoming. *The Puzzle of Conflict Democracies*. Unpublished manuscript, Oxford University and Princeton University.

Berstein, Serge. 1993. *The Republic of de Gaulle, 1958–1969*. Translated by Peter Morris. Cambridge, UK: Cambridge University Press.

Berstein, Serge, and Jean-Pierre Rioux. 2000. *The Pompidou Years, 1969–1974*. Cambridge, UK: Cambridge University Press.

Best, Geoffrey. 1980. *Humanity in Warfare*. New York, NY: Columbia University Press.

Biddle, Stephen, and Stephen Long. 2004. Democracy and Military Effectiveness: A Deeper Look. *Journal of Conflict Resolution* 48 (4): 525–546.

Bien, David. 1979. The Army in the French Enlightenment: Reform, Reaction, and Revolution. *Past and Present* 85: 68–98.

Black, Jeremy. 1994. *European Warfare, 1660–1815*. London: University College London Press.

Blank, Stephen. 1973. *Industry and Government in Britain: The Federation of British Industries in Politics, 1945–65*. Lexington, MA: Lexington Books.

Blanning, T. C. W. 1996. *The French Revolutionary Wars*. London: Arnold.

Blanton, Robert, and Betty Glad. 1997. F. W. de Klerk and Nelson Mandela: A Study in Cooperative Transformation Leadership. *Presidential Studies Quarterly* 27 (3): 565–590.

Blechman, Barry. 1990. *The Politics of National Security: Congress and U.S. Defense Policy*. New York, NY: Oxford University Press.

Boix, Carles, and Susan Stokes. 2003. Endogenous Democratization. *World Politics* 55 (4): 517–549.

Bollen, Kenneth A. 1980. Issues in the Comparative Measurement of Political Democracy. *American Sociological Review* 45 (3): 370–390.

Bolton, John R. 2007. *Surrender is Not an Option: Defending America at the United Nations*. New York, NY: Simon and Schuster.

Bourke, Joanna. 2000. *An Intimate History of Killing*. New York, NY: Basic Books.

Brahimi, Lakhdar. 2000. *Report of the Panel on United Nations Peace Operations*. A/55/305-S/2000/80, 21 August.

Brandis, Buford. 1943. British War Economy: The First Two Years. Ph.D. diss., Duke University.

Brandon, Mark. 2003. War and American Constitutional Order. *Vanderbilt Law Review* 56 (6): 1815–1870.

Bratton, Michael, and Nicolas van de Walle. 1997. *Democratic Experiments in Africa: Regime Transitions in Comparative Perspective*. Cambridge, UK: Cambridge University Press.

Braybon, Gail, and Penny Summerfield. 1987. *Out of the Cage: Women's Experiences in Two World Wars*. London: Pandora Press.

Brehm, John, and Wendy Rahn. 1997. Individual-Level Evidence for Causes and Consequences of Social Capital. *American Journal of Political Science* 41 (3): 999–1023.

Brewer, John. 1989. *The Sinews of Power: War, Money, and the English State, 1688–1783*. New York, NY: Knopf.

Brinkley, Alan. 1995. *The End of Reform: New Deal Liberalism in Recession and War*. New York, NY: Knopf.

Brinton, Crane. 1967. Enlightenment. In *The Encyclopedia of Philosophy*, Vol. 1, edited by Paul Edwards. New York, NY: Macmillan.

Brockner, Joel, and Batia M. Wiesenfeld. 1996. An Integrative Framework for Explaining Reactions to Decisions: The Interactive Effects of Outcomes and Procedures. *Psychological Bulletin* 120 (2): 189–208.

Brooke, Stephen. 1992. *Labour's War: The Labour Party during the Second World War*. Oxford: Clarendon Press.

Brooke, Stephen, ed. 1995. *Reform and Reconstruction: Britain after the War, 1945–51*. New York, NY: St. Martin's Press.

Bruce, Maurice. 1961. *The Coming of the Welfare State*. London: Batsford.

Bryant, Chris. 1997. *Stafford Cripps: The First Modern Chancellor*. London: Hodder & Stoughton.

Bueno de Mesquita, Bruce, and Randolph M. Siverson. 1995. War and the Survival of Political Leaders: A Comparative Study of Regime Types and Political Accountability. *American Political Science Review* 89 (4): 841–855.

Bueno de Mesquita, Bruce, Randolph M. Siverson, and Gary Woller. 1992. War and the Fate of Regimes: A Comparative Analysis. *American Political Science Review* 86 (3): 638–646.

Bullock, Alan. 1967. *The Life and Times of Ernest Bevin*, Vol. 2, *Minister of Labor, 1940–1945*. London: Heinemann.

Burk, James. 2002. Theories of Democratic Civil Military Relations. *Armed Forces and Society* 29 (1): 7–29.

Bushnell, David. 1993. *The Making of Modern Colombia*. Berkeley, CA: University of California Press.

Calder, Angus. 1969. *The People's War: Britain, 1939–1945*. New York, NY: Pantheon.

Calhoun, Frederick. 1990. *The Lawmen: United States Marshals and their Deputies, 1789–1989*. Washington, DC: Smithsonian Institution Press.

Capoccia, Giovanni. 2007. *Defending Democracy: Reaction to Extremism in Interwar Europe*. Baltimore, MD: The Johns Hopkins University Press.

Capoccia, Giovanni, and R. Daniel Kelemen. 2007. The Study of Critical Junctures: Theory, Narrative, and Counterfactuals in Historical Institutionalism. *World Politics* 59 (3): 341–369.

Carbone, Giovanni M. 2005. Continuidade na Renovação? Ten years of Multiparty Politics in Mozambique: Roots, Evolution and Stabilisation of the Frelimo-Renamo Party System. *Journal of Modern African Studies* 43 (3): 417–442.

Carothers, Thomas. 2006. *Confronting the Weakest Link: Aiding Political Parties in New Democracies*. Washington, DC: Carnegie Endowment for International Peace.

Carpenter, Daniel P. 2001. *The Forging of Bureaucratic Autonomy: Reputations, Networks, and Policy Innovation in Executive Agencies, 1862–1928*. Princeton, NJ: Princeton University Press.

Carr, William. 1963. *Schleswig-Holstein, 1815–48: A Study in National Conflict*. Manchester: Manchester University Press.

Cassin, René. 1930. La nouvelle conception du domicile dans le règlement des conflits de lois. *Académie de droit international, The Hague. Receuil des Cours*, 658–809.

Cassirer, Ernest. 1951. *The Philosophy of the Enlightenment*. Princeton, NJ: Princeton University Press.

Cederman, Lars-Erik. 2001. Back to Kant: Reinterpreting the Democratic Peace as a Macrohistorical Learning Process. *American Political Science Review* 95 (1): 15–31.

Centeno, Miguel Angel. 2002. *Blood and Debt: War and the Nation-State in Latin America*. University Park, PA: Pennsylvania State University Press.

Chiozza, Giacomo, and Hein E. Goemans. 2004. International Conflict and the Tenure of Leaders: Is War Still Ex Post Inefficient. *American Journal of Political Science* 48 (3): 604–619.

Chu, Yun-han, et al. 2008. Public Opinion and Democratic Legitimacy. *Journal of Democracy* 19 (2): 74–87.

Clark, Wesley. 2001. *Waging Modern War: Bosnia, Kosovo, and the Future of Conflict*. New York, NY: Public Affairs.

Clarke, Peter. 2002. *The Cripps Version: The Life of Sir Stafford Cripps, 1889–1952*. London: Allen Lane.

Cline, Peter. 1982. Winding Down the War Economy: British Plans for Peacetime Recovery, 1916–19. In *War and the State: The Transformation of British Government*, edited by Kathleen Burk, 157–181. London: George Allen and Unwin.

Cobban, Alfred. 1960. *In Search of Humanity: The Role of the Enlightenment in Modern History*. New York, NY: G. Braziller.

Cohen, Eliot A. 1985. *Citizens and Soldiers: The Dilemmas of Military Service*. Ithaca, NY: Cornell University Press.

——2000. Why the Gap Matters. *The National Interest* 61: 38–48.

Cohen, Jerome B. 1949. *Japan's Economy in War and Reconstruction*. Minneapolis, MN: University of Minnesota Press.

Cole, David. 2005 [2003]. *Enemy Aliens: Double Standards and Constitutional Freedoms in the War on Terrorism*. New York, NY: New Press.

Colley, Linda. 1994. *Britons: Forging the Nation, 1707–1837*. New Haven, CT: Yale University Press.

Collier, David, and Steven Levitsky. 1997. Democracy with Adjectives: Conceptual Innovation in Comparative Research. *World Politics* 49 (3): 430–451.

Collins, Randall. 1999. *Macrohistory: Essays in Sociology of the Long Run*. Stanford, CA: Stanford University Press.

Corner, Paul, and Giovanna Procacci. 1997. The Italian Experience of "Total" Mobilization. In *State, Society, and Mobilization in Europe during the First World War*, edited by John Horne, 223–240. Cambridge, UK: Cambridge University Press.

Correlates of War (COW) Project. 2005. Correlates of War. Available at http://www. correlatesofwar.org/. Accessed August 1, 2009.

Coser, Lewis. 1956. *The Functions of Social Conflict*. Glencoe, IL: Free Press.

Costa Pinto, Antonio. 2001. *O Fim do Império Portugués: A Cena Internacional, As Colonias e a Descolonização 1961–1975*. Lisbon: Livros Horizonte.

Cox, Gary W., and Matthew D. McCubbins. 2005. *Setting the Agenda: Responsible Party Government in the U.S. House of Representatives*. Cambridge, UK: Cambridge University Press.

Craig, Gordon. 1978. *Germany: 1866–1945*. New York, NY: Oxford University Press.

Crenson, Matthew A., and Benjamin Ginsberg. 2002. *Downsizing Democracy: How America Sidelined Its Citizens and Privatized Its Public*. Baltimore, MD: The Johns Hopkins University Press.

——2007. *Presidential Power: Unchecked and Unbalanced*. New York, NY: Norton.

Cropanzano, Russell, and Jerald Greenberg. 1997. Progress in Organizational Justice: Tunneling through the Maze. In *International Review of Industrial and Organizational Psychology*, edited by Cary L. Cooper and Ivan T. Robertson, 317–372. New York, NY: Wiley.

Crovitz, L. Gordon, and Jeremy A. Rabkin, eds. 1989. *The Fettered Presidency: Legal Constraints on the Executive Branch*. Washington, DC: American Enterprise Institute.

Cruz, Consuelo. 2005. *Political Culture and Institutional Development in Costa Rica and Nicaragua: World-making in the Tropics*. Cambridge, UK: Cambridge University Press.

Cuff, Robert D. 1973. *War Industries Board: Business-Government Relations during World War I*. Baltimore, MD: The Johns Hopkins University Press.

Daalder, Ivo H., and Michael E. O' Hanlon. 2000. *Winning Ugly: NATO's War to Save Kosovo*. Washington, DC: Brookings Institution Press.

Dahl, Robert A. 1971. *Polyarchy: Participation and Opposition*. New Haven, CT: Yale University Press.

Dahl, Robert A, ed. 1997. *Toward Democracy: A Journey*. Berkeley, CA: Institute of Governmental Studies Press.

Dahl, Robert A. 1998. *On Democracy*. New Haven, CT: Yale University Press.

Dahl, Robert A., and Edward R. Tufte. 1973. *Size and Democracy*. Stanford, CA: Stanford University Press.

Dallek, Robert. 1998. *Flawed Giant: Lyndon Johnson and His Times, 1961–1973*. New York, NY: Oxford University Press.

Danopoulos, Constantine P. 1983. Military Professionalism and Regime Legitimacy in Greece, 1967–1974. *Political Science Quarterly* 98 (3): 485–506.

——*Farewell to the Man on Horseback: Intervention and Civilian Rule in Greece.* Unpublished manuscript, San Jose State University.

Davenport, Christian. 2007. *State Repression and the Domestic Democratic Peace.* Cambridge, UK: Cambridge University Press.

Davidson, Joel R. 1996. *The Unsinkable Fleet: The Politics of U.S. Navy Expansion in World War II.* Annapolis, MD: Naval Institute Press.

Davis, Vincent, ed. 1980. *The Post-Imperial Presidency.* New Brunswick, NJ: Transaction Books.

de Gaulle, Charles. 1964. *Major Addresses, Statements, and Press Conferences of General Charles de Gaulle: May 19, 1958 – January 31, 1964.* New York, NY: French Embassy, Press and Information Division.

——1971. *Memoirs of Hope: Renewal, 1958–1962.* Translated by Terence Kilmartin. London: Weidenfeld and Nicolson.

de Riz, Liliana. 1984. Notas Sobre Parlamento y Partidos en la Argentina de Hoy. In *Democracia, Orden Político y Parlamento Fuerte,* edited by Hilda Sabato and Marcelo Cavarozzi, 118–126. Buenos Aires: CEAL.

de Tocqueville, Alexis. 1945. *Democracy in America,* Vol. II. Translated by Henry Reeve. New York, NY: Vintage.

de Zeeuw, Jeroen, ed. 2008. *From Soldiers to Politicians.* London: Lynne Rienner.

Degroot, Gerald J. 1996. *Blighty: British Society in the Era of the Great War.* London: Longman.

Desch, Michael C. 2002. Democracy and Victory: Why Regime Type Hardly Matters. *International Security* 28 (1): 5–47.

——2008. *Power and Military Effectiveness: The Fallacy of Democratic Triumphalism.* Baltimore, MD: The Johns Hopkins University Press.

Diamandorous, P. Nikiforos. 1986. Regime Change and the Prospects for Democracy in Greece, 1974–1983. In *Transitions from Authoritarian Rule,* edited by Guillermo O'Donnell, Philippe C. Schmitter, and Laurence Whitehead, 138–165. Baltimore, MD: The John Hopkins University Press.

Diamant, Neill. 2009. *Embattled Glory: Veterans, Military Families and the Politics of Patriotism in China, 1949–2007.* Lanham, MD: Rowman & Littlefield.

Diamond, Larry J. 1999. *Developing Democracy: Toward Consolidation.* Baltimore, MD: The Johns Hopkins University Press.

DiMaggio, Paul, **and** Walter Powell, eds. 1991. *The New Institutionalism in Organizational Theory.* Chicago, IL: University of Chicago Press.

Dobbins, James F. 2003. America's Role in Nation-Building from Germany to Iraq. *Survival* 45 (4): 87–110.

Dobell, Lauren. 1995. SWAPO in Office. In *Namibia's Liberation Struggle: The Two-Edged Sword,* edited by Colin Leys and John Saul, 171–195. Athens, OH: Ohio University Press.

Dolman, Everett Carl. 2004. *The Warrior State: How Military Organization Structures Politics.* New York, NY: Palgrave Macmillan.

Donahue, John. 1989. *The Privatization Decision.* New York, NY: Basic Books.

Donnelly, Mark. 1999. *Britain in the Second World War.* London: Routledge.

Donohue, Laura K. 2008. *The Cost of Counterterrorism: Power, Politics, and Liberty.* Cambridge, UK: Cambridge University Press.

Dower, John. 1999. *Embracing Defeat: Japan in the Wake of World War II.* New York, NY: Norton.

Downes, Alexander B. 2009. How Smart and Tough Are Democracies? Reassessing Theories of Democratic Victory in War. *International Security* 33 (4): 9–51.

Downing, Brian. 1992. *The Military Revolution and Political Change: Origins of Democracy and Autocracy in Early Modern Europe.* Princeton, NJ: Princeton University Press.

Doyle, Michael W., and Nicholas Sambanis. 2000. International Peace-building: A Theoretical and Quantitative Analysis. *American Political Science Review* 94 (4): 779–801.

Dudziak, Mary. 2000. *Cold War Civil Rights: Race and the Image of American Democracy.* Princeton, NJ: Princeton University Press.

Duffield, John. 1994–95. NATO's Functions after the Cold War. *Political Science Quarterly* 109 (5): 763–787.

Dunkerley, James. 1985. Central America: Collapse of the Military System. In *The Political Dilemmas of Military Regimes,* edited by Christopher S. Clapham and George D. E. Philip, 171–200. Totowa, NJ: Barnes and Noble.

Dwork, Deborah. 1987. *War Is Good for Babies and Other Young Children: A History of the Infant and Child Welfare Movement in England, 1898–1918.* London: Tavistock.

Edelstein, David M. 2004. Occupational Hazards: Why Military Occupations Succeed or Fail. *International Security* 29 (1): 49–91.

Edgerton, David. 1984. Technical Innovation, Industrial Capacity, and Efficiency: Public Ownership and the British Military Aircraft Industry, 1935–48. *Business History* 36 (3): 247–279.

——2006. *Warfare State: Britain, 1920–1970.* New York, NY: Cambridge University Press.

Elder, Glenn H., Jr., and Elizabeth C. Clipp. 1988. Wartime Losses and Bonding: Influences across 40 Years in Men's Lives. *Psychiatry: Interpersonal and Biological Processes* 51 (2): 177–298.

Elias, Norbert. 1993. *The Civilizing Process,* Vol. 2. Cambridge, MA: Blackwell.

Ellis, John. 1993. *World War II: A Statistical Survey.* New York, NY: Facts on File.

Ellison, Christopher G. 1992. Military Background, Racial Orientations, and Political Participation among Black Adult Males. *Social Science Quarterly* 73 (2): 360–78.

Elsea, Jennifer K., and Nina M. Serafino. 2007. Private Security Contractors in Iraq: Background, Legal Status, and Other Issues. *CRS Report to Congress,* Order Code RL 32419. Washington, DC: Congressional Research Service, updated 11 July.

Encarnación, Omar G. 2006. Civil Society Reconsidered. *Comparative Politics* 38 (3): 357–376.

Engel, Ulf. 1999. South Africa. In *Elections in Africa,* edited by Dieter Nohlen, Michael Krennerich, and Bernhard Thibaut, 817–842. Oxford: Oxford University Press.

Engelhardt, Tom. 1995. *The End of Victory Culture: Cold War America and the Disillusioning of a Generation.* New York, NY: Basic Books.

Epstein, David, et al. 2006. Democratic Transitions. *American Journal of Political Science* 50 (3): 551–569.

Espinal, Rosario, Jonathan Hartlyn, and Jana Morgan-Kelly. 2006. Performance Still Matters: Explaining Trust in Government in the Dominican Republic. *Comparative Political Studies* 39 (2): 200–223.

Etzioni, Amitai. 1975. *A Comparative Analysis of Complex Organizations*. New York, NY: Free Press.

Evans, Peter, ed. 1997. *State-Society Synergy: Government and Social Capital in Development*. Berkeley, CA: International and Area Studies, University of California.

Feigenbaum, Harvey, Jeffrey Henig, and Chris Hamnett. 1998. *Shrinking the State: The Political Underpinnings of Privatization*. Cambridge, UK: Cambridge University Press.

Feinberg, Richard, and Daniel Kurtz-Phelan. 2006. Nicaragua between Caudillismo and Modernity: The Sandinistas Redux? *World Policy Journal* 23 (2): 76–84.

Feldman, Gerald D. 1966. *Army, Industry, and Labor in Germany, 1914–1918*. Princeton, NJ: Princeton University Press.

Fielding, Steven. 1992. What Did "The People" Want? The Meaning of the 1945 General Election. *Historical Journal* 35 (3): 623–639.

Finkel, Steven, Anibal Perez-Liñan, and Mitchell Seligson. 2008. *Effects of Democracy Assistance on Democracy Building: Final Report*. Washington, DC: USAID.

Finn, John E. 1991. *Constitutions in Crisis: Political Violence and the Rule of Law*. New York, NY: Oxford University Press.

Fischer, David Hackett. 2004. *Washington's Crossing*. New York, NY: Oxford University Press.

Fisher, Irving Nuttall, and George R. Hall. 1968. *Defense Profit Policy in the United States and the United Kingdom*. Santa Monica, CA: The Rand Corporation.

Fisher, Louis. 1975. *Presidential Spending Power*. Princeton, NJ: Princeton University Press.

Flynn, George Q. 1998. Conscription and Equity in Western Democracies, 1940–75. *Journal of Contemporary History* 33 (1): 5–20.

Fones-Wolf, Elizabeth A. 1994. *Selling Free Enterprise: The Business Assault on Labor and Liberalism, 1945–1960*. Urbana, IL: University of Illinois Press.

Fontana, Andres Fuerzas Armadas. 1984. *Partidos políticos y Transición a la Democracia en Argentina*. Buenos Aires: Estudios CEDES.

Forment, Carlos A. 2003. *Democracy in Latin America, 1760–1900*. Chicago, IL: University of Chicago Press.

Forrest, Joshua Bernard. 1992. A Promising Start: The Inauguration and Consolidation of Democracy in Namibia. *World Policy Journal* 9 (4): 748–749.

Forsythe, David. 1992. Democracy, War, and Covert Action. *Journal of Peace Research* 29 (4): 385–395.

Fowler, Dorothy Ganfield. 1977. *Unmailable: Congress and the Post Office*. Athens, GA: University of Georgia Press.

Francis, Martin. 1997. *Ideas and Policies Under Labour, 1945–1951: Building a New Britain*. Manchester: Manchester University Press.

Fraser, Steven. 1991. *Labor Will Rule: Sidney Hillman and the Rise of American Labor*. New York, NY: Free Press.

Frazer, Jendayi. 1994. Sustaining Civilian Control in Africa: The Use of Armed Counterweights in Regime Stability. Ph.D. diss., Stanford University.

Freedom House. 2005. *Freedom in the World 2005*. New York, NY: Freedom House.

Friedberg, Aaron L. 2000. *In the Shadow of the Garrison State: America's Anti-Statism and Its Cold War Grand Strategy*. Princeton, NJ: Princeton University Press.

Frye, Charles E. 1968. The Third Reich and the Second Republic: National Socialism's Impact upon German Democracy. *Western Political Quarterly* 21 (4): 668–680.

Fukuyama, Francis. 1995. *Trust: The Social Virtues and the Creation of Prosperity*. New York, NY: Free Press.

Fulbright, J. William. 1966. *The Arrogance of Power*. New York, NY: Random House.

Fuller, Wayne E. 1972. *American Mail: Enlarger of the Common Life*. Chicago, IL: University of Chicago Press.

Furner, Mary O., and Barry Supple, eds. 1990. *The State and Economic Knowledge: The American and British Experiences*. New York, NY: Cambridge University Press.

Fussell, Paul. 2003. *The Boys' Crusade: The American Infantry in Northwestern Europe, 1944–1945*. New York, NY: Modern Library.

Galassi, Francesco, and Mark Harrison. 2005. Italy at War. In *The Economics of World War I*, edited by Stephen Broadberry and Mark Harrison, 276–309. Cambridge, UK: Cambridge University Press.

Galbraith, John Kenneth. 1978. *The Affluent Society*. Third Edition. New York, NY: Mentor.

Gamba, Virginia, and Richard Cornwell. 2000. Arms, Elites and Resources in the Angolan Civil War. In *Greed and Grievance: Economic Agendas in Civil Wars*, edited by Mats R. Berdal and David M. Malone, 157–172. Boulder, CO: Lynne Rienner.

Ganguly, Sumit. 2001. *Conflict Unending: India-Pakistan Tensions since 1947*. New Delhi: Oxford University Press.

Garrett, Geoffrey, and Barry R. Weingast. 1993. Ideas, Interests and Institutions: Constructing the European Community's Internal Market. In *Ideas and Foreign Policy, Beliefs, Institutions, and Political Change*, edited by Judith Goldstein and Robert O. Keohane, 173–205. Ithaca, NY: Cornell University Press.

Gasiorowski, Mark J. 1996. An Overview of the Political Regime Change Dataset. *Comparative Political Studies* 29 (4): 469–483.

Gastil, Raymond D. 1980, 1990. *Freedom in the World: Political Rights and Civil Liberties*. New York, NY: Freedom House.

Geddes, Barbara. 1999. What Do We Know About Democratization After Twenty Years? *Annual Review of Political Science* 2: 115–144.

Gellman, Barton. 2008. *Angler: The Cheney Vice Presidency*. New York, NY: Penguin.

Gelpi, Christopher F., and Michael Griesdorf. 2001. Winners or Losers? Democracies in International Crisis, 1918–94. *American Political Science Review* 95 (3): 633–647.

Gibler, Doug M., and Marc L. Hutchinson. 2007. Political Tolerance and Territorial Threat: A Cross-National Study. *Journal of Politics* 69 (1): 128–242.

Giddens, Anthony. 1985. *The Nation State and Violence*. Berkeley, CA: University of California Press

Gifford, Brian. 2006. The Camouflaged Safety Net: The U.S. Armed Forces as Welfare State Institution. *Social Politics* 13 (3): 372–399.

Gildea, Robert. 2002. *France since 1945*. Oxford: Oxford University Press.

Gitlow, Benjamin. 1940. *I Confess: The Truth about American Communism*. New York, NY: E. P. Dutton.

Gleditsch, Kristian S. 2002. *All International Politics is Local: The Diffusion of Conflict, Integration, and Democratization.* Ann Arbor, MI: University of Michigan Press.

Gleditsch, Kristian Skrede, and Michael D. Ward. 2006. Diffusion and the International Context of Democratization. *International Organization* 60 (4): 911–933.

Glendon, Mary Ann. 2001. *A World Made New: Eleanor Roosevelt and the Universal Declaration of Human Rights.* New York, NY: Random House.

Gochman, Charles S., and Zeev Maoz. 1984. Militarized Interstate Disputes, 1816–1976: Procedures, Patterns, and Insights. *Journal of Conflict Resolution* 28 (4): 585–616.

Goemans, Hein E. 2000. *War and Punishment: The Causes of War Termination and the First World War.* Princeton, NJ: Princeton University Press.

Goldgeier, James, and Michael McFaul. 1992. A Tale of Two Worlds: Core and Periphery after the Cold War. *International Organization* 46 (3): 467–491.

Goldstein, Norm. 1991. *Marshal: A History of the U.S. Marshals Service.* New York, NY: DSI Publishing.

Goldstone, Jack A. 1991. *Revolution and Rebellion in the Early Modern World.* Berkeley, CA: University of California Press.

Gomez, Jose, and Eduardo Viola. 1984. Transición Desde el Autoritarismo. In *Proceso, Crisis y Transición Democrático,* Vol. 2, edited by Oscar Oszlak, 29–42. Buenos Aires: CEAL.

Good, Kenneth. 1997. Accountable to Themselves: Predominance in Southern Africa. *Journal of Modern African Studies* 35 (4): 547–573.

Goralski, Robert. 1981. *World War II Almanac: 1931–1945.* New York, NY: Putnam.

Gordon, Gilbert Andrew Hugh. 1988. *British Seapower and Procurement between the Wars: A Reappraisal of Rearmament.* Annapolis, MD: Naval Institute Press.

Gospel, Howard F. 1987. Employers and Managers: Organisation and Strategy 1914–39. In *A History of British Industrial Relations,* Vol. II, *1914–1939,* edited by Chris Wrigley, 129–158. London: The Harvester Press.

Gough, Terrence James. 1997. The Battle of Washington: Soldiers and Businessmen in World War I. Ph.D. diss., University of Virginia.

Gowa, Joanne. 1995. Democratic States and International Disputes. *International Organization* 49 (3): 511–522.

Graf, Christoph. 1987. The Genesis of the Gestapo. *Journal of Contemporary History* 22 (3): 419–435.

Green, E. H. H. 1997. The Conservative Party, the State, and the Electorate, 1945–1964. In *Party, State, and Society: Electoral Behavior in Britain since 1820,* edited by Jon Lawrence and Miles Taylor, 176–200. Aldershot: Scholar Press.

Greenberg, Jerald, and Ronald L. Cohen, eds. 1982. *Equity and Justice in Social Behavior.* San Diego, CA: Academic Press.

Griffith, Robert. 1983. The Selling of America: The Advertising Council and American Politics, 1942–1960. *Business History Review* 57 (3): 388–412.

——1989. Forging America's Postwar Order: Domestic Politics and Political Economy in the Age of Truman. In *The Truman Presidency,* edited by Michael J. Lacey, 57–86. New York, NY: Cambridge University Press.

Gross, Oren, and Fionnuala Ní Aoláin. 2006. *Law in Times of Crisis: Emergency Powers in Theory and Practice.* Cambridge, UK: Cambridge University Press.

Gurr, Ted Robert, Keith Jaggers, and Will H. Moore. 1989. *Polity II: Political Structures and Regime Change, 1800–1986.* Inter-University Consortium for Political and Social Research Study No. 9263.

Guttman, Daniel. 2003. Contracting U.S. Government Work: Organization and Constitutional Models. *Public Organization Review* 3 (3): 281–299.

Guttman, Daniel, and Barry Willner. 1976. *The Shadow Government.* New York, NY: Pantheon.

Habermas, Jurgen. 1999. *The Inclusion of the Other.* Cambridge, UK: Polity Press.

Halévy, Elie. 1966. *The Era of Tyrannies: Essays on Socialism and War.* New York, NY: New York University Press.

Hall, Peter A. 1993. Policy Paradigms, Social Learning, and the State: The Case of Economic Policymaking in Britain. *Comparative Politics* 25 (3): 275–296.

——1999. Social Capital in Britain. *British Journal of Political Science* 29 (3): 417–461.

——2003. Aligning Ontology and Methodology in Comparative Research. In *Comparative Historical Analysis in the Social Sciences*, edited by James Mahoney and Dietrich Rueschemeyer, 373–407. New York, NY: Cambridge University Press.

Hammond, Paul. 1961. *Organizing for Defense.* Princeton, NJ: Princeton University Press.

Hanson, Victor Davis. 2000. *The Western Way of War: Infantry Battle in Classical Greece.* Berkeley, CA: University of California Press.

Harmes, Adam. 2006. Neoliberalism and Multi-level Governance. *Review of International Political Economy* 13 (5): 725–749.

Harries, Meirion, and Susie Harries. 1997. *The Last Days of Innocence: America at War.* New York, NY: Random House.

Harrington, Austin. 2005. Introduction to Georg Simmel's Essay "Europe and America in World History." *European Journal of Social Theory* 8 (1): 63–72.

Harris, Howell John. 1982. *The Right to Manage: Industrial Relations Policies of American Business in the 1940s.* Madison, WI: University of Wisconsin Press.

Harris, Nigel. 1972. *Competition and the Corporate Society: British Conservatives, the State, and Industry, 1945–1964.* London: Methuen.

Harrison, Graham. 1996. Democracy in Mozambique: The Significance of Multi-party Elections. *Review of African Political Economy* 67: 19–35.

Hartlyn, Jonathan. 1989. Colombia: The Politics of Violence and Accommodation. In *Democracy in Developing Countries: Latin America*, Vol. 4, edited by Larry Diamond, Juan Linz, and Seymour Martin Lipset, 291–334. Boulder, CO: Lynne Rienner.

Hartzell, Caroline, and Matthew Hoddie. 2003. Institutionalizing Peace: Power Sharing and Post-Civil War Conflict Management. *American Journal of Political Science* 47 (2): 318–332.

Hausner, Jerzy. 1992. *Populist Threat in Transformation of Socialist Society.* Warsaw: Friedrich Ebert Foundation.

Hayward, Jack. 1993. From Republican Sovereign to Partisan Statesman. In *De Gaulle to Mitterand: Presidential Power in France*, edited by Jack Hayward, 1–35. New York, NY: New York University Press.

Hazard, Paul. 1954. *European Thought in the Eighteenth Century: From Montesquieu to Lessing.* New Haven, CT: Yale University Press.

Held, David. 1995. *Democracy and the Global Order: From the Nation-State to Cosmopolitan Governance.* Oxford: Polity Press.

Held, David, Anthony McGrew, David Goldblatt, and Jonathan Perraton. 1999. *Global Transformations: Politics, Economics, and Culture*. Stanford, CA: Stanford University Press.

Henderson, Gordon. 2006. The Public and the Peace: The Consequences for Citizenship of the Democratic Peace Literature. *International Studies Review* 8 (2): 199–224.

Henthorn, Cynthia Lee. 2006. *From Submarines to Suburbs: Selling a Better America, 1939–1959*. Athens, OH: Ohio University Press.

Herbst, Jeffrey. 1997. Prospects for Elite-Driven Democracy in South Africa. *Political Science Quarterly* 112 (4): 595–615.

——2000. *States and Power in Africa*. Princeton, NJ: Princeton University Press.

Higgonet, Margaret Randolph, et al., eds. 1987. *Behind the Lines: Gender and the Two World Wars*. Princeton, NJ: Princeton University Press.

Higgs, Robert. 1989. *Crisis and Leviathan: Critical Episodes in the Growth of American Government*. Oxford: Oxford University Press.

Hintze, Otto. 1975. Military Organization and the Organization of the State. In *The Historical Essays of Otto Hintze*, edited by Felix Gilbert, 178–215. New York, NY: Oxford University Press.

Hirschman, Albert. 1982. Rival Interpretations of Market Society: Civilizing, Destructive or Feeble? *Journal of Economic Literature* 20 (December): 1463–1484.

Hoffmann, Stanley. 1978. *Primacy or World Order: American Foreign Policy since the Cold War*. New York, NY: McGraw-Hill.

Hoge, Charles W., et al. 2004. Combat Duty in Iraq and Afghanistan, Mental Health Problems, and Barriers to Care. *New England Journal of Medicine* 351 (1): 13–22.

Holley Jr., Irving Brinton. 1964. *Buying Aircraft: Matériel Procurement for the Army Air Forces*. Washington, DC: Department of the Army, Office of the Chief of Military History.

Holmes, Stephen. 1991. The Liberal Idea. *The American Prospect* 7: 81–96.

——1995. *Passions and Constraint: On the Theory of Liberal Democracy* Chicago, IL: University of Chicago Press.

——2003. Lineages of the Rule of Law. In *Democracy and the Rule of Law*, edited by José María Maravall and Adam Przeworski, 19–61. Cambridge, UK: Cambridge University Press.

Hooks, Gregory. 1991. *Forging the Military-Industrial Complex: World War II's Battle of the Potomac*. Urbana, IL: University of Illinois Press.

Hornby, William. 1958. *Factories and Plant*. London: Her Majesty's Stationery Office.

Horne, John N. 1991. *Labour at War: France and Britain 1914–1918*. Oxford: Clarendon Press.

Horowitz, David. 1963. *The Italian Labor Movement*. Cambridge, MA: Harvard University Press.

Howard, Michael. 1992. *Lessons of History*. New Haven, CT: Yale University Press.

Howard, Lise Morjé. 2002. UN Peace Implementation in Namibia: The Causes of Success. *International Peacekeeping* 9 (1): 99–132.

Howard, Marc Morjé, and Philip Roessler. 2006. Liberalizing Electoral Outcomes in Competitive Electoral Regimes. *American Journal of Political Science* 50 (2): 365–381.

Howe, Herbert. 2001. *Ambiguous Order: Military Forces and African States*. Boulder, CO: Lynne Rienner.

Howell, William G., and Jon C. Pevehouse. 2007. *While Dangers Gather: Congressional Checks on Presidential War Powers*. Princeton, NJ: Princeton University Press.

Howlett, Peter. 1994. The Wartime Economy, 1939–1945. In *The Economic History of Britain since 1700*, Second Edition, *Vol. 3, 1939–1992*, edited by Roderick Floud and Donald McCloskey, 1–31. New York, NY: Cambridge University Press.

——1995. "The Thin Edge of the Wedge?": Nationalisation and Industrial Structure During the Second World War. In *The Political Economy of Nationalisation in Britain, 1920–1950*, edited by Robert Milward and John Singleton, 237–256. Cambridge, UK: Cambridge University Press.

Huntington, Samuel P. 1961. *The Common Defense*. New York, NY: Columbia University Press.

——1981. *American Politics: The Promise of Disharmony*. Cambridge, MA: Belknap Press of Harvard University Press.

——1991. *The Third Wave: Democratization in the Late Twentieth Century*. Norman, OK: University Press of Oklahoma.

Imlay, Talbot. 2007. Total War. *Journal of Strategic Studies* 30 (3): 547–570.

Inglehart, Ronald. 1988. The Renaissance of Political Culture. *American Political Science Review* 82 (4): 1203–1230.

Iriye, Akira. 2002. *Global Community: The Role of International Organizations in the Making of the Contemporary World*. Berkeley, CA: University of California Press.

Irons, Peter. 1990. *The Courage of Their Convictions: Sixteen Americans Who Fought Their Way to the Supreme Court*. New York, NY: Penguin.

——1999. *A People's History of the Supreme Court*. New York, NY: W. W. Norton.

Jacobs, Meg. 1997. "How About Some Meat?": The Office of Price Administration, Consumption Politics, and State Building from the Bottom Up. *Journal of American History* 84 (3): 910–941.

——2005. *Pocketbook Politics: Economic Citizenship in Twentieth Century America*. Princeton, NJ: Princeton University Press.

Jaggers, Keith. 1992. War and the Three Faces of Power: War Making and State Making in Europe and the Americas. *Comparative Political Studies* 25 (1): 26–62.

Jaggers, Keith, and Ted Robert Gurr. 1995. Tracking Democracy's Third Wave with the Polity III Data. *Journal of Peace Research* 32 (4): 469–482.

James, Patrick, Eric Solberg, and Murray Wolfson. 1999. An Identified Systemic Model of the Democracy-Peace Nexus. *Defence and Peace Economics* 10 (1): 1–37.

James, Scott C., and Brian L. Lawson. 1999. The Political Economy of Voting Rights Enforcement in America's Gilded Age: Electoral College Competition, Partisan Commitment, and the Federal Election Law. *American Political Science Review* 93 (1): 115–131.

Jefferys, Kevin. 1987. British Politics and Social Policy during the Second World War. *Historical Journal* 30 (1): 123–144.

Jennings, M. Kent. 2002. Generation Units and the Student Protest Movement in the United States. *Political Psychology* 23 (2): 303–324.

Jennings, M. Kent, and Gregory B. Markus. 1977. The Effect of Military Service on Political Attitudes. *American Political Science Review* 71 (1): 131–47.

Jervis, Robert. 1997. *System Effects: Complexity in Political and Social Life*. Princeton, NJ: Princeton University Press.

Jhee, Byong-Kuen. 2008. Economic Origins of Electoral Support for Authoritarian Successors: A Cross-National Analysis of Economic Voting in New Democracies. *Comparative Political Studies* 41 (3): 362–388.

Johnman, Lewis. 1991. The Labour Party and Industrial Policy, 1940–1945. In *The Attlee Years*, edited by Nick Tiratsoo, 29–53. London: Pinter.

Johnson, Dominic D. P., and Dominic Tierney. 2006. *Failing to Win: Perceptions of Victory and Defeat in International Politics*. Cambridge, MA: Harvard University Press.

Johnson, Krista. 2003. Liberal or Liberation Framework? The Contradictions of ANC Rule in South Africa. *Journal of Contemporary African Studies* 21 (2): 321–40.

Johnson, Robert David. 2006. *Congress and the Cold War*. Cambridge, UK: Cambridge University Press.

Jonas, Susanne. 2000. Democratization through Peace: The Difficult Case of Guatemala. *Journal of Inter-American Studies and World Affairs* 42 (4): v-38.

Jones, Daniel M., Stuart A. Bremer, and J. David Singer. 1996. Militarized Interstate Disputes, 1816–1992: Rationale, Coding Rules, and Empirical Patterns. *Conflict Management and Peace Science* 15 (2): 163–213.

Jones, Harriet. 1996. A Bloodless Counter-Revolution: The Conservative Party and the Defence of Inequality, 1945–51. In *The Myth of Consensus: New Views on British History, 1945–64*, edited by Harriet Jones and Michael Kandiah, 1–16. New York, NY: St. Martin's Press.

——1999. "New Conservatism?": The Industrial Charter, Modernity, and the Reconstruction of British Conservatism after the War. In *Moments of Modernity: Reconstructing Britain, 1945–1964*, edited by Becky Conekin, Frank Mort, and Chris Waters, 171–188. London: Rivers Oram Press.

Joseph, Richard. 1999. Democratization in Africa after 1989: Comparative and Theoretical Perspectives. In *Transitions to Democracy*, edited by Lisa Anderson, 237–261. New York, NY: Columbia University Press.

Judt, Tony. 1998. *Postwar: A History of Europe since 1945*. New York, NY: Penguin Books.

Kage, Rieko. 2003. Embracing Democracy: The Promotion of Civic Engagement in Occupied Japan. Paper Presented at the Seventh Annual Asian Studies Japan Conference. Tokyo: Sophia University.

——2010. Making Reconstruction Work: Civil Society and Information after War's End. *Comparative Political Studies* 43 (2): 163–187.

Kaiser, David E. 1983. Germany and the Origins of the First World War. *The Journal of Modern History* 55 (3): 442–474.

Kandiah, Michael David. 1995. The Conservative Party and the 1945 General Election. *Contemporary Record* 9 (1): 22–47.

Kant Immanuel. 1949. Eternal Peace. In *The Philosophy of Kant*, edited by Carl J. Friedrich. New York, NY: The Modern Library.

Kapstein, Ethan, and Nathan Converse. 2008. *The Fate of Young Democracies*. New York, NY: Cambridge University Press.

Karakatsanis, Neovi. 2001. *The Politics of Elite Transformation: The Consolidation of Greek Democracy in Theoretical Perspective*. Westport, CT: Praeger.

Kasitsky, Deborah. 2005. *The United States and the European Right*. Columbus, OH: Ohio State University Press.

Kasza, Gregory J. 1995. *The Conscription Society: Administered Mass Organizations*. New Haven, CT: Yale University Press.

——1996. War and Comparative Politics. *Comparative Politics* 29 (1): 355–373.

Katznelson, Ira, Kim Geiger, and Daniel Kryder. 1993. Limiting Liberalism: The Southern Veto in Congress, 1933–1950. *Political Science Quarterly* 108 (2): 283–306.

Katznelson, Ira, and Bruce Pietrykowski. 1991. Rebuilding the American State: Evidence from the 1940s. *Studies in American Political Development* 5 (2): 301–339.

Keane, Terence M., Amy D. Marshall, and Casey T. Taft. 2006. Post-traumatic Stress Disorder: Etiology, Epidemiology, and Treatment Outcome. *Annual Review of Clinical Psychology* 2: 161–197.

Keezer, Dexter M. 1943. Observations on Rationing and Price Control in Great Britain. *American Economic Review* 33 (2): 264–282.

Keizai Antei Honbu Sosai Kanbo Kikakubu Chosaka. 1949. *Taiheiho Senso ni yoru Wagakunino Higai Sogo Hokokusho [Summary Report: Damages to Japan as a Result of the Pacific War]*. In *Shiryo: Taiheiyo Senso Higai Chosa Hokoku [Historical Compendium on Damage to Japan in the Pacific War]*, edited by Takafusa Nakamura and Masayasu Miyazaki, 255–382. Tokyo: Tokyo Daigauk Shuppankai.

Kennett, Lee B. 1967. *The French Armies in the Seven Years War: A Study in Military Organization and Administration*. Durham, NC: Duke University Press.

Kersten, Andrew E. 2006. *Labor's Home Front: The American Federation of Labor During World War II*. New York, NY: New York University Press.

Kestnbaum, Meyer. 2009. The Sociology of War and the Military. *Annual Review of Sociology* 35: 235–254.

King, Gary. 1989. *Unifying Political Methodology: The Likelihood Theory of Statistical Inference*. New York, NY: Cambridge University Press.

King, Gary, and Langche Zeng. 2001. Explaining Rare Events in International Relations. *International Organization* 55 (3): 693–715.

Kirby, D. G. 1979. *Finland in the Twentieth Century: A History and Interpretation*. Minneapolis, MN: University of Minnesota Press.

Kircheimer, Otto. 1961. German Democracy in the 1950s. *World Politics* 13 (2): 254–266.

Kirisutokyo Seinen Undo wa Do Yukuka [Where Is the Christian Youth Movement Headed?]. 1947. Roundtable Discussion. *Kaitakusha* 41 (7): 26–30.

Klarén, Peter F. 2000. *Peru: Society and Nationhood in the Andes*. New York, NY: Oxford University Press.

Klinkner, Philip A., and Rogers M. Smith. 2000. *The Unsteady March: The Rise and Decline of Racial Equality in America*. Chicago, IL: University of Chicago Press.

Knight, Jack. 1992. *Institutions and Social Conflict*. New York, NY: Cambridge University Press.

Kobe YMCA 100nenshi Hensanshitsu. 1981a. *Kobe YMCA no Rekishi wo Kataru: Soritsu 100nen ni Mukete, Zadankai-hen 2 [The History of Kobe YMCA, Roundtable Discussion: Towards the 100-Year Anniversary, Vol. 2]*. Kobe: Kobe YMCA 100nenshi Hensanshitsu.

———1981b. *Kobe YMCA no Rekishi wo Kataru: Soritsu 100nen ni Mukete, Zadankai-hen 3 [The History of Kobe YMCA, Roundtable Discussion: Towards the 100-Year Anniversary, Vol. 3]*. Kobe: Kobe YMCA 100nenshi Hensanshitsu.

———1987. *Kobe to YMCA 100-nen [Kobe and One Hundred Years of the YMCA]*. Kobe: Kobe YMCA.

Kobe YMCA. n.d. Minutes of the Monthly Board Meetings. Internal Documents, courtesy of Kobe YMCA, Kobe, Japan.

———1947. *Showa 21nendo Jigyo Narabini Kaikei Hokoku [Annual Report of the Kobe YMCA: 1946]*. Kobe: Kobe YMCA.

——1969. *YMCA 70yen no Ayumi: 1899–1969 [The 70-Year History of the Kobe YMCA: 1899–1969]*. Kobe: Kobe YMCA.

Kobe-shi Kyoikushi Henshu Iinkai, ed. 1964. *Kobe-shi Kyoikushi Dai 2 shu [The History of Education in the City of Kobe, Vol. 2]*. Kobe: Kobe-shi Kyoikushi Kanko Iinkai.

Kobe-shi, ed. 1965. *Kobe-shi Shi, Dai 3 Shu: Shakai Bunka Hen [History of the City of Kobe, Vol. 3: Culture and Society]*. Kobe: Kobe-shi.

Koh, Harold. 1990. *The National Security Constitution*. New Haven, CT: Yale University Press.

Kohn, Richard H. 1994. Out of Control: The Crisis in American Civil-Military Relations. *The National Interest* 35: 3–17.

——2002. The Erosion of Civilian Control of the Military in the United States Today. *Naval War College Review* 55 (3): 8–59.

Koistinen, Paul A. C. 2004. *Arsenal of World War II: The Political Economy of American Warfare, 1940–1945*. Lawrence, KS: University Press of Kansas.

Korpi, Walter. 1989. Power, Politics, and State Autonomy in the Development of Social Citizenship Social Rights during Sickness in Eighteen OECD Countries. *American Sociological Review* 54 (3): 309–328.

Krahmann, Elke. 2010. *States, Citizens and the Privatization of Security*. Cambridge, UK: Cambridge University Press.

Krebs, Ronald R. 2004. A School for the Nation? *International Security* 28 (4): 85–124.

——2006. *Fighting for Rights: Military Service and the Politics of Citizenship*. Ithaca, NY: Cornell University Press.

——2009. In the Shadow of War: The Effects of Conflict on Liberal Democracy. *International Organization* 63 (1): 177–210.

Krennerich, Michael. 1999. Mozambique. In *Elections in Africa*, edited by Dieter Nohlen, Michael Krennerich, and Bernhard Thibaut, 645–658. Oxford: Oxford University Press.

Kurzman, Charles, and Erin Leahey. 2004. Intellectuals and Democratization, 1905–1912 and 1989–1996. *American Journal of Sociology* 109 (4): 937–986.

Kynaston, David. 2007. *Austerity Britain, 1945–51*. London: Bloomsbury.

Lake, David A. 1992. Powerful Pacifists: Democratic States and War. *American Political Science Review* 8 (1): 24–37.

——2003. Fair Fights? Evaluating Theories of Democracy and Victory. *International Security* 28 (1): 154–167.

Lane, Frederick. 1979. *Profits from Power*. Albany, NY: State University of New York Press.

Langeluttig, Albert. 1929. Federal Police. *Annals of the American Academy of Political and Social Science* 146 (1): 41–54.

Larrabee, F. Stephen. 1981. Dateline Athens: Greece for the Greeks. *Foreign Policy* 45: 158–174.

Lasswell, Harold. 1941. The Garrison State. *American Journal of Sociology* 46 (4): 455–468.

Leal, David L. 1999. It's Not Just a Job: Military Service and Latino Political Participation. *Political Behavior* 21 (2): 153–174.

Lee, Margaret Mikyung, and Ruth Ellen Wasem. 2003. Expedited Citizenship Through Military Service: Policy and Issues. *CRS Report for Congress,* Order Code RL 31884. Washington, DC: Congressional Research Service, updated September 30.

Leech, Daniel D. Tompkins. 1879. *The Post Office Department of the United States of America; Its History, Organization, and Working, from the Inauguration of the Federal Government, 1789, to the Close of the Administration of President Andrew Johnson.* Washington, DC: Judd & Detweiller.

——1976. *The Post Office Department of the United States of America.* New York, NY: Arno Press.

Leff, Mark H. 1991. The Politics of Sacrifice on the American Home Front in World War II. *Journal of American History* 77 (4): 1296–1318.

Legro, Jeffrey W. 2005. *Rethinking the World: Great Power Strategies and International Order.* Ithaca, NY: Cornell University Press.

Levi, Margaret. 1997. *Consent, Dissent, and Patriotism.* New York, NY: Cambridge University Press.

Levitsky, Steven, and Lucan Way. 2010. *Competitive Authoritarianism: Hybrid Regimes after the Cold War.* Cambridge: Cambridge University Press.

Levy, Jack S. 1990. Big Wars, Little Wars, and Theory Construction. *International Interactions* 16 (3): 215–224.

Liang, Hsi-Huey. 1969. The Berlin Police and the Weimar Republic. *Journal of Contemporary History* 4 (4): 157–172.

——1992. *The Rise of Modern Police and the European State System from Metternich to the Second World War.* Cambridge, UK: Cambridge University Press.

Lichtenstein, Nelson. 1982. *Labor's War at Home: The CIO in World War II.* New York, NY: Cambridge University Press.

——1989. Labor in the Truman Era: Origins of the "Private Welfare State." In *The Truman Presidency*, edited by Michael J. Lacey, 128–155. New York, NY: Cambridge University Press.

——1995. *The Most Dangerous Man in Detroit: Walter Reuther and the Fate of American Labor.* New York, NY: Basic Books.

Lindeke, William. 1995. Democratization in Namibia: Soft State, Hard Choices. *Studies in Comparative International Development* 30 (1): 3–29.

Lindsay, James M. 1994. *Congress and the Politics of U.S. Foreign Policy.* Baltimore, MD: The Johns Hopkins University Press.

Linz, Juan, and Alfred Stepan. 1996. *Problems of Democratic Transition and Consolidation.* Baltimore, MD: The Johns Hopkins University Press.

Lloyd, Robert. 1995. Mozambique: The Terror of War, the Tensions of Peace. *Current History* 94 (591): 152–155.

Lowe, Rodney. 1978. The Erosion of State Intervention in Britain, 1917–24. *The Economic History Review* 31 (2): 270–286.

——1990. The Second World War, Consensus, and the Foundation of the Welfare State. *Twentieth Century British History* 1 (2): 152–182.

Lowi, Theodore. 1985. *The Personal President: Power Invested, Promise Unfulfilled.* Ithaca, NY: Cornell University Press.

Lumpe, Lora. 2002. U.S. Foreign Military Training: Global Reach, Global Power, and Oversight Issues. *Foreign Policy in Focus*, Special Report.

Lustick, Ian S. 1997. The Absence of Middle Eastern Great Powers: Political "Backwardness" in Historical Perspective. *International Organization* 51 (4): 653–683.

Lyttelton, Adrian. 2004. *The Seizure of Power: Fascism in Italy.* London: Routledge.

Lyttleton, Oliver. 1962. *The Memoirs of Lord Chandos.* London: Bodley Head.

MacDonald, Donald. F. 1976. *The State and the Trade Unions*. London: Macmillan.

Machin, Howard. 1993. The President, the Parties, and Parliament. In *De Gaulle to Mitterand: Presidential Power in France*, edited by Jack Hayward, 33–54. New York, NY: New York University Press.

MacLean, Alair, and Glen H. Elder, Jr. 2007. Military Service in the Life Course. *Annual Review of Sociology* 33: 175–196.

Mainwaring, Scott, and Timothy Scully. 1995. *Building Democratic Institutions: Party Systems in Latin America*. Stanford, CA: Stanford University Press.

Mann, Michael. 1986. *The Sources of Social Power*, Vol. 1: *A History of Power from the Beginning to A.D. 1760*. New York, NY: Cambridge University Press.

——1992. *States, War, and Capitalism: Studies in Political Sociology*. Cambridge, MA: Blackwell.

——1993. *The Sources of Social Power*, Vol. 2: *The Rise of Classes and Nation-States, 1760–1914*. Cambridge, UK: Cambridge University Press.

Manning, Carrie. 1998. Constructing Opposition in Mozambique: Renamo as Political Party. *Journal of Southern African Studies* 24 (1): 161–189.

——2002. Conflict Management and Elite Habituation in Postwar Democracy: The Case of Mozambique. *Comparative Politics* 35 (1): 63–84.

——2004. Armed Opposition Groups into Political Parties: Comparing Bosnia, Kosovo and Mozambique. *Studies in Comparative International Development* 39 (1): 54–76.

——2008. *The Making of Democrats: Elections and Party Development in Post-War Bosnia, El Salvador, and Mozambique*. New York, NY: Palgrave MacMillan.

Mansfield, Edward D., and Jack L. Snyder. 2005. *Electing to Fight: Why Emerging Democracies Go to War*. Cambridge, MA: MIT Press.

Mansfield Jr., Harvey C. 1989. *Taming the Prince: The Ambivalence of Modern Executive Power*. New York, NY: Free Press.

Marchand, Roland. 1998. *Creating the Corporate Soul: The Rise of Public Relations and Corporate Imagery in American Big Business*. Berkeley, CA: University Press of California.

Marks, Gary. 1989. *Unions in Politics: Britain, Germany, and the United States in the Nineteenth and Early Twentieth Centuries*. Princeton, NJ: Princeton University Press.

Marshall, Monty G., and Keith Jaggers. 2005. POLITY IV: Political Regime Characteristics and Transitions, 1800–2004. Center for International Development and Conflict Management, University of Maryland.

Marshall, T. H. 1950. *Citizenship and Social Class and Other Essays*. Cambridge, UK: Cambridge University Press.

Marwick, Arthur. 1974. *War and Social Change in the Twentieth Century: A Comparative Study of Britain, France, Germany, Russia, and the United States*. London: Macmillan.

Maxwell, Kenneth. 1995. *The Making of Portuguese Democracy*. Cambridge, UK: Cambridge University Press.

Mayhew, David R. 2005. Wars and American Politics. *Perspectives on Politics* 3 (3): 473–493.

Mazower, Mark. 1999. *Dark Continent: Europe's Twentieth Century*. New York, NY: Knopf.

McClintock, Cynthia. 1998. *Revolutionary Movements in Latin America*. Washington, DC: United States Institute of Peace Press.

McGuire, Robert. 2003. *To Form a More Perfect Union: A New Economic Interpretation of the United States Constitution.* New York, NY: Oxford University Press.

McLaughlin Mitchell, Sara, et al. 1999. Evolution in Democracy-War Dynamics. *Journal of Conflict Resolution* 43 (6): 771–792.

McNeil, William H. 1982. *The Pursuit of Power: Technology, Armed Force, and Society since* a.d. *1000.* Chicago, IL: University of Chicago Press.

Meinecke, Fredrick. 1972. *Historicism: The Rise of a New Historical Outlook.* New York, NY: Herder and Herder.

Mercer, Helen. 1991. The Labour Governments of 1945–51 and Private Industry. In *The Attlee Years,* edited by Nick Tiratsoo, 71–89. London: Pinter.

——1996. Industrial Organization and Ownership, and a New Definition of the Postwar "Consensus." In *The Myth of Consensus: New Views on British History, 1945–64,* edited by Harriet Jones and Michael Kandiah, 139–156. New York, NY: St. Martin's Press.

Mercer, Jonathan. 2005. Rationality and Psychology in International Politics. *International Organization* 59 (1): 77–106.

Merritt, Richard. 1995. *Democracy Imposed: U.S. Occupation Policy and the German Public, 1945–1949.* New Haven, CT: Yale University Press.

Mettler, Suzanne. 2005. *Soldiers to Citizens: The G.I. Bill and the Making of the Greatest Generation.* New York, NY: Oxford University Press.

Metz, Edward, and James Youniss. 2003. A Demonstration that School-Based Required Service Does not Deter – But Heightens – Volunteerism. *PS: Political Science and Politics* 36 (2): 281–286.

Micaud, Charles A. 1946. The Launching of the Fourth French Republic. *Journal of Politics* 8 (3): 292–307.

Michaels, Jon D. 2004. Beyond Accountability: The Constitutional, Democratic, and Strategic Problems with Privatizing War. *Washington University Law Quarterly* 82: 1001–1127.

Middlemas, Keith. 1979. *Politics in Industrial Society: The Experience of the British System since 1911.* London: Andre Deutsch.

Milkis, Sidney M., and Michael Nelson. 2008. *The American Presidency: Origins and Development, 1776–2007.* Washington, DC: Congressional Quarterly Press.

Millard, Frances. 1994. The Shaping of Polish Party System, 1989–1993. *East European Politics and Societies* 8 (3): 467–94.

Miller, Benjamin. 2007. *States, Nations, and the Great Powers: The Sources of Regional War and Peace.* New York, NY: Cambridge University Press.

Miller, James. 1986. *The United States and Italy 1940–1950.* Chapel Hill, NC: University of North Carolina Press.

Mills, Geoffrey, and Hugh Rockoff. 1987. Compliance with Price Controls in the United States and the United Kingdom during World War II. *Journal of Economic History* 47 (1): 197–213.

Modell, John, and Timothy Haggerty. 1991. The Social Impact of War. *Annual Review of Sociology* 17: 205–224.

Moe, Terry. 1990. The Politics of Structural Choice: Toward a Theory of Public Bureaucracy. In *Organizational Theory: From Chester Barnard to the Present and Beyond,* edited by Oliver Williamson, 116–153. New York, NY: Oxford University Press.

Moore, James. 2001. *Very Special Agents: The Inside Story of America's Most Controversial Law Enforcement Agency – the Bureau of Alcohol, Tobacco and Firearms*. Urbana, IL: University of Illinois Press.

Moore, K. Michael. 1991. Forward. In *Marshal: A History of the U.S. Marshals Service*, by Norm Goldstein. New York, NY: DSI Publishing.

Morgan, Glenda. 1990. Violence in Mozambique: Towards an Understanding of Renamo. *Journal of Modern African Studies* 28 (4): 603–619.

Morgan, Kenneth O. 1984. *Labour in Power, 1945–1951*. Oxford: Clarendon Press.

——1987. The Rise and Fall of Public Ownership in Britain. In *The Political Culture of Modern Britain: Studies in Memory of Stephen Koss*, edited by J. M. W. Bean, 262–276. London: Hamish Hamilton.

Morley, Morris, and Chris McGillion. 1997. Disobedient Generals and the Politics of Redemocratization: The Clinton Administration and Haiti. *Political Science Quarterly* 112 (3): 363–384.

Mousseau, Michael, Havard Hegre, and John R. Oneal. 2003. How the Wealth of Nations Conditions the Liberal Peace. *European Journal of International Relations* 9 (2): 277–314.

Mousseau, Michael, and Yuhang Shi. 1999. A Test for Reverse Causality in the Democratic Peace Relationship. *Journal of Peace Research* 36 (6): 639–663.

Moyar, Mark. 2006. *Triumph Forsaken: The Vietnam War, 1954–1965*. New York, NY: Cambridge University Press.

Mueller, John. 2004. *The Remnants of War*. Ithaca, NY: Cornell University Press.

Munck, Gerardo L., and Jay Verkuilen. 2002. Conceptualizing and Measuring Democracy: Evaluating Alternative Indices. *Comparative Political Studies* 35 (1): 5–34.

Munck, Ronaldo. 1985. Democratization and Demilitarization in Argentina, 1982–1985. *Bulletin of Latin American Research* 4 (2): 85–93.

Murphy, Mary E. 1943. *The British War Economy, 1939–1943*. New York, NY: Professional & Technical Press.

Murphy, Paul L. 1979. *World War I and the Origins of Civil Liberties in the United States*. New York, NY: Norton.

Murray, Robert. 1955. *Red Scare: A Study in National Hysteria*. Minneapolis, MN: University of Minnesota Press.

Musso, Stefano. 1990. Political Tension and Labor Union Struggle: Working Class Conflicts in Turin During and After the First World War. In *Strikes, Social Conflict and the First World War: An International Perspective*, edited by Leopold Haimson and Giulio Sapelli, 213–246. Milan: Fondazione Giangiacomo Feltrinelli.

Nef, John U. 1963. *War and Human Progress: An Essay on the Rise of Industrial Civilization*. New York, NY: Norton.

Neustadt, Richard. 1990. *Presidential Power and the Modern Presidents: The Politics of Leadership from Roosevelt to Reagan*. New York, NY: Free Press.

NGO Policy Group. 2001. *The Third Sector in Serbia: Status and Prospects*. Belgrade: Center for the Development of the Nonprofit Sector and the NGO Policy Group.

Noguchi, Yukio. 1995. *1940-nen Taisei [The 1940 System]*. Tokyo: Toyo Keizai Shinposha.

Nomura, Takeo. 1975. *Kyoto YMCA 70-nen Shi [The 70-Year History of the Kyoto YMCA]*. Kyoto: Kyoto YMCA.

North, Douglass C. 1990. *Institutions, Institutional Change, and Economic Performance*. Cambridge, UK: Cambridge University Press.

O'Shaughnessy, Laura, and Michael Dodson. 1999. Political Bargaining and Democratic Transitions: A Comparison of Nicaragua and El Salvador. *Journal of Latin American Studies* 31: 91–127.

Ochiai, Shigenobu, and Hajime Arii. 1967. *Kobe Shiwa: Kindaika Urabanashi [The History of Kobe: Modernization and Anecdotes]*. Osaka: Sogensha.

Oe, Shinobu. 1988. *Shina Jihen Daitoa Sensokan Doin Gaishi: Jugonen Senso Gokuhi Shiryoshu Dai 9 Shu [History of Wartime Mobilization in Japan During the War With China and the "Great East Asian War": Secret Documents from the "Fifteen Years' War," Vol. 9]*. Tokyo: Fuji Shuppan.

Office of Homeland Security. 2002. National Strategy for Homeland Security, Washington, DC. Available at www.dhs.gov/xlibrary/assets/nat_strat_hls.pdf. Accessed September 18, 2009.

Ohly, John H. 1999. *Industrialists in Olive Drab: The Emergency Operation of Private Industries During World War II*. Washington, DC: Center of Military History.

Oliver, J. Eric. 2000. City Size and Civic Involvement in Metropolitan America. *American Political Science Review* 94 (2): 361–373.

Olsen, Edward. 1991. South Korea under Military Rule: Friendly Tyrant? In *Friendly Tyrants: An American Dilemma*, edited by Daniel Pipes and Adam Garfinkle, 331–351. New York, NY: St. Martin's Press.

Oneal, John R., and Bruce Russett. 2000. Comment: Why an Identified Systemic Model of the Democracy-Peace Nexus Does Not Persuade. *Defence and Peace Economics* 11 (1): 197–214.

Orwell, George. 1990. *1984*. New York, NY: Signet.

Ottaway, Marina. 1991. Liberation Movements and Transition to Democracy: The Case of the ANC. *Journal of Modern African Studies* 29 (1): 61–82.

Packenham, Robert A. 1973. *Liberal America and the Third World: Political Development Ideas in Foreign Aid and Social Science*. Princeton, NJ: Princeton University Press.

Papilloud, Christina. 2004. Three Conditions of Human Relations: Marcel Mauss and Georg Simmel. *Philosophy and Social Criticism* 30 (4): 431–144.

Paret, Peter. 1992. *Understanding War: Essays on Clausewitz and the History of Military Power*. Princeton, NJ: Princeton University Press.

Patterson, James T. 1972. *Mr. Republican: A Biography of Robert A. Taft*. Boston, MA: Houghton Mifflin.

Payne, Stanley G. 1987. *The Franco Regime, 1936–1975*. Madison, WI: University of Wisconsin Press.

Peacock, Alan T., and Jack Wiseman. 1961. *The Growth of Public Expenditures in the United Kingdom*. Princeton, NJ: Princeton University Press.

Peceny, Mark. 1999. *Democracy at the Point of Bayonets*. University Park, PA: Pennsylvania State University Press.

Peeler, John. 1992. Colombia, Costa Rica, and Venezuela. In *Elites and Democratic Consolidation in Latin America and Southern Europe*, edited by Richard Gunther and John Higley, 81–113. New York, NY: Cambridge University Press.

Peretz, Don, and Gideon Doron. 1997. *The Government and Politics of Israel*. Boulder, CO: Westview Press.

Pernicone, Nunzio. 1974. The Italian Labor Movement. In *Modern Italy: A Topical History Since 1861*, edited by Edward R. Tannenbaum and Emiliana P. Noether, 197–231. New York, NY: New York University Press.

Persson, Kristina. 2003. *The Role of NGOs in HIV/AIDS Work in Cambodia*. Manuscript. Lund University, Sweden.

Pevehouse, Jon C. 2005. *Democracy From Above: Regional Organizations and Democratization*. Cambridge, UK: Cambridge University Press.

Phillips-Fein, Kim. 2009. *Invisible Hands: The Making of the Conservative Movement from the New Deal to Reagan*. New York, NY: Norton.

Pierson, Paul. 1994. *Dismantling the Welfare State*. Cambridge, UK: Cambridge University Press.

——2004. *Politics in Time: History, Institutions, and Social Analysis*. Princeton, NJ: Princeton University Press.

Pion-Berlin, David. 1997. *Through Corridors of Power: Institutions and Civil-Military Relations in Argentina*. University Park, PA: Pennsylvania State University Press.

Pirie, Madsen. 1985. *Dismantling the State*. Dallas, TX: National Center for Policy Analysis.

Pitts, Jennifer. 2005. *A Turn to Empire: The Rise of Imperial Liberalism in Britain and France*. Princeton, NJ: Princeton University Press.

Podgórecki, Adam. 1994. *Polish Society*. Westport, CT: Praeger.

Poole, Michael. 1986. *Industrial Relations: Origins and Patterns of National Diversity*. Boston, MA: Routledge and Kegan Paul.

Porch, Douglas. 1977. *The Portuguese Armed Forces and the Revolution*. London: Croom Helm.

Porter, Bruce D. 1994. *War and the Rise of the State: The Military Foundations of Modern Politics*. New York, NY: Free Press.

Posen, Barry R. 1993. Nationalism, the Mass Army, and Military Power. *International Security* 18 (2): 80–124.

Posner, Eric A., and Adrian Vermeule. 2007. *Terror in the Balance: Security, Liberty, and the Courts*. New York, NY: Oxford University Press.

Postan, M. M. 1952. *British War Production*. London: Her Majesty's Stationery Office.

Postmaster General. 1959. *Annual Report, 1959*. Washington, DC: U.S. Government Printing Office.

Powell, David. 2004. *British Politics, 1910–35: The Crisis of the Party System*. London: Routledge.

Prevost, Gary. 2006. The Evolution of the African National Congress in Power: From Revolutionaries to Social Democrats? *Politikon: South African Journal of Political Studies* 33 (2): 163–181.

Primus, Richard A. 1999. *The American Language of Rights*. Cambridge, UK: Cambridge University Press.

Procacci, Giovanna. 1989. Popular Protest and Labour Conflict in Italy, 1915–18. *Social History* 14 (1): 31–58.

——1990. State Coercion and Worker Solidarity in Italy: The Moral and Political Content of Social Unrest. In *Strikes, Social Conflict and the First World War: An International Perspective*, edited by Leopold Haimson and Giulio Sapelli, 145–178. Milan: Fondazione Giangiacomo Feltrinelli.

——1995. A "Latecomer" in War: The Case of Italy. In *Authority, Identity, and the Social History of the Great War*, edited by Frans Coetzee and Marilyn Shevin-Coetzee, 3–28. Providence, RI: Berghahn Books.

Prost, Antoine. 1973. Combattants et politiciens: Le discourse mythologique sur la politique entre les deux guerres. *Le Mouvement Social* 85 (October/December): 117–154.

——1977. *Les Anciens Combattants et la Sociètè Française, 1914–1939*, 3 Vols. Paris: Presses de la Fondation Nationale de la Science Politique.

Przeworski, Adam, and Fernando Limongi. 1993. Political Regimes and Economic Growth. *Journal of Economic Growth* 7 (3): 51–69.

Przeworski, Adam, et al. 1996. What Makes Democracies Endure? *Journal of Democracy* 7 (1): 39–55.

——2000. *Democracy and Development: Political Institutions and Material Well-Being in the World, 1950–1990.* New York, NY: Cambridge University Press.

Puchalska, Bogusia. 2005. Polish Democracy in Transition? *Political Studies* 53 (4): 816–832.

Pugh, Martin. 2002. *The Making of Modern British Politics, 1867–1945.* Oxford: Blackwell.

Puntila, Lauri Aadolf. 1975. *The Political History of Finland 1809–1966.* London: Heinemann.

Putnam, Robert D. 1993. *Making Democracy Work: Civic Traditions in Modern Italy.* Princeton, NJ: Princeton University Press.

——2000. *Bowling Alone: The Collapse and Revival of American Community.* New York, NY: Simon and Schuster.

Rabinowitz, Mikaela. 2008. Rethinking the Relationship between the Military and the Welfare State. Paper presented at American Sociological Association Annual Meeting, New York, NY.

Rasler, Karen A., and William R. Thompson. 1985. War Making and State Making: Governmental Expenditures, Tax Revenues, and Global Wars. *American Political Science Review* 79 (2): 491–507.

——1989. *War Making and State Making: The Shaping of Global Powers.* Boston, MA: Unwin Hyman.

——2004. The Democratic Peace and a Sequential, Reciprocal, Causal Arrow Hypothesis. *Comparative Political Studies* 37 (8): 879–908.

Raymond, Gino G. 2000. The President: Still a "Republican Monarch"? In *Structures of Power in Modern France*, edited by Gino G. Raymond, 1–18. New York, NY: St. Martin's.

Rehnquist, William H. 1998. *All the Laws but One: Civil Liberties in Wartime.* New York, NY: Knopf.

Reid, Alastair. 1985. Dilution, Trade Unionism and the State in Britain during the First World War. In *Shop Floor Bargaining and the State*, edited by Steven Tolliday and Jonathan Zeitlin, 26–74. Cambridge, UK: Cambridge University Press.

Reilly, Benjamin. 2004. Elections in Post-Conflict Societies. In *The UN Role in Promoting Democracy: Between Ideals and Reality*, edited by Edward Newman and Roland Rich, 113–135. New York, NY: United Nations University Press.

Reiter, Dan. 2001. Does Peace Nurture Democracy? *Journal of Politics* 63 (3): 935–948.

Reiter, Dan, and Allan C. Stam. 2002. *Democracies at War.* Princeton, NJ: Princeton University Press.

——2003. Understanding Victory: Why Political Institutions Matter. *International Security* 28 (1): 168–179.

Reuveny, Rafael, and Quan Li. 2003. The Joint Democracy-Dyadic Conflict Nexus: A Simultaneous Equations Model. *International Studies Quarterly* 47 (3): 325–346.

Ricci, Maria Susana, and J. Samuel Fitch. 1990. Ending Military Regimes in Argentina, 1966–1973 and 1976–1983. In *The Military and Democracy: The Future of Civil Military Relations in Latin America*, edited by Louis Goodman, Johanna Mendelsohn, and Juan Rial, 55–75. Lanham, MD: Lexington Books.

Richards, Paul, and James Vincent. 2008. Sierra Leone: Marginalization of the RUF. In *From Soldiers to Politicians*, edited by Jeroen de Zeeuw, 81–102. London: Lynne Rienner.

Richmond, Al. 1942. *Native Daughter: The Story of Anita Whitney*. San Francisco, CA: Anita Whitney 75th Anniversary Committee.

Ricks, Thomas. 1997. *Making the Corps*. New York, NY: Scribner.

Rogow, Arnold A. 1955. *The Labour Government and British Industry, 1945–1951*. Ithaca, NY: Cornell University Press.

Rose, Richard. 2000. How Much Does Social Capital Add to Individual Health? A Survey Study of Russians. *Social Science & Medicine* 51 (9): 1421–1435.

Rose, Richard, and Doh Chull Shin. 2001. Democratization Backward: The Problem of Third Wave Democracies. *British Journal of Political Science* 31 (1): 331–354.

Rossiter, Clinton L. 1948. *Constitutional Dictatorship: Crisis Government in the Modern Democracies*. Princeton, NJ: Princeton University Press.

Rousseau, Jean Jacques. 1978 (1762). *On the Social Contract*. Translated by Judith R. Masters. New York, NY: St. Martin's.

Rubin, Gerry R. 1984. Law, War and Economy: The Munitions Acts 1915–17 and Corporatism in Context. *Journal of Law and Society* 11 (3): 317–333.

——1987. *War, Law, and Labour: The Munitions Acts, State Regulation and the Unions*. Oxford: Clarendon Press.

Rudalevige, Andrew. 2005. *The New Imperial Presidency: Renewing Presidential Power after Watergate*. Ann Arbor, MI: University of Michigan Press.

Ruggie, John G., ed. 1993. *Multilateralism Matters*. New York, NY: Columbia University Press.

Ruggie, John G. 1998a. *Constructing the World Polity*. London: Routledge.

——1998b. What Makes the World Hang Together? Neo-utilitarianism and the Social Constructivist Challenge. *International Organization* 52 (4): 855–885.

Ruhl, Mark. 2004. Curbing Central American Militaries. *Journal of Democracy* 15 (3): 137–152.

——2005. The Guatemalan Military since the Peace Accords: The Fate of Reform under Arzú and Portillo. *Latin American Politics and Society* 47 (1): 55–85.

Russett, Bruce. 1993. *Grasping the Democratic Peace*. Princeton, NJ: Princeton University Press.

Rustow, Dankwart. 1970. Transitions to Democracy: Towards a Dynamic Model. *Comparative Politics* 2 (3): 337–363.

Ryan, Jeffrey. 1994. The Impact of Democratization on Revolutionary Movements. *Comparative Politics* 27 (1): 27–44.

Sa'adah, Anne. 2003. *Contemporary France: A Democratic Education*. Lanham, MD: Rowman & Littlefield.

Sarkees, Meredith Reid. 2000. The Correlates of War Data on War: An Update to 1997. *Conflict Management and Peace Science* 18 (1): 123–144.

Saul, John, and Colin Leys. 1995. The Legacy: An Afterword. In *Namibia's Liberation Struggle: The Two-Edged Sword*, edited by Colin Leys and John Saul, 196–206. Athens, OH: Ohio University Press.

Savage, Charlie. 2007. *Takeover: The Return of the Imperial Presidency and the Subversion of American Democracy*. Boston, MA: Little, Brown.

Sawyer, Albert E. *Report on Federal Prohibition Enforcement*, 71st Congress, 3rd Session, Senate Document No. 307, Enforcement of the Prohibition Laws, Official Records of the National Commission on Law Observance and Enforcement.

——1932. The Enforcement of National Prohibition. *Annals of the American Academy of Political and Social Science* 163 (1): 10–29.

Scheppele, Kim Lane. 2003. Aspirational and Aversive Constitutionalism: The Case for Studying Cross-Constitutional Influence through Negative Models. *International Journal of Constitutional Law* 1 (2): 296–324.

Schlesinger, Jr., Arthur M. 1949. *Paths to the Present*. New York, NY: Macmillan.

—— 1973. *The Imperial Presidency*. Boston, MA: Houghton Mifflin.

Schlozman, Kay L., et al. 2005. *Inequalities of Political Voice*. Washington, DC: Task Force on Inequality and American Democracy, American Political Science Association.

Schmitter, Philippe C., and Terry Lynn Karl. 1991. What Democracy Is ... and Is Not. *Journal of Democracy* 2 (3): 75–88.

Schreiber, Harry N. 1960. *The Wilson Administration and Civil Liberties, 1917–1921*. Ithaca, NY: Cornell University Press.

Schwartz, Murray L., and James C. N. Paul. 1959. Foreign Communist Propaganda in the Mails: A Report on Some Problems of Federal Censorship. *University of Pennsylvania Law Review* 107 (5): 621–666.

Scott, J. D. 1962. *Vickers: A History*. London: Weidenfeld and Nicholson.

Scott, J. D., and Richard Hughes. 1955. *The Administration of War Production*. London: Her Majesty's Stationery Office.

Searle, G. R. 2004. *A New England? Peace and War, 1886–1918*. Oxford: Clarendon Press.

Secret, Bernard. 1934. Un voyage du souvenir et de l'amitié. *Cahiers de l'Union Fédérale des Associations Francaises d'Anciens Combattants et de Victimes de la Guerre et des Jeunesses de l'Union Fédérale* 4 (55): 6–15.

Segal, David, and Mady Wechsler Segal. 2004. America's Military Population. *Population Bulletin* 59 (4): 3–40.

Seligson, Mitchell. 2005. Guatemala: Democracy on Ice. In *The Third Wave of Democratization in Latin America: Advances and Setbacks*, edited by Frances Hagopian and Scott P. Mainwaring, 202–235. Cambridge, UK: Cambridge University Press.

Seton-Watson, Christopher. 1967. *Italy from Liberalism to Fascism, 1870–1925*. London: Methuen.

Shanahan, William O. 1945. *Prussian Military Reforms, 1786–1813*. New York, NY: Columbia University Press.

Shaw, Martin. 1987. The Rise and Fall of the Military-Democratic State: Britain 1940–85. In *The Society of War and Peace*, edited by Colin Creighton and Martin Shaw, 143–158. London: Macmillan.

Sheehan, James. 2008. *Where Have All the Soldiers Gone? The Transformation of Modern Europe*. Boston, MA: Houghton Mifflin.

Shepard, Todd. 2006. *The Invention of Decolonization: The Algerian War and the Remaking of France*. Ithaca, NY: Cornell University Press.

Shlaim, Avi. 1996. The Likud in Power. *Israel Studies* 1 (2): 278–293.

Sibley, David. 2005. *The British Working Class and Enthusiasm for War*. London: Frank Cass.

Silverstone, Paul H. 1965. *U.S. Warships of World War II*. Garden City, NY: Doubleday.

——1987. *U.S. Warships since 1945*. Annapolis, MD: Naval Institute Press.

Simpson, Mark. 1993. Foreign and Domestic Factors in the Transformation of Frelimo. *Journal of Modern African Studies* 31 (2): 309–337.

Singer, J. David. 1987. Reconstructing the Correlates of War Dataset on Material Capabilities of States, 1816–1985. *International Interactions* 14 (2): 115–132.

Singleton, John. 1995. Labour, the Conservatives, and Nationalisation. In *The Political Economy of Nationalisation in Britain, 1920–1950*, edited by Robert Milward and John Singleton, 13–36. Cambridge, UK: Cambridge University Press.

SIPRI. 1988. *Yearbook: World and Armaments and Disarmament*. Oxford: Oxford University Press.

Skocpol, Theda. 1979. *States and Social Revolutions: A Comparative Analysis of France, Russia, and China*. Cambridge, UK: Cambridge University Press.

——1995. *Protecting Soldiers and Mothers: The Political Origins of Social Policy in United States*. Cambridge, MA: Harvard University Press.

——2003. *Diminished Democracy: From Membership to Management in American Civic Life*. Norman, OK: University of Oklahoma Press.

Skocpol, Theda, Marshall Ganz, and Ziad Munson. 2000. A Nation of Organizers: The Institutional Origins of Civic Voluntarism in the United States. *American Political Science Review* 94 (3): 527–546.

Skocpol, Theda, et al. 2002. Patriotic Partnerships: Why Great Wars Nourished American Civic Voluntarism. In *Shaped by War and Trade: International Influences on American Political Development*, edited by Ira Katznelson and Martin Shefter, 134–180. Princeton, NJ: Princeton University Press.

Slatter, Mick. 1994. Swapo Prepares for Second Win. *Africa Report* 39: 6–10.

Small, Melvin. 1988. *Nixon, Johnson, and the Doves*. New Brunswick, NJ: Rutgers University Press.

Small, Melvin, and J. David Singer. 1982. *Resort to Arms: International and Civil Wars, 1816–1980*. 2nd ed. Beverly Hills, CA: Sage Publications.

Smith, Denis Mack. 1969. *Italy: A Modern History*. Ann Arbor, MI: University of Michigan Press.

Smith, R. Elberton. 1959. *The Army and Economic Mobilization*. Washington, DC: Department of the Army, Office of the Chief of Military History.

Soiffer, Hillel. 2008. Revisiting Infrastructural Power. *Studies in Comparative International Development* 43 (3–4): 231–251.

Sommer, Robin Langley. 1993. *The History of the U.S. Marshals: The Proud Story of America's Legendary Lawmen*. Philadelphia, PA: Courage Books.

Somucho. 1988. *Nihon Choki Tokei Soran [Historical Statistics of Japan]*, Vol. 3. Tokyo: Nihon Tokei Kyokai.

Sparrow, Bartholomew H. 1996. *From the Outside In: World War II and the American State*. Princeton, NJ: Princeton University Press.

——2002. Limited Wars and the Attenuation of the State: Soldiers, Money, and Political Communication in World War II, Korea, and Vietnam. In *Shaped by*

War and Trade: International Influences on American Political Development,
    edited by Ira Katznelson and Martin Shefter, 267–300. Princeton, NJ: Princeton
    University Press.

Sparrow, James T. 2008. "Buying Our Boys Back": The Mass Foundations of Fiscal
    Citizenship in World War II. *Journal of Policy History* 20 (2): 263–286.

Spencer, Elaine Glovka. 1985. Police-Military Relations in Prussia, 1848–1914.
    Journal of Social History 19 (2): 305–317.

Stahler-Sholk, Richard. 1994. El Salvador's Negotiated Transition: From Low Intensity
    Conflict to Low-Intensity Democracy. *Journal of Inter-American Studies and
    World Affairs* 36 (4): 1–59.

Starr, Paul. 2004. *The Creation of the Media: Political Origins of Modern
    Communications*. New York, NY: Basic Books.

——2007. *Freedom's Power: The True Force of Liberalism*. New York, NY: Basic Books.

Stein, Arthur A. 1976. Conflict and Cohesion: A Review of the Literature. *Journal of
    Conflict Resolution* 20 (1): 143–172.

Stein, Arthur A., and Bruce M. Russett. 1980. Evaluating War: Outcomes and
    Consequences. In *Handbook of Political Conflict: Theory and Research*, edited
    by Ted Robert Gurr, 399–422. New York, NY: Free Press.

Stepan, Alfred. 1986. Paths toward Redemocratization: Theoretical and Comparative
    Considerations. In *Transitions from Authoritarian Rule*, edited by Guillermo
    O'Donnell, Philippe Schmitter, and Lawrence Whitehead, 65–85. Baltimore,
    MD: The Johns Hopkins University Press.

——1988. *Re-thinking Military Politics: Brazil and the Southern Cone*. Princeton, NJ:
    Princeton University Press.

——2001. Paths toward Redemocratization: Theoretical and Comparative
    Considerations. In his *Arguing Comparative Politics*, 111–138. Oxford: Oxford
    University Press.

Stevenson, John. 1990. More Light on World War One. *The Historical Journal* 33
    (1): 195–210.

Stone, Geoffrey R. 2004. *Perilous Times: Free Speech in Wartime from the Sedition
    Act of 1798 to the War on Terrorism*. New York, NY: Norton.

Strand, Havard, Lars Wilhelmsen, and Nils Petter Gleditsch. 2002. *Armed Conflict
    Dataset Codebook, Ver. 2.0*. Oslo: International Peace Research Institute.

Strauss, Barry. 2004. The Dead at Arginusae and the Debate over the Athenian Navy.
    Nautiki Epithewrisi [Naval Review] 545.160s: 40–67.

Sugden, Robert. 1986. *The Economics of Rights, Cooperation and Welfare*.
    Oxford: Blackwell.

Sundquist, James L. 1981. *The Decline and Resurgence of Congress*. Washington,
    DC: Brookings Institution Press.

Suri, Jeremi. 2003. *Power and Protest: Global Revolution and the Rise of Détente*.
    Cambridge, MA: Harvard University Press.

Sweeting, George Vincent. 1994. Building the Arsenal of Democracy: The Government's
    Role in Expansion of Industrial Capacity, 1940 to 1945. Ph.D. diss., Columbia
    University.

Szasz, Paul. 1994. Creating the Namibian Constitution. In *The Namibian Peace
    Process: Implications and Lessons for the Future*, edited by Heribert Weiland
    and Matthew Braham, 243–256. Freiburg: Arnold-Bergstraesser-Inst.

Tanner, Duncan. 1990. *Political Change and the Labour Party*. New York,
    NY: Cambridge University Press.

Tansey, Oisín. 2007. Democratization without a State: Democratic Regime Building in Kosovo. *Democratization* 14 (1): 129–150.

Tarrow, Sidney. 2008. War, State-Making, and the "War on Terror." Paper presented at City University of New York.

———2009. War and State-Making: For Tilly, Against Tilly, Beyond Tilly. Unpublished manuscript, Cornell University.

Taylor, A. J. P. 1965. *English History, 1914–1945*. Oxford: Clarendon Press.

Taylor, Brian, and Roxana Botea. 2008. Tilly Tally: War-Making and State-Making in the Contemporary Third World. *International Studies Review* 10 (1): 27–56.

Taylor, Ian. 1991. Labour and the Impact of War, 1939–1945. In *The Attlee Years*, edited by Nick Tiratsoo, 7–28. London: Pinter.

Thayer, John A. 1964. *Italy and the Great War: Politics and Culture*. Madison, WI: University of Wisconsin Press.

Thies, Cameron G. 2006. Public Violence and State Building in Central America. *Comparative Political Studies* 39 (10): 1263–1282.

Thompson, Harry C., and Lida Mayo. 1960. *The Ordnance Department: Procurement and Supply*. Washington, DC: Department of the Army, Office of the Chief of Military History.

Thompson, William R. 1993. The Consequences of War. *International Interactions* 19 (1–2): 125–147.

Thorndike, Joseph Jacobs III. 2005. The Price of Civilization: Taxation for Depression and War, 1932–1945. Ph.D. diss., University of Virginia.

Thucydides. 1954. *History of the Peloponnesian War*. New York, NY: Penguin.

Tilly, Charles. 1975. Reflections on the History of European State-Making. In *The Formation of National States in Western Europe*, edited by Charles Tilly, 3–83. Princeton, NJ: Princeton University Press.

———1985. War Making and State Making as Organized Crime. In *Bringing the State Back In*, edited by Peter Evans, Dietrich Rueschemeyer, and Theda Skocpol, 169–191. Cambridge, UK: Cambridge University Press.

———1992. *Coercion, Capital, and European States, A.D. 990–1992*. Cambridge, MA: Blackwell.

———1993. *European Revolutions, 1492–1992*. Cambridge, MA: Blackwell.

———2004. *Contention and Democracy in Europe, 1650–2000*. New York, NY: Cambridge University Press.

———2006. *Regimes and Repertoires*. Chicago, IL: University of Chicago Press.

———2007. *Democracy*. Cambridge, UK: Cambridge University Press.

Titmuss, Richard. 1958. *Essays on the Welfare State*. London: George Allen & Unwin.

Tomassini, Luigi. 1990. Industrial Mobilization and State Intervention in Italy in the First World War: Effects on Labor Unrest. In *Strikes, Social Conflict and the First World War: An International Perspective*, edited by Leopold Haimson and Giulio Sapelli, 179–212. Milan: Fondazione Giangiacomo Feltrinelli.

———1991. Industrial Mobilization and the Labour Market in Italy during the First World War. *Social History* 16 (1): 59–87.

Tomlinson, Jim. 1993. Mr. Atlee's Supply-Side Socialism. *Economic History Review* 46 (1): 1–22.

———1994. *Government and the Enterprise since 1900: The Changing Problem of Efficiency*. Oxford: Clarendon Press.

Trainor, Joseph C. 1983. *Education Reform in Occupied Japan: Trainor's Memoir*. Tokyo: Meisei University Press.

Treanor, William Michael. 1997. Fame, the Founding, and the Power to Declare War. *Cornell Law Review* 82 (4): 695–772.

Trimble, William F. 1986. The Naval Aircraft Factory, the American Aviation Industry, and Government Competition, 1919–1928. *Business History Review* 60 (2): 175–198.

Truman, Harry S. 1945. *Public Papers of the Presidents of the United States: Harry S. Truman, 1945*. Washington, DC: U.S. Government Printing Office, 1961.

——1946. *Public Papers of the Presidents of the United States: Harry S. Truman, 1946*. Washington, DC: U.S. Government Printing Office, 1962.

——1947. *Public Papers of the Presidents of the United States: Harry S. Truman, 1947*. Washington, DC: U.S. Government Printing Office, 1963.

Turnbull, Stephen. 2006. *The Samurai and the Sacred*. New York, NY: Osprey Publishing.

Turner, Bryan, and Peter Hamilton. 1994. *Citizenship*. London: Taylor and Francis.

Turner, John. 1992. *British Politics and the Great War: Coalition and Conflict*. New Haven, CT: Yale University Press.

United Nations General Assembly Resolution 31/146. 1976.

United Nations Security Council Document S/15287. 1982. *Annex Principles Concerning the Constituent Assembly and the Constitution for an Independent Namibia*. 12 July.

United Nations Security Council Resolution 435/78. 1988. *Agreement among the People's Republic of Angola, the Republic of Cuba, and the Republic of South Africa*. 22 December.

Uppsala Conflict Data Program. 2009. *UCDP Database*. Uppsala University, Department of Peace and Conflict Research. Available at www.ucdp.uu.se/database. Accessed August 8, 2009.

USAID. 1997. *From Bullets to Ballots: Mozambique's Vote for Democratic Governance Electoral Assistance to Post-Conflict Societies*. Washington DC: Center for Development Information and Evaluation.

U.S. Forces in Austria. 1947. *A Review of Military Government Reports*. 1 January.

U.S. Marshals Service. 2009. Operation FALCON. Available at http://www.usmarshals.gov/falcon/index.html. Accessed September 18, 2009.

U.S. Senate. *Senate Executive Document 4*. 37th Cong., 2nd sess.

U.S. Senate. 1944. Special Committee Investigating the National Defense Program. *Third Annual Report* (Senate Report 10, Part 16). 78th Cong., 2nd sess.

Vander Meulen, Jacob A. 1991. *The Politics of Aircraft: Building an American Military Industry*. Lawrence, KS: University Press of Kansas.

Vasquez, Joseph Paul. 2005. Shouldering the Soldiering: Democracy, Conscription and Military Casualties. *Journal of Conflict Resolution* 49 (6): 849–973.

Verba, Sidney, Kay Lehman Schlozman, and Henry E. Brady. 1995. *Voice and Equality: Civic Voluntarism in American Politics*. Cambridge, MA: Harvard University Press.

Veremis, Thanos. 1985. Greece: Veto and Impasse, 1967–74. In *The Political Dilemmas of Military Regimes*, edited by Christopher Clapham and George Philip, 27–45. Totowa, NJ: Barnes and Noble.

Vincent, John. 1966. *The Formation of the Liberal Party, 1857–1868*. London: Constable.

Vinen, Richard. 1996. *France, 1934–1970*. New York, NY: St. Martin's.

Vines, Alex. 1991. *Renamo Terrorism in Mozambique*. London: James Curry.

Vizzard, William J. 1997. *In the Cross Fire: A Political History of the Bureau of Alcohol, Tobacco, and Firearms*. Boulder, CO: Lynne Rienner.

von Doepp, Peter. 2005. Party Cohesion and Fractionalization in New African Democracies: Lessons from Struggles over Third-Term Amendments. *Studies in Comparative International Development* 40 (3): 65–86.

Waddell, Brian. 2001. *The War against the New Deal*. DeKalb, IL: Northern Illinois University Press.

Wade, Christine. 2008. El Salvador: The Success of the FMLN. In *From Soldiers to Politicians*, edited by Jeroen de Zeeuw, 33–54. London: Lynne Rienner.

Waites, Bernard. 1987. *A Class Society at War: England*. New York, NY: Berg.

Waldner, David. 1999. *State Building and Late Development*. Ithaca, NY: Cornell University Press.

Wall, Wendy L. 2008. *Inventing the "American Way": The Politics of Consensus from the New Deal to the Civil Rights Movement*. New York, NY: Oxford University Press.

Wallender, Celeste. 2000. NATO after the Cold War. *International Organization* 54 (4): 705–736.

Walter, Barbara F. 2002. *Committing to Peace: The Successful Settlement of Civil Wars*. Princeton, NJ: Princeton University Press.

Wantchekon, Leonard. 2004. The Paradox of "Warlord" Democracy: A Theoretical Investigation. *American Political Science Review* 98 (1): 17–33.

Ward, Stephen R. 1975. *War Generation: Veterans of the First World War*. Port Washington, NY: Kennikat Press.

Warshauer, Matthew. 2006. *Andrew Jackson and the Politics of Martial Law*. Knoxville, TN: University of Tennessee Press.

Weber, Max. 1978. Discipline and Charisma. In his *Economy and Society*, 2 Vols., edited by Guenther Roth and Claus Wittich, 1148–1156. Berkeley, CA: University of California Press.

Weiland, Heribert, and Matthew Braham, eds. 1994. *The Namibian Peace Process: Implications and Lessons for the Future*. Freiburg: Arnold Bergstraesser Institute.

Weinstein, Jeremy M. 2002. Mozambique: A Fading UN Success Story. *Journal of Democracy* 13 (1): 141–156.

——2007. *Inside Rebellion: The Politics of Insurgent Violence*. Cambridge, UK: Cambridge University Press.

Weir, Gary E. 1993. *Forged in War: The Naval-Industrial Complex and American Submarine Construction, 1940–1961*. Washington, DC: Naval Historical Center.

Wejnert, Barbara. 2005. Diffusion, Development, and Democracy, 1800–1999. *American Sociological Review* 70 (1): 53–81.

Wells, Tom. 1994. *The War Within: America's Battle over Vietnam*. Berkeley, CA: University of California Press.

Wherry, Kenneth S. 1946. Bureaucracy, A National Menace. Unpublished manuscript, box 15, Kenneth Spicer Wherry Papers, RG 3559, Nebraska State Historical Library, Lincoln, NE.

Whitehead, Laurence, et al. 2005. *Perfil de Gobernabilidad de El Salvador*. Madrid: CICODE.

Whiteside, Noel. 1980. Welfare Legislation and the Unions during the First World War. *The Historical Journal* 23 (4): 857–874.

——1990. Concession, Coercion or Cooperation? State Policy and Industrial Unrest in Britain, 1916–1920. In *Strikes, Social Conflict and the First World War: An International Perspective*, edited by Leopold Haimson and Giulio Sapelli, 107–122. Milan: Fondazione Giangiacomo Feltrinelli.

Whittam, John. 1975. War and Italian Society 1914–16. In *War and Society: A Yearbook of Military History*, edited by Brian Bond and Ian Roy, 144–161. London: Croom Helm.

Wildy, Tom. 1992. The Social and Economic Publicity and Propaganda of the Labour Governments of 1945–51. *Contemporary Record* 6 (1): 45–71.

Williams, David C. 2007. U.S. House Committee on Oversight and Government Reform. *Long Statement for the Record on the Status of the United States Postal Service. Hearing before the Subcommittee on Federal Workforce, Postal Service and the District of Columbia.* 110th Cong., 1st sess., 11 April.

Williams, Philip. 1958. *Politics in Post-War France*. London: Longman.

Wilson, O. W. 1951. Progress in Police Administration. *Journal of Criminal Law, Criminology, and Police Science* 42 (2): 141–154.

Wilson, Mark R. 2010. "Taking a Nickel Out of the Cash Register": Statutory Renegotiation of Military Contracts and the Politics of Profit Control in the USA during World War II. *Law and History Review* 28 (2): 1–41.

Winter, Jay M. 1974. *Socialism and the Challenge of War: Ideas and Politics in Britain*. London: Routledge and Kegan Paul.

——1985a. Some Paradoxes of the First World War. In *The Upheaval of War: Family, Work and Welfare in Europe,* edited by Richard Wall and Jay Winter, 9–42. Cambridge, UK: Cambridge University Press.

——1985b. *The Great War and the British People*. London: Macmillan.

——1995. *Sites of Memory, Sites of Mourning: The Great War in European Cultural History*. Cambridge, UK: Cambridge University Press.

——2006. *Remembering War: The Great War between History and Memory in the Twentieth Century*. New Haven, CT: Yale University Press.

Witt, John Fabian. 2007. *Patriots and Cosmopolitans: Hidden Histories of American Law*. Cambridge, MA: Harvard University Press.

Woo-Cumings, Meredith, ed. 1999. *The Developmental State*. Ithaca, NY: Cornell University Press.

Wood, Elisabeth Jean. 2000. *Forging Democracy from Below*. New York, NY: Cambridge University Press.

——2005. Challenges to Democracy in El Salvador. In *The Third Wave of Democratization in Latin America: Advances and Setbacks*, edited by Frances Hagopian and Scott Mainwaring, 179–201. New York, NY: Cambridge University Press.

——2008. The Social Processes of Civil War: The Wartime Transformations of Social Networks. *Annual Review of Political Science* 11: 539–561.

Woodhouse, C. M. 1985. *The Rise and Fall of the Greek Colonels*. New York, NY: Franklin Watts.

Workman, Andrew A. 1998. Manufacturing Power: The Organizational Revival of the National Association of Manufacturers, 1941–1945. *Business History Review* 72 (2): 279–317.

Wrigley, Chris. 1976. *David Lloyd George and the British Labour Movement: Peace and War.* London: The Harvester Press.

——1982a. The Ministry of Munitions: An Innovatory Department? In *War and the State: The Transformation of British Government, 1914–1919*, edited by Kathleen Burk, 32–56. London: George Allen & Unwin.

——1982b. Trade Unions and Politics in the First World War. In *Trade Unions in British Politics*, edited by Ben Pimlott and Chris Cook, 79–97. London: Longman.

——1987a. Introduction. In *A History of British Industrial Relations*, Vol. II, *1914–1939*, edited by Chris Wrigley, 1–22. London: The Harvester Press.

——1987b. The First World War and State Intervention in Industrial Relations. In *A History of British Industrial Relations*, Vol. II, *1914–1939*, edited by Chris Wrigley, 23–70. London: The Harvester Press.

——1987c. The Trade Unions between the Wars. In *A History of British Industrial Relations*, Vol. II, *1914–1939*, edited by Chris Wrigley, 71–128. London: The Harvester Press.

Wunderich, Frieda. 1939. Labor in Wartime. In *War in our Time*, edited by Hans Speier and Alfred Kahler, 245–256. New York, NY: Norton.

Wynn, Neil A. 1977. War and Social Change: The Black American in Two World Wars. In *War and Society: A Yearbook of Military History*, Vol. 2, edited by Brian Bond and Ian Roy, 40–64. London: Croom Helm.

Yale Law Journal. 1942. Legal Techniques for Protecting Free Discussion in Wartime. *Yale Law Journal* 51 (5): 798–819.

Yashar, Deborah. 1997. *Demanding Democracy: Reform and Reaction in Costa Rica and Guatemala, 1870s–1950s.* Stanford, CA: Stanford University Press.

YMCA Japan. Various years. *Annual Reports.* Tokyo: YMCA Japan.

Zakaria, Fareed. 2003. *The Future of Freedom: Illiberal Democracy at Home and Abroad.* New York, NY: Norton.

Zako, Ken. 1990. *"Jugo" no Kiroku: Kobe Sensaiki [Memoirs of the Home Front: Wartime Destruction in Kobe].* Tokyo: Shinjuku Shobo.

Zamagni, Vera. 1993. *The Economic History of Italy, 1860–1990.* Oxford: Clarendon Press.

Zieger, Robert H. 1995. *The CIO, 1935–1955.* Chapel Hill, NC: University of North Carolina Press.

Zweiniger-Bargielowska, Ina. 2000. *Austerity in Britain: Rationing, Price Controls, and Consumption, 1939–1955.* New York, NY: Oxford University Press.

Index